The External Control of Organizations

The External Control of Organizations

A Resource Dependence Perspective

Jeffrey Pfeffer
and Gerald R. Salancik

STANFORD BUSINESS CLASSICS

Stanford Business Books
An imprint of Stanford University Press · Stanford, California

Stanford University Press
Stanford, California

Printed in the United States of America
on acid-free, archival-quality paper.

Library of Congress Cataloging-in-Publication Data

Pfeffer, Jeffrey.
    The external control of organizations : a resource
dependence perspective / Jeffrey Pfeffer and
Gerald R. Salancik.
        p. cm. — (Stanford business books)
    Originally published: New York : Harper & Row,
© 1978.
    "Stanford business classics".
    Includes bibliographical references and index.
    ISBN 0-8047-4789-X (pbk. : alk. paper)
    1. Industries—Social aspects.   2. Interorganizational
relations.   I. Salancik, Gerald R.   II. Title.   III. Series.
HD60.P46   2003
306.3'4—dc21   2002155238

Original Printing 2003
Last figure below indicates year of this printing:
12   11   10   09

Contents

Acknowledgments and Dedication
of the Classic Edition

I am not sure I would have ever even tried to get this book back into print without the encouragement of so many colleagues, many of whom have promised to assign the book in their seminars (and you know who you are!). When Lee Bolman told me that not only was *The External Control of Organizations* highly cited, but used copies were selling on Amazon for $295, I was inspired to make the effort to reclaim the rights and see if we could get the book back into print.

This republication would not have been possible without the enthusiastic support and assistance of Bill Hicks and Kate Wahl of the Stanford University Press. Sofia Salancik, Jerry's daughter, graciously provided her approval for the venture, and Huseyin Leblebici and Cyd Combs helped in my locating Sofia in the first place, as well as providing their own words of encouragement.

Much has changed in the past 25 years since *The External Control of Organizations* was first published. For the past 23 years, I have been fortunate beyond measure to teach at Stanford's Graduate School of Business, where I am surrounded by amazing and remarkable colleagues who mean so much to me. Since January 1985, there is a wonderful new addition to my life, Kathleen, who makes every day a special delight. Whatever I have been able to accomplish, it is because of her love, support, and inspiration.

There is also a sad subtraction. In July 1996, Gerald Salancik died suddenly and tragically. Jerry made the start of my career at the University of Illinois successful. He taught me, encouraged me, and shared his outlook on life with me. His friendship and his amazing wit and intellect made our collaboration a wonderful and enriching experience. On the occasion of the republication of a work that Jerry really brought to life, I remember him with awe and affection. This republication of *The External Control of Organizations* is dedicated to the memory of Gerald R. Salancik. May his memory and his many contributions live on.

Jeffrey Pfeffer
Stanford, California
2002

Introduction to the Classic Edition

The External Control of Organizations had three central themes, each of which represented somewhat of a change in direction for the field of organization studies at the time of its publication. One way of assessing the impact of the book, the evolution of its ideas over time, and exploring its position in the field today is to investigate how these three themes have unfolded over the succeeding years in both empirical research and subsequent theorizing.

The first, and perhaps the most central, theme was the importance of the environment or the social context of organizations for understanding what decisions got made about issues ranging from who to hire (Salancik, 1979; Pfeffer and Leblebici, 1973), the composition of boards of directors (Pfeffer, 1972a; 1973), and what alliances and mergers to seek (Pfeffer, 1972b; Pfeffer and Nowak, 1976). The general premise was that social context mattered (Weick,1996), a theme that can be found in much of the research that Salancik and I did both together and individually. The importance of the environment for understanding organizations was a natural extension of the ideas of open systems theory (e.g., Katz and Kahn, 1978; Yuchtman and Seashore, 1967) then gaining currency. The idea was that if you wanted to understand organizational choices and actions, one place to begin this inquiry was to focus less on internal dynamics and the values and beliefs of leaders and more on the situations in which organizations were located and the pressures and constraints that emanated from those situations. In that sense, *The External Control of Organizations* was quite consistent with the ideas of situationism in social psychology (Bowers, 1973; Jones, 1998). An emphasis on the importance of context for understanding organizations led naturally to questioning the extent to which leaders made a difference in organizational performance (e.g., Lieberson and O'Connor, 1972; Pfeffer, 1977). The shift in direction for the field of organization studies was an increased emphasis on the environment as a way of understanding organizations.

The External Control of Organizations viewed organizations as being embedded in networks of interdependencies and social relationships (Granovetter, 1985). The need for resources, including financial and physical resources as well as information, obtained from the environment, made organizations potentially dependent on the external sources of these resources—hence the characterization of the theory as *resource dependence*. Dependencies are often reciprocal and sometimes indirect. Therefore, the book is filled with network and relationship imagery, even though there was almost no attempt to explicitly employ network methodology to analyze data in the studies summarized therein.

A second important theme was that although organizations were obviously constrained by their situations and environments, there were opportunities to do things, such as coopting (Selznick, 1949) sources of constraint, to obtain, at least temporarily, more autonomy and the ability to pursue organizational interests. Indeed, because of the effect of external constraints on both profits (e.g., Burt, 1983) and decision autonomy (Pfeffer, 1972c), organizations possessed both the desire and, occasionally, the ability to negotiate their positions within those constraints using a variety of tactics. In other words, Salancik and I argued that strategic choice was both possible (Child, 1972) and sometimes, although not inevitably, efficacious because the strategies to overcome constraint sometimes worked (Pfeffer, 1973; Burt, 1983). The change in emphasis for the field was in seeing organizational strategy as focused not just on products and customers but also on suppliers and other entities in the environment, including governmental organizations, that ultimately affected the flow of resources to those organizations. In that sense *The External Control of Organizations* anticipated the growing interest in supply chains and value chain management.

As organizations try to alter their environments, they become subject to new and different constraints as their patterns of interdependence change, which the organizations then try to further negotiate. The image presented is one of dynamic interaction and evolution of organizations, environments, and interorganizational relations over time as the various social actors maneuver for advantage. Again the limits of both the authors' methodological training and the available empirical methods and data did not result in explicitly dynamic models showing the evolution of both environments and organizational decisions and structures over time. But the metaphor of dynamic interaction is implicit in the book as is the image of organizations acting strategically to manage their resource dependencies.

The third major theme was the importance of the construct of power for understanding both intraorganizational and interorganizational behavior. The importance of social power as an idea is an almost inevitable outgrowth of the focus on dependence and interdependence (Blau, 1964; Emerson, 1962) and the constraints that result from dependence and attempts to manage or mitigate those constraints. The emphasis on power as opposed to economic efficiency distinguishes resource dependence from transactions cost theory (Williamson, 1975), which is also concerned with interorganizational relationships among buyers, sellers, and competitors (e.g., Williamson and Ouchi, 1981). The idea that power was important for understanding organizations, as contrasted, for instance, with rationality or efficiency, was yet another way in which resource dependence ideas represented somewhat of a shift in focus for organization studies.

Resource dependence maintained that some organizations had more power than others because of the particularities of their interdependence and their location in social space. For instance, the government was a substantial provider of resources to a number of industries such as defense contractors (and education and health care currently), but itself was less dependent on its suppliers because there were often multiple suppliers of desired goods and services. Hence, organizations that relied heavily on government contracts were typically, although not invariably, more dependent on the government than it was on them (Salancik, 1979). As a consequence, the government could force numerous policies and decisions on those organizations—for instance in education, compelling universities to provide the same athletic opportunities for women as they do for men, and in earlier times, encouraging affirmative action to hire women and minorities.

External resource dependencies also affected internal power dynamics. The people, groups, or departments inside organizations that could reduce uncertainty (Hinings, et al., 1974), manage important environmental dependencies, and help the organization obtain resources held more power as a result of their critical role in ensuring organizational survival if not success (Salancik and Pfeffer, 1974; Salancik, Pfeffer, and Kelly, 1978). So, for instance, power evolved inside electric utilities from engineers to lawyers and business specialists as the critical issues shifted from more technical concerns of building and operating power plants to dealing with an increasingly complex and contentious regulatory environment and managing highly leveraged capital structures in ever more dynamic financial markets (Pfeffer, 1992).

Other Theories of Organizations and Environments

The 1970s saw the emergence of two other important theories that focused on organizations and their environments, population ecology (e.g., Hannan and Freeman, 1989) and institutional theory (e.g., Meyer and Rowan, 1977). There originally were, and to some extent still are, important theoretical differences among the theories, although resource dependence theory and institutional theory have grown somewhat closer together over time. One way of comparing and contrasting the theories is to briefly explore how each deals with the three foci of environmental determinism, strategic choice, and the connection between external constraints and internal dynamics.

Population ecology, like resource dependence, focuses on the effects of the environment on organizations and also shares a concern with the material conditions of that environment, particularly the dimension of population density (e.g., Carroll and Wade, 1991; Hannan and Carroll, 1992), a variable that represents the intensity of competition for resources. Population ecology focuses primarily on organizational birth and mortality of organizational forms or types of organizations as the primary dependent variables. The argument is that it is through differential rates of births and deaths that the prevalence of organizational forms in the population changes (Hannan and Freeman 1989). Organizational adaptation is deemphasized by ecological theory. Adaptation is presumed to be relatively rare both because of inertial forces (Hannan and Freeman, 1984) inside organizations and because change is difficult to accomplish successfully, with evidence indicating that mortality increases when organizations try to change their fundamental characteristics (e.g., Amburgey, Kelly, and Barnett, 1993; Carroll, 1984).

Both resource dependence and population ecology emphasize the importance of the environment for understanding organizations. However, there are some important differences in the perspectives. The five principal differences between population ecology and resource dependence are as follows. First, resource dependence admits much more possibility of organizations altering their environments, while population ecology takes selection processes resulting from competition, for instance, and other dimensions of the environment more as a given. Second, resource dependence includes more possibility and, indeed, likelihood of organizational change and adaptation in response to external forces. In population ecology, by contrast, differential selection through birth and death processes constitutes the primary way in which organizational populations change. Third, resource dependence focuses more on organizational decisions—such as who to put on boards of directors, what other companies to merge with, how to achieve legitimacy through altering internal structures and processes, while population ecology is largely silent about how organizational structures and behaviors emerge to be selected.

These three differences mean that there is much more of a place for strategic choice in resource dependence theory, a somewhat ironic fact given the use of population ecology in understanding corporate strategy (e.g., Burgelman, 1990). However, industrial organization economics, another perspective employed to understand business strategy (e.g., Porter, 1980) also has some of this flavor of environmental determinism. The emphasis in early industrial organization economics conceptions of strategy mostly was on being in the right industry, and once in that industry, except for deciding on whether to compete on the basis of differentiation or cost, organizational decisions were quite circumscribed, dealing mostly with entry and exit into markets. However, particularly in later work Porter (1985) incorporated more possibilities for organizational action with an increased focus on internal processes.

A fourth difference is that population ecology, because of its study of birth and death processes which occur over time, is more explicitly longitudinal than most empirical studies in the resource dependence tradition. However, there is nothing inherently static in resource dependence predictions and, as noted above, there is a dynamic aspect to arguments about changes in organizations and environments over time in response to the actions of the focal and other organizations.

The fifth difference is that population ecology is largely silent about the causes of internal organizational dynamics such as contests for power, leadership succession, and similar issues. In theory, of course, such processes could be modeled using a natural selection logic, but with few exceptions (e.g., Barnett and Carroll, 1995) population ecology has remained true to its name, focused primarily on the dynamics of organizational populations (e.g., Carroll and Hannan, 2000).

Institutional (or as it is sometimes called, neoinstitutional) theory began much like resource dependence with an emphasis on the effects of the social environment on organizations. The environment presumably imposed constraints on organizations that affected how they looked—their structures—and what they did—their practices. The difference was that institutional theory tended to emphasize social rules, expectations, norms, and values as the source of pressures on organizations to conform, rather than the patterns of transactions and exchanges that formed the focus for resource dependence. Scott (1995: 33), for instance defined institutions as "cognitive, normative, and regulative structures that provide stability and meaning to social behavior."

> The cognitive approach focuses on the actors' shared frameworks of interpretation, which allow them to acquire a common definition of the situation. . . . The normative conception is more evaluative in nature, and legitimacy takes on a moral tone—doing what others expect as "appropriate" for one's role. The regulative view looks to formal and informal rules as constraining and regularizing behavior, and legitimacy consists in conforming to those rules (Davis and Greve, 1997: 6).

Note the absence of resource interdependence in the discussions of where constraints originate. Moreover, early institutional theory largely neglected issues of power and interests that were prominent in resource dependence (e.g., DiMaggio, 1988). It was as if institutional rules and social expectations had a life of their own, rather than being themselves the outcomes of contests among various social actors trying to mold the institutional environment to their advantage. In that sense, early versions of institutional theory tended to downplay the potential for strategic choice, for organizations to actively shape their environments, seeing social rules and norms as taken-for-granted and therefore less malleable. More recently, however, institutional accounts have broadened to incorporate the idea of contests over legitimacy, norms, and values, and the possibility of changing the normative order through strategic actions and interactions (e.g., Scott, et al., 2000).

All three theories, then, emphasize the importance of the environment. Resource dependence and recent versions of institutional theory both speak to the possibility of organizations engaging in strategic actions to obtain support from the environment, and both also speak more to the connections between the environment and internal decisions than does population ecology. In fact, legitimacy, something emphasized by institutional analysis, was seen in resource dependence as one more resource to be acquired, possibly through the cooptation (Dowling and Pfeffer, 1975) of elites. The principal difference between resource dependence and recent versions of institutional theory is their relative emphasis on the material conditions of the environment as contrasted with cultural norms, values, and social expectations.

Resource Dependence as Theory and Metaphor

As of the spring of 2002, there were 2,321 citations to *The External Control of Organizations*. Moreover, there was little evidence that the pace of citation to a book almost 25 years old was diminishing. For instance, from 1996 to 2002 there were 846 citations, while from 1992 to 1996 there were 499 citations. Some 58% of the total citations received since the book's publication in 1978 had been received in the most recent ten year period.

On the one hand, one might interpret these data as reflecting the success of resource dependence ideas. Yet, there is a limited amount of empirical work explicitly extending and testing resource dependence theory and its central tenets. Instead, studies of interorganizational relations increasingly rely on ideas from structural sociology that emphasize network position more than resource interdependence (e.g., Anand and Piskorski, 2002). It has been suggested that one of the sources of the success of resource dependence ideas has been that they are as much a metaphorical statement about organizations, not particularly open to being tested or disproved. Without denying the metaphorical use of resource dependence language and ideas, however, it seems clear that the book makes a number of potentially falsifiable empirical predictions.

For reasons of space, it is impossible to review all of the subsequent empirical work that is relevant to evaluating resource dependence theory. In what follows, I selectively summarize some of the major streams of work that has emerged, using the three basic themes of the theory as an organizing framework.

Environmental Effects on Organizations

Although the title of the book speaks to external control, and an important premise is that decisions made inside organizations reflect pressures emanating from the environment, there is actually very little research that has explored the operation of external constraints on organizational decisions (e.g., Pfeffer, 1972c; Salancik, 1979). Rather, much of the empirical exploration has focused on the relationship between resource dependence and organizational decisions that might be construed as being made in response to dependence, such as efforts to absorb or coopt constraint.

There is one important exception to this statement, however, which is Christensen's work on sustaining and disruptive technologies (e.g., Christensen, 1997; Christensen and Bower, 1996). Christensen's study of the disc drive industry revealed an interesting anomaly: the industry's leading, established firms led in the development of sustaining technical changes (Christensen and Bower, 1996: 204) while "the firms that led the industry in introducing *disruptive* architectural technologies . . . tended overwhelmingly to be *entrant* rather than established firms" (p. 205). This occurred even though case study evidence revealed that, in virtually all cases, the new, disruptive technologies had been known by and even, in some instances, developed inside of existing, established firms. The answer as to why new technologies were not adopted by existing firms comes from considerations of resource dependence: "a firm's scope for strategic change is strongly bounded by the interests of external entities (customers, in this study) who provide the resources the firm needs to survive" (Christensen and Bower, 1996: 212). Although Christensen's insights are certainly compatible with resource dependence, to this point there has not been the quantitative empirical work to support the insights generated from the case studies. Specifically, studies of strategic change might consider both the extent to which a given firm is dependent on various customers and the particular demands of those customers to provide further demonstration of the Christensen insights.

The first and most logical extension of the ideas in *The External Control of Organizations* was to take the network imagery implicit in the argument and actually operationalize and extend the ideas using network measures and methods. Ron Burt and I were at the University of California at Berkeley at the same time and knew each other, and he used some of our data on resource flows in the economy in his paper on interlocking directorates (Burt, Christman, and Kilburn, 1980) and in his analysis of mergers (Burt, 1980). Burt (1983) developed much more quantitatively precise measures of external constraint, using the intuition that dependence was a function both of the extent to which a given firm or industry segment had a higher proportion of its transactions with some other segment or set of firms, and with the extent to which that sector was itself concentrated, so that coordinated action could be pursued against the interests of the focal firm.

The availability of data on directors and therefore, the ability to construct data sets assessing the extent and structure of director interlocking produced a surge of research in the relationship between resource dependence and the composition and structure of boards of directors, including the relationship between financial dependence and the presence of bankers on corporate boards (see, for instance, Allen, 1974; Mizruchi and Stearns, 1988). Even though many things have changed in corporate governance and the legal and economic environment over the years, research on interlocking directorates has for the most part has moved on to consider the *effects* of ties on various outcomes such as the diffusion of merger activity (Haunschild, 1993), organizational structures (e.g., Palmer, Jennings, and Zhou, 1993; Burns and Wholey, 1993), and anti-takeover defenses such as poison pills (Davis, 1991). It would be useful to revisit resource dependence and other predictions concerning determinants of the size and composition of corporate boards to see if the original findings are replicated and as a way of exploring scope or moderating conditions for the theory.

Just such a replication and extension was undertaken by Finkelstein (1997) with respect to mergers. His analysis found that resource dependence results were replicated using more recent data. However, using more sophisticated analytical methods and less aggregated data (finer grained industry categorizations) reduced the magnitude of resource dependence effects. Finkelstein (1997: 803) found no evidence that resource dependence effects had diminished over time—"in fact, some of the strongest findings emerged for the three most recent time periods." Finkelstein also found that conditions of anti-trust enforcement affected the ability of resource interdependence to predict patterns of mergers.

Organizational Efforts to Manage Environmental Constraint

In a sense, a number of the studies cited in the preceding section represent organizational efforts to manage constraints. Analyses of mergers, joint ventures, and board of director interlocks often show that these actions follow patterns of transactional interdependence, presumably to cope with that interdependence and the uncertainty that dependence generates. For instance, Gulati and Gargiulo's (1999) study of alliances in three industries spanning several countries and nine years concluded that resource interdependence predicted alliance formation. Their study also showed the effects of network structure, because the specific other organizations that partner in alliances depends on the position those partners have in the social network. In other words, companies seek to build alliances to manage dependence but do so with companies that are in a social position to be trusted.

Other attempts to manage constraints can involve intervening in public policy and the political process. As Schuler, Rehbein, and Cramer (2002: 659) noted: "government policy . . . determines the rules of commerce, the structure of markets (through barriers to entry and changes in cost structures due to regulations, subsidies, and taxation); the offerings of goods and services that are permissible; and the size of markets based on government subsidies and purchases." Unfortunately, the use of political means to manage resource dependence is not often investigated. Apparently many people have bought into the free market rhetoric of business and government and not bothered to note the pervasiveness of quotas, tariffs, and numerous forms of direct and indirect interventions designed to provide one firm or sector advantages. Analyzing the political activities—political action committee contributions, the number of people in a firm's Washington office, and the number of lobbyists and political consultants retained by each firm, Schuler, et al. (2002: 668) found that companies that relied heavily on government contracts "lobbied and contributed to campaigns to maintain close ties with the policy makers responsible for their livelihoods."

Virtually all of the research treating organizational responses to interdependence has a strange omission—any consideration of whether these various cooptive strategies are successful, or at an even more refined level, the conditions under which the various strategies work and when they don't. Two exceptions to this statement would be Burt's (1983) analyses of profits and Pfeffer's (1973) study showing that hospitals that optimally structured their boards to manage interdependence enjoyed greater effectiveness. Although there have been some studies of the effects of, for instance, interlocking directorates on various corporate behaviors (see Mizruch, 1996 for a review), there is much less research than there should be on the effects of various cooptive relations and political strategies on organizational outcomes, including not only profitability but also the reduction of uncertainty, potentially measured as a reduction in variation in performance or other outcomes.

How Environmental Constraint Affects Internal Organizational Dynamics

The External Control of Organizations argued that there was a connection between external interdependence and internal organizational processes, and this connection was mediated by power. Specifically, those people or subunits which could best cope with critical organizational uncertainties came to have relatively more power inside the organization (e.g., Perrow, 1970; Hickson, et al., 1971), and used that power to ensure that their view of what should be done, including who should succeed to various positions, prevailed. Although there have been numerous studies of executive succession since that time, most of those studies have focused on whether insiders or outsiders came to power, with some concern with the functional backgrounds of newly appointed CEOs. The studies have focused their search for explanations on conditions of ownership, financial performance, and the composition of the board of directors (e.g., the proportion of insiders) rather than on the links between the external environment and the frequency and other dimensions of successions (e.g., Ocasio, 1994). Other research has sought to tie the functional backgrounds of senior executives to the strategic decisions (e.g., Hambrick and Mason, 1984) organizations make, but there is little research that attempts to explore the complete connection between environmental constraint and internal organizational dynamics, including outcomes other than who occupies critical organizational positions and their backgrounds.

There is, however, certainly evidence consistent with the resource dependence view of executive succession. Fligstein (1987) traced the rise of finance to power in U.S. corporations to changes in the institutional environment and particularly the rise in power of the capital markets and the need for skill in raising capital and managing relationships with share owners. Thornton and Ocasio (1999), studying the higher education publishing industry, noted that as publishing transitioned from an industry in which books and their quality were important to one in which financial results were viewed as more critical, the determinants of succession changed accordingly.

This quick overview of the basic premises of resource dependence theory indicates that supporting evidence has continued to accumulate. However, there is much less systematic study of resource dependence predictions than there might be, and second, in very few cases are resource dependence predictions tested against alternatives. Therefore, in spite of (or perhaps because of) the widespread acceptance of resource dependence logic, much empirical work remains to be done.

Challenges and Critiques

In the years since *The External Control of Organizations* was published, a number of theoretical challenges and critiques have appeared. Some researchers have argued that resource dependence, with its focus on transactional interdependence, overlooks other important environmental effects on organizations. This must certainly be true, as nowhere did Salancik and I claim that resource interdependence accounted for everything about organizations.

Donald Palmer has offered two alternative views of the environment that are different in their focus from resource dependence. One perspective speaks to the importance of place, of geography, of physical location on interorganizational relations. "Social theory tends to ignore the spatial character of social action and structure. . . . Contemporary organization and class theory are written as if corporations, their administrative and productive activities, and their leaders are not situated in a physical world" (Kono, Palmer, Friedland, and Zafonte, 1998: 865). For instance, Kono, et al. (1998), studying directorate interlocks, found that they had a spatial dimension and the determinants of within locale and across locale directorate ties were different. There is little doubt that geography matters (Friedland and Palmer, 1984), and organizational research would be well served to explore the effects of proximity on numerous phenomena, including interorganizational relations. However, space probably matters more or less depending on the time period, as communication technologies and even norms about economic and social relations at a distance have changed. In that regard, the Kono, et al. study, which used 1964 data, could probably stand replication using more recent data. And the scope conditions for the effects of geography could be profitably explored. Moreover, even in the context of the importance of physical location, "the results indicate that resource dependence relations influence interlocking" (Kono, et al., 1998: 891).

Palmer's second important contribution to the delimiting of resource dependence ideas was to note that resource dependence ignores social class. Again focusing on interlocking directorates, Palmer (1983) argued that director ties did not so much bind organizations together as organizations were places where class relations were formed, reproduced, and reaffirmed. "According to the interorganizational approach, organizations are entities that possess interests. . . . According to the intraclass approach, individuals within the capitalist class or business elite are actors who possess interests. Organizations are the agents of these actors" (Palmer, 1983: 40–42). Palmer found that when directorate ties were broken, they were not often reconstituted, which called into question the idea that interlocking directorates served to manage dependence relations. Of course, it is possible that both perspectives have some validity, and again research could profitably examine the scope conditions of the organizational and the social class approaches.

A third critique of resource dependence comes from those who argue that in the contemporary world, the power of the financial markets and increasingly boundaryless production processes has made the sorts of actions and strategic choices described in *The External Control of Organizations* no longer as important or relevant (e.g., Davis and McAdam, 2000). The basic idea is as follows. Resource dependence presumes some level of managerial discretion—to do things like engage in mergers, constitute boards of directors, and make decisions to manage environmental dependence. This is an accurate statement, and indeed, the assumption of managerial discretion and choice is one important way that resource dependence differs not only from transactions cost theory but many other economic approaches with their presumption that organizations do not invariably or inevitably seek efficiency and are not so constrained that they must do so at all moments. Recently, however, there has been a shift from what might be termed managerial capitalism to investor capitalism (Useem, 1996). This shift has at once reduced the discretion of organizations and increased the role of markets. So, for instance, banks (Davis and Mizruchi, 1999) are no longer as central in the social structure of industry because they are no longer as important in the allocation of financial resources.

But the events of 2001 and 2002 in corporate America speak to the relevance of resource dependence ideas and the importance of social relations even in, or perhaps particularly in, a world dominated by financial markets. As we now know, the market prices of financial instruments were affected by the coverage and recommendations of analysts. These analysts worked for investment banks, securities firms, and commercial banks such as Citicorp that purchased securities firms and investment banks. In order to get underwriting business, analysts provided favorable coverage and banks provided preferred access to initial public offerings for top managers at firms whose business they were seeking. Securities firms such as Merrill Lynch and banks such as J. P. Morgan Chase participated in the underwriting and syndication of complex financial instruments including the off-balance sheet partnership entities at Enron, now known to have been an attempt to artificially inflate the company's financial performance.

At the same time, accounting firms, dependent on companies not only for auditing work but for the more lucrative and higher margin tax and information system consulting business, tended not to be as aggressive as they might be in questioning dubious financial transactions and various maneuvers designed to artificially inflate earnings and hide debt. It would be useful to see the extent to which resource dependence—the extensiveness of financial relations between various entities and the dependence of the firms on those transactions—could account for the variation in the extent to which various accounting firms and investment banks engaged in questionable behavior. It would also be interesting to explore the extent to which director ties help us understand these actions. But the idea that there is some efficient market for corporate control that provides effective discipline over managerial behavior and delimits managerial discretion seems almost ludicrous, given both what occurred with respect to executive compensation and the ties between companies and their bankers and the consequences of those relationships for decisions about investment ratings and financing activities.

This is not to say that resource dependencies will necessarily predict or explain what occurred—we need to do the empirical analyses to answer that question. But at first glance, corporate behavior can be more readily explained by resource dependence ideas than by ideas of efficient markets or even investor capitalism. In the end, managers seemed to have plenty of discretion to both enrich themselves, engage in mergers and other transactions that did not build economic value, and to use their power to influence transactions to constrain the independence of presumably independent entities such as accounting firms, banks, and even, some might argue, federal regulatory authorities such as the Securities and Exchange Commission.

Yet another challenge for resource dependence, somewhat more subtle than those considered to this point, comes from the analysis of social networks and network structures. As Piskorski and Anand (2002: 3–4) noted:

> The resource dependence view . . . suggests that organizations develop relationships with other organizations based on interdependencies between their exogenous endowments or resources. . . . An alternative view . . . emphasizes the role of prior exchanges of an organization determining the structure of subsequent ties.

One alternative is, then, that the history of social ties matters. Another alternative comes from Burt's (1992) analysis of structural holes. Here the idea is that network structure itself provides opportunities for brokerage, and there is an opportunity to profit from linking organizations that are not otherwise linked to each other. Yet a third alternative conceptualization of network relations and social ties comes from Podolny's (1993) emphasis on status. Status is determined by the status of the other organizations the focal organization interacts with. Possession of high status confers a number of benefits including higher revenues and lower costs. There is, therefore, little incentive for high status organizations to form alliances with lower status ones. In each instance, network structure and history are presumed to be critical, *not* the nature or importance of the transactional interdependencies implicated in the network. it would be interesting and useful to see to what extent transactional interdependence moderates or provides even an alternative way of explaining interorganizational relations for those theories that to this point have focused primarily on network structure and status.

With few exceptions (e.g., Piskorski and Anand, 2002), however, these network-social embeddedness theories of interorganizational relations have not been compared with predictions that might emerge from a resource dependence approach. Anand and Piskorski found that, under certain circumstances, resource endowments *can* substitute for network positions in predicting the organization's ability to develop commercial ties. They argued that "both resources and network positions need to be considered in a single model in order to understand the dynamics of interorganizational networks" (Piskorski and Anand, 2002: 33).

Some New Directions for Resource Dependence

My colleague and co-author Jerry Salancik was fond of saying, "success ruins everything." To some extent, the very success of resource dependence theory has also been a problem. The idea, seemingly now widely accepted, that organizations are constrained and affected by their environments and that they act to attempt to manage resource dependencies, has become almost so accepted and taken for granted that it is not as rigorously explored and tested as it might be. In fact, the original work may not even be read. The book has been out of print for a long time. And, as Mizruchi and Fein (1999: 653–654) perceptively noted:

> classic works are frequently described as often cited but rarely read. This accounts for the surprise that readers often experience when they actually go back and read such works. The fact that classic works in a field are often cited and discussed without being carefully read (or read at all) suggests the possibility that these works can become social constructions.

It is quite likely that this is to some extent the fate that has befallen *The External Control of Organizations*. To remedy this problem, throughout this chapter, and in what follows, I provide some suggestions for specific research that might be done that would more directly and proximately engage resource dependence theory.

Finkelstein's (1997) effort to explore the scope or boundary conditions of resource dependence—does the effect vary over time, are there impacts of different public policy regimes—represents only a small beginning to what ought to be a much larger systematic effort to examine resource dependence in context. For instance, we have seen in social psychology that many theories of cognition, with their assumption of individualism, are culturally specific and that phenomena such as the fundamental attribution error—the tendency to overattribute causation to individuals—disappears in other countries (e.g., Morris and Peng, 1994). Resource dependence, and for that matter, other theories of interorganizational relations (e.g., Burt, 1992) begin with an emphasis on the focal organization and how that organization maneuvers to obtain advantage. Perhaps in more collectivist cultures, predictions of resource dependence would not be supported or would look different than they do in cultures in which competition and the seeking of competitive advantage and resource accumulation are emphasized.

Studying the adoption of the multidivisional form, Armour and Teece (1978) found performance effects initially but not subsequently, when adoption was more complete. In a similar way, it may be that the effectiveness of strategies of cooptation for enhancing organizational performance would diminish as such strategies became more widely adopted and implemented. However, as already noted, in order to examine this phenomenon we would need more studies of the *consequences* of organizational efforts to manage environmental dependence.

Resource dependence predicts that organizations will attempt to manage the constraints and uncertainty that result from the need to acquire resources from the environment. However, the theory is largely silent concerning which of the various cooptive strategies organizations will use, and how the use of these strategies varies over time and other circumstances. Haunschild and Beckman (1998) did study whether complementary sources of information affected the impact of interlocks on behavior, but did not study whether complementary sources of information or cooptive relations affected the structure or prevalence of interlocks.

Just as the study of strategy has broadened its focus to consider a range of internal actions organizations may take, to build competencies and internal resources, to enter and leave markets, and to compete on bases ranging from innovation to cost, it would be useful for studies of strategy in a resource dependence tradition to consider the externally-oriented, sometimes non-market based actions companies undertake to provide competitive leverage. Such strategies include political activities, coopting political elites—for instance, by hiring them upon their leaving government service—and even litigation.

It would also be informative to consider how product market competition and capital market changes affect both the ability of resource dependence to explain organizational actions and the effects of those actions on organizational outcomes. To the extent that competition increases pressures for isomorphism, competition might be expected to lead to more similarity in interorganizational behavior. And, Davis's and others' claims about the effects of the changes in the capital markets and other macroeconomic changes on managerial discretion and, consequently, on resource dependence predictions, warrant empirical examination. There is no question that the structure of markets has changed, with increased globalization and with changes in the concentration of share ownership and in the regulatory structure of both financial and product markets. Using resource dependence, and other, theories to empirically explore the effects of such changes on organizations would seem to be a worthwhile undertaking.

To conclude this list of new or expanded directions, I would be remiss if I did not address public policy concerns. Organization theory has been, for the most part, content to be silent in discussions of public policy, particularly policies dealing with economic actors and markets. Instead, discussions of markets, competition, and regulation are left largely to economists. As someone who has personally experienced the results of the deregulation of electricity markets in the form of rolling blackouts and soaring utility bills, and as an observer of the failure of governmental regulation to prevent the continued consolidation of numerous industries or to oversee the operation of markets for the benefits of consumers or the general well being, it seems to me that we ought to offer some competing logics for understanding markets and economic actors. Resource dependence was originally developed to provide an alternative perspective to economic theories of mergers and board interlocks, and to understand precisely the type of interorganizational relations that have played such a large role in recent "market failures."

Providing a detailed road map of what a resource dependence approach to public policy and the analysis of contemporary market failures would look like is well beyond the scope of this brief introductory chapter. Suffice it to say that it would be both informative and useful to examine both interorganizational relations such as mergers and board interlocks and the relations between the regulated and regulators using the basic concepts and hypotheses outlined in this book. We should then take these insights and attempt to derive policy prescriptions based on what we have learned. It seems to me that organization theory generally, and theories of organizations and their environments more specifically, have much to say about the contemporary world of corporate governance, regulatory failure, and self-dealing.

The overriding theme of this introduction to the reissued book is that resource dependence theory, although in many respects quite successful, has been too readily accepted as an obligatory citation and not often enough engaged empirically, either in concert or contrast with other theories of organizations and their environments or to further develop the theory itself. It is my hope that the republication of the original book will make the many ideas and insights of *The External Control of Organizations* accessible to new generations of organizations scholars. By so doing, perhaps the study of resource dependence, as a theory not just as a metaphor, will be reinvigorated.

References

Allen, M. P. 1974. The Structure of Interorganizational Elite Cooptation: Interlocking Corporate Directorates. *American Sociological Review*, *39*, 393–406.

Amburgey, T. L., D. Kelly, and W. P. Barnett 1993 Resetting the Clock: The Dynamics of Organizational Failure. *Administrative Science Quarterly*, *38*, 51–73.

Armour, H. O., and D. J. Teece 1978. Organizational Structure and Economic Performance: A Test of the Multidivisional Hypothesis. *Bell Journal of Economics*, *9*, 106–122.

Blau, P. M. 1964. *Exchange and Power in Social Life*. New York: Wiley.

Bowers, K. S. 1973. Situationism in Psychology: An Analysis and Critique. *Psychological Review*, *80*, 307–336.

Burgelman, R. A. 1990. Strategy-Making and Organizational Ecology: A Conceptual Integration. In J. V. Singh (Ed.), *Organizational Evolution*, 164–181. Newbury Park, CA: Sage.

Burns, L. R., and D. R. Wholey 1993. Adoption and Abandonment of Matrix Management Programs: Effects of Organizational Characteristics and Interorganizational Networks. *Academy of Management Journal*, *36*, 106–138.

Burt, R. S. 1980 Autonomy in a Social Topology. *American Journal of Sociology*, *85*, 892–925

Burt, R. S. 1983. *Corporate Profits and Co-optation*. New York: Academic Press.

Burt, R. S. 1992. *Structural Holes: The Social Structure of Competition*. Cambridge, MA: Harvard University Press.

Burt, R. S., K. P. Christman, and H. C. Kilburn, Jr. 1980. Testing a Structural Theory of Corporate Cooptation: Interorganizational Directorate Ties as a Strategy for Avoiding Market Constraints on Profits. *American Sociological Review*, *45*, 821–841.

Carroll, G. R. 1984. Dynamics of Publisher Succession in Newspaper Organizations. *Administrative Science Quarterly*, *29*, 93–113.

Carroll, G. R., and M. T. Hannan 2000. *The Demography of Corporations and Industries*. Princeton: Princeton University Press.

Carroll, G. R., and J. B. Wade 1991. Density Dependence in the Evolution of the American Brewing Industry Across Different Levels of Analysis. *Social Science Research*, *20*, 271–302.

Child, J. 1972. Organization Structure, Environment, and Performance: The Role of Strategic Choice. *Sociology*, *6*, 1–22.

Christensen, C. M. 1997 *The Innovator's Dilemma: When New Technologies Cause Great Firms to Fail*. Boston: Harvard Business School Press.

Christensen, C. M., and J. J. Bower 1996. Customer Power, Strategic Investment, and the Failure of Leading Firms. *Strategic Management Journal*, *17*, 197–218.

Davis, G. F. 1991. Agents without Principles? The Spread of the Poison Pill Through the Intercorporate Network. *Administrative Science Quarterly*, *36*, 586–613.

Davis, G. F., and H. R. Greve 1997. Corporate Elite Networks and Governance Changes in the 1980s. *American Journal of Sociology*, *103*, 1–37.

Davis, G. F., and D. McAdam 2000. Corporations, Classes, and Social Movements after Managerialism. *Research in Organizational Behavior, Vol. 22*, 193–236.

Davis, G. F., and M. S. Mizruchi 1999. The Money Center Can Not Hold: Commercial Banks in the U.S. System of Governance. *Administrative Science Quarterly, 44*, 215–239.

DiMaggio, P. J. 1988. Interest and Agency in Institutional Theory. In L. G. Zucker (ed.), *Institutional Patterns and Organizations*, 3–21. Cambridge, MA: Ballinger.

Dowling, J., and J. Pfeffer 1975. Organizational Legitimacy, Social Values and Organizational Behavior. *Pacific Sociological Review, 18*, 122–136.

Emerson, R. M. 1962. Power-Dependence Relations. *American Sociological Review, 27*, 31–41.

Finkelstein, S. 1997. Interindustry Merger Patterns and Resource Dependence: A Replication and Extension of Pfeffer (1972). *Strategic Management Journal, 18*, 787–810.

Fligstein, N. 1987. The Interorganizational Power Struggle: The Rise of Finance Personnel to Top Leadership in Large Corporations, 1919–1979. *American Sociological Review, 52*, 44–58.

Friedland, R., and D. Palmer 1984. Park Place and Main Street: Business and the Urban Power Structure. *Annual Review of Sociology, 10*, 393–416.

Granovetter, M. 1985. Economic Action and Social Structure: The Problem of Embeddedness. *American Journal of Sociology, 91*, 481–510.

Gulati, R., and M. Gargiulo 1999. Where Do Interorganizational Networks Come From? *American Journal of Sociology, 104*, 1439–1493.

Hambrick, D. C., and P. A. Mason 1984. Upper Echelons: The Organization as a Reflection of Its Top Managers. *Academy of Management Review, 9*, 195–206.

Hannan, M. T., and G. R. Carroll 1992. *Dynamics of Organizational Populations: Density, Competition, and Legitimation*. New York: Oxford University Press.

Hannan, M. T., and J. H. Freeman 1984. Structural Inertia and Organizational Change. *American Sociological Review, 49*, 149–164.

Hannan, M. T., and J. H. Freeman. 1989. *Organizational Ecology*. Cambridge, MA: Harvard University Press.

Haunschild, P. R. 1993. Interorganizational Imitation: The Impact of Interlocks on Corporate Acquisition Activity. *Administrative Science Quarterly, 38*, 564–592.

Haunschild, P. R., and C. M. Beckman 1998. When Do Interlocks Matter? Alternate Sources of Information and Interlock Influence. *Administrative Science Quarterly, 43*, 815–844.

Hickson, D. J., C. R. Hinings, C. A. Lee, R. E. Schneck, and J. M. Pennings. 1971. A Strategic Contingencies' Theory of Intraorganizational Power. *Administrative Science Quarterly, 16*, 216–229.

Hinings, C. R., D. J. Hickson, J. M. Pennings, and R. E. Schneck. 1974. Structural Conditions of Intraorganizational Power. *Administrative Science Quarterly, 19*, 22–44.

Jones, E. E. 1998. Major Developments in Five Decades of Social Psychology. In D. T. Gilbert, S. T. Fiske, and G. Lindzey (Eds.), *The Handbook of Social Psychology, 4th Edition*, 3–57. New York: McGraw-Hill.

Katz, D., and R. L. Kahn 1978. *The Social Psychology of Organizations, 2nd Ed.* New York: John Wiley.

Kono, C., D. Palmer, R. Friedland, and M. Zafonte 1998. Lost in Space: The Geography of Corporate Interlocking Directorates. *American Journal of Sociology, 103*, 863–911.

Lieberson, S., and J. F. O'Connor 1972. Leadership and Organizational Performance: A Study of Large Corporations. *American Sociological Review, 37*, 117–130.

Meyer, J. W., and B. Rowan 1977. Institutionalized Organizations: Formal Structure as Myth and Ceremony. *American Journal of Sociology, 83*, 340–363.

Mizruchi, M. S. 1996. What Do Interlocks Do? An Analysis, Critique, and Assessment of Research on Interlocking Directorates. *Annual Review of Sociology, 22*, 271–298.

Mizruchi, M. S., and L. C. Fein 1999. The Social Construction of Organizational Knowledge: A Study of the Uses of Coercive, Mimetic, and Normative Isomorphism. *Administrative Science Quarterly, 44*, 653–683.

Mizruchi, M. S., and L. B. Stearns 1988. A Longitudinal Study of the Formation of Interlocking Directorates. *Administrative Science Quarterly, 33*, 194–210.

Morris, M. W., and K. Peng 1994. Culture and Cause: American and Chinese Attributions for Social and Physical Events. *Journal of Personality and Social Psychology, 67*, 949–971.

Ocasio, W. 1994. Political Dynamics and the Circulation of Power: CEO Succession in U.S. Industrial Corporations, 1960–1990. *Administrative Science Quarterly, 39*, 285–312.

Palmer, D. 1983. Broken Ties: Interlocking Directorates and Intercorporate Coordination. *Administrative Science Quarterly, 28*: 40–55.

Palmer, D. P., P. D. Jennings, and X. Zhou 1993. Late Adoption of the Multidivisional Form by Large U.S. Corporations: Institutional, Political, and Economics Accounts. *Administrative Science Quarterly, 38*, 100–131.

Perrow, C. 1970. Departmental Power and Perspective in Industrial Firms. In M. N. Zald (ed.), *Power in Organizations*, 59–89. Nashville, TN: Vanderbilt University Press.

Pfeffer, J. 1972a. Size and Composition of Corporate Boards of Directors: The Organization and Its Environment. *Administrative Science Quarterly, 17*, 218–228.

Pfeffer, J. 1972b. Merger as a Response to Organizational Interdependence. *Administrative Science Quarterly, 17*, 382–394.

Pfeffer, J. 1972c. Interorganizational Influence and Managerial Attitudes. *Academy of Management Journal, 15*, 317–330.

Pfeffer, J. 1973. Size, Composition, and Function of Hospital Boards of Directors: A Study of Organizational-Environment Linkage. *Administrative Science Quarterly, 18*, 349–364.

Pfeffer, J. 1977. The Ambiguity of Leadership. *Academy of Management Review, 2*, 104–112.

Pfeffer, J. 1992. *Managing with Power*. Boston: Harvard Business School Press.

Pfeffer, J., and H. Leblebici 1973. Executive Recruitment and the Development of Interfirm Organizations. *Administrative Science Quarterly, 18*, 449–461.

Pfeffer, J., and P. Nowak 1976. Joint Ventures and Interorganizational Interdependence. *Administrative Science Quarterly, 21*, 398–418.

Piskorski, M. J., and B. Anand 2003. Money Can't Buy Me Love: Relational and Non-Relational Resources in the Formation of Venture Capital Syndicates. Working paper, Graduate School of Business, Stanford University.

Podolny, J. M. 1993. A Status-Based Model of Market Competition. *American Journal of Sociology, 98*, 829–872.

Porter, M. E. 1980. *Competitive Strategy: Techniques for Analyzing Industries and Competitors*. New York: Free Press.

Porter, M. E. 1985. *Competitive Advantage: Creating and Sustaining Superior Performance*. New York: Free Press.

Salancik, G. R. 1979. Interorganizational Dependence and Responsiveness to Affirmative Action: The Case of Women and Defense Contractors. *Academy of Management Journal, 22*, 375–394.

Salancik, G. R., and J. Pfeffer 1974. The Bases and Use of Power in Organizational Decision Making: The Case of a University. *Administrative Science Quarterly, 19*, 453–473.

Salancik, G. R., J. Pfeffer, and J. P. Kelly 1978. A Contingency Model of Influence in Organizational Decision-Making. *Pacific Sociological Review, 21*, 239–256.

Schuler, D. A., K. Rehbein, and R. D. Cramer 2002. Pursuing Strategic Advantage Through Political Means: A Multivariate Approach. *Academy of Management Journal, 45*, 659–672.

Scott, W. R. 1995. *Institutions and Organizations*. Thousand Oaks, CA: Sage.

Scott, W. R., M. Ruef, P. J. Mendel, and C. Caronna 2000. *Institutional Changeand Healthcare Organizations: From Professional Dominance to Managed Care*. Chicago: University of Chicago Press.

Selznick, P. 1949. *TVA and the Grass Roots*. Berkeley, CA: University of California Press.

Thornton, P. H., and W. Ocasio 1999. Institutional Logics and the Historical Contingency of Power in Organizations: Executive Succession in the Higher Education Publishing Industry, 1958–1990. *American Journal of Sociology, 105*, 801–843.

Useem, M. 1996. *Investor Capitalism: How Money Managers are Changing theFace of Corporate America*. New York: Basic Books.

Weick, K. E. 1996. An Appreciation of Social Context: One Legacy of Gerald Salancik. *Administrative Science Quarterly, 41*, 563–573.

Williamson, O. E. 1975. *Markets and Hierarchies*. New York: Free Press.

Williamson, O. E., and W. G. Ouchi 1981. The Markets and Hierarchies Program of Research: Origins, Implications, Prospects. In A. H. Van de Ven and W. F. Joyce (eds.), *Perspectives on Organizational Design and Behavior*, 347–370. New York: Wiley.

Yuchtman, E., and S. E. Seashore 1967. A System Resource Approach to Organizational Effectiveness. *American Sociological Review, 32*, 891–903.

Preface

This book is about how organizational environments affect and constrain organization and how organizations respond to external constraints. It is also a guide to designing and managing organizations that are externally constrained.

Although the ideas of open systems theory, organization, and social constraint are not new, such ideas really have not had much impact on research and training in management and organizational behavior. After some pro forma acknowledgment of social constraints, the environment, and open systems, most authors spend much of their time, space, and research documentation dealing with the same old concepts out of which organizational behavior grew—leadership, motivation, task design, communication, and control. There are no such pro forma bows in this book. We take seriously the idea of social constraint on organizational behavior and design. Our intent is simple—to provoke additional thought, research attention, and concern for the ideas of resource interdependence, external social constraint, and organizational adaptation. In other words, this is not another industrial psychology book in disguise. We hope to set out and to provide empirical demonstrations of an external control perspective for organizational behavior.

In the first chapter, the themes and ideas to be used throughout the book are introduced. We also present some reasons why the external perspective is not more widely adopted for understanding organizational behavior. We define some possible roles for management by introducing the ideas of managers as symbols, managers as adapters to social constraints, and managers as manipulators of their organizational environments.

In the second chapter we examine organizations as coalitions of interests that face an environment of competing, frequently conflicting, demands and that need resources from that environment. Boundaries are defined in terms of survival, for example, the ability to attract and maintain resources.

Chapter Three illustrates how the social control of organizations comes about. The basic components of control—the factors that provide external constraint over organizational actions—are enumerated and described. The framework of social control is illustrated using an empirical study of the autonomy of Israeli managers and the response of United States defense contractors to affirmative action pressure.

The environment and how it is perceived by the organization is considered in Chapter Four. We assert that various dimensions of the environment are not as independent as one might believe from reading the literature and that they become known to the organization through a process of enactment. We explore the various determinants of the enactment process, and include some discussion about how organizations get into trouble with their social environments. We conclude the chapter by describing a framework that may be used descriptively to analyze organizational actions or prescriptively to plan and design strategies.

The next four chapters describe organizational strategies for coping with external constraints. Chapter Five considers the possibilities of adapting to external demands or avoiding demands; Chapter Six examines altering patterns of interdependence through growth, merger, and diversification; Chapter Seven explores the establishment of collective structures of interorganizational behavior through the use of interlocking directorates, joint ventures, industry associations, and normative restraints; and Chapter Eight discusses creating the organizational environment through law, political action, and altering the definitions of the legitimacy.

In examining the external control of organizations and organizational adaptations and responses, one must not neglect the mechanism that produces organizational action. This topic is the focus of Chapter Nine, in which executive recruitment and succession are examined and related to the organization's context and to adaptation and change. The book concludes with a review of the resource dependence perspective, some further analysis of the roles of management, and the implications of this perspective for organizational design and predicting organizational futures.

We have attempted to develop a theoretical perspective that offers new insights for analyzing organizations and to assemble empirical evidence consistent with this perspective. The book is intended as a spur to further research on social constraint and external control.

It is appropriate to conclude by acknowledging gratefully those interdependencies which, rather than acting as constraints, made the end product. Special thanks are in order to Betty Kendall, Ellen McGibbon, and Helen Way, who provided the most extraordinary typing service we have ever seen in the most cheerful and helpful manner, and to Joe Garbarino who graciously made their services available through the Institute of Business and Economic Research at Berkeley. We dedicate this book to Susan, Tina, Sofia, and Fuzzy, those who control our critical contingencies and who have become such important parts of our social context.

Jeffrey Pfeffer
Gerald R. Salancik

The External Control of Organizations

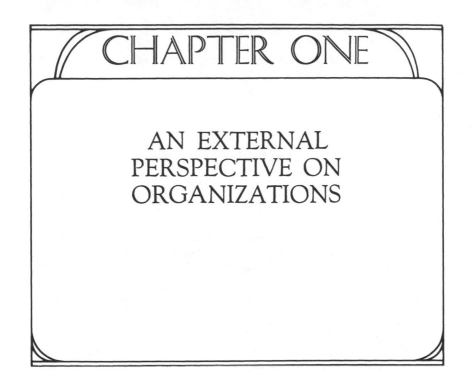

CHAPTER ONE

AN EXTERNAL PERSPECTIVE ON ORGANIZATIONS

The central thesis of this book is that to understand the behavior of an organization you must understand the context of that behavior—that is, the ecology of the organization. This point of view is important for those who seek to understand organizations as well as for those who seek to manage and control them. Organizations are inescapably bound up with the conditions of their environment. Indeed, it has been said that all organizations engage in activities which have as their logical conclusion adjustment to the environment (Hawley, 1950:3).

At first glance, this position seems obvious. An open-systems perspective on organizations is not new (Katz and Kahn, 1966), and it is generally accepted that contexts, organizational environments, are important for understanding actions and structures. One of the purposes of this introductory chapter, besides elaborating the perspective we are going to be developing throughout the book, is to note that, in spite of the apparent obviousness of this position, much of the literature on organizations still does not recognize the importance of context; indeed, there are some reasons why such a neglect of contextual factors is likely to be maintained.

OVERVIEW

Most books about organizations describe how they operate, and the existence of the organizations is taken for granted. This book discusses how organizations manage to survive. Their existence is constantly in question, and their survival is viewed as problematic. How managers go about ensuring their organization's survival is what this book is about.

Our position is that organizations survive to the extent that they are effective. Their effectiveness derives from the management of demands, particularly the demands of interest groups upon which the organizations depend for resources and support. As we shall consider, there are a variety of ways of managing demands, including the obvious one of giving in to them.

The key to organizational survival is the ability to acquire and maintain resources. This problem would be simplified if organizations were in complete control of all the components necessary for their operation. However, no organization is completely self-contained. Organizations are embedded in an environment comprised of other organizations. They depend on those other organizations for the many resources they themselves require. Organizations are linked to environments by federations, associations, customer-supplier relationships, competitive relationships, and a social-legal apparatus defining and controlling the nature and limits of these relationships. Organizations must transact with other elements in their environment to acquire needed resources, and this is true whether we are talking about public organizations, private organizations, small or large organizations, or organizations which are bureaucratic or organic (Burns and Stalker, 1961).

Even seemingly self-contained organizations require some transactions with their environment for survival. The convents and abbeys which flourished during the Middle Ages were designed to be virtually self-sufficient. Needs were kept to a minimum; foods were grown within; and many required utensils, tools, and clothing were made by the abbey's available labor. An attempt was made, consciously, to isolate the organizations as much as possible from the secular world outside. But, abbeys were peopled by people, usually of one sex, and humans are mortal. This meant that new members had to be recruited from the outside, which required the organization to maintain relations with sources of recruits—prisons, wealthy families with illegitimate offspring, and so forth. Recruitment from the outside, therefore, imposed on the organization a need to devote some energy to elaborate socialization and indoctrination procedures. Moreover, these religious organizations had land, and to maintain their land, it was necessary to ensure a position of social legitimacy and political acceptance so that other groups would not attempt to seize the land for themselves.

The fact that organizations are dependent for survival and success on their environments does not, in itself, make their existence problematic. If stable supplies were assured from the sources of needed resources, there would be no problem. If the resources needed by the organization were continually available, even if outside their control, there would be no problem. Problems arise not merely because organizations are dependent on their environment, but because this environment is not dependable. Environments can change, new organizations enter and exit, and the supply of resources becomes more or less scarce. When environments change, organizations face the prospect either of not surviving or of changing their activities in response to these environmental factors.

Despite the importance of the environment for organizations, relatively little attention has been focused there. Rather than dealing with problems of acquiring resources, most writers have dealt with the problem of using resources. Theories of individual behavior in organizations, theories of motivation, leadership, interpersonal communication, theories of organizational design—each concerns the use of resources. The central goal of most theories is the maximization of output from given resources. Questions about how to motivate a worker to be productive are common. But questions about how resources come to be acquired are left unanswered or are completely neglected.

Both problems of using resources and problems of acquiring them face organizations, but the use of resources always presupposes their existence. A good deal of organizational behavior, the actions taken by organizations, can be understood only by knowing something about the organization's environment and the problems it creates for obtaining resources. What happens in an organization is not only a function of the organization, its structure, its leadership, its procedures, or its goals. What happens is also a consequence of the environment and the particular contingencies and constraints deriving from that environment.

Consider the following case, described by a student at the University of Illinois. The student had worked in a fast-food restaurant near the campus and was concerned about how the workers (himself) were treated. Involved in what he was studying the student read a great deal about self-actualizing, theories of motivation, and the management of human resources. He observed at the restaurant that workers would steal food, make obscene statements about the boss behind his back, and complain about the low pay. The student's analysis of the situation was a concise report summarizing the typical human relations palliatives: make the boring, greasy work more challenging and the indifferent management more democratic. The student was asked why he thought management was unresponsive to such suggestions. He considered the possibility that management was cruel and interested only in making a profit (and the operation was quite profitable). He was then asked why the employees permitted management to treat them in such a fashion—after all, they could always quit. The student responded that the workers needed the money and that jobs were hard to obtain.

This fact, that the workers were drawn from an almost limitless labor pool of students looking for any kind of part-time employment was nowhere to be found in the student's discussion of the operation of the restaurant. Yet, it was precisely this characteristic of the labor market which permitted the operation to disregard the feelings of the workers. Since there were many who wanted to work, the power of an individual worker was severely limited. More critical to the organization's success was its location and its ability both to keep competition to a minimum and to maintain a steady flow of supplies to serve a virtually captive market. If the workers were unsatisfied, it was not only because they did not like the organization's policies; in the absence of any base of power and with few alternative jobs, the workers had neither the option of voice nor exit (Hirschman, 1970).

More important to this organization's success than the motivation of its workers was its location on a block between the campus and dormitories, the path of thousands of students. Changes in policies and facilities for housing and transportation of students would have a far greater effect than some disgruntled employees. Our example illustrates, first, the importance of attending to contextual variables in understanding organizations, but also that organizational survival and success are not always achieved by making internal adjustments. Dealing with and managing the environment is just as important a component of organizational effectiveness.

A comparison of the phonograph record and the pharmaceutical industries (Hirsch, 1975) illustrates this point more directly. These two industries, Hirsch noted, are strikingly different in profitability. This difference in profits is more striking because the industries in many ways are otherwise similar: both sell their products through intermediaries, doctors in the case of pharmaceuticals, disc jockeys in the case of records; both introduce many new products; both protect their market positions through patent or copyright laws. What could account for the difference in profit? Hirsch argued that the pharmaceutical industry's greater profits came from its greater control of its environment; a more concentrated industry, firms could more effectively restrict entry and manage distribution channels. Profits resulted from a favorable institutional environment. Aware of the importance of the institutional environment for success, firms spent a lot of strategic effort maintaining that environment. They would engage in activities designed to modify patent laws to their advantage and in other efforts to protect their market positions.

The Environment as Treated in the Social Sciences

The social sciences, even if not frequently examining the context of behavior, have long recognized its importance. The demography of a city has been found to affect the particular form of city government used, and particularly the use of a city manager (Kessel, 1962; Schnore and Alford, 1963). Some political economists have argued that party positions are developed with reference to the distribution of preferences for policies in the population (e.g., Davis and Hinich, 1966), which means that political platforms are affected by context. The importance of external influences on individual voting behaviors has been recognized, while participation in political activities, as well as other forms of voluntary associations, is also partially determined by the context, particularly the demographic and socioeconomic dimensions of the community.

As in the case of political science, some theorists writing about organizational behavior have recognized that the organization's context shapes the activities and structures of formal organizations. Katz and Kahn (1966) argued for the necessity of viewing organizations as open systems, and Perrow (1970) forcefully illustrated the analytical benefits to be gained by considering the environment of the organization in addition to its internal operating characteristics. Bendix (1956) showed how ideologies shaped the use of authority in organizations, and Weber (1930) proposed a theory of economic development that held the religion of a country to be critical. He suggested that the development of mercantile capitalism depended on a legitimating ideology which stressed hard work and delayed gratification, such as that provided by Protestantism, as contrasted with Catholicism.

Economists were even more explicit in giving critical importance to the context of organizations, but they tended to take the environment as a given. Competition is a critical variable distinguishing between the applicability of models of monopoly, oligopoly, imperfect competition, or perfectly competitive behavior. The study of oligopoly is explicitly the study of interorganizational behavior (e.g., Phillips, 1960; Williamson, 1965; Fellner, 1949). And, the study of antitrust policy implicitly recognizes the fact that organizations do make efforts to limit or otherwise manage the competitiveness of their environments.

In recent years, it has become fashionable for those writing about management and organizations to acknowledge the importance of the open-systems view and the importance of the environment, particularly in the first chapter or in a special section of the book. Except for some special terminology, however, the implications of the organization's context for analyzing and managing organizations remains undeveloped. Indeed, if one examines Katz and Kahn's (1966) book carefully, one might argue that the bulk of the material they present in chapters on leadership, communication, and organizational change could have been included with equal ease in any book. This material is not linked to the open-systems perspective Katz and Kahn develop in the beginning of their book. Such a situation is typical of many books, even those with contingency or environment in their titles. Prescriptions for, and discussions of, the operation of organizations remain predominantly concerned with the internal activities, organizational adjustments, and the behavior of individuals.

INTERNAL VERSUS EXTERNAL PERSPECTIVES ON ORGANIZATIONS

The interest in intraorganizational phenomena is not difficult to understand. First, internal processes are the most visible. Walking into any organization, one finds people who are involved in a variety of activities important to the performance of the organization. As Perrow (1970) aptly noted, at first glance, the statement that organizations are, after all, composed of people is patently obvious. The importance of these people to the organization is the logical inference drawn from their very presence. In addition to their visibility, organizational members are also capable of communicating, for they speak the same language as the investigator. They are willing and ready to tell the researcher of their satisfactions and dissatisfactions, their importance to the organization, their feelings toward their work, and their reasons for their decisions. People inside the organization are visible, accessible, and willing to express their opinions. They are a convenient, if not always adequate, research focus.

In addition to convenience, attention to intraorganizational phenomena is fostered by a cognitive bias to attribute causality to the actions of individuals. Research on the behavior of individuals asked to select causative factors suggests that while actors and participants in an event tend to attribute the outcome to situational factors, observers tend to interpret outcomes as the result of the personal motivation and capabilities of the actors (Jones and Nisbett, 1971). The observers of organizations and organizational behavior share this bias. In one recent illustration of this phenomenon (Wolfson and Salancik, 1977), individuals were given the task of controlling an electric car as it traveled over a model track. Unknown to the individuals, their performance was controlled by alterations in the amount of electrical power reaching various sections of the track. All the actual subjects were motivated to do well, but observers tended to see a performer's success as reflecting the amount of effort expended. In fact, it was the result of the experimenter's manipulation of electricity.

In another experimental illustration of the same phenomenological tendency to attribute outcomes to individuals in organizational settings, Staw (1975) set up separate work groups and randomly chose some of the groups to fail and others to succeed. He then asked members of the groups to rate the cohesiveness, leadership, and other attributes of the group. When the groups succeeded, they perceived high cohesiveness and effective leadership, a finding which suggests one reason why organizational analysts have found positive relationships between organizational performance and styles of leaderhip. Individuals in the organization, aware of their own performance, make the same inferences as the theories—if we are doing well, it must be because we are effectively supervised, we are communicating effectively, etc. That such attributional biases can delude organizational actors as easily as observers was shown in a study by Strickland (1958). He assigned two subordinates to a supervisor and then structured the situation so that the supervisor had to spend more time checking on the work activities of subordinate A than on those of subordinate B. The supervisor was given no prior information about the reliability of either worker, and the performance of each was equal. Following the task, the supervisor was asked to make performance evaluations of the two subordinates. The supervisor evaluated subordinate A as less trustworthy than B and recommended that A be watched more closely. The supervisor, in other words, assigned to supervise one subordinate more than another, came to believe that his supervision was both necessary and accomplished something. When individuals assume an organizational role, they came to believe that their performance of the role is having the intended effect and that this effect justifies the role.

Kelley (1971) perceptively noted that attributions are guided not only by the desire to be correct, but also to provide a feeling of control over situations. Clearly, by attributing outcomes to individual action, the observer has a theory of behavior that implies how to control outcomes. When one does not like what is going on, the simple solution is to replace the individual or change the activities. When, on the other hand, a model is used which attributes causality to contextual factors, one faces a much more difficult task in altering activities or outcomes. Therefore, the feelings of control that derive from attributing organizational actions to individuals reinforce the perceptual and cognitive biases, tending to produce a consistent, self-reinforcing system of perception and attribution that emphasizes the importance of individual action.

The consequences of such attributional processes for managerial theory and practice are immediately evident. The concept of the omnipotent actor has led to the search for the unique set of ingredients that produces success in organizations. Originally, the quest was for those traits that distinguished good from poor leaders (Stogdill, 1948). It was believed that if we could isolate and identify those characteristics which made a difference, we could screen and select those individuals who possessed the requisite qualities, ensuring organizational success. Unfortunately, the characteristics could never be found. The trait approach to leadership was finally abandoned, replaced by the belief that it was not personal qualities that mattered but personal behaviors. The search for the unique set of behaviors that constitute leadership or supervisory activities has been well documented (e.g., Carter, 1953; Halpin and Winer, 1952) and, consistent with the original trait perspective, led to the emergence of prescriptions for more consideration, or less close styles of, supervision. Somewhat more recently, contingency theories have become popular, arguing that the appropriate style of behavior depends on the situation, the personalities of the subordinates, the nature of the task, the power of the leader, and so forth. While the quest for the omnipotent actor has become considerably more sophisticated, management researchers continue to trudge after the ever-shifting rainbow's end.

The internal perspective tends to consider that problems can be solved by changing elements within the organization, without regard to their contextual basis. Consider the current problem of motivating workers to engage in menial and boring tasks. The problem seems to be that people are less willing to engage in such work, as evidenced by absenteeism, turnover, and low quality or quantity output. The most common solution advocated for this problem is job redesign, to remove the offending aspects of the tasks (e.g., Hackman and Oldham, 1976). It is a typically internal solution based on the assumption that there is something inherent in the task itself which creates the attitudes of the individual workers, and moreover, that this attitude is some stable characteristic of the individual. Neither assumption is correct. One can create situations experimentally in which persons are induced to do seemingly boring and meaningless tasks for hours. A favorite task requires filling a sheet of graph paper, containing 7000 squares, with random numbers from zero to nine. To make the effort meaningless, the subjects are told that the experimenter will not be able to use their results. Under certain conditions, subjects will express enjoyment in the task and willingly sign up to do it again; while under other conditions, they will label it as unenjoyable (Pallak et al., 1974). The conditions are related to the development of external justification for doing the task in the first place. If a person is induced to do the task with few external constraints or justifications, he tends to find intrinsic features of the task which justify doing it—positive, satisfying reasons. If a person is given considerable external justification for doing the task, he need not attribute interest or enjoyment to the activity, but can explain his behavior by the external constraints. The point is that there are no reactions inherent in an activity. The person, while certainly affected by reality, partially creates interpretations and descriptions of reality.

Why might organizations have problems with worker satisfaction in boring jobs? While the jobs themselves may have something to do with it, it may also be possible that the historical context of the workers and their organizations promotes interpretations of dissatisfaction. The availability of alternative work opportunities, the availability of alternative ways to spend one's time besides working, such as in recreation, and the presence of increasingly powerful labor unions are all characteristics of the present environment. The first two conditions, availability of other jobs and activities, provide individuals with reasons for not being motivated in any particular job. The existence of strong unions provides them with viable political power for expressing and realizing their desires for economic well-being independent of the organization for which they work. Indeed, if one believes the voluminous experimental literature, the ever-increasing levels of pay, by providing increasing external incentives, made it more and more likely that the workers would infer that their activity resulted from the external incentives rather than from the job itself, and would, therefore, come to see the job as less interesting and desirable.

The Importance of Individuals in Organizations

The basic, important question of how much of the variance in organizational activities or outcomes is associated with context and how much with individuals has been infrequently addressed. Pfeffer (1977) noted various theoretical reasons for expecting that individuals would have less effect on organizational outcomes than would an organization's context. First, he argued that both personal and organizational selection processes would lead to similarity among organizational leaders. This means that there is a restriction on the range of skills, characteristics, and behaviors of those likely to achieve positions of importance in organizations. Second, even when a relatively prominent position in the organization has been achieved, the discretion permitted to a given individual is limited. Decisions may require the approval of others in the organization; information used in formulating the decisions comes from others; and persons may be the targets of influence attempts by others in their role set—these social influences further constrain the individual's discretion. Finally, it is simply the case that many of the things that affected organizational results are not controlled by organizational participants. In the case of business firms, the economic cycle, tariff and other regulations, and tax policies are either not subject to control by the organization or are controlled only indirectly through persuasion. In school districts, budgets and educational demands, which are largely a function of state legislative action, local economic growth, and demographic factors are largely outside the control of the district administration. Considering all these factors, it is not likely administrators would have a large effect on the outcomes of most organizations.

In a study of 167 companies, Lieberson and O'Connor (1972) attempted to partition variance in sales, profit, and profit margin to the effects of year (economic cycle), industry, company, and finally, administrators. While the estimate of administrative impact varied by industry and was largest in the case of profit margin, the magnitude of the administrative effect was dwarfed by the impact of the organization's industry and the stable characteristics of a given organization. Extending this perspective, Salancik and Pfeffer (1977) examined the effects of mayors on city budget categories for a sample of 30 United States cities. These authors found that the mayoral impact was greatest for budget items such as parks and libraries not directly the subject of powerful interest-group demands, but that, in general, the mayor accounted for less than 10 percent of the variation in most city budget expenditures.

The conditions under which there would be more or less administrative effect is an important issue, and the theoretical perspective developed in this book will suggest some answers. But, it is fair to state that, based on the presently available research evidence, there is much less evidence for profound administrative effects than is reflected in the predominance of an internal orientation in the literature on organizations.

BASIC CONCEPTS FOR A CONTEXTUAL PERSPECTIVE

We have spent the first part of this chapter discussing the importance of a contextual perspective for understanding organizations and for making them more effective. In the remainder of this chapter, we will briefly describe a number of key concepts that develop this perspective. These concepts will assist in bringing coherence to the large body of work on organization and environment and will provide us with the tools for systematically understanding the effect of environments on organizations and the effect of organizations on environments.

Organizational Effectiveness

The first concept is organizational effectiveness, discussed extensively in Chapter Two. The effectiveness of an organization is its ability to create acceptable outcomes and actions. It is important to avoid confusing organizational effectiveness with organizational efficiency, a confusion that is both widespread and more a real than a semantic problem. The difference between the two concepts is at the heart of the external versus internal perspective on organizations. Organizational effectiveness is an *external* standard of how well an organization is meeting the demands of the various groups and organizations that are concerned with its activities. When the automobile as a mode of transportation is questioned by consumers and governments, this is an issue of the organizational effectiveness of automobile manufacturers. The most important aspect of this concept of organizational effectiveness is that the acceptability of the organization and its activities is ultimately judged by those outside the organization. As we shall see, this does not imply that the organization is at the mercy of outsiders. The organization can and does manipulate, influence, and create acceptability for itself and its activities.

The effectiveness of an organization is a sociopolitical question. It may have a basis in economic considerations, as when an individual declines purchase of a product because it is priced too high. The concept is not restricted, however, to decisions that are economically motivated. Rather, it reflects both an assessment of the usefulness of what is being done and of the resources that are being consumed by the organization.

Organizational efficiency is an *internal* standard of performance. The question whether what is being done should be done is not posed, but only how well is it being done. Efficiency is measured by the ratio of resources utilized to output produced. Efficiency is relatively value free and independent of the particular criteria used to evaluate input and output. Because efficiency involves doing better what the organization is currently doing, external pressures on the organization are often defined internally as requests for greater efficiency. By not questioning the organization's basic activities and operations, the structure of control and influence within the organization can more easily be maintained. Moreover, efficiency is a managerial problem which is perceived as being inherently more tractable.

The difference between efficiency and effectiveness can be illustrated easily. In the late 1960s, Governor Ronald Reagan of California curtailed the amount of money going to the state university system. He was concerned that state university campuses, particularly Berkeley, were indoctrinating students in radical, left-wing ideas. In response to these political pressures and to forestall further budget cuts, the administrators attempted to demonstrate that they were educating students at an ever lower cost per student. Not surprisingly, this argument had little impact on the governor; indeed, it missed the point of his criticism. Producing revolutionaries at lower cost was not what the governor wanted; rather, he questioned whether the universities produced anything that justified giving them state funds.

Organizational Environment

The external basis for judging organizational effectiveness makes the concept of environment important. The concept of environment, however, is elusive. In one sense, the environment includes every event in the world which has any effect on the activities or outcomes of the organization. Primary schools are a part of other organizations' environment. Thus, when primary schools fail to teach reading and grammar properly, some organizations may be affected more than others. An organization which does not require people to read as part of their task may be minimally affected. Other organizations may feel profound effects, as in the case of universities which found themselves spending more and more resources teaching basic reading, grammar, and mathematics skills. Even more affected were publishers, who found it necessary to rewrite many of their textbooks at a seventh- or eighth-grade reading level. The Association of American Publishers had to revise the pamphlet "How to Get the Most Out of Your Textbook" because the college students for whom it was written could not understand it.

Although one can conceive of an organization's environment as encompassing every event that affects it, doing so would not be useful for understanding how the organization responds. Every event confronting an organization does not necessarily affect it. A baking company which has a large inventory of sugar will be less affected by changes in the price of sugar than one which must purchase supplies on the open market continually. Thus, one reason why elements of an environment may have little impact is that the organization is isolated or buffered from them. A second reason why organizations do not respond to every event in the environment is that they do not notice every event, nor are all occurrences important enough to require a response. The term "loosely coupled" has been used to denote the relationship between elements in a social system, such as those between organizations. The effects of organizations on one another are frequently filtered and imperfect (March and Olsen, 1975; Weick, 1976). Loose-coupling is an important safety device for organizational survival. If organizational actions were completely determined by every changing event, organizations would constantly confront potential disaster and need to monitor every change while continually modifying themselves. The fact that environmental impacts are felt only imperfectly provides the organization with some discretion, as well as the capability to act across time horizons longer than the time it takes for an environment to change.

Perhaps one of the most important influences on an organization's response to its environment is the organization itself. Organizational environments are not given realities; they are created through a process of attention and interpretation. Organizations have information systems for gathering, screening, selecting, and retaining information. By the existence of a department or a position, the organization will attend to some aspects of its environment rather than others. Organizations establish subunits to screen out information and protect the internal operations from external influences. Organizational perception and knowledge of the environment is also affected because individuals who attend to the information occupy certain positions in the organization and tend to define the information as a function of their position. If the complaint department is located in the sales division, the flow of information may be interpreted as problems with the marketing and promotion of the product. If it is located in the public relations department, the complaints may be seen as a problem in corporate image. If the function were located in the production department, the complaints might be interpreted as problems of quality control or product design. Since there is no way of knowing about the environment except by interpreting ambiguous events, it is important to understand how organizations come to construct perceptions of reality.

Organizational information systems offer insight to those seeking to analyze and diagnose organizations. Information which is not collected or available is not likely to be used in decision making, and information which is heavily represented in the organization's record keeping is likely to emphatically shape decisions. Some organizations, such as Sears, collect information on a regular basis about worker opinions and morale, while others do not. It is inevitable that those organizations not collecting such information will make decisions that do not take those factors into account. Information systems both determine what will be considered in organizational choice and also provide information about what the organization considers important. The increasing collection of student evaluations of courses and instructors in universities reflects the growing power of students with respect to these organizations and the organizational response of attending more to them. While some would argue that this is a perfect illustration of information that is not used, such is probably not the case. While no definitive studies have been done, it seems clear that the availability of such quantified, concrete information will inevitably intrude to affect the decision-making process and outcomes. Information, regardless of its actual validity, comes to take on an importance and meaning just because of its collection and availability.

The kind of information an organization has about its environment will also vary with its connections to the environment. Organizational members serve on boards of directors, commissions, and are members of clubs and various other organizations. By sending representatives to governmental hearings or investigatory panels, organizations learn about policies that may affect their operations. Research personnel in industry maintain regular contacts with university research projects that may result in knowledge vital to their interests. In one instance, the director of research for the Petroleum Chemicals Research Division of the Ethyl Corporation, a major producer of lead additives for gasoline, made a personal visit to a university research group one month after it had received a large grant to study the impact of lead in the environment (Salancik and Lamont, 1974). Ethyl had learned of the project from contacts in the government. As the project's major objective was to determine the impact of lead on the environment so that policies regarding the manufacture, sale, and distribution of lead might be assessed, the project was of obvious concern to Ethyl.

How an organization learns about its environment, how it attends to the environment, and how it selects and processes information to give meaning to its environment are all important aspects of how the context of an organization affects its actions.

Constraints

A third concept important for understanding organization-environment relationships is constraint. Actions can be said to be constrained whenever one response to a given situation is more probable than any other response to the situation, regardless of the actor responding. That is, constraint is present whenever responses to a situation are not random. A person driving down a city street will tend to drive between 25 and 35 miles per hour. The same person on a state or federal highway will tend to drive between 50 and 65 miles per hour. Whatever the reason, the fact that behavior—of drivers, for example—is not random or, in other words, is somewhat predictable suggests that something is constraining behavior in these situations.

Constraints on behavior are often considered to be undesirable, restricting creativity and adaptation. However, in most cases action is not possible without constraints, which can facilitate the choice and decision process. Consider an undergraduate student attempting to decide on a course of study for a given semester. At a large university, there may be hundreds of courses, and if there were no constraint, literally millions of possible program combinations could be constructed. Deciding among these millions of programs would, of course, be difficult and time consuming, if not impossible. Fortunately, program choices are constrained. First, there may be a limit on the number of courses a student is allowed to take, and then, there is the constraint of not being able to be in two places at the same time. A third constraint is that some courses are defined as being appropriate for certain categories of student, such as graduate courses or freshman courses, while others have necessary prerequisites that limit their being chosen. Further constraints are added by general university requirements, and then, requirements particular to the student's own department and chosen degree program. Thus, out of millions of possible programs of study, only a few options will be feasible, permitted by all the various constraints. Instead of facing a difficult information-processing task, the student need choose only among a very limited set of alternatives.

Behavior is almost inevitably constrained—by physical realities, by social influence, by information and cognitive capacity, as well as by personal preferences. And, in many cases, constraints can be manipulated to promote certain behaviors. In the study of human behavior, when an experimenter designs an experimental situation, he presupposes that he has imposed enough constraints on the situation so that most individuals will behave as he predicts. In a similar fashion, the behavior of larger social units, such as groups and formal organizations, is generally constrained by the interests of others—governments, consumers, unions, competitors, etc.

The concept of constraint explains why individuals account for relatively little variance in the performance and activities of organizational systems. Every individual operates under constraint. Even leaders are not free from it. In a recent study of leadership behavior in an insurance company, it was found that the extent to which supervisors were able to do as their workers wanted was inversely related to the extent to which the supervisors were constrained by other departments (Salancik et al., 1975). Supervisors forced to coordinate and meet the demands of other departments had to behave in ways necessary to meet those demands; they did not have the opportunity to satisfy the desires of their subordinates. The point is that behaviors are frequently constrained by situational contingencies and the individual's effect is relatively small.

THE ROLE OF MANAGEMENT

We have emphasized the importance of contexts, or situational contingencies, as determinants of organizational behavior. We have attempted to question the internal perspective of organizational functioning and the concomitant belief in the omnipotence of individual administrative action. We have not, however, defined the role of the manager out of existence. It is important to conclude this introductory chapter by making explicit our view of the role of the manager within the theoretical perspective we are developing.

The Symbolic Role of Management

As has been noted by others (e.g., Kelley, 1971; Lieberson and O'Connor, 1972), individuals apparently desire a feeling of control over their social environments. The tendency to attribute great effect to individual action, particularly action taken by persons in designated leadership positions, may be partially accounted for by this desire for a feeling of personal effectiveness and control. Thus, one function of the leader or manager is to serve as a symbol, as a focal point for the organization's successes and failures—in other words, to personify the organization, its activities, and its outcomes. Such personification of social causation enhances the feeling of predictability and control, giving observers an identifiable, concrete target for emotion and action.

The idea that administrators serve symbolic functions is not novel. Mintzberg (1973), from detailed observations of managers, specifically listed symbolic activities, though he played down their importance. Gamson and Scotch (1964) have noted that the firing of baseball managers (and we might add, other managers in and out of sports) is a form of scapegoating, which, of course, requires a scapegoat. One of a manager's legitimate roles is to serve as this symbol.

The symbolic role of administrators is, occasionally, constructed with elaborate ritual and ceremony. The inauguration of the president is an uncommon event invested with pomp and expectation. This even though three months earlier both voters and commentators were saying that there was no difference between the candidates. The ritual, however, is necessary.

Why organizations vary in the ritual they associate with their offices of power is little understood. One possibility is that more care and trouble is taken in selecting and installing organizational leaders when they do have influence. Another possibility is just the reverse. The very impotence of leadership positions requires that a ritual indicating great power be performed. People desire to believe in the effectiveness of leadership and personal action. When, in fact, administrators have only minor effects, it might be plausibly argued that ritual, mythology, and symbolism will be most necessary to keep the image of personal control alive. When the administrator really does make a difference and really does affect organizational performance, his effect will be obvious to all and there will be little need to make a show of power and control. It is only when the administrator makes little or no difference that some symbol of control and effectiveness is needed.

It is interesting to note that the ritual of the inauguration of American presidents has grown over time as the executive bureaucracy has grown. The president personally probably has come to have less and less effect on the basic operations of government, while the rituals associated with the office have increased in scope and grandeur.

That managers serve as symbols is not to deny their importance. Important social functions are served by the manipulation of symbols. The catharsis achieved by firing the unsuccessful football coach or the company executive, or by not reelecting some political figure, is too real to dismiss as unimportant. Those who remain in the organization are left with the hope that things will be improved. And, belief in the importance of individual action itself is reinforced—a belief which, even if not completely true, is necessary to motivate individuals to act at all.

The manager who serves as a symbol exposes himself to personal risks. He is accountable for things over which he has no control, and his personal career and fortunes may suffer as a consequence. The sportscasters' cliche that managers are hired to be fired reflects a great amount of truth about all managers. One of the reasons for having a manager is to have someone who is responsible, accountable for the organization's activities and outcomes. If the manager has little influence over these activities or outcomes, it is still useful to hold him responsible. His firing itself may permit loosening some of the constraints facing the organization.

Since most organizational researchers have assumed that managers were the critical element in actual organizational outcomes, the symbolic role of management has been virtually neglected, except for the brief mention by Mintzberg (1973). We would argue that this is one of the more important functions of management, deserving of more explicit empirical attention.

The Possibilities of Managerial Action

Saying that managers are symbols to be held accountable does not suggest many purposeful actions for them; yet, there are many possibilities for managerial action, even given the external constraints on most organizations. Constraints are not predestined and irreversible. Most constraints on organizational actions are the result of prior decision making or the resolution of various conflicts among competing interest groups. For instance, the requirement for companies doing business with the government to develop (and, possibly, implement) affirmative action hiring plans for recruiting minorities and women did not suddenly materialize. This constraint has a lengthy history and resulted from the interaction of a variety of groups and individuals. The fact that a constraint exists indicates that sufficient social support has been mustered to bring it into existence. In the social context of organizations, behind every constraint there is an interest group that has managed to have that constraint imposed. Since this is the case, the constraint is potentially removable if it is possible to organize the social support and resources sufficient to remove it.

The social context of an organization is, itself, the outcome of the actions of social actors. Since many constraints derive from the actions of others, one important function of management is influencing these others as a means of determining one's own environment. Organizations frequently operate on their environments to make them more stable or more munificent. One function of management, then, is to guide and control this process of manipulating the environment. Much of this book will describe just how organizations attempt to influence and control their social context.

Another component of managerial action involves both the recognition of the social context and constraints within which the organization must operate and the choice of organizational adjustments to these social realities. Even when there is no possibility for managerial alteration of the social environment, management can still be difficult, for, recognizing the realities of the social context is not easy or assured. Many organizations have gotten into difficulty by failing to understand those groups or organizations on which they depended for support or by failing to adjust their activities to ensure continued support.

One image of the manager we have developed is that of an

advocator, an active manipulator of constraints and of the social setting in which the organization is embedded. Another image is that of a
processor of the various demands on the organization. In the first, the
manager seeks to enact or create an environment more favorable to the
organization. In the second, organizational actions are adjusted to conform to the constraints imposed by the social context. In reality, both
sets of managerial activities are performed. We would like to emphasize that both are problematic and difficult. It requires skill to perceive
and register accurately one's social context and to adjust organizational
activities accordingly. And, it requires skill to alter the social context
that the organization confronts. Both images of the role of management imply a sensitivity to the social context in which the organization
is embedded and an understanding of the relationship between the
organization and its environment. Both, in other words, require the
adoption of an external orientation to guide the understanding of organizational functioning.

SUMMARY

In this first chapter, we introduced the ideas addressed in the remainder of
the book, ideas necessary for understanding and designing organizational
action. We have noted that we are dealing with the problems of the acquisition of resources by social organizations, of the organization's survival, as
well as of the use of such resources within organizations to accomplish something. To acquire resources, organizations must inevitably interact with their
social environments. No organization is completely self-contained or in complete control of the conditions of its own existence. Because organizations
import resources from their environments, they depend on their environments. Survival comes when the organization adjusts to, and copes with, its
environment, not only when it makes efficient internal adjustments.

The context of an organization is critical for understanding its activities.
Despite considerable pro forma acknowledgement of the environment,
managers and researchers continue to attribute organizational actions and
outcomes to internal factors. Such attributional processes flow from cognitive
and perceptual biases that accompany the observation of organizations, as
well as from the desire to view social behavior with a feeling of control.
These attributions have led to the neglect and serious underestimation of the
importance of social context for understanding organizational behavior.
Studies estimating the effects of administrators (e.g., Lieberson and O'Connor, 1972; Salancik and Pfeffer, 1977) have found them to account for about
10 percent of the variance in organizational performance, a striking contrast
to the 90 percent of the intellectual effort that has been devoted to developing theories of individual action.

While organizational actions are constrained, and contextual factors do predict organizational outcomes and activities, there are several perspectives on the role of management in organizations consistent with such a theoretical position. In the first place, management serves as a symbol of the organization and its actions. Managers are people to fire when things go poorly, an act that reinforces the feeling of control over organizational actions and results. The symbolic role of management, though as yet unexplored, can be systematically empirically examined. In addition to its symbolic role, management can adjust and alter the social context surrounding the organization or can facilitate the organization's adjustment to its context. Both activities require understanding the social context and the interrelationship between context and the organization. Even as a processor of external demands, management has a problematic task. Many organizational troubles stem from inaccurate perceptions of external demands or from patterns of dependence on the environment. Indeed, we would argue that the image of management as a processor of demands is one that implies a high degree of skill and intelligence. After all, anyone can make decisions or take actions—it requires much more skill to be correct.

REFERENCES

Bendix, R. 1956. *Work and Authority in Industry.* New York: Wiley.

Burns, T., and G. M. Stalker. 1961. *The Management of Innovation.* London: Tavistock.

Carter, L. 1953. "Leadership and small group behavior." In M. Sherif and M. O. Wilson (eds.), *Group Relations at the Crossroads,* 257–284. New York: Harper & Row.

Davis, O. A., and M. Hinich. 1966. "A mathematical model of policy formulation in a democratic society." In J. L. Bernd (ed.), *Mathematical Applications in Political Science II,* 175–208. Dallas, Tex.: Southern Methodist University Press.

Fellner, W. 1949. *Competition Among the Few.* New York: Knopf.

Gamson, W. A., and N. A., Scotch. 1964. "Scapegoating in baseball." *American Journal of Sociology,* 70:69–76.

Hackman, J. R., and G. R. Oldham. 1976. "Motivation through the design of work: test of a theory." *Organizational Behavior and Human Performance,* 16:250–279.

Halpin, A. W., and B. J. Winer. 1952. *The Leadership Behavior of the Airplane Commander.* Ohio State University Research Foundation.

Hawley, A. H. 1950. *Human Ecology.* New York: Ronald Press.

Hirsch, P. M. 1975. "Organizational effectiveness and the institutional environment." *Administrative Science Quarterly,* 20:327–344.

Hirschman, A. O. 1970. *Exit, Voice, and Loyalty.* Cambridge: Harvard University Press.

Jones, E. E., and R. E. Nisbett. 1971. *The Actor and the Observer: Divergent Perceptions of the Causes of Behavior.* Morristown, N.J.: General Learning Press.

Katz, D., and R. L. Kahn. 1966. *The Social Psychology of Organizations.* New York: Wiley.

Kelley, H. H. 1971. *Attribution in Social Interaction.* Morristown, N.J.: General Learning Press.

Kessel, J. H. 1962. "Government structure and political environment: a statistical note about American cities." *American Political Science Review,* 56:615–620.

Lieberson, S., and J. F. O'Connor. 1972. "Leadership and organizational performance: a study of large corporations." *American Sociological Review,* 37:117–130.

March J. G., and J. P. Olsen. 1975. "Choice situations in loosely coupled worlds." Unpublished manuscript, Stanford University.

Mintzberg, H. 1973. *The Nature of Managerial Work.* New York: Harper & Row.

Pallak, M. S., S. R. Sogin, and A. Van Zante. 1974. "Bad decisions: effects of volition, locus of causality, and negative consequences on attitude change." *Journal of Personality and Social Psychology,* 30:217–227.

Perrow, C. 1970. *Organizational Analysis: A Sociological View.* Belmont, Calif.: Wadsworth.

Pfeffer, J. 1977. "The ambiguity of leadership." *Academy of Management Review,* 2 (in press).

Phillips, A. 1960. "A theory of interfirm organization." *Quarterly Journal of Economics,* 74:602–613.

Salancik, G. R., B. J. Calder, K. M. Rowland, H. Leblebici, and M. Conway. 1975. "Leadership as an outcome of social structure and process: a multidimensional approach." In J. G. Hunt and L. Larson (eds.), *Leadership Frontiers,* 81–102. Ohio: Kent State University Press.

Salancik, G. R., and V. Lamont. 1975. "Conflicts in societal research: a study of one RANN project suggests that benefitting society may cost universities." *Journal of Higher Education,* 46:161–176.

Salancik, G. R., and J. Pfeffer. 1977. "Constraints on administrator discretion: the limited influence of mayors on city budgets." *Urban Affairs Quarterly,* June.

Schnore, L. F., and R. R. Alford. 1963. "Forms of government and socio-economic characteristics of suburbs." *Administrative Science Quarterly,* 8:1–17.

Staw, B. M. 1975. "Attribution of the causes of performance: a new alternative interpretation of cross-sectional research on organizations." *Organizational Behavior and Human Performance,* 13:414–432.

Stogdill, R. M. 1948. "Personal factors associated with leadership." *Journal of Psychology,* 25:35–71.

Strickland, L. H. 1958. "Surveillance and trust." *Journal of Personality,* 26:200–215.

Weber, M. 1930. *The Protestant Ethic and the Spirit of Capitalism.* New York: Scribner.

Weick, K. E. 1976. "Educational organizations as loosely coupled systems." *Administrative Science Quarterly,* 21:1–19.

Williamson, O. E. 1965. "A dynamic theory of interfirm behavior." *Quarterly Journal of Economics,* 79:579–607.

Wolfson, M. R., and G. R. Salancik. 1977. "Actor-observer and observer-observer attributional differences about an achievement task." *Journal of Experimental Social Psychology,* June.

CHAPTER TWO

ORGANIZATION AND SOCIAL CONTEXT DEFINED

One view of organizations, probably the predominate one, conceives of organizations as rational instruments for achieving some goal or set of goals. Parsons (1956) distinguished organizations from other social collectivities by noting that organizations had some purpose or goal. Perrow (1970) has described organizations in terms of their predominate goal orientations, and the idea that organizations have goals or objectives is one of the most commonly found aspects of the definition of organizations (e.g., Zedeck and Blood, 1974). This goal-oriented or instrumental view of organizations implies that organizations are collections of individual efforts that come together to achieve something which might not otherwise be accomplished through individual action. Just as tools have increased in their complexity and effectiveness for achieving various forms of manual work, so organizations have grown larger and more complex and provide more effective means of accomplishing various social objectives.

The importance of goals as a defining characteristic of organizations has been criticized on several grounds (e.g., Pfeffer, 1977). We prefer to view organizations as coalitions (March, 1962; Cyert and March, 1963) altering their purposes and domains to accommodate new interests, sloughing off parts of themselves to avoid some interests, and when necessary, becoming involved in activities far afield from their stated central purposes. Organizations are social instruments of tremendous power and energy, and the critical issue becomes who will control this energy and for what purpose (Perrow, 1972). To describe adequately the behavior of organizations requires attending to the coalitional nature of organizations and the manner in which organizations respond to pressures from the environment—acceding to the demands of some coalitional interests, avoiding the demands of others, establishing relationships with some coalitions, and avoiding them with others. Managing organizations also is facilitated by recognizing the coalitional nature of organizations.

INTEREST GROUPS AND COALITIONS: ORGANIZATIONS AS MARKETS FOR INFLUENCE AND CONTROL

Parsons (1956) argued that legitimacy was an important concept for understanding organizations and their relationships to their social environments. Parsons noted that since organizations used resources which, presumably, could find alternative uses elsewhere, organizations were continually being assessed on the appropriateness of their activities and the usefulness of their output. In other words, since organizations consumed society's resources, society evaluated the usefulness and legitimacy of the organization's activities.

Parsons's concept raises several questions. Who evaluates the legitimacy of the organization? Who has the right to evaluate organizational legitimacy? Which criteria are to be used in assessing legitimacy? Which organizational activities are to be evaluated, and who chooses them? No answers to these questions apply to all organizations or to the same organization over time. Any interest group, organization, or individual that is in contact with an organization can, and probably will, evaluate the organization, decide what activities and outputs to assess, and determine the criteria that will be used.

Organizations are not so much concrete social entities as a process of organizing support sufficient to continue existence. When one social actor exchanges a product with another for money, it may be convenient to label the situation as one in which an organization is selling its product to a customer, but the point missed is that the very act itself defines the activity of the organization as one of selling. Establishing a coalition large enough to ensure survival is an organization's most critical activity (March and Simon, 1958). The organization as an entity becomes defined only by that activity. March and Simon (1958) talked about organizations in just these terms. They noted that it was necessary to provide inducements for social actors to participate in organizations. In return for these inducements, participants made contributions, and the contributions of some participants became the inducements for others. The organization was the framework, the setting, in which these exchanges of inducements and contributions occurred. Participants would enter and leave the organization depending upon both their assessment of the relative value to be gained by continuing the exchange and the organization's assessment—the assessment of others in the coalition—of the same issue. An organization, according to this perspective, is viable as long as its available inducements are sufficient to elicit the necessary contributions—in other words, to maintain a viable coalition of support.

Organizing coalitions of support can produce strange alliances. One would not, for instance, expect that one purpose of the United States government was to encourage the manufacture and transportation of narcotics for sale to its citizens. Yet, it has promoted such acts wittingly and unwittingly while achieving support for other activities. This illustration comes from a book by Alfred W. McCoy (1972) whose careful study of the politics of heroin in Southeast Asia suggested that the United States made its unwitting contribution to world drug traffic when it struck a bargain with Charles "Lucky" Luciano. During World War II, Luciano was serving time in a federal penitentiary. In return for release and deportation to Italy, he arranged for the Mafia in Sicily to facilitate the landing of United States troops on the island. The reappearance of Luciano in Italy made the reestablishment of the undergrounds of Italy and France easier. These undergrounds became the main worldwide organization for the distribution of heroin. At the end of the war, the missing ingredient was sufficient production to supply the distribution system. Production of opium was spurred by the French and the Americans during their involvement in Southeast Asia. The French secured the cooperation of the Indochinese hill tribes to enter the fight against the Viet Minh by providing support for the production and transportation of what before was only the occasional cultivation of opium. When the French involvement ended, the amount of heroin on the world market dropped. It increased again when the American involvement increased and similar arrangements were made. To obtain support of the hill people for the war, the heroin was allowed to move, with the transport occasionally provided by American aircraft (McCoy, 1972).

An important dimension, then, of the establishment of coalitions is that there is no requirement for the participants to share vested interests or singular, paramount goals. Anything that justifies a participant's involvement is sufficient from an organizing point of view. Some organizational theorists have the idea that everyone who participates in an organization must agree to cooperate in the pursuit of the same goals. This is clearly not the case. Organizational participants may come into the coalition when there is some advantage to be gained and leave when there is no longer any perceived advantage. The gains and costs are defined in terms of the individual participants or groups, not in terms agreed upon by all or promulgated by the organization's management.

Consider again the position taken by Parsons (1956) that legitimacy is necessary for the continued survival of the organization. It should be clear that all members of a society need not agree on the legitimacy of a given organization for it to survive. To survive, the organization need only maintain a coalition of parties who contribute the resources and support necessary for it to continue its activities, activities which themselves are outcomes desired by the coalition members. And, the coalition of interests participating in an organization at a point in time defines the activities of the organization. When an interest group ceases to participate in the organization, the organization either ceases to exist or, more likely, transforms itself into a different organization engaging in different activities relevant to the remaining interests. Sills (1957) described the transformation of the National Foundation for Infantile Paralysis in a way consistent with our argument. To exist, a charitable organization needs beneficiaries, a cause, a purpose. The National Foundation's sole purpose was lost when an effective vaccine for polio was discovered. The very effectiveness of Salk's vaccine diminished the need for the organization. The organization, rather than disappearing, merely located another, related client group—crippled children who suffered from birth defects—and continued anew with this new clientele and coalition participant.

We have described organizations as settings in which groups and individuals with varying interests and preferences come together and engage in exchanges—in March and Simon's (1958) terminology, exchanging contributions for inducements. The difference between these organizational markets of influence and markets in economics is in the extent to which the activities and behaviors exchanged are stable, repeated continually over time. Weick (1969) and Allport (1962) have described the process of organizing as one in which behavior becomes predictable and cyclical—structured. Thibaut and Kelley (1959), with their matrix notation for describing social interaction, proposed an essentially similar framework. Our point is that once established, patterns of interaction are likely to persist if, for no other reason, the persistence of interaction patterns reduces uncertainty for the participants.

It should be clear that not all coalition participants provide contributions that are equally valued; some are valued more, others less. Those coalition participants who provide behaviors, resources, and capabilities that are most needed or desired by other organizational participants come to have more influence and control over the organization, for one of the inducements received for contributing the most critical resources is the ability to control and direct organizational action. It is in this sense that we subtitled this section "organizations as markets for influence and control." Coalition participants are continually engaged in a process of exchange, and as Emerson (1962) and Blau (1964) have suggested, out of these exchanges and the interdependence created by them emerge differences in power among organizational participants. The power of the participant is a function of the dependence of others in the organization on his contributions, activities, capabilities. Control and influence emerge from the interaction of organizational participants and the valuation of the contributions made and inducements demanded by each.

COMPETING DEMANDS

That different people, groups, or organizations may have different criteria for evaluating an organization creates problems for the organization. The problems derive from the fact that the criteria may be incompatible. Faced with conflicting demands, the organization must decide which groups to attend to and which to ignore. When the criteria are compatible, the organization would find that satisfying one group would also increase the satisfaction of others. The existence of incompatible demands raises the possibility that the organization may not be able to maintain the necessary coalition of support. Favoring one group offends another.

There is some empirical evidence consistent with the position that organizations confront incompatible demands. Friedlander and Pickle (1968) studied 97 small businesses in Texas. They identified several internal and external interest groups relevant to the Texas businesses, including the owners, the employees, the customers, the suppliers, the creditors, the local community, and the federal government. For each group, the authors developed a measure of the organization's effectiveness on the group's criteria. For example, the owners were postulated to be interested in profits, while employees were thought to be concerned with their satisfaction with work. Through a combination of direct questioning and the use of records, measures were developed for how effectively the organization was meeting the demands of the various constituent groups. While there are difficulties with some of the measures, the approach employed demonstrated a realization of the interest-group characteristic of organizational effectiveness seldom seen.

Pickle and Friedlander (1967:171) correlated the indices of group satisfaction with each other across the organizations to examine how the satisfaction of one group's demands was related to the satisfaction of others. These correlations are presented in Table 2.1. Three points can be made about the data: (1) the correlations are fairly low, (2) the correlations are generally positive, and (3) the correlations between the satisfactions of some groups are greater than between others. These data suggest that one group's satisfaction implies very little about another group's satisfaction, and their interests, on occasion, will conflict.

While the analysis discussed was made only for the prominent interests of a few Texas small businesses, there is some generality to the idea that the demands of coalition participants will not always be consistent. It is plausible that with increasing size an organization is likely to be confronted with increasingly inconsistent interests. As an

TABLE 2.1 Intercorrelations of Satisfactions of Seven Parties-at-Interest with Ninety-seven Business Firms

	Satisfaction of					
	Community	*Government*	*Customer*	*Supplier*	*Creditor*	*Employee*
Owner satisfaction	.23*	−.12	.37**	.14	.00	.25*
Community satisfaction		.16	.04	.16	.14	.22*
Government satisfaction			−.09	.11	.20*	−.07
Customer satisfaction				.17	.23*	.23*
Supplier satisfaction					.08	.17
Creditor satisfaction						.08

SOURCE: Reprinted from Hal Pickle and Frank Friedlander, "Seven Societal Criteria of Organizational Success," p. 171, Table 1, 1967

* $p < .05$
** $p < .01$

organization becomes large, it generally attracts more attention and establishes coalitions with a more heterogeneous set of organizations.

Because an organization survives only to the extent it creates and maintains the coalition of support necessary for operation, the existence of competing demands can be a problem. Each time the organization satisfies the demands of one participant or interest group it simultaneously constrains its own behavior in meeting other or subsequent demands. To the extent that future demands from other participants will conflict with the first, the constraints on behavior may lessen the ability of the organization to establish the necessary coalitions. The consequences may not appear immediately, and the organization may not be aware of them. In general, however, the constraints imposed by satisfying one set of demands affect the organization's ability to satisfy others.

Many of New York City's troubles in 1975 resulted from the accumulation of concessions made to one part of their constituent environment, placing constraints on the city such that future administrators could not satisfy the demands of other interests. Earlier concessions to city workers and various income groups made it subsequently more difficult to satisfy the demands of creditors. Similar situations exist in home building and railroading, where concessions on work rules, made over the years to various unions, have severely restricted management's ability to adapt to changing competitive and economic conditions.

ORGANIZATIONAL BOUNDARIES AND THE PARTIAL INCLUSION OF PARTICIPANTS

We have argued that organizations are coalitions, maintained by providing inducements (satisfaction) to participants who support the organization. All participants and those affected by the organization can evaluate it, and because of the number and diversity of interests in the coalition constituting most organizations, the managements of organizations face the problem of dealing with inconsistent criteria and competing demands.

We suggest that this perspective on organizations facilitates addressing the problem of precisely what constitutes the organization, or where its boundaries are. The problem of drawing the boundary around a social system has been a perplexing one. Individual boundaries are, apparently, more easily discerned. Nature has neatly packaged people into skins, animals into hides, and allowed trees to enclose themselves with bark. It is easy to see where the unit is and where the environment is. Not so for social organizations. Are suppliers part of the organization, or part of its environment? Consider the case of computer manufacturers who may station personnel for a long time at the "customer's" installation to perform systems engineering work. Are customers part of the organization? In many instances, such as in building a ship, engineers from the customer organization may participate in much of the on-site work, along with the workers from the shipbuilding organization. Not only are organizations not neatly bundled, but they can alter the particular participants in them over time. Thus, descriptions of an organization developed by inventorying its parts at one point in time may describe nothing about the same organization at another point in time.

One solution to the problem of inclusion is that suggested by Haberstroh (1965) and Downs (1967): Draw the organizational boundaries as a matter of analytical convenience, much as analytical boundaries are drawn in the analysis of heat-transfer systems. For some purposes, then, customers might be considered part of the organization, and for others, they might not. Although this particular solution may be useful for a person studying some given aspect of an organization, it is not as helpful for understanding how organizations operate.

The problem of inclusion was recognized by March and Simon (1958) in their discussion of the inducements-contributions balance. For these authors, individuals participated in the organization to the extent they received inducements which exceeded in value, for them, the value of the contributions they were required to make. Thus, customers, for example, make contributions to the organization in the form of money and receive inducements in the form of products and services. Although March and Simon's perspective is an improvement, it still misses an important point by emphasizing the individuals involved rather than the behavior or activities.

The reason there is so much difficulty in drawing social-system boundaries is that it is behaviors that are organized, not individual people. "It is vital to note that it is behaviors, not persons, that are interstructured" (Weick, 1969:46). As Allport (1962) has pointed out, any given individual is only partially included in any system of organized behaviors, being also partly included in many other behavior systems as well. Consequently, it is perfectly possible for a person to be *both* part of an organization and part of its environment through different behaviors occurring at different times. By focusing on distinct physical units, such as individual persons, rather than on behavior patterns, the problems of drawing the boundaries around social systems have been made more difficult.

Discussing the nature of a small group, Allport (1962) and Weick (1969) both persuasively argue that it is cycles of behavior that become organized in a collective structure, and that any given individual is only partly included in the group. "A person does not invest all his behavior in a single group; commitments and interlockings are dispersed among several groups" (Weick, 1969:46). While a group is a concept that becomes, in a sense, less tangible when it is defined in terms of interlocked behaviors or collective structure, it is also probably more valid, because the notion of partial inclusion has been recognized by many persons who have dealt with small-group phenomena.

Recognizing that it is activities that are interstructured in creating organizations is important because under some conditions the particular individuals responsible for those activities can be replaced and the same activities can be continued by others. The organization has the ability to make decisions to initiate activities on its behalf. Because the activities are interstructured, the organization's ability to engage in actions depends on its ability to locate individuals who will do them. What the organization is able to accomplish at any point is the result of the interstructured activities it is able to induce individuals to perform. The work of the organization, then, does not depend completely on individuals but on the activities that the organization is able to initiate and control.

The nature of the partial inclusion is explicitly recognized in the process of the acceptance of legitimate power, or authority, by employees entering an organization. At that time it is recognized that while the organization has the right to coordinate and control some behaviors related to organizational tasks, the individual retains control over other behaviors. A supervisor can tell an employee how to do the job but not what to eat for lunch. The conflict between the requirements of different roles in different behavior structures has been called interrole conflict (Kahn et al., 1964). An individual's partial inclusion in many groups or organizations makes it possible that the demands on behavior made in one structure may be inconsistent or incompatible with demands on behavior made in another group or organization.

The concept of interrole conflict illustrates the basis of power that participants have in determining the organization's activities. Individuals participating in different collective structures with different requirements must choose between the demands of those structures. This ability to choose is the basis of their discretion to create the activities desired by the organization for its operation. Extending this idea to all of the individuals and organizations which transact with a focal organization, it should be clear that the focal organization's activities depend to a great extent on the limits of its discretion and on the discretion of those who interstructure their activities with the other participants and members of the organizational coalition. The organization is, in essence, organizing the activities defining its operation.

When it is recognized that it is behaviors, rather than individuals, that are included in structures of coordinated behavior, then it is possible, at least conceptually, to define the extent to which any given person is or is not a member of an organization. A person's inclusion in a collective structure can be defined as the proportion of his or her behavior included in that structure, or the amount of the person's behavior included in that particular behavior structure divided by the total amount of the person's behavior in all structures.

An important corollary to the notion that participants are partially included in the organization through their activities is: The organization survives to the extent that the activities included are sufficient for the organization to maintain itself. The organization is the total set of interstructured activities in which it is engaged at any one time and over which it has discretion to initiate, maintain, or end behaviors. Although this may seem difficult to visualize, it recognizes the coalitional nature of organizations and that the survival of the organization depends on the set of activities over which it has control. This conceptualization explicitly recognizes the external basis of organizations. The organization ends where its discretion ends and another's begins. The tenuous nature of the organization as an entity can be most easily observed when its own discretion is challenged and others assume control over the activities. One might think that General Motors designs its automobiles. Then, consider the impact of the Environmental Protection Agency, the Department of Transportation and its safety requirements, the various consumer groups, and think again about the extent to which General Motors (or any other automobile manufacturer) has discretion over the design of its automobiles. The discretion of General Motors' management can be limited by those with the means and interest to do so.

When the social-system boundary problem is approached from the perspective of interlocked or coordinated behaviors, rather than from the perspective of individual participants, much of the ambiguity about where the organization begins and the environment ends disappears. The boundary is where the discretion of the organization to control an activity is less than the discretion of another organization or individual to control that activity.

ORGANIZATIONAL EFFECTIVENESS

From the previous discussion it can be seen that a variety of interest groups, individuals, and organizations have contact with a given focal organization; each of these evaluates the organization and reacts to its output and actions. Each has a particular set of criteria of preferences that it uses in this evaluation process, and consequently, organizational effectiveness is a multifaceted concept, where the effectiveness of the organization depends on which group, with which criteria and preferences, is doing the assessment.

Effectiveness and efficiency are terms that are used, and often misused, to analyze and describe organizational behavior. Price (1968) has reviewed a series of studies attempting to determine the correlates of organizational effectiveness. We would argue that few, if any, of the studies reviewed employ measures that assess effectiveness in a meaningful way. In Chapter Four, we will explicate a procedure for assessing the organization's position vis-à-vis its environment—in other words, the organization's effectiveness and the probable consequences of various policies and actions. For the moment, we will concentrate on defining effectiveness and distinguishing it from organizational efficiency.

How well an organization accomplishes its stated, or implied, objectives given the resources used is what efficiency measures. What this means is most easily described by reference to the process for evaluating the efficiency of a machine. Katz and Kahn (1966) used the steam engine as an illustration. A steam engine operates to convert coal or some other fuel into useable power. In the process of the transformation, some of the energic content of the input is lost; therefore, the output energy is less than 100 percent of the energy in the input. The ratio of input to output energy is a measure of the efficiency of the engine. This basic idea, output per unit of input, is used when speaking of the efficiency of an organization. A worker producing seven tin cans per minute is more efficient than one producing five. More output is achieved in the former case per unit labor input.

Efficiency is an internal standard of organizational performance. To develop measures of efficiency, the records of the organization's own activities are all that are needed. The company which manufactures those ubiquitous widgets uses a certain amount of worker hours and material to obtain the output. Its efficiency is determined by counting the number of widgets produced per worker hour and unit of material consumed through use or waste. Different organizations have different outputs and inputs, but the comparing of output to input is common. Schools measure students educated per dollar, while the United States Customs agency measures the efficiency of its agents in terms of the dollar value of confiscated contraband per year.

Although efficiency measures are easy to obtain, they are difficult to interpret. They are easy to obtain because most organizations keep some records on outlays for expenses and on products produced or persons served. Interpretation is difficult because efficiency measures involve assumptions of causality and a level of theoretical understanding seldom possessed by analysts of social systems. In assessing the efficiency of a steam engine, the engineers who design it know various physical laws of energy, heat transfer, and chemistry. From these they can derive both estimates of the energy content of the input and the theoretical maximum efficiency of the device. They can also measure the various sources of energy loss. Social-systems analysts must make similar judgments about the relationships between inputs and outputs and must also make judgments about the transformation process. Unfortunately, they have less knowledge on which to base such judgments. Therefore, most measures of efficiency are open to contest. When management claims a raise is not justified because there is a declining productivity of labor—measured by the output per unit of labor input—labor may counter with the argument that productivity has declined because of lack of maintenance of the machinery or because of errors in management's calculations or competence. Finally, efficiency is problematic to interpret in social systems because the direction of benefit is open to question. In the case of the engine, we can take as given that the less energy lost in the transformation process, or the more output per unit input, the better. But can we so easily assume that the more students taught per dollar, the better; or the lower the cost of treating a hospital patient, the better?

Efficiency is relatively value free. It asks how much is produced at what cost. What is produced is not considered. The output may be antibiotics or atomic bombs, processed food, clothing, or automobiles. The output may be valued by some and not valued by others. Efficiency is taken to be good, so a positive valuation is placed on a larger ratio of output to input. This quest for "bigger is better" reached its ultimate stage when, in virtually a caricature of modern management ideas, the Department of Defense during the Vietnam war reported body counts and worried about the number of enemy killed per thousand dollars of ammunition or bombs expended.

When individuals and organizations consider what is being measured or produced, they are concerned with effectiveness rather than efficiency. Effectiveness is an external standard applied to the output or activities of an organization. It is applied by all individuals, groups, or organizations that are affected by, or come in contact with, the focal organization. Effectiveness as assessed by each organizational evaluator involves how well the organization is meeting the needs or satisfying the criteria of the evaluator.

Of course, efficiency itself may be the standard by which organizational effectiveness is judged. When an engineer orders a machine or when a homeowner buys an air conditioner, one of the criteria may be the efficiency of the appliance, or the amount of work produced per unit of input consumed. The fact that efficiency may itself be a criterion for assessing effectiveness should not be taken to mean that this is always, or even usually, the case. In many instances efficiency of the product is not a criterion, and what is being produced, rather than the ratio of output to input, is of more concern.

Some confusion between effectiveness and efficiency comes about because efficiency itself is valued. Years of Taylorism, scientific management, and now operations research and management science have led to the maximization of efficiency as a value. After literally decades of management ideology venerating efficiency, efficiency has come to be a valued social ideal. In such a climate, efficiency may be used as an argument to achieve objectives sought for other reasons. For instance, as part of an effort to reduce expenditures for programs started under the Johnson administration, President Nixon attempted to merge Volunteers in Service to America (VISTA) with other voluntary programs such as the Peace Corps. The administration maintained in testimony before Congress that the merger was designed solely for greater efficiency in operation by avoiding duplication (*New York Times,* May 24, 1971:1). Two months prior to the administration's proposal to Congress, however, a study by a Pennsylvania State University professor, David Gottleib, had indicated that fully one-third of the volunteers became radicalized by the experience of helping poor people. As one Republican official put it, "VISTA is just a federally financed $36 million-a-year 'hate Nixon' post-graduate school." The proposal to Congress, of course, stressed the cost saving and efficiency, acceptable arguments to remove unacceptable programs.

What this means is that efficiency and effectiveness may be confused because efficiency, as a socially valued ideal, may be used as argumentation to advance or retard proposals or activities which are really being assessed by other criteria. Stating the case in terms of efficiency does not necessarily mean that the issue is being decided on such a basis.

Efficiency and effectiveness are independent standards for evaluating organizations. Organizations can be both efficient and effective, neither efficient nor effective, effective but not efficient, or efficient but not effective. An efficient, but not effective, organization was FAS International (formerly Famous Artists Schools) which, in 1970, filed for reorganization under the bankruptcy laws. FAS advertised in popular magazines for readers to learn to write or draw under the guidance of famous authors and artists, using a correspondence course format. The directors of FAS were well-known artists and authors such as Bennett Cerf, Rod Serling, and Norman Rockwell. The troubles at FAS began in large part when the *Atlantic Monthly* published an article questioning the value of the organization, pointing out that FAS's alluring talent tests were almost always positively evaluated, and more important, explaining that the guidance provided by mail was not from the famous writers or artists, but from staff persons hired at relatively low salaries. Under public criticism, many of the more famous persons disassociated themselves from the company, and the company began to have trouble with regulatory agencies because of its advertising claims. While FAS was quite efficient and profitable, its activities were eventually considered not to be legitimate or effective, and the organization failed.

An example of an effective but possibly inefficient organization was the National Aeronautics and Space Administration during the 1960s. A commitment was made by President Kennedy to land Americans on the moon in a decade, and a tremendous amount of resources was devoted to the space program. The organization was clearly effective—men were landed on the moon in 1969, and the United States had developed an elaborate and sophisticated set of space technology. However, in the drive to meet deadlines and timetables, duplication was encouraged and waste also occurred. In fact, too much efficiency may detract from the effectiveness of an organization. General Motors, with its considerable financial and production resources, could operate so efficiently that it would drive its weaker competitors, such as American Motors and Chrysler, out of business. Such an attempt, however, would probably serve to revive the effort to break up General Motors. Thus, by being too efficient in the car business and controlling too much of the market, General Motors might set in motion actions that would ultimately lead to negative consequences.

SUMMARY

The organization is a coalition of groups and interests, each attempting to obtain something from the collectivity by interacting with others, and each with its own preferences and objectives. The result of these interactions and exchanges is the collectivity we call the organization. In March and Simon's (1958) terms, organizational participants make contributions to the collectivity and receive inducements to ensure their continued participation. Organizations, then, are quasi-markets, in which influence and control are negotiated and allocated according to which organizational participants are most critical to the organization's continued survival and success.

Because organizations are coalitions, management faces the necessity of coping with competing and conflicting demands. Indeed, the management of the organizational coalition, including the resolution of the various conflicts among interests, may be one of the more appropriate conceptualizations of the role of management.

It is important to recognize that it is activities or behaviors, not persons or organizations, that are structured in an organization. The organization's boundary, then, can be defined in terms of its influence over activities compared to the influence of other social actors over the same activities of the same participants. When the focal organization's influence is greatest, we can say that those activities are included within its boundaries. Since organizations are quasi-markets for influence and control, it is altogether appropriate to define boundaries in terms of the relative influence and control over activities.

Organizational effectiveness is the assessment of the organization's output and activities by each of the various groups or participants. Since there are conflicting criteria, effectiveness is inevitably defined only with respect to the assessment of a particular group—what is effective for employees may be ineffective for owners, and what is effective for creditors may be ineffective for owners, and what is effective for creditors may be ineffective for customers. Effectiveness is an external evaluation of what the organization is doing, while efficiency is an internal evaluation of the amount of resources consumed in the process of doing this activity. Because efficiency is a valued social standard, it is occasionally mustered as a rationale for attacking or defending organizations when their activities or outputs are objectionable on other grounds.

The task of organizational management, as developed from this view of organizations, is the management of the coalition to ensure continued support and survival of the organization. This task, which is problematic because of the reality of conflicting and competing demands, is necessary because of the organization's interdependence with other participants and organizations outside of its boundaries—i.e., because of its need for activities that are not completely within its control.

REFERENCES

Allport, F. H. 1962. "A structuronomic conception of behavior: individual and collective." *Journal of Abnormal and Social Psychology*, 64:3–30.

Blau, P. M. 1964. *Exchange and Power in Social Life.* New York: Wiley.

Cyert, R. M., and J. G. March. 1963. *A Behavioral Theory of the Firm.* Englewood Cliffs, N.J.: Prentice-Hall.

Downs, A. 1967. *Inside Bureaucracy.* Boston: Little, Brown.

Emerson, R. E. 1962. "Power-dependence relations." *American Sociological Review*, 27:31–41.

Friedlander, F., and H. Pickle. 1968. "Components of effectiveness in small organizations." *Administrative Science Quarterly*, 13:289–304.

Haberstroh, C. J. 1965. "Organization design and systems analysis." In J. G. March (ed.), *Handbook of Organizations*, 1171–1211. Skokie, Ill.: Rand McNally.

Kahn, R. L., D. M. Wolfe, R. P. Quinn, and J. D. Snoek. 1964. *Organizational Stress: Studies in Role Conflict and Ambiguity.* New York: Wiley.

Katz, D., and R. L. Kahn. 1966. *The Social Psychology of Organizations.* New York: Wiley.

March, J. G. 1962. "The business firm as a political coalition," *Journal of Politics*, 24:662–678.

March, J. G., and H. A. Simon. 1958. *Organizations*. New York: Wiley.

McCoy, A. W. 1972. *The Politics of Heroin in Southeast Asia*. New York: Harper & Row.

Parsons, T. 1956. "Suggestions for a sociological approach to the theory of organizations." *Administrative Science Quarterly*, 1:63–85.

Perrow, C. 1970. *Organizational Analysis: A Sociological View*. Belmont, Calif.: Wadsworth.

Perrow, C. 1972. *Complex Organizations: A Critical Essay*. Glenview, Ill.: Scott, Foresman.

Pfeffer, J. 1977. "Power and resource allocation in organizations." In B. M. Staw and G. R. Salancik (eds.), *New Directions in Organizational Behavior*, 235–265. Chicago: St. Clair Press.

Pickle, H., and F. Friedlander. 1967. "Seven societal criteria of organizational success." *Personnel Psychology*, 20:165–178.

Price, J. L. 1968. *Organizational Effectiveness: An Inventory of Propositions*. Homewood, Ill.: Irwin.

Sills, D. L. 1957. *The Volunteers*. New York: Free Press.

Thibaut, J. W., and H. H. Kelley. 1959. *The Social Psychology of Groups*. New York: Wiley.

Weick, K. E. 1969. *The Social Psychology of Organizing*. Reading, Mass.: Addison-Wesley.

Zedeck, S. and M. R. Blood. 1974. *Foundations of Behavioral Science Research in Organizations*. Monterey, Calif.: Brooks/Cole.

CHAPTER THREE

SOCIAL CONTROL
OF ORGANIZATIONS

The theme of this book, and the underlying premise of the external perspective on organizations, is that organizational activities and outcomes are accounted for by the context in which the organization is embedded. While some empirical attention has been paid to the effects of environment on organizational structures, and there has been some theoretical emphasis on the importance of environment, there are remarkably few studies of interorganizational influence activities. This is especially remarkable since many organizations have as their primary function and purpose the control and alteration of the activities of other organizations. Wiley and Zald (1968) have examined the operation of two regional college and university accrediting organizations; Zald and Hair (1972) have written of the various external controls on hospitals. But these two case studies are rare.

The number of organizations attempting to control other organizations is large. There are, first, all the various accrediting organizations, such as those operating to accredit educational organizations, hospitals, and social service agencies. There are regulatory bodies that function to control at least some of the activities of the organizations they regulate. Regulatory bodies include those established by law and those established by the agreement of the organizations themselves, such as the NCAA, established by university athletic departments to regulate the conduct of interscholastic sports. Various advocate and interest groups, such as the Sierra Club, Common Cause, and others of narrower interests and shorter duration, operate to attempt to affect the decisions and activities of business and government organizations. In addition to organizations that explicitly and openly seek to control other organizations, interorganizational influence attempts are frequent among organizations interacting for other purposes. Thus, banks may attempt to control the dividend policies of firms to which they lend money.

In this chapter, we will present the basic theory we propose to explain the operation of interorganizational influence, or social control processes. Although we will also present some relevant empirical evidence, it should be clear that many aspects of these ideas have yet to be empirically examined. Thus, the material is presented as a way of organizing thinking and understanding of the process of interorganizational influence.

INTERDEPENDENCE

Interdependence is the reason why nothing comes out quite the way one wants it to. Any event that depends on more than a single causal agent is an outcome based on interdependent agents. Interpendence is the reason you cannot find the word in the *American Heritage Dictionary*—an outcome which depends both on your obtaining the dictionary and looking up the word and on the publishers' having included the word in the volume. In social systems and social interactions, interdependence exists whenever one actor does not entirely control all of the conditions necessary for the achievement of an action or for obtaining the outcome desired from the action.

Virtually all organizational outcomes are based on interdependent causes or agents. Interdependence characterizes the relationship between the agents creating an outcome, not the outcome itself. A seller is interdependent with a buyer because the outcome of concluding a sale depends on the activities contributed by each. A seller is also interdependent with another seller if each is negotiating with the same buyer for a sale.

There are various ways of categorizing interdependence. One way is to distinguish between outcome interdependence and behavior interdependence. These two forms of interdependence are themselves independent, meaning that they can occur either alone or together. In a situation of outcome interdependence, the outcomes achieved by A are interdependent with, or jointly determined with, the outcome achieved by B. Consider a market of a given size in which there are two participants; the quantity sold is determined by the price charged; and the profits earned by the participants are determined by the amount sold, the price charged, and the quantity produced. In such a situation, the two participants, A and B, are in a situation of outcome interdependence. While each independently may make price and quantity decisions, the outcome—profit—will be a function of both the participant's own decisions and those of his or her competitor. In the case of behavior interdependence, the activities are themselves dependent on the actions of another social actor. Organizing a poker game is an example of behavioral interdependence. In order for one person to play poker, it is necessary that he or she convince others to participate in the game, which involves having them at a certain place at a certain specified time. If the others do not cooperate, then the person cannot engage in the activity of playing poker.

A further distinction can be made between kinds of outcome interdependence by whether the participants are in a competitive or symbiotic relationship. In a competitive relationship, the outcome achieved by one can only be higher if the outcome achieved by the other is lower. In the terminology of game theory, this is a fixed sum, or zero sum, game. In a situation of symbiotic interdependence, the output of one is input for the other. It is possible for both to be better off or worse off simultaneously. Many efforts have been made to define competitive and symbiotic relationships (e.g., Hawley, 1950). In terms of human ecology, competitive relationships exist when the actors each require identical resources for survival. Symbiotic relationships involve one actor's using the by-products of the other, or in other words, using different resources.

Interdependencies are not necessarily symmetric or balanced. They can be asymmetric. Moreover, interdependence existing between two social actors need not be either competitive or symbiotic—frequently, relationships contain both forms of interdependence simultaneously. For instance, a conglomerate firm may sell the product of one of its divisions to another firm, thereby existing in a symbiotic relationship, and at the same time, be in competition with that other firm in the sale of the product of a different division.

Interdependence is important to an organization because of the impact it has on the ability of the organization to achieve its desired outcomes. Consider the following illustration:

In a small town in Maine there is one seller of a perishable product and one buyer. The buyer requires 100 units of product every two days, with the probability of his needing the 100 units on any given day being .5. The supplier has a .9 probability of having 100 units of the product on hand on any given day. The probability of the buyer, buyer A, being able to obtain what he wants is .9 and results from his dependence on the supplier. One day a new buyer, buyer B, comes into town. Buyer B also needs 100 widgets on average every two days, with demand varying randomly. Buyer A's probability of now getting what he wants is a function of his getting to the supplier either on a different day or, if on the same day as B, on the probability of getting there before B. The probability of A now getting what he wants is reduced to .675. This added uncertainty is troublesome to A, so he decides to find an alternate source of supply for the product. Meanwhile, the first supplier notes that his sales have fallen from the time when both A and B bought from him. When A and B were both in the market, there was only a .25 chance of not selling the product that day, but with only B in the market, there was a .5 chance of not selling the product. The supplier, therefore, decides to cut down on the amount of product he carries, so if B does not come in, he will not be out so much inventory. This, in turn, reduces the likelihood of a B getting what he wants. Eventually, it is likely that the buyer and supplier will work out some arrangement to coordinate their behaviors so that neither faces as much uncertainty. In short, to cope with the interdependence of outcomes, the two will probably decide to make their behaviors more inter-dependent.

This simple illustration demonstrates a number of important points about the consequences of interdependence for analyzing organizational behavior. First, we can see that interdependence varies with the availability of resources relative to the demands for them. When there is a large amount of resources relative to the demand, interdependence between actors who need the same resource is reduced. Second, interdependence characterizes individuals transacting in the same environment, with the connection being through the flow of transactions. We can also see that interdependence can create problems of uncertainty or unpredictability for the organization. This uncertainty, which is typically troublesome to organizations, derives from the lack of coordination of activities among social units. Organizations facing uncertainty attempt to cope with it on occasion by restructuring their exchange relationships. The solution to one organization's uncertainties—for instance, finding a new supplier—can create new uncertainties for other organizations. Most importantly, the example illustrates how organizations, to solve their problems of uncertainty regarding outcomes, are likely to be led to increase their interdependence with respect to behavior, that is, to interstructure their behaviors in ways predictable for each. The typical solution to problems of interdependence and uncertainty involves increasing coordination, which means increasing the mutual control over each others' activities, or, in other words, increasing the behavioral interdependence of the social actors.

Interdependence is a consequence of the open-systems nature of organizations—the fact that organizations must transact with elements of the environment in order to obtain the resources necessary for survival. It might be noted that interdependence has been increased with the increasing specialization and division of labor among organizational entities. In the days of the pioneers on the American frontier when a family grew and made most of the things it required, the interdependence between the family and the various organizations it dealt with was less than for a family·in the present, where there are specialized organizations providing a variety of goods and services, as well as organizations that purchase labor. To the extent that social organizations are self-contained, there is less interdependence between them. The amount of interdependence existing between organizations is not a given, but can change over time as organizations become more or less self-contained.

THE SOCIAL CONTROL OF
ORGANIZATIONAL CHOICE

Organizations engage in exchanges and transactions with other groups or organizations. The exchanges may involve monetary or physical resources, information, or social legitimacy. Because organizations are not self-contained or self-sufficient, the environment must be relied upon to provide support. For continuing to provide what the organization needs, the external groups or organizations may demand certain actions from the organization in return. It is the fact of the organization's dependence on the environment that makes the external constraint and control of organizational behavior both possible and almost inevitable.

Organizations could not survive if they were not responsive to the demands from their environments. But, we have noted that demands often conflict and that response to the demands of one group constrains the organization in its future actions, including responding to the demands of others. This suggests that organizations cannot survive by responding completely to every environmental demand. The interesting issue then becomes the extent to which organizations can and should respond to various environmental demands, or the conditions under which one social unit is able to obtain compliance with its demands. By understanding the conditions of the social control of organizations, we believe it is possible to understand how organizations decide to comply with, or attempt to avoid, influence.

The nature of control and influence in social processes has been explored in a variety of disciplines, including social psychology, political science, sociology, and economics. In the study of interorganizational influence, there have been some preliminary attempts to develop an adequate theory. Most of these theories assume that some form of interdependence is a necessary condition for exerting influence (e.g., Emerson, 1962; Jacobs, 1974; Blau, 1964). As Hawley wrote, "Dominance attaches to the unit that controls the conditions necessary to the functioning of the other units" (1950:221). We would concur that, in general, organizations will tend to be influenced by those who control the resources they require. But there are a number of other conditions which increase the likelihood of the influence being successful. Below is a list of the conditions which affect the extent to which an organization will comply with control attempts:

1. The focal organization is aware of the demands.
2. The focal organization obtains some resources from the social actor making the demands.
3. The resource is a critical or important part of the focal organization's operation.
4. The social actor controls the allocation, access, or use of the resource; alternative sources for the resource are not available to the focal organization.
5. The focal organization does not control the allocation, access, or use of other resources critical to the social actor's operation and survival.
6. The actions or outputs of the focal organization are visible and can be assessed by the social actor to judge whether the actions comply with its demands.
7. The focal organization's satisfaction of the social actor's requests are not in conflict with the satisfaction of demands from other components of the environment with which it is interdependent.
8. The focal organization does not control the determination, formulation, or expression of the social actor's demands.
9. The focal organization is capable of developing actions or outcomes that will satisfy the external demands.
10. The organization desires to survive.

It is not necessary that all conditions be present for influence to be observed. We would argue, however, that as more of the conditions are met, the probability of external control becomes more and more likely. These conditions are not themselves unalterable givens in a situation. Social actors can and do attempt to affect the conditions in order to create greater likelihood of being able to exert control success-fully over other organizations. Attempts are made to obtain more con-trol over important resources, to obtain better access to information in order to assess the organization's actions and outcomes, and to increase the importance of what the influencing organization supplies. Social control involves a process in which both the influencer and the fo-cal organization act to affect the conditions governing the influence process.

These conditions have parallels in other discussions of interorgani-zational power. Thompson (1967:31) noted that "an organization is dependent on some element of its task environment 1) in proportion to the organization's need for resources or performances which that ele-ment can provide, and 2) in inverse proportion to the ability of other elements to provide the same resources or performance." Blau (1964:119–125), in specifying the conditions for independence, the converse of dependence, states that 1) strategic resources promote independence; 2) the fact that there are alternative sources from which a needed service can be obtained fosters independence; 3) the ability to use coercive force to compel others to dispense needed ser-vices is another condition of independence, where the inability to use force may be due to weakness or to normative restraints; and 4) a lack of need for various services also fosters independence.

The conditions are also partly consistent with various models of intraorganizational power—that is, power of various subunits within the organization. Hickson et al. (1971) noted that power accrues to those in the organization able to reduce uncertainties for the organiza-tion, and the more central the uncertainty and the more irreplaceable the actor, the more influential he will be. Salancik and Pfeffer (1974) have indicated that the power of a department in an organization is a function of the amount of important resources contributed by the de-partment. In both formulations, the concepts of alternative sources and the importance of what the actor controls are present.

The argument that the organization is a coalition of support im-plies that an important factor determining the organization's behavior is the dependencies on the various coalition participants. An organiza-tion's attempts to satisfy the demands of a given group are a function of its dependence on that group relative to other groups and the extent to which the demands of one group conflict with the demands of another. Three factors are critical in determining the dependence of one organization on another. First, there is the importance of the re-source, the extent to which the organization requires it for continued operation and survival. The second is the extent to which the interest group has discretion over the resource allocation and use. And, third, the extent to which there are few alternatives, or the extent of control over the resource by the interest group, is an important factor determining the dependence of the organization.

Resource Importance

An organization's vulnerability to extraorganizational influence is partly determined by the extent to which the organization has come to depend on certain types of exchanges for its operation. There are two dimensions to the importance of a resource exchange—the relative magnitude of the exchange and the criticality of the resource. These two dimensions are not completely independent.

The relative magnitude of an exchange as a determinant of the importance of the resource is measurable by assessing the proportion of total inputs or the proportion of total outputs accounted for by the exchange. An organization that creates only one product or service is more dependent on its customers than an organization that has a variety of outputs that are being disposed of in a variety of markets. Similarly, organizations which require one primary input for their operations will be more dependent on the sources of supply for that input than organizations that use multiple inputs, each in relatively small proportion. Single-material organizations—two examples are wood-product and petrochemical firms—are less common than single-output organizations. Historically, universities have defined themselves as processing a relatively narrowly defined input—people between 18 and 22 years of age. As the supply of people in that cohort has decreased, relative to capacity to process it, universities have faced problems. One response has been to broaden the range of needed inputs to include older people in adult education and continuing education programs.

The second dimension of importance concerns the criticality of the input or output to the organization. The criticality of a resource in the functioning of an organization is more difficult to determine than the sheer magnitude of its use. Criticality measures the ability of the organization to continue functioning in the absence of the resource or in the absence of the market for the output. A resource may be critical to the organization even though it comprises only a small proportion of the total input. Few offices could function without electric power, even though the utility may be a relatively small component of the organization's expenditures.

The criticality of a resource for an organization may vary from time to time as conditions in the organization's environment change. A lawyer may be relatively unimportant until the organization is confronted with a major lawsuit that threatens its survival. In Crozier's (1964) example of the maintenance workers in a French factory, the workers were important only when and if the machinery broke down. As the environmental contingencies change, what is a critical resource may change also.

The fact that a resource is important to the organization's functioning is, in itself, not the source of the organization's problems. Problematic conditions of resources come from the environment. When the supply of a resource is stable and ample, there is no problem for the organization. Organizational vulnerability derives from the possibility of an environment's changing so that the resource is no longer assured. Forms of organization which require scarcer resources, for which acquisition is more uncertain, would be less likely to survive than those that require resources in more stable and ample supply. One might expect, then, to see a succession of organizations until one evolves that requires resources that are more stable and more abundant in the environment.

Achieving stability in the supply of a resource or in the absorption of an output is problematic for an organization that requires steady resource exchanges to operate. Instability may change a situation of adequate supply to one of insufficiency. For some organizations, stability is a more important dimension of its operation than either profitability or growth. Instability with respect to an important resource means the organization's survival has become more uncertain. The apparent desire for stability and certainty noted by many observers of organizations (e.g., Hazard, 1961; Cyert and March, 1963) derives, then, not just from the desire of management to have an easier job or more security. Rather, it is in the interests of all coalition participants to have the organization survive, for their continuing participation in the organization indicates that they are obtaining benefits they would like continued. Uncertainty or instability with respect to an important resource threatens the continued existence of the organization, because it makes the participation of coalition members more doubtful. If participants have come to rely on an organization for performances or resources and these become unpredictable, the benefits of participation in the coalition diminish, and it is in the interests of all participants either to abandon the unstable organization for a more stable coalition or to stabilize the uncertainty confronting the organization. It is the necessary responsibility of management to ensure the survival of the coalition, and this entails working to minimize the possibilitiy of resources becoming scarce or uncertain.

Discretion over Resource Allocation and Use

The second major determinant of dependence is the extent of discretion over the allocation and use of a resource possessed by another social actor. There are many forms of discretion over a resource, which is the capacity to determine the allocation or use of the resource. Such discretion is a major source of power and is more important when the resource is more scarce. In an environment dense with organizations and interest groups with a variety of laws and norms, discretion is rarely absolute. More commonly, there are degrees of shared discretion.

One basis for control over a resource is possession. Knowledge is one resource controlled in this fashion. An individual possesses his knowledge in a direct and absolute manner. He is the sole arbiter of its use by others. The basis for the power of such professionals as doctors, lawyers, and engineers, with respect to their clients, lies in the access to knowledge and information. Ownership or ownership rights are also a means of possessing a resource and therefore controlling it. However, unlike the case of knowledge and information, ownership is a form of indirect discretion in that it depends on a social-political conception and on enforceable social consensus. American and British oil firms that built and owned production facilities in other countries were only able to maintain their ownership while the legal and social foundations permitting their ownership existed. When their Middle East hosts passed a law giving themselves 51 percent ownership, the oil industry dramatically learned the tenuous nature of property rights. Thus, although ownership provides a basis for exerting control over a resource, it is not absolute and depends on the consent of others in the social system.

Another basis for control is access to a resource. It is possible to regulate access to a resource without owning it. Any process that affects the allocation of a resource provides some degree of control over it. An executive secretary gains considerable power from the ability to determine who is permitted access to the boss. The agents of organizations who influence the allocation of the organization's contracts develop personal power from their positions, a point noted by Thompson (1962) in his discussion of organizations and output transactions. Thus, salesmen attempt to win the favor of purchasing agents because the purchasing agents influence the allocation of resources even though they do not own them. Lockheed's bribes to Japanese intermediaries were their means of gaining access to the government which purchased their planes.

Another important basis for control is the actual use of the resource and who controls its use. It is possible for a resource to be used by other than the owners, in which case the users have some measure of control over the resource. Although both the owners of taxis and city police departments, which regulate cab drivers, may prefer drivers to accept fares throughout the city, the fact is that, in many cities, taxi drivers refuse fares in what are considered dangerous areas.

The ability to control the use of a resource is a major source of influence for some interest groups. Employees are frequently in a position to control use most directly and occasionally obtain satisfaction of their demands by using the power such use confers. In the fall of 1974, the air traffic controllers in Chicago staged what might be described as a slowdown, though it was accomplished merely by precisely following procedures specified for their jobs. At issue was the withdrawal of familiarization passes by the air carriers. These passes allowed the controllers to become familiar with problems involved in air transport by riding in the cockpit of airplanes, frequently to places such as Miami and Denver.

The final source of control derives from the ability to make rules or otherwise regulate the possession, allocation, and use of resources and to enforce the regulations. In addition to being a source of power, the ability to make regulations and rules can determine the very existence and concentration of power. Laws permitting, if not facilitating, the organization of workers into unions permit the concentration of power, while laws regulating interactions among competitors presumably limit the concentration of buyer and seller power. The ability of rules to affect the concentration of power against organizations is nicely illustrated in a recent case decided by the Supreme Court. In a case that took eight years to resolve, Morton Eisen, a New York shoe salesman, filed a class action complaint on behalf of all the people who had bought or sold odd lots of stock (less than 100 shares) on the New York Stock Exchange in dealings with the defendants, two brokerage houses accused of controlling odd-lot trading and illegally fixing prices that resulted in increased fees. While Eisen's damage was only $70, the total class could have been entitled to almost $8 million. The Supreme Court ruled that the plaintiff filing on behalf of a class had to give individual notice to all class members who can be identified with reasonable effort and must bear the cost of such notification. In this particular case, that would have required $272,000 for the preparation and mailing of notices. Of course, such a rule makes the prosecution of such actions much less likely.

Rules also determine the extent to which dependence relations, developing from resource exchanges, can be used to accomplish the external control of behavior. In a series of cases brought under the antitrust laws, it has been determined that franchisors cannot compel their franchisees to buy machinery or other inputs from them. Other cases have held that sales territories cannot be restricted. In the absence of such prohibitions, the franchisors, with their greater power, would be able to control the activities of the franchisees much more tightly. Normative restraints also occasionally operate to limit the use and scope of interorganizational influence attempts.

Concentration of Resource Control

That an interest group or organization controls a resource and that the resource is important, still does not assure that it will be able to create a dependency for another organization. The dependence of one organization on another also derives from the concentration of resource control, or the extent to which input or output transactions are made by a relatively few, or only one, significant organizations. The sheer number of suppliers or purchasers is not the critical variable. Rather, the important thing is whether the focal organization has access to the resource from additional sources. There are many rules and regulations that can restrict access despite the availability of alternatives. For instance, a law governing the shipment of freight traveling between two points on an American coast requires that the cargo be carried on a United States ship. This law requires shippers transporting goods between the mainland and Hawaii to use more expensive American shipping. Concentration of resource control, then, refers to the extent to which the focal organization can substitute sources for the same resource.

Economists have typically measured concentration in terms of the proportion of the market accounted for by the largest four or eight organizations (Adelman, 1951). Alternative measures might include the Gini ratio of concentration, which measures the extent to which a distribution departs from a uniform distribution. The relative number of alternatives available, as well as the size or importance of these alternatives, has consequences for the extent to which organizational behavior is constrained.

Concentration can arise in a multitude of ways. An organization can have a monopoly position legally protected or legally established, as in the case of electric and telephone utilities. Or, a group of firms can act together as one, constituting a cartel. For coordinated action to develop, it is not necessary for the organizations to communicate with one another. As Phillips (1960) has noted, when there are a small number of firms with similar goals and similar cost structures, implicit coordination is possible. Collective organizations and associations are another form of achieving concentration over some resource. Unions and, to a lesser extent, trade and professional associations are instances of these attempts to achieve coordinated action, or to have many organizations or individuals act as one.

With mass coverage of social activities by television, it is increasingly possible for large numbers of individuals to engage in collective action without interpersonal communication and without the need to form an association. In 1974, for example, farmers across the United States took action to reduce their supply of livestock in order to increase prices, and they did so, not only as a result of communications within farm organizations, but also because they learned on the evening news of such actions taken by other farmers.

Any system that regulates resources and their exchanges, in effect, concentrates influence over those resources. If an organization wanted to influence a class of organizations when there are many such organizations to be influenced, it would be in a better position to exert influence if the multitude of organizations were regulated by a single agency or governed by a single law. Instead of having many targets for influence, there would be only one. Concentration of resource control means that influence attempts can be concentrated similarly, with the possessor of the resource control as the target.

As an illustration of this effect, consider the issue of controlling hospital costs and activities. In most states there are thousands of hospitals, and the task of influencing decisions at each hospital would be enormous. However, most hospitals are now largely reimbursed by third-party payers, Blue Cross, some other private insurance firm, or the federal government through the Medicare and Medicaid programs. Furthermore, reimbursement is based on defined standards for service and allowable costs. Instead of having to influence thousands of individual hospitals in order to have an impact on the activities of the medical system, it is only necessary to influence two organizations— Blue Cross and the Department of Health, Education, and Welfare. Although these are larger organizations and, therefore, perhaps more difficult to influence, it is clear that influence attempts can be focused on fewer targets.

Dependence

Concentration of the control of discretion over resources and the importance of the resources to the organization together determine the focal organization's dependence on any given other group or organization. Dependence can then be defined as the product of the importance of a given input or output to the organization and the extent to which it is controlled by a relatively few organizations. A resource that is not important to the organization cannot create a situation of dependence, regardless of how concentrated control over the resource is. Also, regardless of how important the resource is, unless it is controlled by a relatively few organizations, the focal organization will not be particularly dependent on any of them. When there are many sources of supply or potential customers, the power of any single one is correspondingly reduced.

The dependence we are describing results from exchange processes and from the requirements of organizations to acquire resources and engage in exchange with their environments. Dependence, then, measures the potency of the external organizations or groups in the given organization's environment. It is a measure of how much these organizations must be taken into account and, also, how likely it is that they will be perceived as important and considered in the organization's decision making.

Countervailing Power and Asymmetric Dependence

Some writers have maintained that the concentration of resources is the basis of interorganizational influence (Mintz and Cohen, 1971). We disagree. The problems associated with concentrated power do not arise because the power is concentrated but because others are not able to muster equal power or equal concentration of opposition. The concentration of power itself is inevitable. It arises from a need to take organized action in cases where the interests of a number of parties are involved. And to the extent that the interests of one party cannot be achieved without other parties, concentration is necessary. The basis of organization is the concentration of effort, coordinating some set of activities to achieve some outcomes of interest to the participants. Perrow (1972) has seen this clearly and has consequently noted that the critical issue in organizations is not whether there will be a concentration of control but, rather, whose interests are being served by the organized, coordinated activities.

A variety of decision mechanisms have been invented to resolve differences in interests and preferences, ranging from using some random selection device, such as coin flipping or dice rolling, to relying on accepted, legitimate authority, to using power based on the control over resources vital to the organization. The point is that some concentration of power is inevitable to achieve collective outcomes. The mechanisms through which effort is organized and coordinated are varied and are not the topic we are examining.

It is the case, however, that the concentration of force to accomplish something is more likely to cause those in opposition to concentrate and coordinate their actions also. Galbraith (1967) has spoken of this in terms of the notion of countervailing power—that the concentration of power or resources in one sphere tends to set up forces that result in a countervailing, concentrated opposition. There are many anecdotal instances of this occurring, though the phenomenon has not been subjected to systematic empirical testing. For instance, in the area of labor-management bargaining, it is known that if employers move to industry-wide bargaining, the union will also concentrate its bargaining efforts and work for industry-wide settlements. As companies have expanded abroad, developing production facilities for a product in many countries, unions have begun to explore the possibility of developing cross-national federations to engage in worldwide bargaining with a company or an industry, which would prevent a company facing a strike in one country from making up the production in its plants in other countries.

For the dependence between two organizations to provide one organization with power over the other, there must be asymmetry in the exchange relationship. If organization X sells to organization Y and is dependent on Y for absorbing its output, it is simultaneously true that Y purchases from X and is, therefore, dependent upon X for the provision of some required input. Asymmetry exists in the relationship when the exchange is not equally important to both organizations. This may occur because the organizations differ greatly in size, so that what is a large proportion of one's operations is a small proportion of the other's. For instance, General Motors purchases many components from a wide variety of relatively small suppliers. Many of these suppliers furnish virtually 100 percent of their output to General Motors, although each contributes only a small fraction to the total input of General Motors.

Without asymmetry in the exchange relationship neither organization possesses a particular power advantage, reducing the likelihood that one organization will dominate interorganizational influences. Of course, there can be asymmetries with respect to one resource, though the net relationship between the two organizations is counterbalanced because of corresponding asymmetries for other resources. Thus, an organization may exchange information for sales or may exchange purchases of a product from one organization for sales of some other product to the same organization. This reciprocity is quite common among industrial concerns and is frequently encouraged.

When the net exchange between organizational entities is asymmetrical, some net power accrues to the less dependent organization. This power may be employed in attempting to influence or constrain the behavior of the other more dependent organization. To summarize the preceding discussion, the potential for one organization's influencing another derives from its discretionary control over resources needed by that other and the other's dependence on the resource and lack of countervailing resources or access to alternative sources. Perrow (1970) reports on a striking example of interorganizational influence deriving from asymmetrical exchanges. He reported that it was the practice of the large automobile-manufacturing firms to audit the records of their small suppliers, thereby ensuring that the small suppliers were not earning excessive profits on their transactions. In fact, it has been argued that the profitability of General Motors derives not so much from its production efficiencies but from its market position. It can take advantage of its suppliers' production efficiencies by using its influence to control the price at which it buys. General Motors absorbs much of the output of the small suppliers, while each supplier provides only a fraction of the input to General Motors. Further, while General Motors confronts a large number of firms competing for its business, the suppliers must sell to only three major automobile companies, with General Motors accounting for more than half the market. The small suppliers are quite dependent on General Motors, which, in controlling the market for cars, also controls the market for parts. Since General Motors can always decide the quantity to be purchased from each supplier, it can maintain the size and number of suppliers at a level sufficient to continue its position of relative power.

EMPIRICAL EXAMINATIONS OF INTERORGANIZATIONAL INFLUENCE

The concept of dependence is useful in understanding how organizational decision making is constrained by the environment. If organizations achieve their own ends by using their power to affect the behavior of other organizations, then it is possible to conceive of organizational behavior as the consequence of influences. While it is more common to view organizations as self-directed, making strategic decisions and vigorously pursuing courses of action, the concept of dependence suggests that organizations are partly directed by elements in their environment. Organizations formulate their own actions in response to the demands placed upon them by other organizations. The extent to which a given organization will respond to the demands of other organizations can be explained by the variables we have described previously, particularly focusing on the dependence of the organization on the various external organizations. Below, we describe two studies testing these ideas.

Israeli Managers

Aharoni (1971) interviewed the general managers of the 141 largest manufacturing plants in Israel and, as part of this study, asked them what they might do in a variety of hypothetical situations. These data were used in a study of the extent to which sales interdependence, foreign ownership, and financial problems could explain the managers' expressed willingness to comply with various governmental requests and policies (Pfeffer, 1972).

Each manager was presented with a hypothetical decision situation in which he was asked what level of profit he would be willing to accept on an investment in a development area. The Israeli government had designated certain areas for development and had encouraged firms to invest in these areas. Managers were asked to answer, along a seven-point scale, what rate of return they would be willing to forego to invest in the development area, assuming that, after government incentives and other considerations, they would earn 15 percent in the development area. An expressed willingness to accept lower returns was assumed to be a measure of the managers' commitment to accede to government demands.

Two sources of interdependence with the government were used to examine variation in the answers to this question. The government was both a purchaser of goods and a source of financing. We would expect that firms which sell a large proportion of their goods to the government would be more willing to comply with the government's request concerning plant location. And, we would also expect that firms which were in worse financial condition and were restricted in finding sources of financing would be more dependent on the government for financial assistance and would also be more willing to comply with the government's wishes.

To examine the hypothesis that dependence affects organizational decisions, the managers' responses regarding the size of the return they would be willing to give up to invest in the development area were correlated with the proportion of the firm's sales to the government. In Table 3.1, rank-order correlations are presented.

For total government sales combined, the correlation of .21 indicates that firms selling a larger proportion of their output to the

TABLE 3.1   Correlations of Percentage Sales to Various Governmental Agencies and Willingness to Invest in Development Area

Government Agency	Correlation[a]	Level of Significance[a]
Defense	+.110	.04
Shekem	+.325	.001
Other government	+.160	.005
Total government	+.211	.001

[a] Kendall rank-order correlations

government were willing to give up larger yields from investment else-where in order to comply with the government's request. The correla-tions in Table 3.1 also indicate that the proportion of sales to defense were the least related to willingness to comply, while sales to the Shekem, the Israeli equivalent of the American commissary or PX, were most related. This result is not surprising if we consider that a large number of firms can potentially supply the commissary, while there were only a few large firms selling to defense. Because the de-pendence was more asymmetrical in the case of firms selling to the commissary, those firms were more willing to comply as a function of their dependence on government sales.

The firms' potential reliance on the government for financing was also related to their willingness to comply. The managers were asked, "Do you think your firm is limited in choosing its sources of funds?" and were given four responses, ranging from "No" to "Yes, always." This question was assumed to measure the firms' dependence on the government for assistance in financing. The correlation with the ex-pressed willingness to invest in the development area was .11 ($p <$ .04), consistent with our expectations but not a very strong relation-ship. Answers to another question asking about the influence the Ministry of Finance had on the firms' decisions correlated .17 ($p <$ .003) with a question about access to alternative funding sources.

Although the strength of the relationships were not large, the results of the study of responses of Israeli managers (Pfeffer, 1972) were consistent with our argument that organizational actions are con-strained by the environment to the extent the organization is depen-dent on the environment. The Israeli managers study has a number of limitations. Data were collected for other purposes; organizational be-havior was assessed by asking about responses in hypothetical situa-tions, even though the answers were provided by the same people who would make the actual decisions; and the data were collected by a respected professor of business who had been Dean of the Business School at Tel Aviv University. This last fact may have affected the responses given; for instance, the managers may have been reluctant to admit their willingness to forego higher profits or may have wanted to appear even more loyal to the interests of the country. Such factors would introduce randomness into the responses, attenuating the strength of the correlations.

Sales Interdependence and Affirmative Action

An attempt to gather more evidence on the effects of dependence (Salancik, 1976) was made shortly after the study of the Israeli man-agers. The context in this case was American firms and their responses to the government's requirement for affirmative action regarding the employment of women. In a series of presidential executive orders, first blacks and then women were included in the requirement that organizations doing business with the government not only cease discriminatory hiring practices but also engage in affirmative action to increase the proportion of such people in the work force.

To obtain some indication of the extent of response to these governmental demands, the top 100 defense contractors were examined. Letters were mailed to the executive vice-president inquiring about the firm's plans for hiring women MBA graduates in June. The letter, from a university department of business administration, implied the purpose in writing was to find out how to advise female graduates regarding job opportunities. The letter also asked for any information or brochures the firm might have. Careful records were kept of replies, including weighing the response and noting the time required to respond. Some firms did not reply, others sent short notes explaining they were not hiring, while others sent long letters from their affirmative action directors. Some firms sent brochures describing management opportunities for women in their organizations. From this information, each organization was rated according to how actively it appeared to be in pursuit of female management graduates. One measure of response was the length of time it took to obtain a reply. Another measure was the extent to which the response encouraged female management students to seek employment, with the most encouraging being those responses from the director of equal employment opportunity accompanied by brochures describing opportunities for women, while the least responsive was either no reply or a short note from a secretary indicating there were no positions. These two measures correlated highly ($r = .89$).

From the original sample of 100, some firms had to be dropped: some were only holding companies and did no direct hiring; some were engineering firms and did not hire people with only MBA degrees; for others sales information about them could not be publicly obtained. In all, 78 firms were examined. For each of these firms, 1970 information was collected on their total sales, sales to the government, and the proportion of the total procurement in the defense department each furnished. From these data, the following were computed: (1) the firm's percent of sales to the government, a measure of its dependence on the government; (2) the dollar amount of nongovernment sales, a measure of its potential visibility to the public; and (3) the firm's contribution to the total defense expenditures, a measure of the government's dependence on the firm. The one-third of the firms with the largest amount of dollar sales to nongovernment organizations were designated as large, visible organizations, while the remainder were considered to be less visible, smaller organizations. Within each category, the firms were further categorized according to their control of the market. A firm controlled the market to the extent it had a larger proportion of the total sales of that commodity. For instance, Colt Industries, in 1970, accounted for more than 50 percent of the small arms business with the government. Such concentration, we assumed, indicated greater government dependence on the firm for purchases.

As in the case of the decisions of the Israeli managers, our interest is in the way the organization's responsiveness to government demands varies with dependence on the government. One would expect firms to respond more to government pressures according to how dependent they were on the government for their business, which is measured by the proportion of their sales to the government. At the same time, one might expect that if the Department of Defense were dependent on a contractor because of the contractor's control of the production of a given item, the government would be less likely to pursue compliance vigorously. Some contractors, of course, because of pressures from other groups, might comply even if not under pressure from the Department of Defense. Large consumer goods firms, for instance, because of their public visibility, might be more inclined to comply even without government pressure. Thus, we would expect that the degree of responsiveness of contractors to affirmative action pressures as a consequence of their dependence on the government to itself vary with the visibility of the contractor and with his importance as a source of supply. For large, visible firms that are not major sources of defense supplies, the enforcement pressures should be greatest; for less visible contractors that are major suppliers of defense requirements, the enforcement should be least. From the point of view of the contractors confronted with pressures to comply, the decision should depend on how much they need the government as a purchaser of their output. Those firms very dependent on the government should be more responsive than those not so dependent. But we should also expect that, as the enforcement demands are less, the relationship between a firm's dependence and its compliance would also diminish.

The data testing this argument are presented in Table 3.2. The four types of firms are ranked according to our assumptions about the amount of enforcement pressure they are likely to face, and the correlations represent the extent to which the firms of each type respond as a function of the proportion of their total sales to the government. As can be seen, when enforcement pressures are assumed to be greatest, responses evidencing concern for affirmative action are strongly related to the degree of the organization's dependence on the government ($r = .84$). This relationship diminishes as firms face less enforcement pressure. Indeed, for small firms that are important

TABLE 3.2   U.S. Defense Contractors' Responsiveness to Inquiry About Employment Opportunities for Women as a Function of Proportion of Sales to the Government, Firm Size, and Control of Production

Type of Firm	Correlation	Sample Size
Large, visible firm, not controlling production of items	.84[a]	13
Large, visible firm, with control of production of items	.46[b]	13
Small, less visible firm, not controlling production of items	.02	26
Small, less visible firm, with control of production of items	−.67[a]	26

[a] $p < .01$ [b] $p < .05$

sources of supply, the relationship between the firm's dependence and the response to our inquiries about affirmative action is actually negative.

SUMMARY

The concept of the social control of organizational choice is well illustrated by the data from the Israeli managers and the American defense contractors. To the extent that the focal organization depended on the government, a greater influence on the decisions of the managers and the behavior of the contractors could be observed. Randall (1973), in a study of the responsiveness of state employment service officers to headquarter's requests for more training activity, found a similar result. It is exactly such influences on behavior, resulting from the organization's transactions or exchanges with external organizations, that are what is meant when we say that organizational behavior is constrained and shaped by the demands and pressures of organizations and groups in its environment.

Descriptively, it has been proposed that constraints on behavior result from situations of asymmetric interdependence, when there exists the discretion to control resources and enforce demands and when the focal organization's behavior is not already tightly constrained. In this setting, it is hypothesized that the organization will tend to be influenced more the greater the dependence on the external organization, or alternatively, the more important the external organization is to the functioning and survival of the organization. It is evident that effectiveness, as defined in the last chapter—meeting the objectives or requirements of various groups or organizations—is sought as a natural outcome of the organization's requirements for maintaining exchanges with its environment and with its requirements for survival.

The effective organization, then, is the organization which satisfies the demands of those in its environment from whom it requires support for its continued existence. But how does an organization become effective? In this chapter we have said little about how to manage an organization to achieve effectiveness. We have not yet done this primarily because the first task of being effective is to have an adequate model of the reality within which you operate. Without an adequate model of the world, effective action is certainly unlikely. In the next chapter, we will describe how organizations know their environments—the demands and constraints they confront—because the first step in effective management is being able to perceive the environment accurately and to understand the factors that determine how the organization defines its world. Then, in the following chapter, we will consider some other issues in effectively managing the organization. There are several aspects to managing the organization's relationships with its environment. First, there is the question of knowing on what the organization's effectiveness depends. Then there is the question of when to respond to environmental demands and when not to. And, third, there is the issue of how to avoid environmental constraints that force actions which limit the chances for effectiveness and survival.

REFERENCES

Adelman, M. A. 1951. "The measurement of industrial concentration." *Review of Economics and Statistics*, 33:269–296.

Aharoni, Y. 1971. *The Israeli Manager*. Israeli Institute of Business Research, Tel Aviv University.

Blau, P. M. 1964. *Exchange and Power in Social Life*. New York: Wiley.

Crozier, M. 1964. *The Bureaucratic Phenomenon*. University of Chicago Press.

Cyert, R. M., and J. G. March. 1963. *A Behavioral Theory of the Firm*. Englewood Cliffs, N.J.: Prentice-Hall.

Emerson, R. E. 1962. "Power-dependence relations." *American Sociological Review*, 27:31–41.

Galbraith, J. K. 1967. *The New Industrial State*. Boston: Houghton Mifflin.

Hawley, A. H. 1950. *Human Ecology*. New York: Ronald Press.

Hazard, L. 1961. "Are big businessmen crooks?" *Atlantic Monthly*, 208: 57–61.

Hickson, D. J., C. R. Hinings, C. A. Lee, R. E. Schneck, and J. M. Pennings. 1971. "A strategic contingencies' theory of intraorganizational power." *Administrative Science Quarterly*, 16:216–229.

Jacobs, D. 1974. "Dependency and vulnerability: an exchange approach to the control of organizations." *Administrative Science Quarterly,* 19: 45–59.

Mintz, M., and J. S. Cohen. 1971. *America, Inc.: Who Owns and Operates the United States.* New York: Dial Press.

Perrow, C. 1970. *Organizational Analysis: A Sociological View.* Belmont, Calif.: Wadsworth.

Perrow, C. 1972. *Complex Organizations: A Critical Essay.* Glenview, Ill.: Scott, Foresman.

Pfeffer, J. 1972. "Interorganizational influence and managerial attitudes." *Academy of Management Journal,* 15:317–330.

Phillips, A. 1960. "A Theory of interfirm organization." *Quarterly Journal of Economics,* 74:602–613.

Randall, R. 1973. "Influence of environmental support and policy space on organizational behavior." *Administrative Science Quarterly,* 18:236–247.

Salancik, G. R. 1976. "The role of interdependencies in organizational responsiveness to demands from the environment: the case of women versus power." Unpublished manuscript, University of Illinois.

Salancik, G. R., and J. Pfeffer. 1974. "The bases and use of power in organizational decision making: the case of a university." *Administrative Science Quarterly,* 19:453–473.

Thompson, J. D. 1962. "Organizations and output transactions." *American Journal of Sociology,* 68:309–324.

Thompson, J. D. 1967. *Organizations in Action.* New York: McGraw-Hill.

Wiley, M. G., and M. N. Zald. 1968. "The growth and transformation of educational accrediting agencies: an exploratory study in social control of institutions." *Sociology of Education,* 41:36–56.

Zald, M. N., and F. D. Hair. 1972. "The social control of general hospitals." In B. S. Georgopoulos (ed.), *Organizational Research in Health Institutions,* 51–81. Institute for Social Research, University of Michigan.

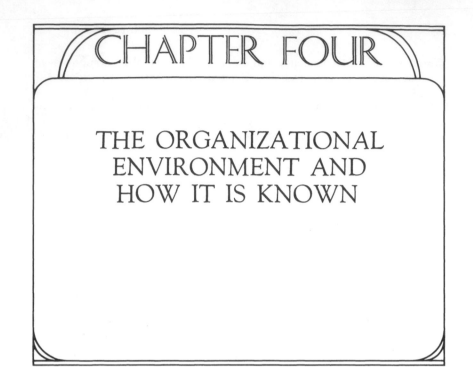

CHAPTER FOUR

THE ORGANIZATIONAL ENVIRONMENT AND HOW IT IS KNOWN

We have described the importance of context for understanding organizational behavior; yet, it is not sufficient to talk about context or organizational environment in general terms. Two issues confront us. First, what are the dimensions of context, or the environment, which are important—how can organizational environments be described and measured? Second, there is the important issue of how organizational environments are known by the organization and how they come to influence decision making. In this chapter we will deal with how the environment can be described and how it comes to be known by the organization.

Part of the problem in understanding the environment as a concept is that the environment of an organization can affect an organization's outcomes without affecting its behavior. It is necessary to distinguish between behavior and outcomes. Important elements of the environment may be invisible to organizational decision makers, and hence, not considered in determining organizational actions, but these same elements can affect organizational success or failure. It is unlikely that firms purchasing coal mines in the early 1960s thought much about the Arab world when deciding their purchases. Nevertheless, when Arab governments raised oil prices, investors in coal profited. The outcomes were affected, even though it is unlikely the original decisions had been.

To understand how the environment of an organization affects organizations, it is useful to distinguish three levels of the environment. On one level, the environment consists of the entire system of interconnected individuals and organizations who are related to one another and to a focal organization through the organization's transactions. The next level is the set of individuals and organizations with whom this organization directly interacts. It is on this level that the organization can experience its environment. The environment comprised of organizations transacting with the focal organization is, however, not the environment that determines organizational action, for this environment, in order to affect action, must be observed and registered. Observation, attention, and perception are active processes which must occur for events to exist in the experience of any social actor. Thus, the third level of the organization's environment can be characterized as the level of the organization's perception and representation of the environment—its enacted environment.

The three characterizations of the organization's environment are, of course, related. The larger environmental system can impact the set of transactions between the focal organization and its organization set, and these transactions are the raw material out of which the enacted environment is formed. The enacted environment influences organizational actions, while events in the other levels of environment may affect outcomes.

DIMENSIONS OF THE ENVIRONMENT

Many authors have attempted to describe or dimensionalize organizational environments. One of the earliest and most influential attempts was the work of Emery and Trist (1965). Emery and Trist described four types of environments, which differed according to the source and nature of the interdependence between the environment and the organization. The first type, called placid-randomized, referred to a situation in which the resources desired by the organization were randomly distributed throughout the environment, with a constant probability of uncovering necessary resources as the organization searched the environment. In this environment, organizations survive to the extent they can use different kinds of resources, can store a single resource, or can use an abundant resource, one which they are likely to encounter frequently in the environment. The second type of environment, called placid-clustered, referred to an environment in which the pattern of resources was sequentially predictable. Interdependence with such environments involves the sequential probabilities of the shifts in resource availability and the relationship to the organization's requirements. Single organizations survive by accumulating enough resources to survive the periods of resource scarcity or by reducing their need for resources during lean periods. H. & R. Block, the tax preparation firm, is an excellent example of such an organization. With activities clustered by the calendar for filing tax returns, the firm must earn enough during this period to last the entire year and also must expand and contract operations with this seasonality.

The third type of environment, called disturbed-reactive, is fundamentally different from the first two. In this environment, the distributions and probabilities of resources are created by the actions of the organizations themselves. Competitive interdependence characterizes such environments. Members of the same organizational class transact with the same environment, compete for resources, and can transact with each other. Predictability in such an environment derives from the ability of organizational actors to identify their interdependencies and to anticipate the sequence of actions and reactions of competitors. In economics, this environment is represented by the concept of oligopoly.

The final type of environment described by Emery and Trist, called turbulent, differs from the third environment in that it involves the connection of sets of actors to other sets of actors, such that any one actor is connected to the set of actors with which he is immediately interdependent, and the environment itself is interconnected with other sets of interdependent actors. The important difference is that even greater uncertainty is created for the organizations. Actions in other parts of the interconnected system, while largely invisible, can have impact on the organization's immediate exchanges. Although Emery and Trist describe a turbulent field as one in which changes can occur from the field itself rather than from the interconnected components, their examples are not consistent with this argument. Their illustration of a turbulent environment and its effects is the case of a vegetable canning company which had enjoyed a large market share for many years and suddenly found its sales and market share declining. In interpreting how this decline in position came about, Emery and Trist noted a number of factors: the end of wartime controls on steel and tin, allowing cheaper cans; an end to import quotas on vegetables; increased affluence; development of quick-freeze technology;

displacement of small stores by large supermarkets. The canner, rather than recognizing these events as part of the environment, continued to concentrate on its immediate competitors in the vegetable canning business. While the events noted took place outside the immediate set of transacting organizations related to the canner, the outcome faced by the canner could have been predicted from knowledge of such events, and these events were clearly in the immediate environment of the canner.

The important contribution of Emery and Trist was the recognition of a distinction between the set of transacting organizations, the organization set (Evan, 1966), and the larger social context within which both the organization and its organization set are embedded. The interconnectedness of one set of actors wth other sets increases the interdependence among all and may increase the uncertainty of outcomes. While interdependence is increased, whether predictability or uncertainty is increased is partially a function of the organization's ability to recognize and control the increased number of actors which may affect its operation.

Terreberry (1968) extended Emery and Trist's arguments, claiming that the four types of environments described by Emery and Trist were stages in an evolutionary chain and that organizational environments were becoming increasingly turbulent. She further argued that organizations were increasingly less autonomous and that other organizations were increasingly important components of the environment of formal organizations. Warren (1967; Warren, Rose, and Bergunder, 1974) has also considered the effect of the general network in which interorganizational activity is embedded. Unlike many who have commented on the problems caused by interconnectedness, Turk (1970) found that being embedded in a richly connected interorganizational network can benefit organizational achievement. Cities linked to larger national social service networks through the presence of many national headquarters and containing many community associations were more likely to have an active poverty program. Turk argued that it was easier to introduce new organizations into an environment that was already richly connected. This result might, in part, be a consequence of the fact that it is easier to found organizations or programs in a context which has more organizational experience (Stinchcombe, 1965).

In addition to the interconnectedness of the organizational environment, writers have examined the effects of other properties of the interorganizational field. Hawley (1963), for instance, defined power as a property of the interorganizational field, measured by the concentration of authority. He measured the concentration of power in a city as the ratio of managers, proprietors, and officials to the total labor force; and he found that the concentration of power was positively related to the probability of the city undertaking and completing urban renwal projects. Presumably, the ability to coordinate the necessary commitment and support was easier with concentrated authority.

Concentration has been the primary dimension used by economists to describe organizational environments. Economic concentration (Adelman, 1951) has been defined as the proportion of an industry's output, value added, sales, assets, or employment which is controlled by the largest four, eight, or any number of firms. While there is a diversity of concentration ratio measures thus available, typically four-firm ratios based on sales output or a value-added basis have been used. Concentration is, in a sense, related to Hawley's measures of the concentration of power, for the inference is that the more concentrated a market, the more economic power is in the hands of a few dominant organizations. However, concentration also is a measure of uncertainty, as has been shown by Bernhardt and Mackenzie (1968). Stigler (1964) noted, in discussing oligopolistic pricing practices, that with fewer major customers (rather than firms), policing such pricing arrangements became easier.

The measurement of economic concentration has become quite refined, with Weiss (1963) introducing adjustments for over and under aggregation in industrial categories and for geographic characteristics of the competition in the industry. Research has utilized industry concentration as an independent variable and traced, for instance, the impact of concentration on profitability and price-cost margins (Weiss, 1963; Collins and Preston, 1968; Bain, 1968).

Concentration in organizational systems has been associated with the ability to achieve desired outcomes by the organizations in that system. The reason for this should be evident from our description of interdependence and its effect on achieving outcomes. Concentration reduces some of the problems of interdependence for organizational actors by reducing the number of separate social units that must be coordinated. The ultimate form of concentration, of course, is that of a single organization with the legitimacy and power to coordinate all of the behaviors under its control.

A related characteristic of organizational systems is conflict and dissensus. In one sense, conflict is the opposite of concentration, for it signifies a lack of ability to coordinate interdependent activities. Coordination is diminished by the presence of conflict. Conflict differs from interdependence in that conflict refers to disagreements about the ends or goals of the social system. Interdependence need not result in conflict if the interdependent actors share similar preferences. On the other hand, conflict is not possible without interdependence, for unless social actors are interdependent, there is no connection between them and hence no basis for conflict. Interdependence, therefore, is a necessary but not sufficient cause of conflict in social systems.

Political scientists have examined the degree of conflict or dissensus existing in the environments of political organizations. Kessel (1962), for example, found that city manager forms of government were used in cities with relatively less conflict over fundamental values and objectives. The governmental function in such settings was to administer; in cities with diverse populations and conflicts over goals, a politically more sensitive mayor-council form of government was needed to resolve conflicts and make decisions. On the level of state government, Walker (1969) observed that innovation among American states was partly predictable from the political conflict or consensus in the state.

One source of conflict in interorganizational fields derives from resource scarcity. Interdependent organizations faced with the problem of resource scarcity frequently seek ways to coordinate their conflict. Litwak and Hylton (1962) argued that coordinating agencies, such as the United Fund, developed and included more of the local agencies when resources were either very plentiful or very scarce. Agencies affiliated with strong national organizations, like the American Cancer Society, were less willing to participate in the United Fund. Integration with the national organization provided these agencies with resources and a buffer against uncertainty which local agencies could achieve only through coordination. The adequacy of resources has been observed by Assael (1969) to be a major determinant of the level of conflict between automobile dealers and manufacturers. However, there has been relatively little empirical attention to the effects of scarcity or munificence on organizational actions (e.g., Staw and Szwajkowski, 1975).

One of the more prominent themes in the literature has been the description of organizational environments in terms of their uncertainty. Uncertainty refers to the degree to which future states of the world cannot be anticipated and accurately predicted. Uncertainty, according to the prevailing literature, tends to be associated with decentralized, less formalized organizations. Uncertainty has been used by a number of authors (Lawrence and Lorsch, 1967; Duncan, 1972) to explain organizational structures. Occasionally, uncertainty has been confused with change (e.g., Osborne and Hunt, 1972). It is, of course, quite possible to have rapid change which is predictable and, therefore, not uncertain. Uncertainty is determined by the level of forecasting capability of the organization at a given point in time; as forecasting techniques improve, uncertainty diminishes.

Uncertainty itself is not problematic. It is a problem for organizations only when the uncertainty involves important interactions with other environmental elements that are important for the organization. Uncertainty is only problematic when it involves an element of critical organizational interdependence.

From the preceding discussion of the various environmental dimensions that have been used in the organization-environment literature, it should be evident that the dimensions are not really independent of each other. In fact, one can argue that the dimensions are likely to be causally related. In Figure 4.1, the simple linear relations among environmental dimensions is presented. In that figure, structural characteristics of the environment are distinguished from relationships among social actors, and both are distinguished from uncertainty, which is viewed as a result. Such conceptual distinctions are not frequently observed in the current literature.

The three most elemental structural characteristics of environments are concentration, the extent to which power and authority in the environment is widely dispersed; munificence, or the availability or scarcity of critical resources; and interconnectedness, the number and pattern of linkages, or connections, among organizations. These three structural characteristics, in turn, determine the relationships among social actors—specifically, the degree of conflict and interdependence present in the social system. Conflict and interdependence, in turn, determine the uncertainty the organization confronts. Uncertainty, then, can be viewed as one outcome of other environmental dimensions. Demands on the focal organization is another possible outcome. From the viewpoint of the external control of organizational behavior, the importance of concentration, munificence, and interconnectedness as basic dimensions describing the environment should be clear.

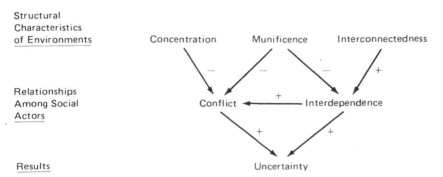

FIGURE 4.1   Relationships Among Dimensions of Organizational Environments

THE INTERCONNECTEDNESS OF ORGANIZATIONS

The interconnectedness of the environment is a dimension that is attracting growing research concern as empirical investigations of organization-environment activity move from analyzing the strategic actions taken by single organizations to consider the design of networks of organizations. The concept of interconnectedness is well illustrated by the following sequence of events occurring while wage and price controls were in effect in the early 1970s. Under the wage and price regulations, prices were controlled so as to prevent margins from expanding from their precontrol levels. However, margins were defined on an organization-wide basis. It so happened that a company operating primarily in the Northeast was found by the Price Commission to be making too much profit and, under the prevailing regulations, was told to cut prices so that its margins would be reduced and the excess profit returned to consumers. The regulations, however, did not specify how or where price was to be cut. The corporation was expanding its retailing activities into the South and had not yet established a firm position there. So, the decision was made to slash prices in the few stores in the South, thereby attracting additional business and gaining a more secure market position. The consequence of this strategy was that some small competing stores in the region were forced out of business. Thus, stores in one region were adversely affected by policies implemented because of events taking place literally thousands of miles away. Moreover, the foundation for these events had been laid months earlier by officials attempting to halt inflation.

Interconnectedness results in problems for organizations because, as can be seen in our example, the greater the level of system connectedness, the more uncertain and unstable the environment for given organizations. Changes can come from anywhere without notice and produce consequences unanticipated by those initiating the changes and those experiencing the consequences. Simon (1969) argued persuasively that systems were more likely to survive if they were loosely connected. In a system with n elements, the number of possible connections between the elements is: $n(n-1)/2$. If each link were actually effective, if the system were tightly interconnected, then any disturbance entering the system at any point would quickly affect every element. If the system were loosely coupled, on the other hand, disturbances would have more chance of being localized, and the system would be more stable and more certain.

Furthermore, adaptation is likely to be easier in a loosely joined system. When everything is connected to everything else, it is difficult to change anything because there are more constraints, deriving from the large number of interrelationships. On the other hand, in a loosely joined system, subsystem adaptation is better able to proceed, as there are not so many constraining links to be confronted. Simon (1969) argued that a loosely joined set of elements would evidence short-run independence of subsystems from each other and long-run dependence only in the aggregate. There is some limited empirical evidence that is consistent with our portrayal of organizational environments as loosely coupled networks of clusters of organizations which are themselves more closely interconnected (Freeman, 1968).

Organizations that are only loosely coupled, or networks of organizations that are not tightly interconnected, produce situations in which the actions of one element bears little predictable relationship to the actions of other elements or agents. When a system of organizations is not tightly interconnected, the actions of the organizations are less predictable given an external stimulus on one, or some subset, of them. Because of this unpredictability, loose-coupling may be perceived as a problem by managers of organizations or organizational systems. After all, if you are an agency head attempting to introduce change into the organizational system, the fact that loose-coupling makes the system more stable (i.e., less responsive to your interventions) will probably be seen as a problem rather than as an advantage. Social stability is not favorably perceived by those attempting to introduce change.

It is our impression that organizations are becoming more interconnected and that the cause of this increasing system connectedness is most often government action. In the example at the beginning of this section, we saw how the wage and price controls made economic areas more interconnected. Other governmental laws have similar effects. Certainly, regulations requiring similar responses from all organizations lead to more system responsiveness, though less variation within the system. We would argue that the increase in connectedness derives from the motivation we have described: managers want control and predictability and want to be able to intervene with effect relatively rapidly. To the extent the system is interconnected, just such results will be observed. System connectedness, then, is a substitute for concentration in that both assure predictability and provide increasingly powerful levers for change.

Organizations employ a variety of strategies for bringing stability and certainty to their environments. They may restructure the organization to avoid instability or its consequences; stabilize exchange relationships; or restructure the set of exchange relationships to enhance stability. Each organizational action taken to reduce uncertainty or manage problematic transactions may alter the connectedness of the system, possibly altering the transaction flows to other organizations.

In other words, actions taken to manage interdependence may, in the long run, increase the interdependence among environmental elements, requiring further actions to manage the new uncertainties. Two sellers merging, thereby reducing competitive interdependence, increases the interdependence among the buyers previously served by the two. The buyers may in turn form cooperatives, merge themselves, or undertake a variety of other actions. Such actions over time may lead to the creation of new forms of organization or, even more likely, new forms of managing interdependence among organizations.

THE ENACTMENT PROCESS—HOW ENVIRONMENTS ARE KNOWN

One of the least discussed topics is the interface between the organization and the environment, particularly how the environment or context comes to affect the structures or decisions of organizations. We shall consider this issue in more detail in Chapter Nine. There is some evidence that the power of internal subunits varies with their relationship to critical environmental problems (Hinings et al., 1974; Perrow, 1970, Pfeffer and Salancik, 1977). Since organizational decisions are based, at least partly, on subunit influence (Stagner, 1969; Pfeffer and Salancik, 1974), one might suggest that organizational environments come to affect organizational actions partly by affecting the distribution of power and influence inside the organization.

Having influence within an organization determined by external pressures is important because such concentrated influence within the organization can be used to organize the activities necessary to cope with these external pressures. Reorganizing is not a trivial matter when survival itself may be at stake. While marketing departments may have dominated many corporations during the 1950s and 1960s, there are indications that financial and legal departments may be increasing in importance. The increasing concentration of power throughout the economic system has created both a need for expertise to deal with it and to avoid losing it. *Fortune* magazine (Carruth, 1973) has estimated that the companies they surveyed increased their legal bills 75 percent in six years. The interests of corporate executives have changed with changes in pressure—the chairman of the board of American Can said that he spent 60 percent of his time on legal matters in 1972, twice what he estimated he had spent five years earlier.

A lawsuit is not hard to notice. It comes neatly prepared and delivered by a process server. Most demands and changes in the environment, however, are not as readily noticeable. If organizations adapt to their environments and if environments constrain and affect behaviors, then the question of how organizations learn about their environments is an important one.

The Enacted Environment

The events of the world around us do not present themselves to us with neat labels and interpretations. Rather, we give meaning to the events. Weick has noted that environments are enacted. He stated that "the human *creates* the environment to which the system then adapts. The human actor does not *react* to an environment, he *enacts* it" (1969:64). There are two general meanings to the term enactment, and both are implied by Weick's argument. One is to decree as by legislative process; and the other is to recreate or represent as by staging a play. Both processes are involved when one interprets events from the environment. An individual answering the question, "What did you see?" is forced both to reconstruct the image he recalls as occurring and to decree existence to some of the images he may have forgotten.

Weick attributes his development of the enactment concept to Schutz's (1967) discussion of time and the development of meaning. "The creation of meaning is an attentional process, but it is attention to that which has already occurred. Second, since the attention is directed backward from a specific point in time (a specific here and now), whatever is occurring at the moment will influence what the person discovers when he glances backward" (Weick, 1969:65). The implication of this argument is that meaning is retrospective, or that actions are known only after they have been completed.

Giving meaning to events after they have occurred is an inherent aspect of human information processing. All perceptions of visual and auditory information from the environment are representations. What a person sees is not the stimulus external to himself but a representation of that stimulus. The particular representation does not last long unless the person stores the information in memory.

In considering information processes more complex than simple perception, the extent to which the environment is enacted is considerable. Attention is a limiting process; when one perceives one thing, simultaneous exposure to something else is impossible. Most information systems are designed with substantial redundancy to compensate for this fact of limited attention. Moreover, people fill in what they expect to perceive. Illusions and reality are constructed in this way. As one moves from simple, observable processes to complicated interpretations of events spanning time and involving multiple observations, the necessity for summarizing, selecting, discarding, and simplifying becomes predominant. As one deals more with things that are not directly observable but must be inferred from observables, there is no recourse but to use accumulated knowledge about how the world operates to make sense out of it. There are no meanings that the world gives to us as valid. There are only our created beliefs, more or less supported by what we consider as evidence, and held with more or less conviction or doubt. The meaning is created by the observer.

One other important point that Weick makes about the enactment process is that the equivocal material we work on to extract meaning is, of necessity, always a representation of the past. Nothing that has not occurred is available for processing. Thus, the material for decision making is always an enacted environment of the past. The question, what is the environment, should more properly be, what was the environment. Many find this argument difficult to understand or accept because they envision decision making as a forward looking process in which future actions and their possible consequences are considered. In fact, the conceptions both of future actions and of future consequences are based on prior experience. The ability to make accurate predictions about what will happen in the future depends on the development of a description of reality, a theory which reflects attention to the details of events previously observed. Planning is based on a theory of the past, and when plans go awry, it is the theory and not the environment that is wrong.

Weick's concept of enactment provides important implications for understanding organizational actions in environments. The question of what the environment is, is meaningless without regard to the focal organization which enacts it, or more precisely, the individuals who enact it in planning the activities of the organization. If organizations can plan behavior only with respect to their constructions of the environment and its meaning, then to speak of contexts separate from a particular focal organization makes little sense. If environments are enacted, then there are as many environments as there are enactors, which may explain why there are so many typologies of organizational environments, as well as why different organizations and even different individuals within each may react differently to what appears to be the same context.

Determination of what the environment is rests with the organization. It may be wrong in its particular enactment and unable to predict its outcomes because it has a poor theory of its own reality. For an external observer predicting the behavior of the organization, the prediction and explanation of organizational behavior will be enhanced if the attentional process, as well as the objective setting, is included in the analytic framework. Something not attended to by the organization cannot affect its actions, even though it may subsequently affect its outcomes.

Weick's description of environment is similar to an analysis by Dill (1962). Dill thought the environment should be examined as it affects the organization being studied and treated as information which becomes available to the organization or which the organization seeks out. There is a great deal of information, but only some of this comes to the attention of the organization and is, therefore, relevant for understanding its behavior. "Because of the sheer quantity and diversity of the inputs that are accessible and relevant, no organization is likely to notice or attend to more than a small proportion of them" (Dill, 1962:97). To link organizational actions to environmental inputs, it is necessary to analyze an organization's exposure to information, its readiness to attend to and store various environmental inputs, and its strategies for searching the environment (Dill, 1962:97). It is also necessary to recognize that individuals and subgroups within organizations do not access the same environments and that the information they have varies. Individuals and subgroups have their own goals and activities that may bring them into contact with different aspects of the organization's environment. Thus, it may be more reasonable to speak of different environments, attended to or enacted by different individuals and groups within the organization.

DETERMINANTS OF THE ENACTMENT PROCESS

Noting that an organization's environment is enacted, or created by attentional processes, tends to shift the focus from characteristics of the objective environment to characteristics of the decision process by which organizations select and ignore information. There are several important dimensions to this decision: some are relevant when the attentional process is considered at a point in time; and others are relevant when the attentional process is considered over time.

At a given point in time, the attentional process is determined largely by the structure of the organization, the structure of the information system in the organization, and the activities of the organization. The information system is conceptualized as the reports, statistics, facts, or information that are regularly collected and their pattern of transmission through the organization. The fact that certain information is regularly collected focuses the organization's attention on it. The collection of certain information occupies the time and attention of the organization, which necessarily restricts the time and attention devoted elsewhere. Second, the fact of its existence and prominence conveys the impression that the information is somehow important. New entrants to the organization will accept this importance and begin to construct their perceptions of the organization and its problems around the available information. Third, the availability of the information will create a demand for the use of the information. It is evident that the information system creates a demand for certain details, as well as their supply. If reports on market share are prepared monthly, when they are not prepared on time, there will probably be a demand within the organization for them. Theoretically information systems are designed and created to provide the information the decision maker requires, but that is an impossible task because the decision maker does not know what he needs but only what is available. The available information provides cues to what is considered organizationally important and provides the information which will tend to be used by decision makers.

The information system also focuses attention on some aspects of the organization's environment, and since attention requires time and resources, both of which are scarce, it can be reasonably argued that certain things are noticed while others are not, with a trade-off being made in the attention process. Seen as similar to one of Cyert and March's (1963) standard operating procedures, the information system can be viewed as providing a memory for the organization. The information system indicates what aspects of the environment the organization believes are important and provides information on what portions of the environment are considered by the organization.

An organization's information system focuses not only the attention but also the behavior of organizational members. Ridgway (1956), who examined some of the functions and dysfunctions of performance measurement within organizations, noted that the act of measurement frequently had unanticipated consequences. An example is Blau's (1955) observations about a public employment agency. At one point in this agency's history, employment interviewers were appraised by the number of interviews they conducted. As a consequence, they interviewed as rapidly as possible. The specific needs of job seekers or employers for a certain job or certain skills were overlooked. Later, in addition to sheer numbers of interviews, the agency kept records on other performance information, including referrals of applicants which were weighted according to their difficulty of placement. Behavior of interviewers changed accordingly. Blau (1955) also looked into a federal investigative agency, where he noted that employee's behavior was structured around the cycle of accounting periods. At the end of an accounting period when pressured to look good, employees took on easy jobs to fill the records; difficult cases were tackled only at the beginning of a measurement period. Granick (1954) found that the glory of setting a new production record in a Soviet factory led managers to go all out one month, pushing both the men and equipment quite hard. After the record was established, production fell off. Berliner (1956) found that even without trying for a record, Soviet administrators practiced "storming" just to meet production quotas, neglecting repairs and maintenance at the end of the month. Then, the following month, the overdue maintenance was done early, the factory fell behind, and a new cycle of storming began.

The important point is not merely that measurement affects behavior, but that what gets measured focuses activity and behavior. When the employment agency studied by Blau began to collect eight measures of performance, behavior adjusted to fit each aspect of performance measured. "Even where performance measures are instituted purely for purposes of information, they are probably interpreted as definitions of important aspects of that job or activity and hence have important implications for the motivation of behavior" (Ridgway, 1956:247). Moreover, the collection of information on something means that it can be included in organizational decisions. Without information about it, it is not likely that the factor will be used in determining organizational behavior.

Since organizations adapt to, or deal with, environments they enact, the analysis of organizational behavior will be enhanced by a descriptive analysis of the determinants of organizational information systems and other elements that help to determine the attentional process in the organization. What factors may lead organizations to collect information on certain aspects of their environment or their operations? One is the sheer ease of collecting the information. Reports about production are more readily collected and, therefore, more likely to be than reports about markets. Another possible dimension is the ease of processing the information, or fitting it into a presentable and transmittable form. This would place a premium on information which is quantifiable and easily measurable. Information about markets and production are more likely, then, than intelligence reports on government activities and possible legislation.

In addition to these simple features of the information, the attention of the organization is also likely to be determined by the necessity for the information, that is, its relevance to problems and operations. There are two aspects to the necessity dimension. One is that the activity being monitored is critical to the operations of the organization, either because it represents a dominant portion of the activity or because it is central to all other activities. Many universities, for instance, collect information on the publishing activities of their faculty and relatively little information about teaching. Obviously, this priority for information reflects the organizations' definition of their critical functions. As these definitions change, frequently in response to environmental demands, so does the information system. The second aspect of necessity is the utility of the information in decision making. Information reduces uncertainty. If no uncertainty is experienced with respect to a certain sphere of activity, collecting information is unnecessary. A firm which never experiences difficulty in disposing of its products or services does not need a lot of market research. Data about the market becomes necessary only when the organization has difficulty predicting future demand relative to planned production, particularly when production schedules and levels cannot be altered easily.

Another critical determinant of the decision to collect information is the structure of the organization. Information is not neutral. The more important a problem is, the more important it becomes to have information about the problem, and the more important are those who control or gather the information. One would suspect that subunits, which are themselves concerned with their own survival and power in the organization, would collect information which enhances their own value in organizational decision making or which convinces others in the organization that they have information needed for organizational problems. In either case, attentional processes are determined by the organization's own structure of influence. As Katz and Kahn (1966) and Downs (1967) have noted, organizational subunits have dynamics of their own; they act to enhance their power and prestige relative to other departments in the organization. Subunits established to examine or deal with some aspect of the environment, then, will attempt to show that (a) that aspect is the most important part of the environment for the organization, and (b) the subunit is doing a good job of dealing with it. It is almost a management adage that when something becomes a problem, one establishes a department to deal with it. A converse implication is that organizational units already dealing with some aspects of the environment will emphasize those environmental aspects as meriting the organization's attention. A public relations department, once established, makes public images a more important concern of the organization. If a department of market research is established, the customer will become a more salient and important part of the environment. If a legislative relations unit is established, the legislatures with which the organization deals will now become more important to it.

Organizations also establish units to screen out information and protect the organization's operations from external influences. The Nixon White House has been characterized as an elaborate filtering mechanism for protecting its occupant from external information. When critical comments were made by outsiders, these would be clarified by pointing out the questionable sources that produced them. Many business firms establish consumer complaint divisions to achieve the same purpose. The complaints received by the organization are routed to the complaint division where they are handled. The complaints, however, rarely arouse organizational action because the individuals responsible for handling the complaints are used to seeing them and, moreover, the complaints are localized in a subunit which is seldom structurally well connected to the operating units of the organization.

The establishment of departments and the development of information systems are both partly guided by considerations of adaptation. Organizations learn what portions of the environment to attend to through past experience. Caught off guard by some consumer organization, an organization will probably develop a surveillance system to keep that portion of the environment in focus. Organizations learn to attend to new sectors of their environments when these sectors begin to demand certain performances of the organization. Those that do not develop new, appropriate information systems are less likely to survive. Either through adaptation or selection a similar result will emerge—as environments change, organizational information processing and attentional mechanisms will change.

Because the environment is enacted through organizational processes of attention and because these processes themselves are developed as organizations respond to the environment, the organization is, in a sense, always lagging. It's attentional processes are inevitably focused on what *had been* important in the past. Weick has argued that planning is retrospective. One reason for this should be apparent. Planning is customarily done with the information and organizational structures that developed to deal with past environmental contingencies. The environment enacted for planning is some portion of the organization's past environment, which will not necessarily be relevant to the changing context of the organization's future. It takes time to build new information structures, and the structures that exist are guarded by the departments representing them. The failure of the canning company which Emery and Trist (1965) described may not have been caused by a turbulent environment so much as by the organization's being trapped in the history of its own success.

PROBLEMS IN ENVIRONMENTAL ENACTMENT

Although organizational decisions and actions are determined by the enacted environment—that set of definitions of the world constructed by the organization's attention process—organizational outcomes can be affected by parts of the environment not noticed or heeded. There are several types of problems that may arise in the process of enacting the environment which may adversely affect the organization's adaptation to the environment and its prospects for continued survival and success. Problems may arise because the organization misreads its situation of interdependence, or it misreads the demands being made on it. Organizations also face problems arising from a commitment to the past and from the necessity to balance conflicting demands. Each of these kinds of problems will be considered in turn.

Misreading Interdependence

The first type of problem an organization confronts arises when it does not perceive correctly all the external groups it depends on or the relative importance or potency of each. This is especially likely when new organizations are developing that are interested in the activities of the focal organization or when the focal organization itself enters a new field of activity. There are many examples of organizations which had difficulty because of a failure to recognize important external groups or to attribute enough potency or importance to certain groups. Certainly, the lack of concern with safety and pollution matters demonstrated by the automobile industry in the early 1960s and the subsequent problems the industry faced, illustrate well the type of problem involved.

Cordtz (1966) has nicely summarized both the problem and the consequences. Focusing particularly on General Motors, Cordtz points out that "G. M. officials . . . are products of a system that discourages attention to matters far outside the purview of their jobs" (1966:118). Because of the insensitivity to the demands of various external groups and organizations for increased product safety, the automobile industry was "saddled with the one thing it most abhors: government instructions on how to build cars" (1966:117). Cordtz further provides evidence to indicate that there was some advance warning of coming problems, but that the company either put aside such warnings or was ignorant of them.

> To a company with a sharp ear cocked, there have been two decades of warnings of possible trouble to come on safety. As early as 1946, a national traffic safety conference called by President Truman recommended that "motor vehicles should be progressively designed and constructed for safer operation and maximum protection from injury in an accident." But the manufacturers—and G. M. most of all—concentrated on "safer operation" and for years ignored "protection from injury." By 1949, the Indiana State Police and the University of California had undertaken independent studies of the nature and causes of injuries in auto accidents and discovered that many of the manufacturers' assumptions about how to build safe cars were very questionable indeed (1966:206).

Subsequently, the automobile industry was also burdened with demanding regulations concerning the pollution produced by the vehicles being manufactured. One must conclude, after looking at a history of the industry, that the problems and demands were recognized, but the industry grossly underestimated the ability of the various organizations to mobilize public support and enforce their demands on the companies.

While the automobile industry is the subject of this particular example, few industries have completely escaped being caught by surprise when suddenly confronted by demands and influences of a group, or organization, which in reality had more power than was previously believed. In addition to misreading the potential potency of a particular interest group, organizations may have poor knowledge about their vast and often complex effects on the rest of the world. In many instances the activities of the organization actually have effects which contradict their own stated goals and purposes. Consider organizations involved in the control of drug abuse. One of the major problems of illegal drug use is that the expensive habit is supported through other illegal activities, such as robbery. Drugs follow the laws of supply and demand like other commodities. When a major police raid reduces the flow of drugs, the likely outcome is a rise in price. These higher prices translate into the addict's need to commit more crimes to raise the additional funds needed to support a habit. To the extent that demand for drugs is inelastic, a reasonable assumption, restrictions in supply may actually increase the related crime activity.

Thus, there are two components to the first problem, misreading interdependence: Organizations may underestimate their dependence on, or the potency of, various external groups or organizations; and, organizations may not even perceive the complex relationships their activities have on other groups and organizations in the environment.

Misreading Demands

The second kind of problem occurs when a group or organization is recognized as being potent, but the focal organization misreads the criteria or demands being made. The misunderstanding frequently involves a response stressing greater efficiency and missing the point that the output itself is being questioned. This condition describes many American universities today. Whether rightly or wrongly, the products and services themselves have been called into question by organizations and segments of the American population. During the antiwar rallies of the late 1960s and early 1970s, there were many Americans who believed that universities were training revolutionaries. Students themselves frequently complained that the universities were committed to the rigorous pursuit of irrelevancy. Budgets, enrollments, and alumni contributions fell, and universities characteristically responded by tightening managerial controls and reevaluating program costs, attempting to do the same things at less cost. Producing revolutionaries more efficiently was not what was being requested, and the relevance of irrelevant education was not increased by doing the same thing for less money. Demands for changes in output were read as demands for more efficiency.

Misunderstanding the requests being made of an organization arises from the mechanism of selective perception we have already discussed. Information filters leave out some information and alter other information; people in organizations focus on what they have been trained to notice and on those things relevant to their jobs. When problems originate outside the organization, subunits within the organization will use these problems as opportunities to demonstrate their own capabilities, and the external problems are perceived in a form which supports the pet positions of groups within the organization. Accustomed to examining only certain information and limited in information, individuals attend to the subproblem they can deal with even when it is not the source of the difficulty. Thus, universities, which are well equipped to provide cost-student data, defined the problems in these terms. Information about service rendered to various groups is less easily obtained. That which is measured is attended to, and that which is not measured is ignored. Most formal organizations generally have very good internal reporting systems, while they are relatively weak in attending to changes in the environment. It is, therefore, not surprising that the first reaction to organizational problems typically involves solutions focusing on efficiency dimensions, for frequently, that is about the only thing the organization can measure.

Organizations differ in the speed with which they notice changes in the environment. Few major shifts come about all at once, and ample cues indicate that important components of the environment are changing. The difficulty is that these cues may exist in a part of the environment that is not being watched, or that they may be filtered or distorted in the process of being assimilated into the organizations' information system. To the extent that information systems are closed and well structured, novel or different information is not as likely to be correctly perceived. Thus, the dilemma between structure and flexibility noted by Weick (1969) with respect to the organizing process is also apparent in the enactment and attention process—if the organization attends to everything, it will be swamped with information and will be unable to function; if the information system is so tightly structured that environmental changes are consistently missed, the organization will be unprepared to face threats to survival.

Commitment to the Past

A further limitation on organizational adaptation derives from a commitment to doing things a certain way. Organizations differ in their commitments to the past. Some become superstitious, believing that what worked in the past will work forever. Most build up traditions, mythologies, and rituals. More than mere psychological recalcitrance is involved in commitment. In many instances, the beliefs and successes of the past become entrenched in physical and managerial structures. When they do, they are nearly impossible to change. The railroads were not entirely surprised when trucks emerged as major competitors in the 1940s. But, the railroads were stuck with a commitment to fixed networks of track and were prohibited for a long time by regulatory authorities from diversifying. Sometimes commitments may be more a matter of preference than of necessity, as in the case of Henry Ford and his early commitment to providing only a single model and color of automobile.

Commitments build in the relationships within the organization. Changes which dislodge personnel or disrupt power structures are likely to take a long time to implement. From observations about the speed with which computer technologies were introduced into organizations, Whisler (1970) noted that an important source of resistance to change was the fact that some people would gain and some would lose as a result of the change.

John Tuthill, a former American ambassador to Brazil, learned about commitments to the past during an uphill battle to reduce the staff of the embassy (1973). Because of growing nationalism in Brazil, the ubiquitous American presence was becoming an irritation. Seeking to reduce a staff of over 900 personnel to about half that size, Tuthill sought approval from Secretary of State Dean Rusk in 1966. Although Rusk gave immediate approval, it took Tuthill three years to bring about even a 20 percent reduction in his office and another three years to achieve a similar reduction in the other United States missions. The greatest opposition came from the lower bureaucratic levels in Washington because these were the people who sent the instructions and chose the personnel to staff the foreign missions. The personnel that Tuthill wanted to cut were the home-front bureaucrats' reason for existence and an important source of their power and status.

Conflicting Demands

Another problem in adapting to demands of external groups is the problem of balancing the demands of many organizations or groups simultaneously. The organization, in responding to one set of pressures, may set in motion actions that will turn some previously satisfied group into a very unhappy one. To overlook satisfied interest groups is easy for an organization because demands that are currently being well met are not as likely to be strongly voiced. It is, therefore, imperative for the organization to consider the implications of any given action or decision on *all* the groups and organizations with which it is interdependent.

Pittsburgh Brewing makes and sells Iron City beer. It was the beer of the working man and had been the top selling brand in Pittsburgh for twenty years. As reported in the *Wall Street Journal,* sales fell about 15 percent from February to June and twice that much in some blue-collar areas. The fall in sales was explained by the *Journal:*

> And everyone knows the reason. They say the trouble started when Pittsburgh's black community ended an 11-month boycott against the beer.
>
> That's right, when the boycott *ended.* Iron City, it seems, is the victim of barroom backlash, a boycott by whites who don't like what they've heard about the agreement Pittsburgh Brewing signed with black tavern owners and the National Association for the Advancement of Colored People. "People more or less want to punish the brewery for the settlement," one Iron City salesman laments (Harris, 1972:30).

In a settlement with the black community, Pittsburgh Brewing agreed to hire two blacks for each white put on the payroll during the next two years and thereafter to hire one of every two new employees from the black community until the proportion of blacks employed was 25 percent, about equal to the representation of blacks in the Pittsburgh community. The company also agreed to advertise in more black-oriented media and to hire a black marketing assistant. The settlement aroused the opposition of other groups.

> The biggest booster of the boycott has been Harvey F. Johnston, a McKees Rocks, Pa., real estate salesman and white supremist who heads a group called the National Association for the Advancement of White People. He has given the anti-Iron campaign top billing in the last four editions of the newspaper he publishes (claimed circulation: 75,000), and has put out 100,000 circulars in western Pennsylvania bars blasting the beer.

The problem of striking a balance between the conflicting demands of various groups and organizations is exacerbated when the organization has not engaged in any type of planning. Unintended repercussions are completely unanticipated. Under the not-so-secure blanket of ignorance, the solutions to one set of problems create the conditions for new difficulties.

THE ASSESSMENT OF EXTERNAL DEMANDS

Many of the problems organizations face in attempting to adapt to their environments stem from the inability to predict or assess the potency and demands of various interest groups, how these demands conflict, or how they constrain the organization's actions. Operating in ignorance of its interdependence and constraints, the organization can make strategic errors. It can fail to satisfy some demands and heed others when that is not necessary. It can place itself in positions of interdependence that would be better avoided. It may provide information to groups which leaves the organization vulnerable to future influence. Often the critical problem is not that the organization is immobilized but that it is ignorant.

We have argued that the effective organization is one which responds to the demands from its environment according to its dependence on the various components of the environment. We presented this as a model which could predict organizational behavior, as illustrated in the case of the Israeli managers and their accession to government demands. This model also serves, however, as a framework for what the organization should do to ensure its survival and success. The extent to which such a model can serve as a guide to action is affected by the organization's own awareness of its environment and the manner in which it enacts that environment. The increasing diversity of interest groups and their distance from the organization's immediate activities make the enactment process problematic. We shall suggest a methodology which can serve both as a guide to organizations and as a method for assessing organizational effectiveness. It is a methodology designed to increase awareness of the contingencies facing an organization. The procedure may be applied to actions of organizations that have already occurred as well as to possible future actions.

Determining Interest Groups

The first task in assessing external demands is to ascertain those groups or organizations that are relevant for the functioning of the focal organization or for a particular activity. Friedlander and Pickle's (1968) study provides one such list for small businesses on an aggregated level. A useful guide for developing a list of relevant interest groups is to consider what resources and activities are critical to the organization and what individuals or groups do at present, or could potentially, provide or affect those resources. For example, in one study of a university applied-research organization that conducted research on the distribution and accumulation of lead in the ecosystem, the following groups were recognized as affecting the activities of the research group: faculty from various departments in the university; the professional groups and decision makers affecting faculty careers, such as editors of scientific journals; the funding agency, the RANN division of the National Science Foundation; Congress which appropriated funds to the funding agency; the various federal and state agencies involved in the regulation of environmental effects, including the Environmental Protection Agency; the industrial organizations which produced the lead; the industrial organizations that used lead, including those that used lead in gasoline; and the research divisions and associations of these various governmental and industrial organizations. In an analysis of the organization over a four-year period, it was evident that all these groups affected both what the organization did and how its basic structure evolved (Salancik and Lamont, 1975). Recognizing interdependence is not always easy, and a sequential questioning of the key actors in the organization may be a useful beginning.

Weighting Interest Groups

Having determined who is relevant to the organization, the next step is to recognize that all may not be of equal importance. It becomes necessary to weight the relative power of the various groups. One possible method is to have representatives from each group rate all the other groups in terms of their assessment of each group's importance for the organization. An averaging of the responses of all group representatives will generally be found to be very reliable, as most participants in a situation are fairly accurate estimators of their relative positions. One problem with this method, however, is that the less visible interest groups may be ignored or underestimated.

Another procedure would involve identifying the critical resources which the organization needs and analyzing which groups or individuals control them. For example, a radio station depends on advertising revenue. But this does not tell one how critical advertisers are to the organization. If advertisers are difficult to get, then they may have a great deal of influence over the station's programming. On the other hand, the advertisers are interested in a radio-time purchase primarily because of the ability to reach an audience. The size of an audience itself may depend on the presence of a good disc jocky or the radio station's restriction of competition.

The Criteria of Groups

The next task is to determine the criteria or values by which each group evaluates the organization. Measures may be obtained both by using the perceptions of the organization and by directly asking group representatives. One should expect to find differences and even inconsistencies in the criteria used by the various groups to evaluate the organization. A generalized approach to the measurement of group values has been demonstrated by Rokeach (1968) in a study of the values of citizens in the United States. Rokeach had individuals rank order 18 generalized values in terms of their importance to their daily lives. He found that the values held by groups varied. Rokeach also found that various political philosophies varied in their ranking of values. Rokeach's approach of having individuals rank a set of standard values is useful when it is possible to develop a set of criteria that are relevant to several groups. Salancik (1975) has shown that Rokeach's values can validly distinguish the interests of social groups toward future events.

The Impact of Actions on Criteria

Information about different groups and their values is useful only when it is applied to assessing potential reactions to activities or outputs of the focal organization. The next step, then, is to assess, for a given action or result, how it will affect the various criteria of the groups. This task of judgment can be accomplished using either experts or representatives from the various groups. Essentially, it requires asking a question of the following form: If this event (outcome) were to occur, would it increase, decrease, or have no effect on this criterion? The question, of course, is repeated for each criterion for each group.

Information about the impact of events on criteria can be usefully incorporated with the information about the groups and their preferred interests. Three things can be derived: (1) estimates of the extent to which a given event potentially satisfies any given interest group; (2) estimates of the extent to which a particular event potentially satisfies some groups while simultaneously dissatisfying others; and (3) estimates of the extent to which the event potentially satisfies groups that are important to the organization.

A final useful assessment to make in evaluating the effectiveness of organizational actions is to obtain measures or estimates of the interdependence between the various interest groups. Interdependence among the criteria of the groups means that in attaining one criterion, the criteria important to another group must also be attained. For instance, if it is the case that customers are the most important determinant of a firm's profits, then the owner's interest in profits will be served only as the customers' interests are also served. One generalized method for determining interdependencies is the cross-impact method. This procedure involves listing the events (or organizational interest groups) along a vertical and horizontal array, and then considering for each group in the vertical array its interdependence with each group on the horizontal list. Thus, for one group the question is asked: If this group's criteria are met, what impact will it have on the ability to meet the criteria of each other group?

The asssesment procedure we have described is diagrammed in Figure 4.2. We have elaborated this assessment procedure partly because it can be a useful systematic way of evaluating the potential effects of proposed or completed actions. However, this procedure also forces an explicit recognition of the basis of organizational behavior. The central questions of organizational action are, we believe: who wants what and how important is it that the demand be satisfied? and what are the implications of the satisfaction of one demand for the satisfaction of other demands?

It may be difficult for the reader to appreciate how easily organizations may mislead themselves about their own situations. We can illustrate this point by examining a typical response of a public university to what is being called a crisis in higher education. For specific details, we shall consider the University of Illinois at Urbana-Champaign, but the scenario is essentially being repeated, with few variations, throughout the country.

For many years public universities received ever-increasing bud-

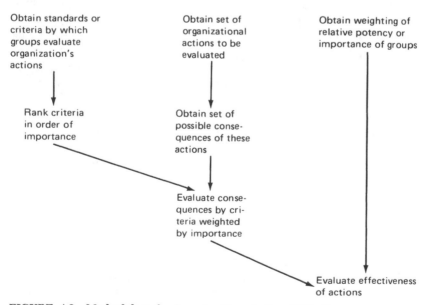

FIGURE 4.2   Methodology for Assessing Organizational Effectiveness

get allocations, based not only on their ever-increasing student enrollments but also on an ability to command a great deal of legislative
support. This period of receiving virtually all the budget requested
ended in the late 1960s. The retirement of a state senator from St.
Joseph, who was the ranking member and chairman of the appropria-
tions committee, may have been a contributing factor to the problem
in Illinois. St. Joseph is only eight miles from Urbana-Champaign, and
the university was a pet project of the senator. For whatever reason,
the budget increases soon began to fall behind the rate of inflation.
But, what is interesting is not the problem but the response. The
university responded to the withdrawal of financial support by initiating measurement procedures to guide internal budget allocations and
reallocations and to document its cost efficiency. Program budgeting
experts were hired at the top administrative levels, and information
systems were expanded. While the procedures, and even the preliminary report leading to their development, are lengthy, one salient feature can be briefly described: there was *no* provision for the assessment of organizational effectiveness using the opinions, beliefs, or
values of the groups or organizations relevant to the university. Rather,
all procedures relied on essentially internal accounting standards and
measurements, such as student/faculty ratios, student failure ratios,
students educated per dollar, and so forth. Thus, the university had
followed many other organizations down the path of mistaking cost-
efficiency for effectiveness.

By way of contrast, it should be noted that other government
agencies have not placed themselves in the same trap. When the
soaring costs of the public medical or welfare programs were called
into question, frequently the programs were justified by statements
such as, "all Americans have a right to adequate medical care," or "all
Americans have a right to an adequate living." In these instances, the
values or objectives themselves were justified, regardless of the cost or
considerations of efficiency that were involved. Later, the university
attempted to point out the achievements of the organization and how
it had helped the state, but frequently the achievements were couched
in terms of criteria important to the faculty rather than to the general
public.

SUMMARY

If organizations are constrained by their context, it is important to assess
how the context becomes known, what important dimensions of the environment affect organizations, and how organizations may be managed to avoid
making mistakes in attending to the environment. It is important to recognize

that organizational actions are determined by an enacted environment—the organization responds to what it perceives and believes about the world. The fact that environments are enacted does not mean that individual differences come into prominence. The enactment process, we would argue, is largely determined by the existing organizational and informational structure of the organization. But, enactment does suggest that more attention be devoted to the management of information acquisition activities and to the determinants of enactment and attentional processes in organizations.

Organizations may misread interdependence, misinterpret demands, remain committed to past practices, or fail to see the various conflicts in demands. While attention is inevitably retrospective, focused on the process of creating meaning out of past action and using structures and information adapted to dealing with past problems, it is possible to develop procedures for assessment that may overcome some of the problems commonly encountered in designing organizational actions. The outlined procedure for assessing organizational effectiveness represents both a model of organizational behavior and a prescription for managing organizations to ensure their continued survival.

REFERENCES

Adelman, M. A. 1951. "The measurement of industrial concentration." *Review of Economics and Statistics*, 33:269–296.

Assael, H. 1969. "Constructive role of interorganizational conflict." *Administrative Science Quarterly*, 14:573–582.

Bain, J. S. 1968. *Industrial Organization*, 2nd ed. New York: Wiley.

Berliner, J. S. 1956. "A problem in Soviet business management." *Administrative Science Quarterly*, 1:86–101.

Bernhardt, I., and K. D. Mackenzie. 1968. "Measuring seller unconcentration, segmentation, and product differentiation." *Western Economic Journal*, 6:395–403.

Blau, P. M. 1955. *The Dynamics of Bureaucracy*. University of Chicago Press.

Carruth, E. 1973. "Legal explosion has left business shell shocked." *Fortune*, 87:65–69 ff.

Collins, N. R., and L. E. Preston. 1968. *Concentration and Price-Cost Margins in Manufacturing Industries*. University of California Press.

Cordtz, D. 1966. "The face in the mirror at General Motors." *Fortune*, 74:117 ff.

Cyert, R. M., and J. G. March. 1963. *A Behavioral Theory of the Firm*. Englewood Cliffs, N.J.: Prentice-Hall.

Dill, W. R. 1962. "The impact of environment on organizational development." In S. Mailick and E. H. Van Ness (eds.), *Concepts and Issues in Administrative Behavior*, 94–109. Englewood Cliffs, N.J.: Prentice-Hall.

Downs, A. 1967. *Inside Bureaucracy*. Boston: Little, Brown.

Duncan, R. 1972. "Characteristics of organizational environments and perceived environmental uncertainty." *Administrative Science Quarterly,* 17:313–327.

Emery, F. E., and E. L. Trist. 1965. "The causal texture of organizational environments." *Human Relations,* 18:21–32.

Evan, W. M. 1966. "The organization-set: toward a theory of interorganizational relations." In J. D. Thompson (ed.), *Approaches to Organizational Design,* 173–191. University of Pittsburgh Press.

Freeman, L. 1968. *Patterns of Local Community Leadership.* Indianapolis: Bobbs-Merrill.

Friedlander, F., and H. Pickle. 1968. "Components of effectiveness in small organizations." *Administrative Science Quarterly,* 13:289–304.

Granick, D. 1954. *Management of the Industrial Firm in the U.S.S.R.* New York: Columbia University Press.

Harris, R. J. 1972. "Barroom backlash: some blue-collar workers shun their favorite beer after the brewery signs a pact to hire more blacks." *Wall Street Journal,* 86 (June 8, 1972):30.

Hawley, A. H. 1963. "Community power and urban renewal success." *American Journal of Sociology,* 68:422–431.

Hinings, C. R., D. J. Hickson, J. M. Pennings, and R. E. Schneck. 1974. "Structural conditions of intraorganizational power." *Administrative Science Quarterly,* 19:22–44.

Katz, D., and R. L. Kahn. 1966. *The Social Psychology of Organizations.* New York: Wiley.

Kessel, J. H. 1962. "Government structure and political environment: a statistical note about American cities." *American Political Science Review,* 56:615–620.

Lawrence, P. R., and J. W. Lorsch. 1967. *Organization and Environment.* Boston: Harvard University Press.

Litwak, E., and L. F. Hylton. 1962. "Interorganizational analysis: a hypothesis on coordinating agencies." *Administrative Science Quarterly,* 6:395–420.

Osborne, R. N., and J. G. Hunt. 1972. "Quantifying the environment of health care systems." Paper presented at the 41st National Meeting, Operations Research Society of America, New Orleans, April 1972.

Perrow, C. 1970. "Departmental power and perspective in industrial firms." In M. N. Zald (ed.), *Power in Organizations,* 59–89. Nashville, Tenn.: Vanderbilt University Press.

Pfeffer, J., and G. R. Salancik. 1974. "Organizational decision making as a political process: the case of a university budget." *Administrative Science Quarterly,* 19:135–151.

Pfeffer, J., and G. R. Salancik. 1977. "Organizational context and the characteristics and tenure of hospital administrators." *Academy of Management Journal,* 20:74–88.

Rokeach, M. 1968. *Beliefs, Attitudes, and Values.* San Francisco: Jossey-Bass.

Salancik, G. R. 1975. "Liberation or poverty: an indirect assessment of the impact of potential future events on society." *Journal of Applied Social Psychology*, 5:173–185.

Salancik, G. R., and V. Lamont. 1975. "Conflicts in societal research: a study of one RANN project suggests that benefitting society may cost universities." *Journal of Higher Education*, 46:161–176.

Schutz, A. 1967. *The Phenomenology of the Social World*. Evanston, Ill.: Northwestern University Press.

Simon, H. A. 1969. *The Sciences of the Artificial*. Massachusetts Institute of Technology Press.

Stagner, R. 1969. "Corporate decision making: an empirical study." *Journal of Applied Psychology*, 53:1–13.

Staw, B. M., and E. Szwajkowski. 1975. "The scarcity-munificence component of organizational environments and the commission of illegal acts." *Administrative Science Quarterly*, 20:345–354.

Stigler, G. 1964. "A theory of oligopoly." *Journal of Political Economy*, 72: 44–61.

Stinchcombe, A. L. 1965. "Social structure and organizations." In J. G. March (ed.), *Handbook of Organizations*, 142–193. Skokie, Ill.: Rand McNally.

Terreberry, S. 1968. "The evolution of organizational environments." *Administrative Science Quarterly*, 12:590–613.

Turk, H. 1970. "Interorganizational networks in urban society: initial perspectives and comparative research." *American Sociological Review*, 34:1–19.

Tuthill, John W. 1973. "The repeal of Parkinson's Law." *Intellectual Digest*, 3 (April):34–35.

Walker, J. L. 1969. "The diffusion of innovations among the American states." *American Political Science Review*, 63:880–899.

Warren, R. 1967. "The interorganizational field as a focus for investigation." *Administrative Science Quarterly*, 12:396–419.

Warren, R., S. Rose, and A. Bergunder. 1974. *The Structure of Urban Reform*. Lexington, Mass.: Heath.

Weick, K. E. 1969. *The Social Psychology of Organizing*. Reading, Mass.: Addison-Wesley.

Weiss, L. W. 1963. "Average concentration ratios and industrial performance." *Journal of Industrial Economics*, 11:237–254.

Whisler, T. 1970. *Information Technology and Organizational Change*. Belmont, Calif.: Wadsworth.

CHAPTER FIVE

MANAGING ENVIRONMENTAL DEMANDS:
Adaptation and Avoidance

As organizations become more interdependent with greater numbers of organizations and as those with whom they are interdependent become less visible because of their distance from the immediate sphere of organizational activity, the problem of managing organizations and their relationships with the environment increases. As a consequence of the growing interdependence, organizations make more demands on one another to obtain some degree of control over each other's activities so that the needs and interests of each can be predictably met.

In this chapter, we shall describe some possible organizational responses to the demand environment confronted. The possibility of compliance with external constraints, or adaptation, will be considered, as well as the possibilities for avoiding influence and for managing and avoiding dependence. This chapter is the first in a series of chapters in which we will use our model of the external control of organizations to examine organizational responses and the problems of managing the organization's institutional environment.

AN ENVIRONMENT OF
CONFLICTING INTERESTS

Awareness of the enormous concentrated power of large organizations has made them targets for many who want to control or use that power. Perrow (1972) pointedly argued that the critical question concerning bureaucracies was not whether or not they would disappear, to be replaced by some other organizational form, but rather, who would control and use the enormous power inherent in these large social organizations. Industrial organizations are not merely economic entities that produce goods cheaply. They are places in which people work. They are polluters of the environment, sources of military and economic power, creators and distributors of wealth, and places in which the statuses of persons become defined through work.

As the impact of organizations on other social actors becomes more noticeable, there is evidence that we are moving from a concern with organizational efficiency to a concern with organizational effectiveness. Instead of asking how much is being produced at what cost, the question increasingly is: What is being produced? The demands placed on organizations have become greater and more insistent. The legitimacy of social organizations, always problematic (Parsons, 1956), has become even more so. That different groups and organizations have different criteria for evaluating an organization, and consequently make different demands of it, makes the resolution of these conflicts not amenable to maximization or other simple computations. When there are conflicts about outputs and legitimacy, the conflicts are not resolved by producing the same output with lower cost.

There are empirical indications of the increasing interdependence of organizational action. For instance, the General Electric Company experienced a strike lasting 101 days during 1969–1970. This strike did not involve just General Electric and the unions. One of the factors enabling workers to withstand the personal financial impact of the strike was their ability to collect various forms of relief from the states and the federal government. The strikers collected an estimated $30 million of publicly financed aid from food stamps, welfare checks, and unemployment compensation (*Wall Street Journal,* July 14, 1971:1). To help link the strikers to these sources of support, the AFL–CIO developed a nationwide network of 180 full-time community service representatives and had the local United Fund organizations pay their salaries. The United Funds agreed because the unions were important in their own annual fund drives. The same unions, because of their importance in political campaigns, were able to thwart attempts in Congress to exclude strikers from relief eligibility. The only real opposition to the strike came from the states paying the bill. A long strike against General Motors cost the state of Michigan $25 million in added public assistance and $100 million in lost tax revenues. Thus, in current society, disputes between private interests can erupt into national conflicts, and decisions made by centralized decision bodies far removed from the questions at hand can help to determine the final outcome.

The density and interconnectedness of interorganizational fields today derives from adaptations to past problems. In a world characterized by competition for scarce resources, the predominant adaptations were developments to achieve control over the availability of resources. Technologies were developed to produce foodstuffs to improve the yield, and then to distribute and store them efficiently to guard against periods of unfavorable weather. The developments that provided more control over production and availability themselves created new interdependencies. The efficiency of production deriving from the use of chemical fertilizers and herbicides and insecticides made the agricultural industry dependent on the chemical firms. Furthermore, as the fertilizers drain into the water supply, further dependencies are created with suppliers of drinking water and with those who fish the affected waterways. As these interdependencies become known, still other organizations are created to regulate and adjudicate the conflicts among the contesting interests.

In the current dense environment, efficiencies are no longer the solution to organizational problems, for the efficiencies have created interdependencies with other organizations, and these interdependencies are the problem. The dominant problems of the organization have become managing its exchanges and its relationships with the diverse interests affected by its actions. Because of the increasing interconnectedness of organizations, interorganizational effects are mediated more by regulation and political negotiation than by impersonal market forces. The increasing density of relationships among diverse interests has led to less willingness to rely on unconstrained market forces. Negotiation, political strategies, the management of the organization's institutional relationships—these have all become more important.

ORGANIZATIONAL COMPLIANCE

Management of environmental demands does not in itself imply that the organization should rush to comply with them. There are times when compliance, although important for maintaining an immediately critical exchange relationship, may not be in the long-term interests of the organization.

Compliance is a loss of discretion, a constraint, and an admission of limited autonomy. To the extent that the focal organization is subject to *successful* external influence attempts, it places itself in a situation in which its long-term survival may be threatened. Kahn et al. (1964) found that persons who were influenced in their role behavior once, tended to be subjected to relatively more influence attempts. Thus, one's vulnerability can increase as it is exploited. An organization is likely to confront additional interorganizational influence attempts after being influenced once. As a consequence, organizational autonomy may be lost progressively as behaviors and decisions are increasingly constrained by the context in which the organization operates. The power of the OPEC oil cartel grew in just such a manner. Although the cartel had been organized for years, it was not until 1970 that the first test of its power was successfully accomplished. The Persian Gulf countries and Libya made a few price increases; the United States State Department convened a meeting of the importing countries and they agreed to allow the price to rise, primarily because the OPEC move was interpreted as a threatened embargo. Emboldened by this success, the 1971 Tehran and Tripoli agreements were made, granting large increases in the price and setting the tone for diminished control by the oil companies (Adelman, 1972).

The fact that organizational behavior is constrained by the demands and influences of external groups and organizations has consequences both for the later actions of the focal organization and for the development and growth of influencing organizations. Moreover, influence attempts are more likely to be made when they have a greater probability of success. One indicator of success probability is the past history of influence attempts in the interorganizational relationship. Organizations can, however, develop prior estimates of their expected success in interorganizational influence and use these estimates to decide whether or not they will make demands on the focal organization. To the extent that the discussion of factors affecting constraints on behavior is correct, then variables are also provided that can be used to predict when demands and influence attempts will actually be voiced. Influencing organizations will develop and will articulate demands, we would argue, when the factors are propitious for them to successfully influence their targets.

AVOIDING INFLUENCE AS AN ORGANIZATIONAL RESPONSE

Just as influencing organizations can develop prior estimates of their probable success and use these to guide their behavior, so can the focal organization. To forestall a loss of autonomy and to remove some of the contextual constraints on behavior, the focal organization may take actions to reduce the probability of being subject to successful enforcement of external demands. To the extent that the conditions leading to the social control of organizations outlined in Chapter Three are valid, we would expect the organization to operate on one or more of the variables to reduce the probability that an influence attempt would result in actual constraints on behavior.

When the organization faces conflicting demands, compliance can be a serious restriction on subsequent adaptation to other demands. By implication, the organization must either choose which of the various competing demands to attend to or somehow avoid the conflict or demands. In this section, we will discuss some of the means by which organizations manage demands without necessarily satisfying them and, thereby, provide themselves with the discretion they require to attend to those demands which cannot be ignored.

Organizations may solve the problem of conflicting demands by employing the mechanism of sequential attention to the demands of the various subgroups (e.g., Cyert and March, 1963). Instead of always satisfying one group at the expense of some other, the organization may attend to one set of demands at one point in time and to some other set when they become more pressing. At one time, an organization may face pressing financial demands and may attend to strengthening its financial position. While it is doing that, its market share may fall, and then it may subsequently attend to its products and markets. Just as conflict does not have to be completely resolved within the organization, it is also true that conflicts among the demands of various external groups and organizations do not have to be solved all at once but can be attended to sequentially.

In the balancing of demands of the various groups, nondisclosure of what each group is actually getting can be a strategy employed to lessen the demands of the other groups. A group's satisfaction is largely determined by its aspiration level; a group is satisfied relative to what it expects to get. Aspiration levels are affected both by what the group has obtained in the past and by what competing groups obtained. Thus, employees may be willing to forego pay increases when the company is near bankruptcy and suppliers, creditors, and owners are also suffering. If the employees found that the owners were really secretly profiting, they would be quite irate. It is in the organization's interests to make each group or organization feel it is getting relatively the best deal. Knowledge of what each group is getting is best kept secret.

Another strategy for balancing demands is to play one group off against another explicitly. As an example, organizations under federal pressure to hire more minority individuals frequently claimed that hiring was controlled by the union. The union, in turn, claimed that the company had responsibility for hiring. While the arguments go on, the demands of minorities go unmet. Or, the demands of public employees for higher wages can be juxtaposed with the demands of local citizens' groups for lower taxes. Even if the balancing of demands is not done explicitly, it is probably true that the resultant organizational decisions represent an implicit weighting of the forces that impinge upon and constrain its administration.

MANAGING THE CONDITIONS OF SOCIAL CONTROL

While balancing conflicting demands will forestall some problems of lost autonomy, perhaps the most effective way of avoiding the constraints of external demands is to avoid the conditions which demand compliance in the first place. In Chapter Three, we discussed a model of the social control of organizations and presented some conditions which would tend to increase the external control of organizational behavior. At that time, we focused on the situation of interdependence existing between the focal organization and its environment. Now, we turn our attention to the various situational characteristics which facilitate the exercise of influence. When these characteristics are not present, influence is made difficult. We will review these conditions and how their manipulation helps to maintain organizational autonomy. The conditions deal with the organization's control over the generation of demands, the determination of satisfaction with demands, and the discretion in the organization's behavior.

Control of Demands

Several of the conditions manipulated by organizations relate to control over the demands which are likely to be made on an organization. The first of these has to do with the organization's awareness of demands. While it may seem superfluous to include this condition, awareness of demands by the organization is an important precondition for affecting control and an equally important condition for avoiding influence.

Interest groups vary in making their demands known, and organizations vary in the extent to which they find out about the demands. On one level, interest groups may not make demands simply because other demands are being satisfied and the interest group either feels morally compelled not to make a demand or feels that the satisfied demands will be threatened if other claims are made. Thus, the

Alaskan state government was reluctant to constrain the behavior of the oil companies building the thousand-mile pipeline because of its importance to the Alaskan economy. The builders pumped billions of dollars into the state, which gave them a considerable influence with its policy makers. As the president of the Alaskan State Senate put it, "There's still the underlying fear that if we assert ourselves too much, we'll kill the goose that lays the golden egg" (*Time*, June 2, 1975:18).

Organizations may purposely manipulate the illusion of satisfaction to avoid the open expression of some demands. Patients in a psychiatric hospital may be drugged to reduce their demands on the staff. At the same time, relatives may be told about all the fine therapeutic activity going on. Again, restriction on the availability of information is helpful in using this strategy.

Organizations also may avoid demands by controlling the extent to which interest groups have access to communication channels. Most organizations possess a crew of stoutly protective executive assistants and receptionists whose effect, if not intent, is to route individuals away from their bosses. Another effective mechanism for avoiding demands is actually to convene a meeting to air the demands, but either schedule the meeting for times and places inconvenient for undesired interest groups or pack it with individuals more favorable to the organization. Making the cost of communicating high is a common device for reducing expressions of displeasure. Costs of communication may be high because of uncertainty about where and how to communicate, the necessity of filing special forms or making an appointment, or the necessity of obtaining specialized help in registering one's demands. The cost of litigation, for instance, may stop a dissatisfied person or group from using the courts to force compliance from the focal organization.

Many organizations do not actively attempt to avoid input from interest groups. Indeed, many take active steps to determine demands from the environment, through market research and surveys of attitudes among employees, stockholders, customers, and suppliers. The extent to which organizations encourage or discourage the expression of demands, we would argue, is a function of their resource dependence on those groups. An informal study of the posted office hours of professors in a department in one large state university indicated that those who were known for their research tended, *more than others*, to post student visiting hours during prime class time and lunch periods ($r = .48$).

It is usually better to avoid the expression of demands than to face the necessity of refusing the demands of a potent interest group. Refusal is a much more final, potentially hostile action. Thus, subordinates will seldom say, no, outright to their employers—rather, the employees merely avoid the boss so no requests for work can be made.

Controlling the Definition of Satisfaction

A second method for managing demands is to define the request as being satisfied. In this situation, the organization controls the satisfaction of its interest groups without losing discretion over its behavior. Many professional groups use a device of this type. State laws that regulate the licensing and practice of medicine explicitly define the treatment of a patient as satisfactory if the physician uses standard medical procedures. The patient with a question about the level of care received confronts a panel of experts who are doctors, like his or her own, to decide whether the care has been adequate or not. More often, people will simply ask their own doctor, who reassures them that everything is going fine.

The professional-client relationship is typical of a very general problem in social influence, the uncertainty of evaluation and judgment. Evaluation is a process of applying some criterion or criteria to an output to determine the fit. When operational measures can be taken, the satisfaction of the criteria may be easy to assess. A British and French airplane manufacturing joint venture lost potential sales of $20 billion because the plane failed to meet the speed specifications. Speed is an easy criterion to assess. On the other hand, another airplane, manufactured in Sweden, lost out in the competition because the NATO purchasers did not want to rely on a neutral country to manufacture arms for their arsenals. There are no operational measures for determining the reliability of intentions. Sweden simply lost the argument about its future reliability.

Whenever ambiguity exists either in the statement of criteria or in their application to a particular output, there will exist the possibility of equivocality in interpretation. Both interest groups and the focal organization will have discretion in determining whether a demand is satisfied. The focal organization, then, has some control over the interpretation of outcomes and may direct its behavior as it wants while contending that the demands have been satisfied. The power to control its own behavior is enhanced to the extent that those making the demands are not well equipped to determine when, or if, they have been met.

Because of equivocality, it is difficult to call an organization's output into question. Even when its output is questioned, the organization may control the evaluation partly to ensure that support is obtained from the environment. One of the more fascinating attempts to question an organization is the investigation of the effects of television violence. To resolve the hotly debated issue of the effects of televised violence, such as seen on the police and Western shows, on behavior, the Surgeon General of the United States commissioned an expert panel to investigate the question. After thousands of dollars had been spent on research, the Surgeon General's report made only tentative and limited conclusions, suggesting that children already predisposed to violence may, perhaps, develop more aggressive tendencies, which might produce violent behavior in circumstances which incite to violence. In this case, as in many instances, the government investigative agency found it necessary to rely on some of the television industry's own technical experts. The investigating commission permitted the industry, particularly the National Broadcasting Company (NBC), to consult with it on the selection of appropriate panel members. For a number of years, NBC had been conducting a series of studies of its own and knew who would be sympathetic panel members. One of the persons explicitly denied participation, although he requested inclusion, was Albert Bandura, a noted psychologist from Stanford who had repeatedly documented the fact that when children observed films depicting aggression, they tended to imitate the behavior (e.g., Bandura and Walters, 1959).

Controlling the Formation of Demands

Yet another source of discretion for the focal organization is to actually take part in the formulation of the interest group's demands. Three ways in which organizations may take part in the creation of the demands to which they must then respond are: (1) professionalization and self-regulation; (2) involvement in setting standards and regulatory policies; and (3) advertising and other merchandising.

This source of organizational power and discretion is made possible by the same condition of uncertainty that makes the determination of satisfaction difficult. As a consequence of uncertainty, we rely on others more knowledgeable to give us advice. The problem of obtaining advice from those who are affected by the person's actions has been well illustrated. In medicine, there is concern about unnecessary surgery performed by surgeons who find it in their economic self-interest. In an article in the *Saturday Review*, appropriately titled "Never ask a barber if you need a haircut?" Daniel Greenberg (1972) noted that the National Aeronautics and Space Administration (NASA), which favored the growth of space-related research and development, attempted to resolve a seemingly technical question by giving the task to Lockheed, a firm in financial trouble, and Mathematica, a consulting firm that had previously done work for NASA. The question was whether the space program should be based on reusable shuttles or expendable boosters. The shuttle would take longer to develop and involve greater exploratory research and development, ensuring a longer survival of NASA's role. Not surprisingly, the shuttle was the answer that emerged from the scientific study.

The discretion permitted organizations because of an interest group's reliance on them for their expertise derives partly from the amount of resources that would be required for others to develop similar expertise. When the massive oil spill occurred off the Santa Barbara coast in 1969, the Western Oil and Gas Association contributed to a $250,000 study of the ecological effects. While the validity of the conclusion that the impact was negligible was questioned by a southern California scientist (*New York Times*, March 22, 1971:1), neither he nor any other interest group could amass the resources necessary to offer equal expertise.

Another way of controlling demands is by controlling the legislative and administrative bodies empowered to define organizational output. Universities, for instance, control demand for courses by setting requirements for student graduation. Banks have come to be major backers of guaranteed student-loan programs, and the movement of personnel between regulatory boards or commissions and the companies being regulated is well known.

A final important mechanism by which organizations gain discretion over the demands they face is through advertising and promotion. Beliefs about products and services are created, and beliefs about the value provided by a given organization and its products are similarly created. While we do not want to review the extensive literature on advertising, it seems that public relations and advertising are methods of controlling the demands of external groups and organizations, though such methods are more indirect and riskier than simply legislating requirements or advising on demands.

Factors Affecting Discretion in Behavior

Another set of conditions which can affect the ability of one organization or interest group to influence another derives from the context of the behavior itself. Two important dimensions of the context in which the behavior takes place are the observability, or visibility, of the focal organization's behavior to the influencing organization and the discretion possessed by both the influencing organization and the focal organization. If the influencing organization is prevented from using its position of power or if the focal organization is prevented from complying, no effect will be observed. Similarly, to the extent that the compliance of the focal organization is difficult to observe, effective influence is less likely.

One of the easiest ways to avoid being influenced is not to possess the capacity to comply with the demands being made. Though this may seem obvious, it represents an important source of discretion for organizations. Except in those cases where physical or technological capability does not exist, what can or cannot be done is the result of legal or other social constraints and subject to some uncertainty and differing judgments. Legal constraints forbid certain actions both of influencing organizations and of the organization which is the target of the influence. The existence of those who break the laws, however, suggests that the presence of constraint is not necessarily binding.

Enforcement of legal constraints is selective. For instance, there is some indication that the Federal Trade Commission has most frequently prosecuted smaller firms, frequently engaging in less serious but more easily proven violations of various regulations (Posner, 1969). Other examples of selective enforcement abound. Furthermore, the willingness of organizations to expose themselves to possible prosecution is variable, and Staw and Szwajkowski (1975) have shown that firms operating in less munificent environments are more likely to engage in illegal activities.

The willingness of some organizations to ignore constraints and of other organizations to ignore their violations are only two factors that influence whether sanctions really affect organizational discretion. Equally important is the process by which the constraints are imposed in the first place. The very determination of what is and what is not legitimate or legal is likely to be the result of political processes in which organizations press for rules which benefit their interests. At any time, organizations with power will probably advocate rules which permit them the widest possible use of their power, while those organizations in less powerful positions seek rules that protect them from the more powerful.

A good example of a situation in which the balance of power between organizations was asymmetrical but where no freedom to influence behavior existed is in the area of antitrust law. In the case of Eastman Kodak Company v. Southern Photo Material Company (1927), Kodak, with a virtual monopoly of the photographic film industry, attempted to convince a dealer to sell his business. When the dealer refused, Kodak then refused to sell its supplies to the dealer. Antitrust law compelled Kodak to do business with the dealer. Otherwise, Kodak's monopoly power would have forced the dealer to sell out or go out of business. Kodak sold to thousands of dealers, but Southern Photo Material could buy only from Kodak. Prohibitions against interorganizational influence are most strictly interpreted when one party's economic power is overwhelming compared to other social actors, as in the case of manufacturers' attempts to influence local dealers in setting retail price or in limiting their sales territory (Areeda, 1967).

In addition to legal restrictions on interorganizational influence, important normative social restraints also operate. Perrow (1970) illustrated some of these norms in his discussion of social rules of the game among businesspeople. Perrow described a manufacturer whose plant was destroyed by fire. Competitors volunteered the use of their manufacturing facilities during the off-shifts, while the manufacturer's were being rebuilt. These norms do not actually serve the immediate self-interest of all the participants. Rather, they function to serve the long-run welfare of the businesses by establishing general norms which limit predatory competitive behavior.

Latitude in the behavior of a focal organization may not exist for several reasons. First, the organization may be completely regulated in the particular area in which influence is being attempted. Railroads, airlines, trucking firms, and electric and telephone utilities are only a few of the lines of business in which the organization itself has relatively little direct control over important service and pricing policies. Attempts to alter the rates charged by public utilities by acting directly on these organizations are likely to be unsuccessful, since rates can be altered only with the approval of the regulatory agency. While the utility may play an active and influential role in the activities of the rate setting commission, it remains the case that the utility cannot unilaterally alter many aspects of its behavior.

Being subjected to pressure without having the ability to respond may expose organizations to a great deal of frustration. Yet, this very lack of decision-making power can operate as a shield against interest-group demands. The attempts at influence are shifted from the organization to its regulators. Those who wish to control the organization must attempt to control the commissions. And the bases of control shift from resources necessary to the organization to those resources which are important to the policy setting commissions.

A second limitation or constraint on the behavior of an organization is the existence of a highly competitive environment. The theory of perfect competition (e.g., Stigler, 1966) states that in the long run, for firms to remain in business, they must operate at the minimum point on their long-run average cost curves and must sell at the price determined in the competitive marketplace. Economic theory also states that these cost curves will be identical across firms, so that each firm will be producing at the same cost and selling at the same price. Their behavior is thus constrained. While these long-run equilibrium conditions presumed to occur given various restrictive assumptions, are admittedly abstractions, it does seem plausible to presume that operating freedom will be less in more competitive markets which affect the latitude of an organization's behavior when confronted by external influence. Control will be more difficult over firms in competitive environments.

A third form of limitation on the organization's behavior is powerful influences from other organizations in the environment, where these organizations do not have regulatory control. To the extent that the organization's behavior is already constrained and determined by external demands and influence, behavior can not vary a great deal in response to additional external pressures. The situation may be one in which the organization is constrained beyond what it might otherwise desire or one where it can play various external pressures off against one another. Many organizations claim that union hiring and seniority rules limit their ability to comply with government pressures for affirmative action, while the same companies may later attempt to use integration requirements to bring in nonunion workers and attempt to diminish the union's power.

Visibility of Behaviors and Outcomes

In the research on social influence among individuals, one of the more consistent findings is that public behaviors are more influenceable than private behaviors (Kiesler and Kiesler, 1969). There are any reasons why this might be true. The ability of the actor demanding compliance to apply sanctions against noncompliance is reduced when it is difficult or impossible to monitor that compliance. Furthermore, the publicness of an activity produces a commitment to continue the activity (Salancik, 1977). Thus, if one behaves in one way and that has been observed, to behave in another way would create an inconsistency. For an influencing agent requesting action which is incompatible with prior organizational actions, the fact that the prior action and potential future action are public, limits the compliance. But if prior and future actions are compatible, compliance is more likely. A third reason that visibility of behaviors might affect influence attempts is that actors other than the one attempting influence can view public behaviors and evaluate them and apply their own sanctions. These three factors act, one can see, in opposite directions. The visibility of action so compliance can be observed increases the likelihood of influence in public actions. At the same time, commitment to past public actions limits the likelihood of changing activities, and the same public visibility that makes it possible for the influencing agent to observe compliance also means the organization can be assessed by other social actors. In general, if an interest group's power to apply sanctions is greater than that of all others and past behaviors were private while current activities are public, compliance will be greatest. Least compliance will be observed when past behaviors were public and current behaviors are private.

To be visible, behavior does not have to be directly observed. Very often, activity is not directly observed but inferred from the presence of certain effects. The important thing about visibility for it to constrain behavior is that the social actor thinks the behavior can be observed or inferred from observable outcomes. When behavior and outcomes are not visible, the organization is in a position to be the interpreter of its own actions and effectiveness. Organizations can also be interpreters of outcomes which are themselves visible but which present ambiguities in assessing who is responsible. A bookstore servicing a university campus makes money by selling books to students while, at the same time, not overstocking. To keep overstocking to a minimum, bookstores may order quantities smaller than the expected demand. It is very clear to disgruntled students that they cannot get needed books. But what is not clear is who is responsible. Customer dissatisfaction may be turned away from the bookstore by attributing the problem to professors who order books late or who have over-ordered in the past. Whatever the truth of the situation, the important point is that the difficulty of observing its behavior places the organization itself in the primary position for interpreting its activities to the various groups.

Many organizations find secrecy a necessary condition for maintaining the discretion required to operate within a set of conflicting demands. The latitude afforded for complying or not complying is important. Not surprisingly, the disclosure of information itself is one of the major sources of conflict between organizations which wish to influence and the organizations which seek to avoid influence and maintain discretion. The inability of regulatory agencies to acquire information about the activities of the organizations which they ostensibly regulate hampers the development and implementation of public policy. One of the greatest difficulties faced in planning energy policy during the early 1970s was that most of the estimates of energy reserves came from the energy companies themselves. Public utilities were given permission to pass along fuel cost increases immediately, without the requirement of going through the regulatory proceedings. Not surprisingly, after the fact it was found that there was evidence of substantial overcharging. Even in the context of normal proceedings, the limited staff of the commissions and their reliance on the regulated firms for virtually all the data permits the regulated organizations additional control over regulatory outcomes. It can be seen why regulation is so desirable. The regulatory commission buffers the organization from influence attempts since the commission ostensibly controls the organization's behavior; yet, because of the information and visibility advantages accruing to the regulated organization, it can actually retain much discretion and influence over regulatory results.

Information control, then, is an important mechanism for both the exercise and the avoidance of influence. One might argue that organizations will release information when it is in their best interests to do so and will attempt to obtain information that enables them to exercise influence. What information is available about organizational actions is the outcome of a political process in which social actors, each trying to advance its interests, attempt to acquire or withhold information as it serves their position in the political struggle. While the public interest, confidentiality, and other claims are asserted in the contest over information availability, it must be remembered that these are arguments and, like all arguments, are used selectively to enhance the interests of those raising the argument.

MANAGING AND AVOIDING DEPENDENCE

The strategies we have discussed for avoiding influence may be effective in avoiding the influence of relatively less powerful groups. Such strategies are less likely to work when dealing with powerful interests controlling critical organizational dependencies. General Motors' power over its automotive suppliers was great enough that it could not only make demands about permissible prices but also enforce demands to audit the suppliers' books and ensure they were not making excessive profits (Perrow, 1970). Confronted by powerful external organizations, organizational adaptation requires managing the interdependencies themselves, as avoidance may no longer be possible.

Organizational Change Strategies

There are two broadly defined contingent adaptive responses—the organization can adapt and change to fit environmental requirements, or the organization can attempt to alter the environment so that it fits the organization's capabilities. The "marketing concept" (Kotler, 1967) is an example of the former strategy. According to the marketing concept, which is a derivative of classical economics, the firm assesses the needs of the marketplace, and then adapts its products and production process to fill some of these needs. In an extension to nonprofit marketing (Kotler and Levy, 1969), the social organization assesses what the social needs are, and defines as its market segment some set of those needs which it will attempt to meet. The concept is that of the organization as an adapter or responder to the signals provided it by consumers and other organizations. As the firm is said to be a price taker in classical economics, the organization can be characterized as a need taker, or an environmental requirement taker, responding to demands that are implied by the context in which it operates.

Alternatively, the organization can adapt by attempting to operate on that environment. If the organization and the environment must be mutually compatible, then either the organization can change or the environment can be changed. Galbraith's (1967) notion of demand creation is consistent with this second strategy. If rapidly changing environments require certain kinds of organizational structures, the organization can adapt its structure to fit the environment or it can alter the environment so that it becomes compatible with the present structure. Since the environment is enacted, the potential for adapting the environment is greatly expanded, as the organization can choose which parts of the environment to attend to.

In one sense, organizations create the environments to which they adapt by selecting the market segment they will serve—by excluding some elements of the environment and including others. Universities which obtain major portions of their resources from alumni, for instance, institute selection procedures which ensure adequate supplies. Many private universities have quotas which provide favorable treatment to the children of their own alumni. Since the occupational backgrounds of the parents are reliable predictors of the success of the offspring, such an admissions policy ensures a potential source of funding for the future. A similar strategy may be employed by job training agencies. To make sure they can demonstrate their effectiveness, only the most trainable applicants are accepted for the program, and difficult cases are excluded. Such a strategy is similar to market segmentation, in which the organization searches for a market within which it can successfully operate.

Within each of these broad categories of altering the organization or the environment, there are many subsets of possible organizational responses. The organization can adapt its structure, its information system, its pattern of management and human relations, its technology, its product, its values and norms, or its definition of the environment. In attempting to affect the environment, the organization can engage in strategies of diversification, total absorption of the environment as in merger, partial absorption as in cooptation, or in activities that are designed to influence the rules under which interorganizational action takes place. Organizations can lobby to have the government control the environment in their interest or can persuade established regulators to create favorable environmental contexts.

Not only are organizations constrained by the political, legal, and economic environment, but, in fact, law, legitimacy, political outcomes, and the economic climate reflect, in part, actions taken by organizations to modify these environmental components for their interests of survival and growth.

The forms which organizational adaptations take are contingent on the environment and depend on the nature and amount of interdependence confronted by the organization. Organizational adaptations are discussed in the remainder of this book, and we will briefly outline these responses in this chapter. Recall that the two major components of interorganizational power are (1) the focal organization's dependence on important critical resource exchanges, and (2) the control which other organizations might possess over the exchange of that resource. Organizational attempts to manage and avoid dependencies focus on these two components of interorganizational power.

Strategies for Avoiding Resource Dependence

Organizations can take a number of actions to avoid dependence that results from reliance on a single critical resource exchange. A common solution to the problem of overreliance on single sources or markets is to buffer the organization against possible instability. In the case of input, this is accomplished by developing inventories of sufficient size to permit the organization to continue operating even when supplies are scarce (Thompson, 1967). Generally, the more unstable the source of supply, the larger the inventory must be. In the case of output, a similar degree of stability may be attained by committing the organization to long-term contracts for disposal of the output.

While buffering may provide the organization with the capability to survive periods of uncertainty or instability, buffering does not remove the basic source of the vulnerability. A somewhat more adequate strategy is to control the input or output exchange itself, to control the stability and predictability of the exchange relationships. One method of achieving this predictability is to control rules of trade using either formal or informal, legal or illegal means. Industries with sizeable investments in single purpose technologies, such as oil, steel, or utilities, tend to operate under protection from foreign competition and with either formal regulation or informal interfirm organizations that manage competition and markets. Control over extraorganizational influences provides some measure of protection from the problems resulting from unstable input or output exchanges.

Like buffering, control over demand and supply exchanges still leaves the organization somewhat vulnerable. Cartels can disband, government regulators can become hostile, and informal arrangements can be broken. Another, more direct form of controlling input and output exchanges is to take control of the organizations which either provide the needed resource or absorb the output. However, even such merger or vertical integration has limitations. The organization merely alters its interdependence, but does not eliminate its reliance on the environment.

The most effective strategies for dealing with dependence which arises from reliance on a single product or market are those which alter the purposes and structure of the organization so that it no longer requires only a limited range of inputs or serves only a few markets. Given that the organization's vulnerability derives from dependence on single exchanges, the most direct solution is to develop an organization which is dependent on a variety of exchanges and less dependent on any single exchange. A family with two of its members working at different jobs will be less vulnerable to shifts in employment conditions than a family dependent on a single individual.

The two ways of diminishing dependence are the development of substitutable exchanges and diversification. Developing substitutable resources, such as oil to replace natural gas, is essentially the redefinition of an exchange so that it is no longer critical. The ease of developing the capacity to accept other inputs or for creating other outputs depends on the current state of knowledge and the flexibility of the organization's technology. Cereal firms, for instance, found it relatively easy to manufacture natural cereals and to market cereal products as snack foods in addition to marketing cereal as breakfast food. The major change was in marketing strategy.

The more radical form of dependence avoidance is through diversification into different lines of business. The effectiveness of this strategy is enhanced to the extent the new businesses are different from the current set of activities, presumably using different resources, supplying different markets, and facing different competitors. The range of possible diversification is great, extending from expansion into a related geographic area, or market, to the conglomeration of the firm so that it includes diverse lines of business with practically no resource exchanges in common.

Strategies for Avoiding Control

The problems which arise for an organization because of its dependence on a single exchange in part arise because the exchange is controlled by some other organization. Many of the adaptations which interdependent organizations undertake focus on diminishing the control of others or of obtaining control for the focal organization.

When the interdependence an organization faces derives from the concentration of power possessed by other organizations, one approach is to eliminate the concentration of control through antitrust suits. Most antitrust suits are filed by large organizations attempting to reduce the control of other large organizations. In just this way Budget Rent-A-Car (a division of Transamerica) successfully entered airports with its concession stands. The courts agreed that it was unlawful for the three major car rental firms to control all the leases for booth rental space at airports and that other competitors must have the opportunity to compete on the premises.

A less direct method of restricting another's control is through cooptation, in which members of the controlling organization are invited to participate in various activities of the vulnerable organization, to sit on the board of directors, advisory panels, and so forth. The aim of bringing in potentially hostile outsiders is to socialize them and to commit them to provide assistance to the focal organization.

More direct means for avoiding unfavorable situations of control involve acquiring countervailing control or otherwise regulating control. Many of the oil companies own the pipelines through which oil and gas must be transported to markets. While these firms could, potentially, use their control of vital transportation links to eliminate competition from smaller independent firms, this is not possible because pipelines are regulated and must provide nondiscriminatory access for all users. Mergers and acquisitions not only control asymmetrical interdependence by absorbing it, but also make the surviving organization more powerful since it now possesses more resources and more resource control itself. Control may also be limited through the socialization of executives, causing them to avoid using interorganizational power, through informal agreements and arrangements, and through the development of norms and values which restrict the exercise of interorganizational influence.

SUMMARY

Organizations confront an environment of conflicting demands in which interacting organizations are increasingly mutually interdependent. This interconnectedness makes the management of the focal organization more difficult because a variety of possible consequences of actions must be considered and, occasionally, the organization finds itself confronted by powerful external organizations making inconsistent demands. While compliance with the demands of a powerful external group is a possible course of action, compliance is likely to generate additional demands for various actions and, more important, may restrict the organization's ability to adapt to other demands made by other external groups in the future.

Organizations may attempt to avoid influence attempts in a variety of ways. Many of the techniques involve the use of secrecy or the restriction of information, so that those making the demands do not know what others are receiving or, in fact, may not know how well their own requests have been satisfied. Demand avoidance may entail balancing conflicting organizations against each other, as in the case of the equal employment organizations and the unions. Demands may be managed by attending to them sequentially. Organizations may place themselves in situations in which they can claim limited discretion, making them uninviting targets for influence. Alternatively, they can seek to have laws enacted or norms developed limiting the discretion of more powerful external organizations in their attempts to achieve specific actions from the focal organization. The antitrust laws present illustrations of instances in which concentrated economic power is limited in its use.

The determinants of the dependence can be addressed directly by the focal organization attempting to maintain discretion. Alternative sources of supply, alternative resources, or diversification may be sought to diminish the criticality of a particular exchange relationship. Or, the control that others have over the exchange can be attacked through the use of laws, norms, or strategies of absorption and regulation such as merger, cooptation, and the exchange of personnel.

In the next three chapters, we will present extensive empirical evidence on the strategies used by organizations to avoid and manage their interdependence with other organizations. These data are consistent with the arguments we have developed concerning the sources of dependence and the requirements necessary for organizations to maintain discretion and autonomy. Our model of the social control of organizations permits us, then, not only to predict organizational compliance, as we saw in Chapter Three, but also to explain the occurrence of organizational actions taken to manage the social control relationships. In Chapter Ten we shall consider the implications of our perspective on social control and organizational response for the management of organizations.

REFERENCES

Adelman, M. A. 1972. *The World Petroleum Market*. Baltimore: Johns Hopkins University Press.

Areeda, P. 1967. *Antitrust Analysis*. Boston: Little, Brown.

Bandura, A., and R. H. Walters. 1959. *Adolescent Aggression*. New York: Ronald Press.

Cyert, R. M., and J. G. March. 1963. *A Behavioral Theory of the Firm*. Englewood Cliffs, N.J.: Prentice-Hall.

Galbraith, J. K. 1967. *The New Industrial State*. Boston: Houghton Mifflin.

Greenberg, D. 1972. "Don't ask the barber whether you need a haircut." *Saturday Review*, 55 (Nov. 25, 1972):58–59.

Kahn, R. L., D. M. Wolfe, R. P. Quinn, and J. D. Snoek. 1964. *Organizational Stress: Studies in Role Conflict and Ambiguity*. New York: Wiley.

Kiesler, C. A., and S. B. Kiesler. *Conformity*. Reading, Mass.: Addison-Wesley.

Kotler, P. 1967. *Marketing Management: Analysis, Planning, and Control*. Englewood Cliffs, N.J.: Prentice-Hall.

Kotler, P., and S. J. Levy. 1969. "Broadening the concept of marketing." *Journal of Marketing*, 33:10–15.

Parsons, T. 1956. "Suggestions for a sociological approach to the theory of organizations." *Administrative Science Quarterly*, 1:63–85.

Perrow, C. 1970. *Organizational Analysis: A Sociological View*. Belmont, Calif.: Wadsworth.

Perrow, C. 1972. *Complex Organizations: A Critical Essay*. Glenview, Ill.: Scott, Foresman.

Posner, R. A. 1969. "The Federal Trade Commission." *University of Chicago Law Review*, 37:47–89.

Salancik, G. R. 1977. "Commitment and the control of organizational behavior and belief." In B. M. Staw and G. R. Salancik (eds.), *New Directions in Organizational Behavior*, 1–54. Chicago: St. Clair Press.

Staw, B. M., and E. Szwajkowski. 1975. "The scarcity-munificence component of organizational environments and the commission of illegal acts." *Administrative Science Quarterly*, 20:345–354.

Stigler, G. J. 1966. *The Theory of Price*. New York: Macmillan.

Thompson, J. D. 1967. *Organizations in Action*. New York: McGraw-Hill.

CHAPTER SIX

ALTERING
ORGANIZATIONAL
INTERDEPENDENCE:
Controlling the Context
of Control

We have argued that the organization ends and the environment begins at that point where the organization's control over activities diminishes and the control of other organizations or individuals begins. At this point, exchanges with the environment take place, and the organization is vulnerable. It is open to influence; it can fail to achieve the needed exchange. If the exchange is important for the organization, the organization should attempt to manage its interdependence by extending its own control into those vital areas. Alternatively, the organization might alter its own situation of interdependence. It might increase its own dominance so that those with whom it exchanges become relatively more dependent on it. And finally, the organization might reduce the domination of other organizations by decreasing its reliance on single critical exchanges. These three strategies can be viewed as means by which the organization attempts to restructure the conditions of interdependence with its environment. The three occasionally manifest themselves as growth accomplished through merger.

In this chapter we discuss merger and growth as strategies for managing interorganizational dependence. We argue that *vertical* integration represents a method of extending organizational control over exchanges vital to its operation; that *horizontal* expansion represents a method for attaining dominance to increase the organization's power in exchange relationships and to reduce uncertainty generated from competition; and that *diversification* represents a method for decreasing the organization's dependence on other, dominant organizations. We will present data which suggest that merger is undertaken to accomplish a restructuring of the organization's interdependence and to achieve stability in the organization's environment, rather than for reasons of profitability or efficiency as has sometimes been suggested.

USING MERGER TO COPE WITH INTERDEPENDENCE

One of the problems faced by organizations interdependent with other organizations is that the exchanges required for maintaining operations are uncertain and potentially unstable. Coping with organizational environments requires stabilizing them somehow or, as Thompson (1967) has suggested, reducing the uncertainty confronting the organization. When the conditions of the environment are mediated by social actors, as is increasingly the case for modern organizations, uncertainty derives not only from the vagaries of nature but from the actions taken by others. In such cases, the uncertainty resulting from the unpredictable actions of others is reduced by coordinating these actors. Observations of most environments suggest that they tend, over time, to move from instability to stability because the various participants develop stable interaction patterns.

One way of achieving increased stability and predictability in organization-environment relationships is through growth (Katz and Kahn, 1966), and one form of growth is through merger, which involves the acquisition of another firm or organization. Merger typically involves a restructuring of organizational dependence. There are three general types of merger between organizations, involving vertical integration, horizontal expansion, and diversification or conglomeration. Each merger has the effect of managing interdependence, though each is focused on a different form of interdependence and operates differently. Companies may merge vertically, forward or backward, in the production process in an attempt to deal with symbiotic interdependence, or the "mutual dependence between unlike organisms" (Hawley, 1950:36). Steel companies may merge with producers of coal, and oil companies may acquire systems for petroleum distribution. Paper companies may buy lumber firms while textile firms purchase fabric stores. The second form of merger is horizontal expansion,

in which organizations acquire their competitors to reduce com-
mensalistic interdependence—the interdependence which derives from
the competitive relationship of outcomes obtained by two or more
parties. The structure of an industry becomes increasingly concentrated as horizontal mergers reduce competitive interdependence.
Mergers among similar organizations not only reduce competitive interdependence by absorbing competition, such mergers also increase
the power of the resulting larger organization in its symbiotic relationships as well. The third form of merging involves diversification, in
which an organization acquires another organization which is neither
in the same business nor in a direct exchange relationship with it. A
firm dependent on a single, critical exchange can reduce its dependence on any single exchange through diversification by engaging in
activities in a variety of different domains.

Nelson (1959) noted that mergers followed the economic cycle,
occurring more frequently when stock prices were high and interest
rates low, or when the costs of merger were reduced. Nelson further
noted that there had been three major merger movements, the first
accomplishing the consolidation of competitors, the second achieving
vertical integration, and the third involving an expansion and diversification into other sectors of the economy.

We argue that merger is a mechanism used by organizations to
restructure their environmental interdependence in order to stabilize
critical exchanges. It is possible to analyze the extent to which actual
mergers are consistent with this argument. There are alternative
theories of merger, including those that hypothesize that mergers are
undertaken to increase profits or to achieve economies of scale. While
these arguments are not necessarily incompatible with our interdependence management hypothesis, the available data do not support these
other two interpretations of merger activity.

PATTERNS OF VERTICAL MERGERS

The merger data used for this analysis were drawn from the Federal
Trade Commission's (FTC) *Report on Large Mergers in Manufacturing and Mining, 1948–1969* (1970) and were first analyzed by
Pfeffer (1972). Mergers of manufacturing companies with other manufacturing firms and mergers of petroleum refiners with producers of
gas and oil were examined, a total of 854 mergers, representing
acquisition of $44.9 billion in assets over the twenty-year period.

To examine whether mergers represent a response to environmental interdependence, the question was asked whether organizations acquired firms in industries with which they transacted. If organizations merge to control interdependence, then they should acquire

organizations in areas with which they exchange resources. Moreover, they should make such acquisitions more often when the exchanges are problematic. While there are many resources of concern to organizations, such as information and legitimacy, we restricted the analysis to only those resources that are exchanged for money through the buying and selling of goods. White (1974) and Levine and White (1961) have suggested that resource exchange is a useful perspective for analyzing interorganizational behavior. To estimate resource exchanges between organizations, we used measures of transactions derived from Leontief's (1966) input-output tables of the United States' economy. These tables estimate the dollar amount of goods which each industry purchases from every other industry. They can thus be used to describe the resource dependencies faced by firms in a given industry. Because the input-output information is obtainable only at an aggregated level, we must conduct our analysis of patterns of merger activity on that level. This requires the assumption that the organizations within the industries face relatively similar exchange patterns and that mergers by particular organizations within those industries will, therefore, reflect these same exchange patterns.

The firms involved in the 854 mergers from 1948 to 1969 were grouped by the two-digit level of the Standard Industrial Code (SIC). This aggregates our measures of merger activity to the same level as measures of resource exchanges among economic sectors. Bain (1968) has noted that when industrial behavior is analyzed at the two-digit SIC level, the results have been biased to underestimate individual relations between variables. The results presented are likely to be conservative estimates of the effect of resource interdependence on merger activity because of the requirements for aggregation and because we are forced to assume that the exchange patterns of the merging firms are reflected in the average of all firms.

From the FTC data, we computed the proportion of one industry's acquisitions, industry i, made in another industry, j. The proportion of acquisitions was computed both for the number of mergers and for the total assets acquired. From Leontief's input-output tables, we developed for each industry (i) measures of (1) the proportion of its output sold to each other industry (j), (2) the proportion of its input purchased from each other industry, and (3) the proportion of total transactions (both output and input) with each other industry. From this information it is possible to assess the extent to which the distribution of mergers made by an industry corresponds to the distribution of its resource transactions with other industries. That is, if textile firms sell most of their output to firms in the apparel industry, do textile firms also tend to a greater extent to acquire firms in the apparel industry?

Let:

M_{ij} = the percentage of mergers which industry i made with industry j.
A_{ij} = the percentage of total assets acquired by firms in industry i that come from industry j.
S_{ij} = the percentage of industry i's sales made to industry j.
P_{ij} = the percentage of industry i's purchases made from industry j.
T_{ij} = the percentage of industry i's total transactions that are with industry j.

If firms are merging to absorb interdependence, then we have hypothesized that merger of firms in an industry, i, with industry j are a function of industry i's transactions with industry j, or:

$$M_{ij} = a + b_1 S_{ij} + b_2 P_{ij} + b_3 T_{ij} + u \qquad (6.1)$$
$$A_{ij} = a' + b'_1 S_{ij} + b'_2 P_{ij} + b'_3 T_{ij} + u \qquad (6.2)$$

where u is a random disturbance term or error. We are not a priori certain which measure of resource dependence is most responsible for merger behavior in the whole sample. Below, however, we develop some hypotheses seeking to account for the relative importance of sales or purchase interdependence for explaining merger activity by industry.

Alternative Explanations for Mergers

We shall also consider three alternative reasons for merger. The first is that mergers occur on a random basis. Because there are differing numbers of large firms in different industries, the observed patterns of merger behavior would not be equal across industries even if mergers were occurring randomly. In other words, the supply of potential merger candidates large enough to be reported in the FTC series differs across industries. Data on the number of firms with assets over $10 million were collected from the Internal Revenue Service Statistics of Income, and used as a control variable in the analysis. The variable N_j represents the number of large firms in industry j. If mergers only followed available supply, one would expect a positive correlation between patterns of merger activity and N_j.

A second alternative is that the profitable industries are likely to attract firms interested in acquisitions. If mergers are being made to enhance firm profitability, it is likely that the acquisitions would be made in industries with higher rates of return. Indeed, rates of return are supposed to attract entry according to economic theory, thereby increasing competition and reducing returns to an equilibrium level. Industry profitability, measured by the rate of return earned on equity, was included as an additional control and denoted by E_j.

Finally, the concentration of firms within target industries was employed as another control variable. It was thought that concentration might be a surrogate for difficulty of entry into an industry. A concentrated industry with a few large firms may be more difficult to enter than one with many small firms, so that firms desiring entry might be compelled to merge if they are to succeed. The concentration ratios used were those developed by Weiss (1963), which correct for geographic and aggregation effects. The concentration ratio is denoted by C_j, and concerns the proportion of industry i's sales made by the top four firms.

Results

The results of the analysis of merger as a correlate of organizational interdependence are quite striking. For all manufacturing industries, the following Pearson correlations were obtained:

	S_{ij}	P_{ij}	T_{ij}	$E_{i,j}$	N_j	C_j
M_{ij}	.65	.62	.66	.01	.16	.01
A_{ij}	.59	.52	.57	.03	.21	.04

All three correlations of merger activity with transactions are statistically significant ($p < .001$). A stepwise regression analysis indicated that the percentage of sales (S_{ij}) made to other industries accounted for 41.8 percent of the variation in acquisitions across industries; the percentage of purchases (P_{ij}) accounted for another 5.9 percent of the variation; and total transactions (T_{ij}) added another 1.5 percent to the explained variance. Together the three measures of resource interdependence accounted for 49.2 percent of the variation in merger activity across industries. A similar analysis indicated that 39.4 percent of the variation in patterns of merger activity measured by assets acquired could be explained by resource exchange patterns.

Although the transactions measures do account for the variation in patterns of merger activity, the other industry characteristics do not explain much. Both profitability and industry concentration were uncorrelated with merger behavior. While the correlations with the number of large firms are statistically significant, this variable was substantially less predictive than the resource dependence measures.

Specific Industry Results

The general analysis of patterns of merger activity is consistent with the argument that organizations attempt to manage their dependence by absorbing this interdependence through acquisition. In this section we consider the patterns and correlates of merger activity on an industry by industry basis. Industries differ in their concentration and in other characteristics. We suspected that the pattern of merger activity exhibited would differ depending on the context of the specific industry. Examination of the correlates of merger activity on a specific industry basis will enable us to test more refined hypotheses derived from the perspective of acquisition activity as a form of interdependence management.

Eighteen manufacturing industries had enough total mergers to analyze separately. For these industries, the distribution of mergers made by firms in that industry with firms in every industry were correlated with the distribution of transactions across the same industries and also with the other characteristics of the other industries in which firms were acquired. These results are presented in Tables 6.1 and 6.2. Table 6.1 presents the results for the analysis of the percentage of

TABLE 6.1   Correlations of M_{ij} (Percentage of Total Mergers of Industry i with Industry j) with Transactions and Other Variables for Each Manufacturing Industry

Industry	S_{ij}	P_{ij}	T_{ij}	E_j	N_j	C_j
Food	.98**	.95**	.97**	−.13	.56**	.00
Textile	.67**	.94**	.86**	−.52	.07	−.26
Apparel	.93**	.74**	.91**	−.72	−.18	−.46
Lumber	.76**	.60**	.69**	.09	−.05	−.35*
Paper	.86**	.98**	.96**	.13	.12	−.10
Printing	.98**	.53**	.78**	.20	.03	−.16
Chemicals	.96**	.98**	.97**	.28	.38*	.24
Petroleum	.68**	.73**	.82**	.03	.01	.20
Rubber	.32	.22	.36*	.26	.16	.37
Leather	.88**	.86**	.88**	−.73	−.36	−.38*
Stone, Clay, and Glass	.80**	.95**	.95**	.30	.25	.22
Primary Metals	.81**	.99**	.95**	.07	.33	.31
Fabricated Metals	.46*	.15	.31	.29	.49**	−.01
Machinery	.96**	.78**	.91**	.24	.52**	.08
Electrical Machinery	.91**	.85**	.93**	.29	.39*	.20
Transportation Equipment	.61**	.63**	.63**	.34	.46*	.36
Instruments	.61**	.56**	.67**	.21	.21	.14
Miscellaneous Manufacturing	.31	.29	.38*	.04	−.07	−.10

* represents significance at the .05 level in the expected direction
** represents significance at the .01 level in the expected direction

TABLE 6.2 Correlations of A_{ij} (Percentage of Total Assets Acquired by Industry i That Were in Industry j) with Transactions and Other Variables for Each Manufacturing Industry

Industry	S_{ij}	P_{ij}	T_{ij}	E_j	N_j	C_j
Food	.98**	.96**	.98**	−.11	.60**	.00
Textile	.64**	.78**	.78**	−.58	.28	−.27
Apparel	.86**	.86**	.97**	−.74	−.14	−.46*
Lumber	.44*	.24	.34	.11	.04	−.19
Paper	.81**	.95**	.92**	.12	.16	−.00
Printing	.97**	.53**	.77**	.18	.01	−.18
Chemicals	.91**	.96**	.94**	.31	.38*	.29
Petroleum	.86**	.31	.43*	.22	−.02	.31
Rubber	.19	.34	.40*	.24	.43*	.42
Leather	.91**	.88**	.90**	−.70	−.36	−.36*
Stone, Clay, and Glass	.64**	.90**	.83**	.32	.35*	.21
Primary Metals	.78**	.98**	.93**	.08	.35*	.32
Fabricated Metals	.48*	.03	.22	.31	.44*	.05
Machinery	.95**	.77**	.90**	.28	.58*	.16
Electrical Machinery	.92**	.77**	.90**	.30	.46*	.18
Transportation Equipment	.73**	.83**	.80**	.34	.46*	.36
Instruments	.48*	.27	.44*	.22	.37*	.07
Miscellaneous Manufacturing	.08	.29	.26	.16	−.02	.00

* represents significance at the .05 level in the expected direction

** represents significance at the .01 level in the expected direction

mergers by number, while Table 6.2 presents the analysis for the percentage of assets acquired in the various industries. In virtually all industries, the pattern of merger activity is significantly related to at least one measure of resource interdependence. More mergers are made in industries with which the acquiring firm does business than in industries with which it does not do business. The other variables considered do not explain the variation in merger behavior nearly as well. The arithmetic average of the correlations over the 18 industries between M_{ij} and A_{ij} and the various explanatory factors are listed below:

	S_{ij}	P_{ij}	T_{ij}	E_j	N_j	C_j
M_{ij}	.75	.71	.77	.04	.19	.02
A_{ij}	.70	.65	.71	.06	.24	.05

The fact that mergers are associated with transactions does not in itself conclusively demonstrate that those mergers were made to control sources of organizational dependence. Quite possibly, firms acquire other firms that are familiar to them; these would most likely be firms with which they do business. There are, however, some hypotheses which can be used to distinguish between the familiarity argument and the thesis that mergers are made to cope with problematic interdependence. These hypotheses deal with the extent to which mergers follow patterns of sales or purchase interdependence.

To the extent that the organization operates in a relatively concentrated environment, we argue that its interdependence with suppliers of input will be relatively more important and problematic than its interdependence with customers. Consequently, we predict that there will be a higher correlation between merger activities and purchase interdependence the higher the concentration of the organization's economic environment. The concept of concentration means that the organization has relatively few competitors for sales. In turn, concentration presumably gives it market power (Caves, 1970), but this market power is with respect to those organizations to which it sells. Its power with respect to customers comes from the fact that these customers have few alternative sources of supply. Since the organization in a more concentrated industry has power with respect to customers, it would be expected that it would focus its attention in managing dependence on those organizations from which it buys input.

This hypothesis is consistent with the data. If we split the 18 industries by industrial concentration, as measured by Weiss (1963), the following results are obtained. Considering the correlations for the percentage of mergers by number, the average correlation between proportion of mergers made and proportion of purchase transactions for the more highly concentrated industries is .762, while this same correlation is .652 for the less concentrated industries. In other words, for the more highly concentrated industries, the purchase transactions interdependence variable accounts for 58 percent of the variation in observed merger behavior, while this variable accounts for only 42 percent of the variation in the case of the less concentrated industries. A similar result holds when we examine merger activity using the proportion of total assets acquired in each industry. For this dependent variable, purchase interdependence accounts for 49 percent of the variation for the more concentrated industries and 35 percent for the less concentrated. Consistent with our argument, the data indicate that firms operating in more highly concentrated industries use mergers more to cope with exchange dependence with respect to organizations providing input.

A second testable derivative of our hypothesis that mergers are made to control sources of problematic interdependence is that mergers should be made to enhance market power when it is lacking but necessary to alleviate unpredictable sales. When concentration is intermediate, sales interdependence should better account for patterns of merger activity and sales interdependence should be more important than purchase interdependence in accounting for merger activity. At very high levels of industry concentration, as just noted, the firms have market power with respect to customers. Consequently, dependence with customer organizations is not problematic, and there should be less strategic attention focused on managing sales interdependence. At very low levels of industrial concentration where there are a large number of competitor organizations, the firm becomes a passive taker of price and other competitive factors and sales interdependence can not be managed through interfirm linkages. As Stern and Morgenroth (1968) have suggested, we argue that sales uncertainty is greatest when concentration is intermediate in value, and consequently, it is under those conditions that we would expect merger to be most accounted for by sales interdependence.

This prediction is also consistent with the data. We again split the sample, this time identifying nine industries in which concentration was closest to the average value of 41 percent and nine industries that had either very high or very low levels of industrial concentration. In Table 6.3, we present the data both for proportion of mergers and for proportion of assets acquired, indicating the correlations between sales interdependence, purchase interdependence, and the pattern of merger activity for industries both intermediate and extreme in industrial concentration. As can be seen in that table, sales interdependence is more highly correlated with merger activity for industries intermediate in concentration, and the difference between sales and purchase interdependence is also greater for industries intermediate in

TABLE 6.3   Correlations Between Sales and Purchase Interdependence and Patterns of Merger Activity in Industries of Differing Levels of Concentration

	Intermediate Concentration		Extreme Concentration[*]	
	Sales (S_{ij})	Purchase (P_{ij})	Sales (S_{ij})	Purchase (P_{ij})
Number of Mergers (M_{ij})	.866	.781	.633	.633
Assets Acquired (A_{ij})	.841	.749	.562	.544

[*] Either extremely high concentration or extremely low concentration

concentration. These results hold whether number of mergers or assets acquired are considered.

The argument that firms merge according to patterns of familiarity would not explain the differential effects of salses and purchase dependence. Rather, the grouped and individual industry analyses of merger activity suggest that merger activity is undertaken to manage interorganizational dependencies, with more activity being undertaken to manage the more critical aspects of the dependence. In short, firms merge into those industries which create the biggest problems for them. This basic theme will be pursued in subsequent chapters as we analyze additional forms of interfirm linkage activity.

MERGERS WITHIN THE SAME INDUSTRY: REDUCING COMPETITIVE UNCERTAINTY

Some industrial mergers are made between organizations in the same industry. Such within-industry mergers can represent either attempts to gain control over organizations with which one does business, as there are with in-industry transactions, or attempts to gain control over competitor organizations to increase the firm's dominance in exchange relationships. Because of the large numbers of firms and activities included in the same two-digit SIC classifications, significant transactions occur between firms in the same industry, and thus the management of symbiotic interdependence must be considered along with the management of competitive uncertainty in developing predictions about the extensiveness of within-industry merging.

Symbiotic Interdependence

Following the previously developed arguments about the relationship between transactions interdependence and merger patterns, we would expect to observe a relationship between the proportion of mergers made within the same industry and the proportion of transactions within the industry. This hypothesis assumes that mergers are being made to control symbiotic interdependence. Examining the proportion of mergers made within the same industry as the dependent variable, the following correlations were observed:

	S_{ii}	P_{ii}	T_{ii}	E_i	N_i	C_i
M_{ii}	.22	.46*	.36*	−.30	.38*	−.14
A_{ii}	.35*	.33*	.34*	−.17	.42*	−.06

* Significantly different at .05 level

As with the entire sample of mergers, within-industry mergers are significantly related to patterns of resource exchange, although the relationships are not as strong. Again, the level of industrial concentration does not predict the extent to which firms merge within their own industries, nor is profitability significantly related to merger activity. If anything, the negative correlation with profitability indicates that contrary to what might be predicted from economic theory, there is a greater tendency to merge within the same industry in those industries that are relatively *less* profitable. The number of large firms in the industry also predicts mergers within the industry and does so independently of resource exchange patterns, as these variables are uncorrelated.

These results tend to reduce the likelihood that the familiarity argument is the explanation for merger activity. In considering mergers made only within the same industry, we can more plausibly argue that the degree of familiarity within each industry is constant. Differences in within-industry merger rates, therefore, can more confidently be attributed to variables other than familiarity, such as the pattern of resource interdependence.

Competitive Interdependence

The weaker relationship between mergers and resource exchanges for within-industry mergers suggests that other factors are operating. One such factor is competitive interdependence. Organizations may be acquiring firms within the same industry in order to reduce some of the uncertainty that derives from competition. Firms would acquire other firms in the same industry to manage competitive uncertainty when competitive uncertainty was most problematic. Previous research (Stern and Morgenroth, 1968; Pfeffer, 1972; Pfeffer and Leblebici, 1973) has suggested that uncertainty is curvilinearly related to industrial concentration, in an inverted U-shaped relationship. When there are many firms in an industry and concentration is relatively low, the actions of any firm represents only a small proportion of the total industry; thus, any firm has few consequential effects on most of the other firms. As concentration increases, an oligopolistic market structure is reached, in which firms have increasing impact on each other. As concentration increases even more, uncertainty begins to decrease. With only a very few large firms operating, tacit coordination becomes possible, and each develops stable expectations concerning the others' behavior.

Stigler (1964) found that when there were few firms, the probability of detecting deviations from standard industry practice or pricing is greater than when there are many firms. The inverted U-shaped relationship between concentration and uncertainty, then, derives from two factors. As concentration increases, the impact of any one firm's activities on the others increases. Similarly, as concentration increases, the ability to coordinate interfirm activity increases even in the absence of interorganizational structures or interfirm linkages. The greatest uncertainty arises when there are enough large firms to have major impact on each other but too many separate organizations to be tacitly coordinated.

To test our argument concerning the relationship between mergers within the same industry and intermediate levels of concentration, a graph was drawn with the proportion of mergers within the same industry on one axis and the concentration ratio on the other. It was graphically determined that within-industry merger activity peaked at about the 40 percent ratio for four-firm concentration. This is approximately the same as the mean value of concentration for industries in the study, which was 41 percent. The absolute value of the difference in industry concentration from this intermediate value of 40 percent was computed for each industry in the sample. This variable, the difference in concentration, represents the deviation in concentration from an intermediate level. This difference in concentration measure correlated -.38 ($p < .05$) with the proportion of mergers within the same industry and -.39 ($p < .05$) with the proportion of acquired assets in the same industry. Both relationships are in the predicted direction, indicating that the proportion of mergers within the same industry is highest when concentration is intermediate and lowest when concentration deviates most from intermediate. The difference in concentration measure is uncorrelated with the measures of resource exchanges, indicating that it adds to the explanatory power of the other variables in accounting for mergers within the same industry. The difference in concentration is correlated with the number of larger firms, N_i, which may explain why N_i had such a high correlation with the proportion of mergers within the same industry.

The measures of resource interdependence and difference in concentration are uncorrelated with each other, and they can be combined into a single regression equation to estimate the proportion of the variance in merger activity within the same industry that can be explained. When the measures of sales and purchase interdependence are combined with differences in concentration in a multiple regression, 37.8 percent of the variation in the proportion of mergers made within the same industry for the 20 industries is explained, while the formulation accounts for 35 percent of the variation in the proportion of assets acquired within the same industry.

Although considerations of symbiotic and competitive interdependence accounted for a significant portion of the pattern of merger activity, there was unexplained variance, or some mergers unaccounted for by the model. Not represented in the formulations considered so far are acquisitions of organizations outside the industries with which the organizations transacted or operated. Mergers outside the pattern of transactions may be undertaken to move into new, more promising lines. By diversifying, firms may avoid previous patterns of dependence or diminish their importance. Since organizations facing dominant resource exchanges are more vulnerable to influence and lack the autonomy necessary for survival, they may enhance their survival by restructuring dependencies to counteract previously dominant exchanges.

DIVERSIFICATION: DETERMINING INTERORGANIZATIONAL DEPENDENCE

Diversification is similar to merger in our analysis of organization-environment interaction. The subject, primarily studied by economists, has not been viewed in the broader context of an organizational response to resource interdependence. One of the most comprehensive examinations of diversification was Gort's (1962) study for the National Bureau of Economic Research. Gort examined diversification achieved through product additions and abandonments for various time periods up until 1954, looking at differences among large corporations and among industries. He concluded that the factor most able to account for variations in diversification activity was technology. Technological intensity was measured as the ratio of technical personnel to total employees and, also, as the rate of change in productivity. Industries that were very technological diversified more and were more often entered by diversifying companies. Companies did not primarily diversify into industries that were countercyclical to eliminate some of the variations resulting from the business cycle affecting their own industries. And, while companies did tend to diversify into growing industries, the growth was primarily due to technological change. Diversified companies were not more or less profitable than other firms.

While Gort's study indicates that technological intensity is related to diversification, there are few theoretically useful cues given to interpret these results. The one position consistently used to explain economic activity—profit maximization—is inconsistent with the data. One can make sense out of Gort's results by assuming that diversification is a strategy used for avoiding constraining resource dependence. Technologically intense manufacturing organizations, firms which employ numerous technical skills to produce high-technology goods, tend also, though not invariably to be firms which sell much of their output to the government. Diversification, then, may represent an attempt to reduce the dependence on single customers or concentrated sales markets. In other words, the correlation between technological intensity and diversification may be spurious, as both may be related to selling to the government or to other dominant customers.

Diversification can be viewed as another organizational response to the environment. It is a strategy for avoiding interdependence. Diversification buffers the organization against the potential effects of dependence by putting the organization into another set of relationships that are presumably different. Diversification is a way of avoiding the domination that comes from asymmetric exchanges when it is not possible to absorb or in some other way gain increased control over the powerful external exchange partner. Diversification is most likely to be used when exchanges are very concentrated and when capital or statutory constraints limit the use of merger or other strategies for managing interorganizational relationships.

If diversification is a response to organizational interdependence, then the extent of diversification should be related to the proportion of resources exchanged with one or a few dominant organizations. One organization which can create significant problematic interdependence for other organizations is the government, particularly the federal government. Since priorities change and the government is frequently the only buyer for output, selling to the government presents an uncertain situation. Moreover, the government can not be acquired, and the use of cooptation and joint ventures is also not possible. We would, therefore, hypothesize that firms or industries which sell a larger proportion of their output to the government would be more likely to use diversification as a means of coping with interdependence.

To test this possibility as an explanation for Gort's (1962) results, we used Gort's measure of diversification for 13 manufacturing industries and correlated it with the proportion of business these industries did with the federal government, as estimated from the input-output tables. The correlation was .58, statistically significant even with this small sample, suggesting that industries diversify more, the more they sell to the government. A similar analysis was conducted to examine the proportion of business which industries conducted outside their primary activity, which can be used as another measure of diversification. The industry's proportion of sales to the government was correlated .55 with the extent to which it engaged in business outside its primary activity. Both analyses suggest that industries doing more business with the government tend to diversify more and to have less of their activity concentrated in one industry group.

The merger data displayed previously in Tables 6.1 and 6.2 can also be examined using this perspective on diversification. Although all industries tended to follow patterns of resource exchange in choosing merger partners, this varied from industry to industry. The magnitude of the correlations between merger and resource exchange measures can be used as an estimate of the extent to which organizations made acquisitions among the set of firms with which they engaged in resource exchanges. When the correlation between mergers and exchange is low, it suggests firms may have selected mergers outside their exchange set for purposes of diversification. Following our preceding argument about doing business with the government as a stimulus to diversification, we should find that lower correlations between merger and resource exchange patterns are exhibited for industries that do more business with the federal government. The industries which transacted more with the government had, in fact, lower correlations between mergers and resource exchanges, suggesting that a pattern of diversification was more likely to be pursued.

Diversification by Israeli Firms

The general finding that industries diversify more, the more business they do with a single dominant output market can be examined also with the data Aharoni (1971) collected from Israeli manufacturing firms. When we considered these data in Chapter Three, we found that firms doing business with the government tended to be more constrained in their decision making, the higher the proportion of sales made to the government. If diversification represents an attempt to avoid such loss of autonomy, we would expect to observe diversification among firms doing more business with the Israeli government.

A more general perspective would argue that firms would seek to sell relatively less to any market to which they currently sell a great deal. The greater the current percentage of sales to a class of customers, the less the firm should desire to sell to that same customer class. Aharoni asked each Israeli manager he interviewed what percentage his firm now sold and what percentage he would like it to sell to each of the following customer types: (1) retailers, (2) wholesalers, (3) other manufacturers, (4) Shekem (military commissary), (5) defense, and (6) foreign customers. To estimate how much managers would like to reduce their sales to each customer class, we can subtract the percentage desired from the percentage currently sold to each class. The larger this difference, the more the manager would like to reduce sales to that class of customer. If the desired percentage is greater than the current percentage, it would suggest the manager would like to increase sales to some customer with which it is now doing little business. The correlation of this difference with the amount currently sold to each customer class would indicate whether firms desire to decrease their sales more when they are more dependent on a particular class of customers. These correlations are presented in Table 6.4. As seen in that table, the correlations are all positive and all but one are statistically significant ($p < .001$). The greater the proportion of sales currently being made to a given customer class, the more the managers desired to reduce their firm's business to that class.

The magnitude of the relationship between the proportion of current business and desired reductions varies for the six customer classes. The correlation is highest for business conducted with the Shekem (.34) and for business with wholesalers (.34), and is lowest for business with foreign customers (.01). The pattern of results is consistent with our argument that firms seek to avoid constraining dependence when it is most uncertain and problematic. The Shekem represents a concentrated purchasing organization. Unlike the case of defense, however, the Shekem can be supplied by a larger number of firms. Moreover, in the case of defense suppliers, the government is more dependent on the small number of possible suppliers for this critical resource than it is on a larger number of suppliers who can furnish supplies. A similar interpretation can be applied to the difference in correlations between wholesale and retail organizations. Wholesalers represent a more concentrated customer class than do retailers, and therefore, firms are more interested in reducing their dependence on this class of customer.

Firms which sold their output to foreign customers were not as interested in changing this position. This apparent anomaly may be

TABLE 6.4   Correlations of the Percentage Sold with the Difference Between Desired Percentage Sold and Actual Percentage Sold for Customer Types

Customer Type	Kendall Rank-Order Correlation
Defense	.152***
Shekem	.339***
Retailers	.190***
Wholesalers	.341***
Other Manufacturers	.232***
Foreign Customers	.012
Total Government	.275***

*** Statistically significant at less than the .001 level of probability due to the Israeli government's policy of actively encouraging exports to earn foreign exchange. Export incentives, favorable treatment by the ministries, and strong normative values all reinforced the desirability of selling abroad. Because of these factors, interdependence with foreign customers was more acceptable.

Another way of examining these data is to note the percentage of sales desired compared with current sales. In all cases except foreign sales, the preferred mean proportion of sales is less than the actual mean. The average percentage by which the 141 Israeli managers wanted sales decreased to government markets was 21.8 percent, much more than to any other market. The desired reduction to other organizations, excluding foreign customers, was 9.2 percent. For foreign customers, an increase of 3.5 percent was desired. The managers were most dissatisfied with selling to the most concentrated market and were most satisfied with selling to that market in which they earned normative rewards and other incentives.

United States Government Contractors and Diversification

Hunt and Hunt (1971) examined the pattern of relations existing between major contractors and the Department of Defense (DOD) and the National Aeronautics and Space Administration. They observed a great deal of stability in the contractual relationships. Their analysis of the top 50 contractors from 1959 to 1968 indicated a tendency among DOD contractors to reduce their share of business with the DOD during the period. No such tendency was evident among NASA contractors. The difference between NASA and DOD contractors is explainable by the difference in the size of the two markets and their consequent impact on organizations, as well as with the fact that production for the Viet Nam War was declining. From data compiled by Leon Reed for the Council on Economic Priorities, an analysis of the top 100 DOD contractors from 1962 to 1971 suggests that contractors who experienced the greatest rises in sales during the escalation of the Viet Nam War (1964–1968) were more likely than other contractors to be diversified, as measured by their proportion of sales to DOD and by the number of consumer products. The effect of the growth and subsequent decline in spending on defense were felt most by those firms which were least diversified, particularly the aircraft manufacturers. Other contractors, such as Bendix, acquire additional lines of business in an attempt to reduce reliance on government procurement. Bendix proudly reported its diversification every year, noting in its annual reports its decreasing reliance on government business.

The various studies suggest that diversification represents an explicit attempt to avoid uncertainty and the control by others who control critical resource exchanges. Product and industry diversification, mergers outside the firm's own industry, reductions in sales and the expression of a desire to reduce sales all suggest firms' attempts to move away from relationships in which they are at a relative power disadvantage. Such a result is well predicted by Blau's (1964) discussion of the consequences of power differences emerging in social relationships.

There are other mechanisms of diversification not discussed here, including product development and diversified marketing strategies. Decisions to market different products for different market segments represent not only attempts to achieve profits but also attempts to diversify dependence and increase stability and certainty. Another form of diversification involves the succession of goals—the tendency for organizations to redefine their stated goals to fit new contingencies in the environment. The restructuring of goals permits the organization to take on new tasks or activities, lessening dependence on old environments and activities.

ORGANIZATIONAL GROWTH

The acquisition of organizations accomplished through merger is only one instance of organizational growth. Another method of growth, of course, is to expand present operations through direct capital investment. In this section we will discuss organizational growth, a more general concept than merger. We argue that growth, whether accomplished by merger or direct expansion, represents an attempt to cope with problematic dependence. We also examine the competing argument that growth is undertaken to increase organizational profitability. Growth, regardless of how it is achieved, provides organizations with additional control over their environments and enhances their likelihood of survival. Large organizations, because they are interdependent with so many other organizations and with so many people, such as employees and investors, are supported by society long after they are able to satisfy demands efficiently.

Some writers have argued that growth arises from an inevitable internal pressure for expansion of organizational activities. Katona (1951), for instance, maintained that organizations grew for self-realization. Growth is a way of justifying the worth of the organization and its present activities. Growth, in this sense, can be viewed as a form of commitment. An organization, engaging in some activities, becomes committed to these activities. This commitment means that the activities come to be viewed as worthwhile and important, and therefore, the organization seeks to expand to perform even more of these worthwhile activities. Katz and Kahn (1966) expressed a similar idea when they noted that technological progress frequently fosters growth, even when it might not be desirable. New technologies and improved methods are incorporated because they relate to the organization's work. Frequently, these advances increase production capacity. Katz and Kahn cited the example of the expansion of steel manufacturing capacity as a consequence of the adoption of technological advances at a time when the industry was already suffering from excess capacity.

While it may be true that growth stems from the internal dynamics of the organization, merely attributing growth to these forces neglects the issue of growth in what areas or what activities, as well as the fact that in social systems, as opposed to biological systems, growth is frequently the outcome of decisions. While the size of a plant may be genetically determined, as well as limited by the resources the plant is given, in the instance of organizational growth, there is some choice concerning how large the organization is to become. As Starbuck has said, "Growth is not spontaneous. It is the consequence of decisions" (1965:453). It is reasonable to argue that organizational growth occurs because size fosters the achievement of either organizational goals or the goals of some members of the organization (McGuire, 1963).

The possibility that growth is not inevitable, but rather the result of choice, has led writers to offer motivations for growth. Starbuck (1965) enumerated ten possible goals served by growth, though he did not empirically distinguish their importance. One often-cited class of reasons for growth deal with the individual motivations of the organization's executives and include such elements as adventurousness, desire for prestige, power, and increased compensation. Other motives posit objectives such as profitability or the achievement of economies of scale in operation. Unfortunately, evidence will not permit determination of what intentions executives had in mind when decisions were made to expand the organization. Most of the research has been addressed to the consequences of growth, with the expectation that motivation can be inferred from consequences. Such an inferential process, however, can possibly be misleading. Observing no relationship between growth and profitability does not, inevitably, mean that profitability was not the reason for the expansion—only that the result was not achieved. For instance, observing that most small investors lose money in the stock market should not imply that people invest in order to lose money.

Our own view is that expansion represents an intentional response to organizational interdependence, but a response which is neither inevitable nor constant. Rather, when organizations experience problems as a consequence of interdependence, such as uncertainty or external control, an attempt is made to manage the interdependence. Depending on how the environment is enacted and the organization's capabilities and resources, different strategies for managing the interdependence will be adopted. Growth is but one solution and, represents, as seen from the data on merger, an attempt to directly control the interdependence by either the domination or avoidance of exchanges.

Mergers, Growth, and Profitability

Mueller (1969) has argued that conglomerate mergers are made only for growth, and Reid (1968) found that merger active firms were not more profitable than firms that were less active in acquiring other organizations although they were superior on indices of growth. Reid's analysis suggests that if mergers, a form of capital investment, are undertaken to increase profits, they are notably unsuccessful in doing so. Dewing (1921) found that the earnings of firms engaging in mergers declined after the consolidations, and that the anticipated benefits of the mergers had been overestimated before the merger occurred. Livermore (1935) studied 328 firms which merged during the period 1890 to 1904. Successful surviving mergers accounted for less than 50 percent of the total. Reid (1962) examined 66 firms between 1950 and 1959. The more successful firms in terms of profits were more likely to be those not active in making acquisitions. Kelley (1967) concluded that merger active firms were neither more nor less profitable than other comparable firms in their industry, and Hogarty (1970) observed that the performance of stock prices of merger active firms was not superior to the performance of stock prices of less active firms. The available evidence suggests that mergers increase organizational size, of course, but do not consistently increase profitability.

If mergers represent a strategy of growth undertaken to control environmental interdependence, it is clear why profitability is not necessarily enhanced. Acquiring firms are not free to select firms based on considerations of profitability alone. Mergers undertaken to absorb interdependence are limited to acquisitions from the group of firms which affect an organization's business. Even if business organizations desire to acquire the most profitable ventures, other things being equal, the requirement of coping with resource interdependence imposes a search rule which limits the set of potential acquisitions. Merging to manage symbiotic interdependence limits firms to acquiring others in industries with which they transact. If a firm merges to cope with competitive interdependence, it must obviously acquire competitors.

Firms merging to control interdependence are limited to selecting from the set of firms on which they are dependent. On the other hand, firms which merge to diversify into other activities are less restricted. Diversification may permit considering a greater number of firms than those with whom resources are exchanged. A larger set of alternatives should permit firms to select more profitable merger candidates. The difference in size of potential sets of acquisitions, therefore, should lead to differential profitability of merger targets depending upon whether the firms are merging for reasons of diversification or of horizontal or vertical integration.

To examine this argument, an analysis of the profitability of acquired firms was made. The Federal Trade Commission has published profitability levels of companies acquired in mergers of various types (Federal Trade Commission, 1969). Their listing includes 401 mergers in manufacturing and mining during 1950–1968 in which the assets of the acquired company were $25 million or more. In Table 6.5, we have reduced the FTC data to show the rate of return of firms acquired in two types of acquisitions—those acquired in horizontal and vertical mergers and those acquired in mergers made for purposes of diversification. A chi-square test of the difference in the distributions indicates that firms acquired for horizontal expansion or vertical integration are less profitable than firms acquired for diversification ($p < .02$).

As noted previously, merger is only one form of growth, and we can ask the more general question of whether growth increases profitability. Growth might allow economies of scale to be realized, per-

TABLE 6.5   Profitability of Acquired Companies, Asset Size of $25 Million or More, in the Year prior to Acquisition, 1950–1968

Profitability (rate of return on equity)	Horizontal and Vertical Mergers	Conglomerate and Product Extension
20% and over	6 companies	13 companies
15%–20%	12	44
10%–15%	38	92
5%–10%	45	83
0%– 5%	21	31
Not profitable	11	5
Total companies	133	268

mitting profit margins to increase. Growth may also increase the market power of a firm, and this market power may lead to increased profits. Growth, of course, leads to larger size, so the issue can be recast as the relationship between size and profitability. A number of studies have examined this relationship, where profitability has been considered either before or after taxes and as a percentage of sales or assets. Regardless of how profits were assessed, these studies (Stekler, 1963; Stekler, 1964; Sherman, 1968; Alexander, 1949) all indicated that firms' average profit rates increase until some relatively modest size is achieved and then remain roughly constant or decline slightly. Moreover, considering only those corporations that report positive net income, average profits actually decline as size increases.

The argument that increasing size is necessary to achieve economies of scale is also suspect. While cost reductions do occur as firms increase in size from being quite small to more moderate size, such economies of scale are achieved at relatively small firm sizes and do not increase thereafter with further growth. Bain (1954; 1956) has conducted some of the most extensive examinations of economies of scale. He concluded that the economies to be gained can not account for the very large firm sizes observed. In part, this may be due to the fact that economies arise in production facilities more so than for the entire firm. It may also be due to the fact that economies are not the reason for growth.

Large size may not necessarily increase profits because economic power may tend to be confronted by countervailing power (Galbraith, 1952). We have already noted that organizations facing concentrated power in industries with which they transact may move to concentrate power themselves to deal with the situation. Power, especially the power of large economic units, is further limited by government regulation and the antitrust laws. When interest groups conflict, one party always will attempt to stimulate government action if the opposition develops too much power. Thus, business and labor each have attempted to have Congress limit or break up the power the other has obtained. In the early 1900s, labor was ruled to be subject to the Sherman Antitrust Act to prevent collective action against employers. By 1914, labor was exempted from this restriction under the Clayton Act. The subsequent growth of labor unions was somewhat checked by the Taft-Hartley law of 1948; right-to-work provisions were directed at preventing the use of legal coercion to create complete monopolies of unionized labor. Size, and the concomitant visibility, makes an organization a more likely target for groups ranging from consumer rights' organizations to antitrust enforcement agencies. So, with the economic power that accompanies the attainment of large size comes additional scrutiny and constraints on the utilization of that power.

Executive Motivation and Organizational Growth

While size has not been correlated with organizational profitability, some writers have attempted to explain organizational decisions favoring growth in terms of the motivations of individual organizational executives. The motivations most commonly used involve individual goal maximization, such as increasing salaries, which are presumed to be negatively related or unrelated to overall organizational performance. One individual motivation for organizational growth is the desire for prestige, power, and job security. Executives in larger companies have more prestige and power than those in smaller firms, as they control more resources. Executives from larger firms are respected and are more often invited to serve on both advisory and policy-making committees and in federal executive positions. Gordon (1945) has argued that the desire for personal power and prestige is one of the more important motives of businesspeople. Williamson (1963) has provided some evidence that managers do use organizational resources and slack (excess resources) for their own prerogatives, including automobiles and travel. He also noted, however, that this feathering of one's nest is constrained by both competitive conditions and shareholder demands. While the effect of size on power and prestige is clear, it is less clear whether size enhances or decreases managerial discretion, as described by Williamson. Large firms may have widely dispersed shareholdings, which may increase the control of managers over the firm. On the other hand, the larger firms are also more visible, and this increased public scrutiny may diminish the autonomy of managers with respect to their own perquisites as well as to decisions made for the organization.

The explanation most commonly advanced to account for organizational growth is that executive compensation is related to organizational size, and consequently, executives seek organizational growth for the purpose of maximizing their own salaries. Roberts (1956; 1959) noted that the salary of the highest paid executive in a firm was independent of the profit earned by the firm but increased with sales volume. McGuire, Chiu, and Elbing (1962) also showed that executive incomes were more closely related to organizational size, as measured by sales revenues, than they were to profits. Simon (1957) argued that Roberts' results were not well explained by economic variables alone. Employing three mechanisms of salary determination, Simon found that the salaries of executives were partly determined by social comparison with other organizational members. Lowest level salaries were determined by competitive market conditions, while higher executive salaries depended on the steepness of the organizational hierarchy and a stable organizational norm for maintaining executives' salaries some ratio above the salaries of sub-

ordinates (1957:34–35). The correlation of size and salaries may, therefore, be a spurious result of the effect of size on hierarchical structure.

But more recent evidence indicates that these earlier conclusions
concerning the relationship between executive compensation and size
were naive, in that salary is only one form of executive compensation.
Lewellen (1968; 1969) noted that the compensation of executives had
become increasingly weighted toward ownership participation in the
form of the corporation's shares. Compensation data were obtained for
the five highest paid positions every year between 1940 and 1963 for 50
of the nation's largest manufacturing firms. Lewellen concluded,
"While in the 1940's and up to the mid-1950's, compensation and
ownership income were about equally important, thereafter the
balance shifted strongly toward the latter. Since 1955, the average
annual increments to top executives' wealth resulting from their hold-
ings of their firms' stock has been *twice* as great as the increments
generated by their compensation" (1969:316). Thus, "a separation of
ownership and management *functions* clearly exists; it seems that a
significant separation of their pecuniary interests does not"
(1969:320).

While any given executive may not hold much of the total shares
of the firm, his shareholdings of the corporation are likely to be a
significant component of his own personal wealth. Lewellen argued
that since most executives had large shareholdings of the firm that they
managed, and since, moreover, many compensation schemes relied on
share price (such as stock options, which are worthless if the market
price for the shares falls), the executives would have interests in share
price equivalent to that of the owners of the firm, the shareholders in
general.

Lewellen's findings are, of course, inconsistent with the argument
that growth, even when unprofitable, will be pursued to enhance executive compensation. Since neither merger nor size seems to lead to
either profitability or increased stock valuation (Hogarty, 1970),
Lewellen's results would tend to be consistent with a profit maximization goal for managers, and would argue against growth for its own
sake. As a final note, we should comment that recently there has been
increasing attention to the use of monetary compensation again, particularly after the change in tax laws concerning stock options and the
poor stock market performance of the early 1970s.

Growth and Stability

If growth and size provide no apparent advantage in terms of economies of scale, profits, or executive compensation, what can account for
growth? One possibility is, as we have argued, that growth increases

the organization's control over critical activities and reduces problematic dependence. The available evidence does suggest that size provides advantages in stability and the reduction of uncertainty. Caves (1970:286) found that the variance in profit rates among firms declines as one goes from small to larger corporations. Samuels and Smyth (1968) analyzed 186 British companies and found that the variability of profits over time decreased as the organization's size increased. Caves (1970) concluded that the monopolistic power enjoyed by large business enterprises is taken in the form of risk avoidance or uncertainty reduction rather than in the form of increased profits.

Starbuck (1965:463) has noted that the desire for stability may be one of the most important considerations in choosing the direction for growth. Osborn (1951) found that both the rate of profit for corporations that earned income and the rate of loss for corporations that suffered losses varied inversely with size. Stability is also evident in the pricing in oligopolistic markets. "The significance of price rigidity is that, in oligopolistic markets with partial collusion or imperfectly recognized mutual dependence, the immobility reduces the risks of misunderstanding and subsequent 'destructive competition' in the process of adjusting prices" (Caves, 1970:290).

Stability is also sought in market shares of industrial firms. Gort (1963) calculated for each of the 205 four-digit SIC industries two measures of stability of market shares from 1947 to the 1954 Census of Manufacturers. The first measure was the correlation coefficient between the 1947 and 1954 shares, and the second was the geometric mean of the regression coefficient of 1947 shares on 1954 shares and 1954 on 1947. The 1954 level of industry concentration was highly related to either measure of market share stability. Gort tested absolute size as an additional variable, but it accounted for little additional variance, indicating that the critical variable is control and stability of markets, which is enhanced by large size.

Saying that growth brings stability begs the question of why organizations desire stability and certainty. The reason why stability, or the reduction of uncertainty, is so important to organizations has already been implied. First, planning is largely impossible because organizational environments are enacted and can be anticipated only retrospectively. Second, the interdependence in environments that are composed of large organizations is more complex and more threatening to organizational survival, necessitating strategies to stabilize interorganizational relations. And, to the extent that organizational choice is constrained by the patterns of interdependence and influence emanating from the social context, then changes or disruptions in the patterns of influence and/or interdependence require new organizational adaptations to the social context, and there is always the risk that a new successful adaptation may not be found, leading to the disappearance of the organization.

Organizational size, in addition to providing stability, itself enhances the organization's survival value. As Starbuck has noted, "The importance of survival to an organization cannot be overstated" (1965:463). Steindl (1945) found the small firms were more likely to disappear than large ones. Large firms, because of their size, have larger constituencies to look after them, as well as more important and established relations with other segments of the business community.

Organizations that are large have more power and leverage over their environments. They are more able to resist immediate pressures for change and, moreover, have more time in which to recognize external threats and adapt to meet them. Growth enhances the organization's survival value, then, by providing a cushion, or slack, against organizational failure. Large organizations also develop larger sets of groups and organizations interested in their problems with willingness to assist in survival. For even interest groups making demands on large organizations are better off with the survival of the organization than without it. This is illustrated nicely by the rush of labor unions to petition the government to save Lockheed. The unions' demands for wages have a better chance of being met by a surviving firm than by one that is bankrupt.

Growth enhances an organization's survival potential because it provides additional stability and reduces uncertainty and also provides leverage for the organization in managing interorganizational relationships. This is not to say that growth is equally efficacious in providing these benefits to all types of organizations. Organizational growth potentially raises some problems for organizations. As organizations grow, they may require additional funding and be unable to generate this funding internally. Thus, growth may make the organization more dependent on its environment rather than less. But these new interdependencies can be, in turn, addressed, and in general, growth provides the ability for the organization to deal with its interdependence with the environment by absorbing portions of the interdependence and developing additional power with respect to those other organizations with which it is interdependent.

SUMMARY

One organizational response to interdependence is to absorb it. The available evidence on patterns of merger activity among industrial firms is consistent with this position. Mergers follow patterns of resource interdependence. Mergers made to cope with competitive interdependence are most likely when competitive uncertainty is highest—at intermediate levels of industrial concentration. It is possible to further refine the analyses, to consider the conditions under which purchase or sales interdependence will be most critical and, therefore, most correlated with patterns of mergers. Purchase interdependence is more important when the firm operates in a concentrated industry, thereby already possessing power with respect to customer organizations. Mergers to cope with sales interdependence are more likely when firms operate in industries with intermediate levels of concentration, where market uncertainty and, consequently, sales interdependence are most problematic.

Additional considerations of the profitability of mergers of various types and consideration of other forms of organizational growth are consistent with the basic theoretical position. Organizational growth and large size enhances the survival capacity of organizations, providing them with more power with respect to their environments and with more parties interested in their continuation. Size was found to be positively related to stability but unrelated to profitability. The evidence is consistent with the argument that firms grow and merge, a specific form of growth, to manage environmental dependence, but it is not consistent with many of the other arguments advanced to account for the behavior.

REFERENCES

Aharoni, Y. 1971. *The Israeli Manager.* Israeli Institute of Business Research, Tel Aviv University.

Alexander, S. 1949. "The effect of size of manufacturing corporations on the distribution of the rate of return." *Review of Economics and Statistics,* 31:229–235.

Bain, J. S. 1954. "Economies of scale, concentration, and the condition of entry in twenty manufacturing industries." *American Economic Review,* 44:15–39.

Bain, J. S. 1956. *Barriers to New Competition.* Cambridge: Harvard University Press.

Bain, J. S. 1968. *Industrial Organization,* 2nd ed. New York: Wiley.

Blau, P. M. 1964. *Exchange and Power in Social Life.* New York: Wiley.

Caves, R. E. 1970. "Uncertainty, market structure and performance: Galbraith as conventional wisdom." In J. W. Markham and G. F. Papanek (eds.), *Industrial Organization and Economic Development,* 283–302. Boston: Houghton Mifflin.

Dewing, A. S. 1921. "A statistical test of the success of consolidations." *Quarterly Journal of Economics,* 36:231–258.

Federal Trade Commission. 1970. *Large Mergers in Manufacturing and Mining, 1948–1969.* Statistical Report No. 5. Washington, D.C.: Bureau of Economics, Federal Trade Commission.

Galbraith, J. K. 1952. *American Capitalism: The Concept of Countervailing Power.* Boston: Houghton Mifflin.

Gordon, R. A. 1945. *Business Leadership in the Large Corporation*. Washington, D.C.: Brookings.

Gort, M. 1962. *Diversification and Integration in American Industry*. Princeton University Press.

Gort, M. 1963. "Analysis of stability and change in market shares." *Journal of Political Economy*, 71:51–63.

Hawley, A. H. 1950. *Human Ecology*. New York: Ronald Press.

Hogarty, T. F. 1970. "The profitability of corporate mergers." *Journal of Business*, 43:317–327.

Hunt, R. G., and G. W. Hunt. 1971. "Some structural features of relations between the Department of Defense, the National Aeronautics and Space Administration, and their principal contractors." *Social Forces*, 49:414–431.

Katona, G. 1951. *Psychological Analysis of Economic Behavior*. New York: McGraw-Hill.

Katz, D., and R. L. Kahn. 1966. *The Social Psychology of Organizations*. New York: Wiley.

Kelley, E. M. 1967. *The Profitability of Growth Through Mergers*. Pennsylvania State University Press.

Leontief, W. 1966. *Input-Output Economics*. New York: Oxford University Press.

Levine, S., and P. E. White. 1961. "Exchange as a conceptual framework for the study of interorganizational relationships." *Administrative Science Quarterly*, 5:583–601.

Lewellen, W. G. 1968. *Executive Compensation in Large Industrial Corporations*. New York: National Bureau of Economic Research and Columbia University Press.

Lewellen, W. G. 1969. "Management and ownership in the large firm." *Journal of Finance*, 24:299–322.

Livermore, S. 1935. "The success of industrial mergers." *Quarterly Journal of Economics*, 50:68–96.

McGuire, J. W. 1963. *Factors Affecting the Growth of Manufacturing Firms*. University of Washington, Bureau of Business Research.

McGuire, J. W., J. S. Y. Chiu, and A. O. Elbing. 1962. "Executive incomes, sales, and profits." *American Economic Review*, 52:753–761.

Mueller, D. C. 1969. "A theory of conglomerate mergers." *Quarterly Journal of Economics*, 83:643–659.

Nelson, R. 1959. *Merger Movements in American Industry*. Princeton University Press.

Osborn, R. C. 1951 "Efficiency and profitability in relation to size." *Harvard Business Review*, 29:82–94.

Pfeffer, J. 1972. "Merger as a response to organizational interdependence." *Administrative Science Quarterly*, 17:382–394.

Pfeffer, J., and H. Leblebici. 1973. "Executive recruitment and the development of interfirm organizations." *Administrative Science Quarterly*, 18: 449–461.

Reid, S. R. 1962. *Corporate Mergers and Acquisitions Involving Firms in Missouri, 1950–1959*. Ann Arbor: University Microfilms.

Reid, S. R. 1968. *Mergers, Managers, and the Economy*. New York: McGraw-Hill.

Roberts, D. R. 1956. "A general theory of executive compensation based on statistically tested propositions." *Quarterly Journal of Economics*, 20: 270–294.

Roberts, D. R. 1959. *Executive Compensation*. New York: Free Press.

Samuels, J. M., and D. J. Smyth. 1968. "Profits, variability of profits and firm size." *Economica*, 35:127–139.

Sherman, H. J. 1968. *Profits in the United States: An Introduction to a Study of Economic Concentration and Business Cycles*. Ithaca, N.Y.: Cornell University Press.

Simon, H. A. 1957. "The compensation of executives." *Sociometry*, 20:32–35.

Starbuck, W. H. 1965. "Organizational growth and development." In J. G. March (ed.), *Handbook of Organizations*, 451–533. Skokie, Ill.: Rand McNally.

Steindl, J. 1945. *Small and Big Business*. Oxford: Blackwell.

Stekler, H. O. 1963. *Profitability and Size of Firm*. Institute of Business and Economic Research, University of California.

Stekler, H. O. 1964. "The variability of profitability with size of firm, 1957–1958." *Journal of the American Statistical Association*, 59:1183–1192.

Stern, L. W., and W. M. Morgenroth. 1968. "Concentration, mutually recognized interdependence and the allocation of marketing resources." *Journal of Business*, 41:56–67.

Stigler, G. J. 1964. "A theory of oligopoly." *Journal of Political Economy*, 72:44–61.

Thompson, J. D. 1967. *Organizations in Action*. New York: McGraw-Hill.

Weiss, L. W. 1963. "Average concentration ratios and industrial performance." *Journal of Industrial Economics*, 11:237–254.

White, P. E. 1974. "Resources as determinants of organizational behavior." *Administrative Science Quarterly*, 19:366–379.

Williamson, O. E. 1963. "A model of rational managerial behavior." In R. M. Cyert and J. G. March, *A Behavioral Theory of the Firm*, 237–252. Englewood Cliffs, N.J.: Prentice-Hall.

CHAPTER SEVEN

THE NEGOTIATED ENVIRONMENT:
Establishing Collective Structures of Interorganizational Action

The most direct method for controlling dependence is to control the source of that dependence. One is not always in a position to achieve control over dependence through acquisition and ownership, however. Mergers require resources and may be proscribed in various circumstances. Courts can not merge with police, nor can district attorneys directly merge with either. Yet, from the point of view of each organization, being able to control the others would facilitate its own activities. If police could control prosecution and conviction, it would certainly ease their task of arrest; if prosecutors could control police, it would ease their function. Just because organizations can not merge with each other does not mean that mutual interdependence can not be coordinated. There are many informal mechanisms and semiformal interorganizational linkages that can be employed to coordinate the respective interests of various social actors.

Social coordination of interdependent actors is possible as a means for managing mutual interdependence. Behavior, in this instance, is not determined by hierarchical mandate but by agreements to behave in certain ways. Some of these agreements may be tacit, taking on the characteristics of social norms. Others may be more or less explicit. The bases for coordinating interorganizational behavior are so numerous and varied that they appear to be a natural part of organizational activity. It is expected that prior to negotiating a large contract, a salesman might take a customer to lunch, during which they might discuss the order and exchange information about the industry in general. It might be less expected that the two individuals would agree to purchase each other's products and not to sell or buy from each other's competitors. Each interaction, though varying in legality, represents an attempt to stabilize the transactions of organizations through some form of interfirm linkage. We call this the negotiated environment (Cyert and March, 1963) of organizations. We argue that the development of coordination among organizations derives from the same requirements for controlling interdependence that leads to merger and growth. When situations of exchange and competition are uncertain and problematic, organizations attempt to establish linkages with elements in their environment and use these linkages to access resources, to stabilize outcomes, and to avert environmental control. This chapter will present evidence indicating that coordination between organizations, like mergers, follows patterns of interdependence.

Organizations coordinate in many ways—cooptation, trade associations, cartels, reciprocal trade agreements, coordinating councils, advisory boards, boards of directors, joint ventures, and social norms. Each represents a way of sharing power and a social agreement which stabilizes and coordinates mutual interdependence. Such strategies are much more common than total absorption, as in merger, and are particularly useful when coordination is needed only occasionally. Organizations that need occasional access to the capital markets do not need to own or control financial institutions. Rather, what they need are assurances of support and capital when it is required. In other circumstances, coordination is achieved more readily when accomplished through a central coordinating organization. If there are many small competitors, merger, or acquisition, to substantially concentrate the industry is not feasible. Under such conditions, the development of strong business associations, such as the various farmer organizations or professional associations, is more likely.

Coordination has the advantage of being more flexible than managing dependence through ownership. Relationships established through communication and consensus can be established, renegotiated, and reestablished with more ease than the integration of organizations by merger can be altered. The disadvantage of these less complete absorptions of interdependence is the less than absolute control it provides over the other organizations. Interdependence is a situation in which another has the discretion to take actions which affect the focal organization's interests. For the organizations seeking greater autonomy, the critical task is how to reduce the other's discretion and simultaneously align it with the focal organization's own interests. The problem is how to coordinate the other's actions so that they are compatible with what the focal organization wants. Ownership solves the problem directly; compliance comes through the authority established by owning the other organization. Coordination through interfirm linkages depends on voluntary behavior; significant discretion remains with external organizations who may withdraw from the coordinated interaction.

Linkages to other organizations provide four primary benefits to organizations in their activity of managing environmental interdependence. First, a linkage to another organization provides information about the activities of that organization which may impinge on or affect the focal organization. Thus, interlocking directors among competitors may provide each with information about the other's costs and pricing and market strategy plans. Second, a linkage provides a channel for communicating information to another organization on which the focal organization depends. A banker sitting on the board of the local hospital is easily informed about the hospital's need for funds. Third, a linkage and the exposure it provides is an important first step in obtaining commitments of support from important elements of the environment. The board member, exposed to the problems and viewpoints of the focal organization, identified with the organization because of his visible board membership, naturally becomes committed to the perspective and needs of the focal organization. The fourth result of interorganizational linkage is that it has a certain value for legitimating the focal organization. Prestigious or legitimate persons or organizations represented on the focal organization's board provide confirmation to the rest of the world of the value and worth of the organization.

Linkages help stabilize the organization's exchanges with its environment and reduce uncertainty. Through negotiation and the arrangement of agreements with others, uncertainty is reduced directly. It is frequently in the interests of all parties to a relationship to have some degree of assurance and predictability regarding what they can expect from one another. Part of the interaction between individuals serves the purpose of maintaining the relationships and exchanging information about each other and their activities. Thus, the polite banter between a salesperson and a customer is not, strictly speaking, part of the business relationship, but it is important for maintaining the social bond between them, so that each knows he or she can rely on the other. The more each becomes enmeshed in the social networks of the other, such that there are overlaps in friendship networks and other business acquaintances, the more binding their relationship becomes and the more stable and predictable it is likely to be. It has been argued that one of the reasons for the high rate of divorce in industrial societies is that individuals are so mobile they are no longer enmeshed in the social networks of their families and friends. No longer bound together by the linkages among families and friends, a married couple are committed only by their own interpersonal linkage. At one time, marriage represented political alliances between families. The bond that linked the two individuals was not left to the chance of attributed affection and compatibility, but was the result of a public commitment enforced by the network of friends and families with a stake in the relationship and the alliance it created.

Interpersonal linkages play a psychological role in reducing uncertainty. People tend to prefer conducting their business with people familiar to them. Granovetter (1974) has illustrated this effect in his study of the process of getting a job. He found that a higher proportion of the higher paying jobs were obtained through personal contacts. He argued that the use of relatively short networks for recruitment provided advantages to the recruiting organization. The reliance on personal recommendations would give the person doing the hiring more confidence in the veracity of the recommendations and more knowledge about the person being recommended, since he would at least be somewhat familiar with the person doing the recommending. Festinger (1954) was one of the first social psychologists to systematically pursue the idea that the very process of attempting to make the right decision leads people naturally to seek out other individuals to determine what is the best thing to do. Under conditions of uncertainty, particularly, the use of social networks in decision making will be more pronounced. In Granovetter's study, it appeared that there was less tendency for technical jobs to be found through contacts than for managerial jobs. One might presume that technical skills are more readily assessable and that management talent is a more uncertain quantity to evaluate.

The tendency for organizations to develop and establish linkages with the environment, to associate with interdependent others, and to negotiate and standardize relationships, itself stems from the conditions of the environment and the situation of interdependence confronting the organization. When interdependence is problematic because it can lead to uncertain or unfavorable outcomes, the need to coordinate through social mechanisms is greatest, and this is particularly true when alternative ways of coping with the interdependence are not available. Linkages to the environment are channels of communication, and linkages arise when communication is most necessary between interdependent others. Linkages also serve as channels for persuasion and negotiation, and in these ways also stabilize interdependent relationships. By exchanging information about each other's activities, the organizations are in a position to plan more predictably. By obtaining commitments from each other, each organization develops certainty about the future course of the exchange.

NORMATIVE COORDINATION OF INTERDEPENDENCE

One simple and direct way to regulate behavior is to generate common expectations for all individuals operating within a certain set of circumstances. A norm is developed, and social actors are socialized to behave as prescribed by the norm. If most actors conform to normative expectations, then it becomes feasible for stable and regular relationships to be maintained.

There are three important theoretical issues regarding the norms that develop to regulate interorganizational relations. When do norms arise? What aspect of relationships is covered by the content of the norms? Under what conditions do social actors violate norms so that the preservation of the norm is threatened? The limited information available suggests that norms develop under conditions of social uncertainty to increase the predictability of relationships for the mutual advantage of those involved, and that norms break down when they cease to serve those interests. It is difficult to know whether a norm is operating to influence behavior. The presence of a norm may be inferred by two means. When all social actors behave in a similar way in a particular situation there is a possibility that they are being influenced by a norm. This is an imperfect way of knowing that a norm exists, for in fact the actors could be behaving independently, having arrived at the same decision because it represents the best way to behave. When theatergoers arrive for a play at eight, they are not following a norm, but rather responding to the schedule established by the producer. More telling evidence of a norm is discovered when the norm is violated. If sanctions are applied when the actors behave in certain ways, it is likely that a commonly shared norm is operating. Even this method, however, fails to distinguish between norms and the power of another to impose constraints. Norms˙ are commonly or widely shared sets of behavioral expectations. Although it is possible to be sanctioned by a single social actor, it is only when most social actors sanction the behavior that we can say a norm exists.

The earliest experiments dealing with the formation of norms were those conducted in the 1930s by Muzafir Sherif (1935). Sherif placed individuals in a darkened room and asked them to look at a single point of light projected on a screen. They were told to report how much movement they observed in the point of light. The light, in fact, never moved, but the normal visual process gave the appearance of movement. The situation is ambiguous because each individual's eye movements are random and uncoordinated with any other's. When estimates of the amount of movement were reported in the presence of others, the reports initially differed but over time became more similar. In this situation, every person provides a framework for the judgments of every other person. Since every person believes he or she is seeing the same phenomenon, each tends to adjust the judgments to accommodate the information received from the other people. Mutual adjustment results in a stable pattern of reporting. Sherif (1935) describes this phenomenon as the development of a social norm and indicates that it develops directly out of the situation of ambiguity and uncertainty facing the subjects.

Other research has been addressed to the issue of the transmission of norms from one generation of actor to another. Jacobs and Campbell (1961), working with the Sherif experiment, found that norms decay slowly as new persons enter a group and the original group members leave. In their experimental situation, confederates of the experimenter originally were involved in establishing the norm regarding the amount of distance the light was observed to move. On each trial, one of the confederates was replaced by a naïve subject, and after four trials, only subjects were in the group. This process of substituting a new subject for a previous member of the group continued for thirty trials. By that time, the group norm had moved very close to the answer normally given by subjects viewing the light and responding alone. Jacobs and Campbell showed the transmission of norms across experimental generations. Such transmission occurs because each individual is influenced by the judgments of the others as well as by what he or she observes. The verbal reports represent a compromise between what the others believe and what the individual sees. Over time, the artificially established norm is violated because it does not represent the world as the subjects experience it.

In a novel extension of the Jacobs and Campbell experiment (Zucker, 1975), it was found that artificially created norms will persist across generations with virtually no decay when the subjects believe themselves to be involved in a permanent social system. In this extension, individuals were told that they belonged to an organization and that the judgments of distance were made as part of this organization. Under these conditions, the norms persisted over the thirty trials. The subjects accepted the framework of observation because that framework was part of the accepted social structure of the organization. Adherence to norms is, then, in part an unintentional result of the acceptance of a larger social system as a frame of reference.

The norms which have evolved to coordinate interorganizational behavior are general in content and apply to issues of trust and predictability. Macaulay (1963), for instance, has examined noncontractual relations among business firms, relationships where there was little formalized planning or prescriptions concerning how the parties should behave. He noted that the customs which operate fill the gaps in the express agreements between transacting parties. Two of the most widely accepted norms were: "(1) Commitments are to be honored in almost all situations; one does not welsh on a deal. (2) One ought to produce a good product and stand behind it" (1963:63). It is interesting that these norms both stress the meeting of expectations in an exchange relationship. Both norms are related to the concept of trust. It can be argued that predictability in social relationships rests on the ability of the social actors to trust one another, so that each can rely on the assurances provided by the other.

Normative arrangements, assured by implicit understandings, are useful when formal arrangements are not permitted. Perrow (1970) noted that many large, diversified organizations have what are known as trade relations people. These individuals are responsible for managing the organization's exchanges with other firms so that firms which do business with the organization receive, in turn, the focal organization's business. Such arrangements are particularly important between diversified organizations when there is a good possibility of each firm being able to use some of the other's products. A firm, for example, may be both a builder of ships and a manufacturer of heavy equipment. If the firm buys its steel from a particular company for the ships, it may expect the steel manufacturer to purchase its heavy machinery in return. Although less common, there may even be cases of complex patterns of reciprocity among a number of firms simultaneously. Thus, the transport firm that purchases the ships from the ship manufacturer might be given the hauling business of the steel firm. Such reciprocal trade arrangements are illegal. Rather than make explicit contracts, a norm of reciprocity develops, over time, which is understood and accepted by all but is left implicit.

The norm of reciprocity is ubiquitous in social arrangements (Gouldner, 1960). Reciprocal agreements stabilize interorganizational relationships by providing an element of commitment that binds the transacting parties together. Doctors, for instance, engage in a form of reciprocity in their system of patient referrals. Sometimes the exchanges are asymmetric, so that some form of kickback mechanism is required. While we know of no studies of referral networks, we suspect that the frequency and cohesiveness of such networks would increase when competition is high and communications facilities are available, such as local organizations where the parties can get together.

The existence of reciprocal exchanges and referral networks need not develop from the explicit assignment of individuals (Perrow, 1970) to such tasks. It is likely that the development of the trade relations function occurred when organizations missed complying with the norms of reciprocity because of the increasing size, diversity, and complexity of their operations. Reciprocity could arise because a firm, in disposing of its product to another business, learns about that other business and how it can benefit the focal organization. Reciprocity can also develop from the sense of obligation that arises when one party does a favor for another. Several studies of individuals suggest that the acceptance of a favor implies an obligation to return it (Wicklund, 1974). We suspect that this tendency for acting on such implicit obligations, however, is dependent upon the extent of interdependence and the amount of communication among a set of social actors. Referral networks would be unnecessary if there was no interdependence and would be unstable if the actors did not communicate enough to know what each was referring to the other. There is considerable evidence that norms are more likely to be adhered to when individuals expect to interact in the future (Kiesler and Kiesler, 1969), and that sanctions are more likely to be applied against violators of norms when future interaction is anticipated (Kiesler, Kiesler, and Pallak, 1967).

A good deal of competition among organizations is eliminated through nothing more than the existence of norms against cutthroat competition. Professional groups and organizations frequently have explicit norms against competition, maintained through proscriptions against advertising. Doctors, lawyers, and architects all have restrictions on advertising, though recently federal agencies have attacked these restrictions for their anticompetitive impact. Kessel (1958) has described how norms developed in the medical profession so that one doctor would not testify against another in a malpractice case. Lawyers overcome such reluctance by bringing into their firms nonpracticing physicians who could provide the necessary medical expertise.

It has been demonstrated experimentally that stable patterns of behavior will evolve among individuals competing with one another (Rabinowitz et al., 1966). Each individual learns over time that by trying to maximize an individual outcome in an interdependent situation neither participant fares very well. As a consequence, patterns of action develop which stabilize the individual outcomes and permit stable outcomes to the competitors. These studies, using the minimal social situation in which outcomes are interdependent but no communication is permitted, illustrate the basis for the development of norms against competition. The norm formalizes a recognized need for stability and predictability in organizational operations.

In addition to norms against overly competitive behavior, there are also normative restraints on the use of interorganizational influence. Conflicts between organizations are occasionally governed by normative restrictions. Public agencies, and particularly those concerned with public safety and welfare, such as hospitals, police and fire departments, and public schools, do not face the same degree of strike threat from unions as economic organizations, partly because it is less acceptable to strike against public organizations. Thus, when workers for these organizations do strike, they generally attempt to develop elaborate social justifications for their deviant behavior, aligning their actions with the socially justifiable goal of improving service or helping the clients. When doctors withheld services in California in 1975 to protest rapidly increasing malpractice insurance rates, it was done, so it was claimed, to hold down the cost of medical care since the doctors could have passed the higher rates along to their patients.

One can hypothesize that the more normative constraints there are against a given interorganizational influence attempt, the more justification will be mustered to legitimate it. In a recent teachers' strike in Urbana, Illinois, the teachers passed out literature to citizens in shopping centers outlining their demands. There were six demands listed on the sheet. The first five dealt with dimensions which people tend to associate with the quality of education—class size, preparation time, facilities, etc. The last item on the list was salaries. When the school board agreed to meet the first five demands completely, the teachers, of course, still refused to settle. The board had cleverly caught the teachers at the game of attempting to cloak private demands in socially legitimate trappings.

Norms that arise in interorganizational relationships serve to alleviate the incidence of drastic change or surprise. Although we have no systematic data about their formation and alteration, an analogy to individual normative situations suggests that norms arise when uncertainty must be stabilized. When norms change, it is because they no longer serve the interests of the parties to the relationships and there is not sufficient social support to apply sanctions to violators.

From a managerial point of view, norms are not a particularly useful mechanism for coping with interdependence. Since norms represent a social consensus, it is not possible simply to mandate a normative environment to suit an organization's needs. Management's task is to become aware of the normative constraints affecting relationships among organizations, recognizing when and whether the norms are beneficial, and if not, taking an active role in attempting to change them by establishing a new social consensus through persuasion.

More direct methods of achieving interorganizational coordination are available. These methods involve developing interfirm organizations (Phillips, 1960) in a process involving the exchange of information, resources, and other commitments. Though the specific linkage mechanisms used may vary, in each instance there is some mechanism for exchanging information and some motivation to develop coordinated structures of interorganizational behavior.

INTERORGANIZATIONAL COOPERATION: THE CASE OF JOINT VENTURES

If communication among organizations is a necessary ingredient for achieving coordinated behavior, then vehicles which facilitate information exchange are likely to arise in the organizational field. One such mechanism for achieving coordination among organizations through a sharing of information and resource commitments is the joint venture. The term "joint venture," sometimes also referred to as a joint subsidiary, refers to the creation of a new organizational entity by two or more partner organizations (Boyle, 1968). We can refer to the creating organizations as the parents and the created organizations as the progeny. The joint venture involves the creation of a new, separate, organizational entity, jointly owned and controlled by the parent organizations. This new entity can incur debt, sign contracts, or undertake other activities in its own name and without consequence to the financial or legal position of the parents, except, of course, for their investment in the joint venture. The Arabian-American Oil Company (ARAMCO), formerly owned jointly by the Saudi Arabian government and four large oil companies, is an example of a joint venture. Bernstein (1965) distinguished joint ventures from mergers by noting that in joint ventures, only a portion of the parent companies' assets are pooled, while in a merger, complete pooling of assets takes place. However, Mead (1967) has argued that there is little significance in the distinction between joint ventures and mergers.

The joint venture permits the exchange of information between the parent organizations in the following ways. First, the joint venture may be staffed by top executives drawn from the various parent firms. Thus, since these executives obviously retain their contacts with the parent organizations, the joint venture becomes a forum in which executives from interdependent firms can meet. More important, the management of the joint venture requires the setting of price and the establishment of production targets and product policies which are similar to decisions that must be made in the parent organizations. If the joint venture is created in the same industry as the parent firms, it is unlikely that it will compete with them. Further, executives from the parent firms will be jointly involved in making decisions on pricing and production policies. It has been judicially recognized that in such a setting, the zeal of competition if it existed among the parent organizations may well be reduced. Not only is there an effect of information sharing, but since assets have been pooled, the parent organizations are likely to be bound together through such commitments. Mead (1967) examined joint bidding for oil and gas leases and found that in cases of joint bidding, the same firms were not likely to bid against each other on other leases in the same sale. Mead further found that such restriction on competitive activity persisted for as long as two years after the joint action, suggesting the amicable consequences of such alliances.

There are essentially three theories to describe why two or more formal organizations form joint ventures. Each is partially correct. The first theory derives from economics. Economists have argued that joint ventures may be established to spread the risks of new industrial developments, to establish joint or combined facilities for greater economy, to accumulate large amounts of needed capital, and to undertake programs that are too expensive for individual companies (Pate, 1969:16). Joint ventures, then, are economically justified when there are economies of scale in operation, when capital requirements are too large for a single organization, and when there is great technological risk from the joint venture. The risk factor is the one cited to justify joint ventures in oil and gas exploration. Joint ventures are justifiable if undertaken for these reasons, for they facilitate activities that would not otherwise occur at all.

Sociologists have infrequently examined joint ventures. When examined at all, it was from the perspective of both interorganizational and intraorganizational factors. Aiken and Hage (1968) studied joint activities (not quite the same thing, as they do not involve the creation of separate entities) among health and social welfare organizations. These authors proposed that common programs were undertaken to overcome the resource limitations of a single agency, while still maintaining the autonomy of the originating organizations. The question posed was what types of organizations would seek to overcome resource limitations, and the answer suggested was the more professional, complex organizations. Aiken and Hage (1968) focused on the structural correlates of the extent of participation in joint activities and found that complexity and professionalization of the staff both increased the likelihood that the organizations would engage in joint programs. This analysis, of course, does not directly test their central point that joint programs are a consequence of resource limitations.

The third conceptual framework for analyzing joint venture activity is similar to the one used to examine patterns of merger activity. This perspective assumes that joint ventures are another form of interorganizational coordination. If the principal problem organizations face is competitive and symbiotic interdependence, then it can be presumed that joint ventures are undertaken to reduce uncertainty and promote stability in the environment. Joint ventures are likely to evolve between organizations for which the cooperative exchange is mutually reinforcing. Organizations will interlock around joint ventures which coordinate otherwise problematic interdependence and are, therefore, primarily exchanges which reduce uncertainty about resource transactions.

Pate (1969) concluded that most joint ventures were not being undertaken for purposes of spreading investment risk or for undertaking technological development, but rather, were occurring among firms in a position either of competitive or of symbiotic interdependence with each other. Pate found that 80 percent of all joint ventures were between firms in competitive or buyer-seller relationships to each other. A similar result was reported by Boyle (1968), who also noted that for those joint subsidiaries for which size data were available, there was little evidence to support the conclusion that joint ventures were being undertaken because of resource limitations. The fact that joint ventures occur between organizations doing business or competing with each other does not necessarily imply that a collective structure has developed to manage interdependence. It may well be that the most likely candidates for projects involving risk or facilities sharing are other organizations with familiarity and interest in such undertakings. To determine whether joint ventures represent an attempt to reduce uncertainty among interdependent organizations, we must examine how the level of joint venture activity varies as a function of the potential for reducing uncertainty.

A Model of Uncertainty Reduction

Interorganizational behaviors, such as joint venture activities, can be analyzed from the perspective of uncertainty reduction and the development of interorganizational collective structures. The number of interorganizational behaviors linking organizations varies considerably across contexts, and it is our hypothesis that this variation can be partially explained by considerations of uncertainty reduction. The model proposed derives from considerations of *when* it is most advantageous to engage in activities for the purpose of interorganizational coordination and the reduction of environmental uncertainty. We expect the propensity of firms to engage in joint ventures would be a function of both the need for reducing uncertainty and the feasibility of doing so effectively through interfirm linkages. As we have argued in the case of mergers, the need for reducing uncertainty is a function of the industry structure. Uncertainty is greatest for organizations operating in industries of intermediate concentration, when there are enough large firms to affect one another's outcomes but too many to coordinate tacitly. At very high levels of concentration, uncertainty is reduced since each firm can observe the others' behavior and accommodate. Planning is possible because stable and accurate conjectural variations develop. Conjectural variations are defined as "one firm's conjecture (or expectation) of how the other firm's output will alter as a result of its own change in output" (Cohen and Cyert, 1965:231). When markets are not changing very fast and there are only a few participants, stability can be achieved through tacit coordination.

The uncertainty in organizational fields characterized by many small participants of relatively equal size is not likely to be troublesome. If firms are completely interdependent in an industry of 1000 firms, then when one changes, it will alter the business of the others by .1 percent. If the firms are not completely interdependent, the impact of change will have even less effect on the others. Thus, in unconcentrated industries, uncertainty *deriving from interdependence* is minimal, and hence the need for interfirm coordination is low. We would, therefore, expect that the need for coordination would be greatest in cases of intermediate concentration.

The need for interorganizational communication by itself would not necessarily lead to cooperative ventures, as there is also the consideration of the feasibility of coordinating interdependence. The ability to develop an effective and stable collective structure is, in part, restricted by the number of others that must be coordinated. If only two organizations are involved, the possibility that some set of activities could be found around which they could interact to mutual advantage would be higher than if there were four organizations. As the number of firms in the organizational field to be coordinated increases, the probability of developing an interorganizational structure through informal or semiformal linkages decreases. Conversely, the more concentrated the industry, the more easily a stable structure can emerge through pair-wise interactions. The greater the number of organizations there are which can affect the interests of the focal organization, the less likely it is that interfirm linkages will improve the situation.

The ability of n number of organizations to communicate with each other decreases as the number of organizations increases. The number of links required to fully connect a network of n organizations is: $n(n-1)/2$. When two organizations are involved, only one interchange is necessary. With 10 organizations, 45 linkages must take place to connect the organizations fully. Thus, the feasibility of developing an interfirm organization is increased when there are fewer firms to be organized.

The expectation that intermediate concentration in an industry is related to higher numbers of joint ventures is possibly contradictory to the prediction of other theories of joint venture activity. If joint ventures were, in fact, primarily designed to spread the risk of new ventures or technology, they would arise more when there were many small organizations which could not afford to absorb the risks alone.

To summarize the argument, we expect joint ventures (and other forms of interorganizational linkage) to be most likely when they are necessary and feasible, that is, to be a function of both the level of potential uncertainty and the number of firms with which it is necessary to communicate to achieve effective coordination. We propose, then, that the extensiveness of interorganizational communication through interlocking activities across industries can be explained by:

$$Y_i = aX_1^{b_1}X_2^{b_2} \tag{7.1}$$

where X_1 is the concentration in the industry, and X_2 is the absolute value of the difference in concentration from an empirically determined top of the hypothesized inverted U-shaped relationship. Transformed by logarithms, we have hypothesized that:

$$\ln Y_i = a + b_1 \ln X_1 + b_2 \ln X_2 \tag{7.2}$$

It is this form of the equation that will be estimated.

The Federal Trade Commission (1970) published data on the amount of joint venture activity by two-digit SIC manufacturing industry. Using data from 1966 through 1969, to avoid choosing an unrepresentative year, the total number of joint ventures by industry was computed. Concentration data from Weiss (1963), used in the study of merger activity, were again employed. If we let Y_1 be the *number* of joint ventures in each industry during the period, then the regression equation estimated is:

$$\ln Y_i = 1.953 + \underset{(.504)}{.940} \ln X_1 - \underset{(.377)}{1.156} \ln X_2 \quad r^2 = .57 \tag{7.3}$$

The numbers in parentheses are the standard errors of the respective regression coefficients. Both coefficients have the expected sign, indicating that joint ventures are more likely when concentration is higher and when there is less deviation from intermediate concentration. The two-variable formulation accounts for nearly 60 percent of the variation in the amount of joint venture activity across industries.

PATTERNS OF JOINT VENTURE ACTIVITY

Considerations of uncertainty reduction and interdependence management should not only permit the analysis of the number of joint ventures across industries, but, in a formulation similar to that used to analyze mergers, should explain patterns of joint venture activity as well. In a study of joint ventures among manufacturing and oil and gas exploration companies, Pfeffer and Nowak (1976) provided support for this theoretical position.

In a study of 166 joint ventures which took place during the period 1960 to 1971, Pfeffer and Nowak found that patterns of joint venture activity corresponded to patterns of transactions interdependence. To the extent organizations in industry A were more interdependent with organizations in industry B, a higher proportion of industry A's joint ventures were with industry B. The explanation for the observed relationship is the same as in the case of mergers. In order to manage resource interdependence with other organizations, linkages are used to stabilize exchange relationships. The pooling of resources, as in a joint venture, constitutes one viable form of interfirm linkage to manage transactions interdependence. In Table 7.1, correlations between transactions interdependence and joint venture activity are presented, as well as correlations examining the relationship between the concentration ratio and the proportion of employment engaged in research and development. This latter variable was included in the analysis to consider the explanation that joint ventures were undertaken to manage technological risk and uncertainty, as well as resource interdependence. In a multiple regression equation, both resource interdependence and technological intensity were statistically significant in explaining patterns of joint venture activity while the two variables were virtually uncorrelated.

In Table 7.2, correlations are presented for each of the 15 industries in which there were at least 3 joint ventures undertaken. As in the case of merger, there are profound differences across industries in the extent to which observed patterns of joint venture activity were accounted for by sales interdependence, purchase interdependence, both, or neither. As we did for our analysis of merger activity, we can

TABLE 7.1   Correlations of the Proportion of Industry *i*'s Joint Ventures with Industry *j* with Other Variables

Variable	Correlation	Level of Significance
Proportion of industry *i*'s sales to industry *j*	.28	$p < .001$
Proportion of industry *i*'s purchases from industry *j*	.25	$p < .001$
Proportion of industry *i*'s total transactions with industry *j*	.28	$p < .001$
Concentration ratio in industry *j*	.16	$p < .05$
Proportion of total employment engaged in research and development in industry *j*	.25	$p < .001$

consider which interdependence is likely to be more uncertain and derive hypotheses to account for these variations in correlations over industries.

First, paralleling our discussion for mergers, we can hypothesize that there will be a higher correlation between patterns of joint venture activities and purchase interdependence the higher the concentration of the organization's economic environment. The concept of concentration means the organization has few competitors for sales and, therefore, has market power with respect to its customers. Since the organization operating in a more concentrated environment faces little uncertainty in its transactions with customer organizations because of its power, it would be likely to focus its attention on managing its interdependence with sources of supply. This argument is confirmed by the data. For these 15 industries, there is a correlation of .50 ($p <$ .10) between the industry concentration ratio and the magnitude of the correlation between purchase interdependence and joint venture activity.

Sales interdependence is most problematic and uncertain when organizations are operating in an industry of intermediate concentration. This point has been developed both earlier in this chapter and in our discussion of patterns of merger activity. As predicted by this argument, there is a statistically significant correlation ($r - .41$, $p < .10$) between the difference in concentration from the median value and the extent to which joint ventures are related to sales interdependence

TABLE 7.2 Correlations Between Patterns of Joint Venture Activity Among Parent Organizations and Independent Variables for Individual Industries

Industry	s_{ij}	p_{ij}	t_{ij}	sci_j	c_j	Number of Joint Ventures
Oil and natural gas extraction	.61**	.40*	.62**	.57**	.32+	28
Food	.93**	.91**	.92**	−.08	.04	7
Lumber and wood products	−.07	−.06	−.07	.27	.36+	6
Paper	−.14	−.02	−.09	−.24	−.48**	4
Printing and publishing	.76**	.36*	.56**	.30+	.04	8
Chemicals	.93**	.97**	.96**	.56**	.21	64
Petroleum refining	.90**	.82**	.88**	.45*	.22	24
Rubber and miscellaneous products	.18	−.11	−.01	.37+	.25	3
Stone, clay, and glass products	.86**	.69**	.84**	−.07	.21	7
Primary metals	.68**	.92**	.83**	.13	.34+	23
Fabricated metals	.42*	−.01	.17	.73**	.26	5
Machinery, except electrical	.83**	.67**	.78**	.48*	.13	16
Electrical machinery	.89**	.90**	.95**	.58**	.31+	28
Transportation equipment	−.09	.48*	.07	.40*	.29	8
Instruments	.61**	.47*	.62**	.60**	.20	5

** $p < .01$ s_{ij} = proportion of industry i's sales to j
* $p < .05$ p_{ij} = proportion of industry i's purchases from j
+ $p < .10$ t_{ij} = proportion of i's total transactions with j
            c_j = concentration ratio of industry j
            sci_j = proportion of total employment in R&D for industry j

Since a joint venture involving industry i and industry j counts for both i and j when $i \neq j$, the numbers of joint ventures in the table add up to more than 166.

in each of the 15 industries. In short, joint ventures follow sales inter-dependence more closely in industries where concentration is inter-mediate and, consequently, where sales are more problematic and uncertain.

We can further parallel the analysis of merger activity by ex-amining the use of joint ventures to manage competitive interdepen-dence. While symbiotic relationships can exist between organizations in the same industry or with organizations in different industries, competitive interdependence occurs with respect to organizations operating in the same industry. Consequently, to consider the use of joint ventures to manage competitive interdependence, we consider only the proportion of joint ventures occurring between organizations operating in the same industry. We have argued that interorganiza-tional linkages to reduce competitive interdependence are more likely to be undertaken when industrial concentration is at an intermediate range. At very low levels of industrial concentration, when there are many firms active in the market, interorganizational linkages through joint ventures or other devices will accomplish little because there are so many organizations to be coordinated. On the other hand, with only a few firms, formal interfirm linkage, such as with a joint venture, is not required. In these highly concentrated environments, tacit inter-firm coordination can be achieved without semiformal mechanisms of interfirm communication.

The above argument is supported. The proportion of joint ven-tures made between firms in the same industry (two-digit SIC) is least at high and low levels of concentration ($r - .55; p < .01$). Further-more, in contrast to mergers, the proportion of joint ventures within the same industry is virtually uncorrelated with the proportion of transactions within the industry ($r = .07$). These results suggest that joint ventures are being used, even more than merger, to coordinate competitive interdependence and reduce competitive uncertainty. The correlation with industry structure is higher, and the correlations with transactions interdependence measures are lower, than in the case of mergers.

The results presented above are virtually unchanged when the relationship between the parent firms and the joint subsidiaries them-selves is considered. Overall, patterns of joint venture activities follow patterns of resource exchange. The proportion of joint subsidiaries founded in the same industry as the parent organizations is negatively related to the difference in concentration from the median value and is unrelated to transactions interdependence.

In considering joint ventures, we have found that both the num-ber and pattern of joint venture activity can be explained by considerations developed from our theoretical schema. Joint ventures can be analyzed as mechanisms for achieving interfirm coordination and can be predicted by considerations of resource interdependence, competitive uncertainty, and conditions that make various forms of interdependence more or less problematic.

COOPTATION: THE USE OF INTERLOCKING BOARDS OF DIRECTORS

Joint ventures represent, of course, only one form of interorganizational linkage; and involving a partial pooling of assets, they are only slightly less powerful interfirm linkages than merger. Somewhat less involving are the placing of representatives from environmental groups or organizations on advisory committees or boards of directors. Although interlocking directorates do not involve the same degree of commitment of resources as joint ventures, they do facilitate interactions between the organizations over time. Thus, the practice of interlocking boards provides opportunity to evolve a stable collective structure of coordinated action through which interdependence is managed. The establishment of friendships, the exchange of information, and the identification with the focal organization would all facilitate stable relationships among organizations. In royal houses, the practice of arranging marriages with members of other royal families to cement alliances was quite common. This practice of placing in one organization a representative from another to cement the bond between them continues to the present.

Interlocking directorates, we would argue, are one form of a more general tendency to manage the environment by appointing significant external representatives to positions in the organization. Known as cooptation, this is a strategy for accessing resources, exchanging information, developing interfirm commitments, and establishing legitimacy. Of all forms of interorganizational coordination, it is one of the most flexible and easiest to implement, two advantages that have made its use pervasive. The flexibility derives from the fact that any organization can create advisory or directing boards and appoint outsiders to them. The organization has considerable discretion and can choose to appoint representatives from the environment as dependence requires. Of course, individuals may refuse the invitation to join the board, but they would not be likely to do so if the linkage would offer advantages to them and their organizations as well.

There are three points of view which might explain the appointment of outsiders to an organization's advisory or governing board.

The first recognizes the possibility of appointing people with managerial skills to provide the organization with managerial expertise. For small organizations, with limited resources to develop a bank of management talent itself, this may be an important reason for selecting board members. We know of a small, privately held consulting firm which appointed to its board a vice-president of the World Bank, a major contributing author to *Fortune* magazine, and one of New York's top corporate lawyers. The board members were all friends of the president of the firm, and the appointments were made to tap their business expertise. The first advice the board offered was to get out of the business of selling time and develop a marketable product which could be leased for a fee. This was an idea that had not occurred to the president, and he accepted the advice. As a result, his business was transformed from one of consulting for a few hundred dollars a day to one of selling standardized information and analytic services to corporations throughout the world, with a tremendous increase in income.

Another perspective emphasizes the controlling or governing function of the board. Publicly held corporations, for instance, are required to establish boards which are elected by the shareholders, the owners of the corporation. The board's ostensible function is to oversee the organization's operations and ensure that the interests of the owners are served. Boards are empowered to choose the management of the corporation and to vote on major corporate decisions. In public organizations as well, the board may be viewed as a means of control over the organization. Indeed, advocates of greater social responsibility for business firms have occasionally held that boards of directors could accomplish this objective.

This second perspective ignores the fact that executives in organizations frequently have considerable control over the board. Not only does management itself own stock and occasionally sit on the board, but also management controls the information that the board members receive about the organization and its operations. Through the control of information, management can see to it that board members, who are only associated with the organization on a part-time basis, are essentially prevented from exercising control except under the most extreme circumstances.

Cooptation describes a situation in which a person, or set of persons, is appointed to a board of directors, advisory committee, policy making or influencing group, or some other organizational body that has at least the appearance of making or influencing decisions. Such appointment may occur either by means of an election or by direct invitation. Through providing at least the appearance of participating in organizational decisions, cooptation tends to increase support for the organization by those coopted. The perspective of gaining support is the third that one can use to analyze boards of directors. When an organization appoints an individual to a board, it expects the individual will come to support the organization, will concern himself with its problems, will favorably present it to others, and will try to aid it. Many aspects of the situation promote commitment to the organization (Salancik, 1977). A board member is publicly identified with the organization, and thus may be expected to accept some responsibility for its actions. The board meeting itself places the member in the presence of others, and one might expect the normal situational influences producing conformity, adherence to norms, and cooperation to operate. The individual is placed in a role, and the expectations associated with that role determine his or her behavior. Finally, the feeling of participating in setting organizational policy makes the individual both more identified with, and more committed to, that policy. The link between participation and cooptation, and the consequence for achieving support has been noted by Gamson (1968), among others. The individual has been coopted; the organization's interests become his or her interests.

How cooptation works is nicely illustrated by the following example. In a large state university in the early 1970s, various pressures were being felt by campus administrators from women faculty, nonacademic staff, and students who were concerned with discrimination in hiring, promotion, and pay, as well as in the recruitment and financing of graduate students. Since there were various federal regulations also proscribing discrimination, the university administration felt under some pressure to accommodate at least some of the demands. Furthermore, as a public university, it could not well afford to have active and vocal opposition. This university's solution (a strategy adopted by many others as well) involved the creation of a Committee on the Status of Women. To this committee were appointed the most vocal, well-connected, and powerful women active in this area. The committee was given some stationery, some research assistant support, and various other trappings of legitimacy, including occasional meetings with the chancellor and official recognition in university publications and documents.

While not completely successful in defusing the demands, as the women, after all, were not strictly coopted but were left on a committee to talk to each other, the strategy did substantially reduce the level of activity. The committee became concerned with maintaining its position in the organization, its recognition, its research assistance, its access to the chancellor. Given a stake in the organization, the group became concerned with maintaining that stake. Procedural issues began to dominate substantive concerns, the demands and complaints gave way to concern with bureaucratic procedures, and the level of opposition was significantly reduced. The quieting of opposition through the technique of setting up a subunit within the organization to absorb the protest has been described by Leeds (1964) and has been used in the War on Poverty to absorb active community political leaders. Participation, it seems, has two effects. First, persons become committed to organizational actions because they are identified as having cooperated in their formulation. Second, persons become committed to the organization to maintain their perceived access or influence. It becomes possible for individuals to justify going along on the basis that if they did not participate and comply, things would be even worse, and that it is worth some level of compromise to maintain the limited degree of access and influence that has been granted.

It customarily takes time to develop the degree of commitment to the organization that is required to obtain continuing support from significant segments of the environment, and appointments to boards offer two advantages in this regard. First, the appointment forces regular and legitimate contact with the organization, which provides opportunities for information sharing. The organization is in a position to obtain information from important interest groups and at the same time present information and persuade representatives to its own position. The second advantage is that potentially hostile elements can be neutralized by the fact that any one board member represents only a small proportion of the entire board in most cases. The forced need to make decisions may create pressures for uniformity (Festinger, 1950). The more integrated the person becomes with the organization and the fewer the ties to other organizations, the more likely will initial opposition be neutralized through conformity pressures. Select groups of elite who participate in decision making in secrecy with few ties to other group invariably develop social consensus. Selznick (1949) has described in detail the manner in which interests initially hostile to the Tennessee Valley Authority were coopted and convinced to support the project.

Loss of Organizational Autonomy

By appointing persons to the organization's governing board, particularly those with initially incompatible interests, the organization becomes susceptible to the influence of these individuals. While the organization may be in a position to socialize and obtain the support of external groups through cooptation, the organization may be altered by the bringing of external organizations into its councils. Selznick (1949) has noted the dilemma posed by the use of cooptation. While support may be achieved, the original aims of the organization may be diverted. In the instance of the Tennessee Valley Authority, local conservative agrarian interests, initially hostile to the project, were coopted but in the process many of the New Deal aims and objectives of the program were diverted, and many of the project's activities ultimately benefited these agrarian interests.

Possibly it is the belief that one can influence the organization that motivates outsiders to accept appointments to boards. Dooley (1969), who examined interlocking directorates among the 200 largest manufacturing corporations, noted that the interlocks between manufacturing organizations and financial institutions have been consistently maintained since the 1930s. Dooley also noted that these enduring networks limited the organization's autonomy and imposed restraint from the outside community on the organization. Our own analysis would suggest that such mutual exchanges are designed to impose constraint because it is simultaneously constraining (organizing) the actions of interdependent organizations that enables each to face a stable, certain environment. Having a bank representative on the board may help the organization obtain financing, but it also helps the bank place loans. While there is no specific evidence, it would seem that the stability observed by Dooley (1969) would be a function of the extent to which the network served the interests of all parties simultaneously. Levine (1972), using a smallest space analysis, developed a map of the sphere of influence derived from the patterns of interlocking among manufacturing and financial institutions. Levine found there was a great deal of geographic clustering, with banks occupying central positions in the networks. This geographic clustering may derive from the fact that organizations in the same area are most interdependent with each other, being more in competition for labor, capital, and markets.

INTERLOCKING DIRECTORATES AND COMPETITIVE UNCERTAINTY

Our argument is that directors are another form of interfirm linkage, used to manage the organization's relationships with the environment. If that is the case, then we should be able to use the same basic theoretical ideas, developed first to explain merger and then joint venture activities, to account also for variations in director interlocking. Such is the case, as can be seen in an analysis of the extensiveness of interlocking among competing organizations.

In our development of a model to predict the amount of joint venture activity, we argued that competitive uncertainty was highest when industrial concentration was intermediate (see Stern and Morganroth, 1968). At very low levels of concentration, there was little direct interdependence among individual firms; while in very concentrated environments, patterns of tacit interfirm coordination could develop without formal mechanisms (Phillips, 1960). We also noted that the effectiveness of a single interorganizational linkage in coordinating interdependent organizations would increase as the number of organizations to be coordinated decreased. These factors led to the development of Equation 7.2, which was estimated to explain the number of joint ventures undertaken in various industries. We can estimate a similar equation to see how much variation in the amount of interlocking among competitors can be explained.

The House of Representatives (1965) has published data on the number of interlocks among officers and directors of companies which operate in the same industry, defined on the five-digit SIC level of detail. The data focus on the director or officer as the interlocking agent. These data were aggregated to the two-digit industry basis, so for each two-digit industry, we have the number of interlocks among competitors, defined on a five-digit level of detail.

If we let Y_2 be the number of total interlocks, both officer and director, in each two-digit SIC category, and Y_3 be the number of officer interlocks, then estimating regression equations for the uncertainty reduction model yields:

$$\ln Y_2 = .453 + 1.286 \ln X_1 - 1.076 \ln X_2 \ r^2 = .51 \qquad (7.4)$$
$$(.604) \qquad (.451)$$

$$\ln Y_3 = 1.536 + 1.039 \ln X_1 - .466 \ln X_2 \ r^2 = .36 \qquad (7.5)$$
$$(.511) \qquad (.382)$$

Again, the numbers in parentheses are the standard errors of the regression coefficients and X_1 is the concentration ratio and X_2 is the absolute value of the difference in concentration from the median value; ln means the analysis uses the natural cog of the value. The model accounts for a significant proportion of the variation, and both variables enter the equation with the predicted sign. The amount of competitor interlocking is positively related to the level of concentration and negatively related to the difference in concentration from an intermediate level. For the 20 industries constituting the sample, all the coefficients except that for X_2 in Equation 7.5 are statistically significant.

SIZE AND COMPOSITION OF CORPORATE BOARDS OF DIRECTORS

Our hypothesis is that formal organizations use their boards of directors as vehicles for coopting important external organizations with which they are interdependent. Cooptation is likely to be used as a tactic when total control of interdependence through ownership is (1) legally proscribed, (2) impossible due to resource constraints, or (3) when partial inclusion is sufficient to solve the organization's problems of dealing with the external organizational context. Business organizations could be expected to use cooptation (1) with very large organizations, which would be costly to acquire; (2) with financial institutions, where total absorption is frequently forbidden by law; (3) with political bodies important to the organization, where merger is not feasible; and (4) with special interest groups that are temporarily politically potent.

Other studies of cooptation are consistent with this argument. Price (1963) noted that commissioners on the Oregon Fish and Game Commissions primarily served the function of a buffer between the staff which enforced the policies and the public. Commissioners were selected for their social positions and apparent legitimacy. While commissioners did effectively buffer the executive functions of the agencies, there was a cost to their use. The commissioners frequently "were acting for the benefit of their home communities and requiring a great deal of attention from the staff in order to keep informed on the problems of wild life management" (Price, 1963:378). Zald (1967), examining the boards of YMCAs in Chicago, found that the percentage of the board members who were business leaders was positively correlated with financial support of the organization. However, boards comprised primarily of business leaders tended to participate less in YMCA programs and suffered lower attendance at board meetings. Zald (1969) later attempted to specify the conditions under which board members would serve a direct administrative or environmental linking function. He suggested that board members would exercise more direct administrative control over the organization's functioning when they possessed access to external resources and the contingencies confronting the organization required those resources. Such a conceptualization is consistent with a contingency theory of power (Hickson et al., 1971). The argument is that control, or power, goes to those who can best cope with critical organizational uncertainties.

To examine if environmental influences were coopted, Pfeffer (1972) studied the size and composition of the boards of directors of 80 randomly selected nonfinancial corporations. The sample was drawn from *Dun and Bradstreet's Reference Book of Corporate Managements, 1969* and included large companies for which stock ownership was not concentrated in the hands of officers and directors.

Board size was taken to be a measure, albeit imperfect, of the organization's attempt to link itself with its environment. Presumably, a board could be kept to a nominal size, such as that required by law (in California, the minimum board size allowed is three). However, to the extent the organizational environment was heterogeneous, the need for representatives from the environment would be increased. Large organizations are more likely to be visible targets for the demands of others in the social context and thus need to establish linkages to the social context. Similarly, one might expect board size to increase as a function of the financial requirements and health of the organization. A large organization, regardless of its current financial position, has needs for greater access to capital and could be expected to appoint more representatives of financial institutions. Similarly, the worse the financial position of the organization, the more it would need the same financial representation. In the 80 firms sampled, the proportion of board members representing financial institutions was correlated .21 ($p < .04$) with the debt/equity ratio of the corporation, which means that the higher the proportion of debt in the capital structure, the higher the proportion of representatives from financial institutions there were on the board. The size of the board was correlated .47 ($p < .001$) with the sales of the firm, or its size, and .18 ($p < .05$) with the debt/equity ratio. The size of the board, then, was related to the organization's need for linkage to the environment, determined both by its capital structure and by its size and visibility.

In addition to the size of the board, relative proportions of inside and outside directors can be examined. Inside directors are those directors who are also managers of the corporation. Outside directors are persons who neither currently manage nor are retired managers of the firm. One would expect that as the potential environment pressures confronting the organization increase, the need for outside support would increase as well, leading to a larger proportion of outisde directors on the board. Firms with a larger debt/equity ratio had a higher proportion of outside directors on their boards, with the correlation being .34 ($p < .001$). In addition to financial position, one would also expect the size of the organization and whether or not it was regulated to affect the need for outside board members. Regulation, as a political process, should require organizations to be more concerned about their relationships with the external environment. A multiple regression equation was estimated to predict the proportion of inside directors from the factors of firm size, capital structure, and the presence or absence of either national or local regulation. The equation estimated was:

$$PI = 59.93 - .00373\ S - 5.560\ D - 27.12\ NR - 22.84\ LR\quad r^2 = .29$$
$$\qquad\qquad (.00301)\quad (4.899)\quad (7.39)\quad (7.665)$$

$$(7.6)$$

The signs on the coefficients were all in the expected direction, in that the prediction was that the proportion of inside directors would be reduced the larger the organization, the higher the proportion of debt in the capital structure, and if the organization were regulated. Almost 30 percent of the variance was explained by these few characteristics of the organization's context. These variables are only imperfect measures of the organization's requirement for environmental linkage, and of course, it is possible that the organization coordinates interdependence using other mechanisms besides director interlocks. In a subsequent study, Allen (1974) replicated the finding relating the size of the board to the size of the organization, but did not replicate the finding relating inside directors and directors from financial organizations to the capital structure. However, Allen considered only manufacturing corporations and may, therefore, have been confronted with less variation than in the sample used in the earlier study.

Cooptation and Organizational Performance

Numerous management writers have stressed the administrative role of boards of directors rather than the political or representational function (e.g., Koontz, 1967; Brown and Smith, 1957; McDougall, 1969; Juran and Louden, 1966). While we would not deny the importance of administrative expertise, our argument is that the board is primarily of use to provide linkage to the environment. Further, we would argue that an organization which does not effectively manage its environmental relationships would be less successful than one which does. Effectively managing environmental relationships implies that the organization is neither too closely nor too loosely linked with the appropriate context. An organization which has too many external members may be unduly constrained, while an organization with too few external board members may be unable to attain necessary support.

To examine the relationship between organizational performance and the structure of the board, we first have to determine what the optimal board structure would be for each firm. This was done by assuming that Equation 7.6, representing the pooled experience of the 80 firms, provides a means for estimating the optimal board structure for any given firm. The technique of using pooled estimates to derive an optimal policy is known as "bootstrapping" and has been employed in studies of production planning (Bowman, 1963) and in decision making (Slovic and Lichtenstein, 1971). Essentially, the pooled equation predicts what the ratio of inside directors should be, given those variables included in the model.

Our prediction is that deviations from optimal board structure, as estimated from Equation 7.6, will be negatively related to the organization's performance. To assess whether this hypothesis was consistent with the data, the estimated proportion of inside directors was subtracted from the organization's actual proportion of inside directors, and the absolute size of this deviation was used in the analysis. Two performance measures were used: the ratio of net income to sales (the profit margin), and the ratio of net income to stockholders' equity. Of course, there are large differences in profitability and profit margins across industries. Therefore, the two measures were standardized by comparing the performance with the average for the industry characterizing the firm. Eight firms had to be eliminated at this point because they were so diversified that no meaningful industry comparisons could be made. For the remaining 72 firms, both performance measures were significantly correlated with the organization's deviations from optimal board composition ($r = -.30, p < .005$). The direction of the correlation indicates that the greater the deviation from optimal board structure, the lower the organization's performance compared to the industry average.

HOSPITAL BOARDS OF DIRECTORS

There are some problems with the previous analysis of corporate boards which are not present in a subsequent study of the size, function, and composition of hospital boards of directors (Pfeffer, 1973). The analysis of corporate boards considered only a few dimensions of composition, such as the proportion of insiders and the proportion of persons from financial institutions. Furthermore, a cooptative intent was assumed in the study. In the study of hospital boards of directors, a questionnaire was mailed to hospitals in Illinois asking about the structure of the board, its function, and other aspects of the hospital's context. The 57 responses were used in the analyses.

One focus of this study was to examine whether the function of the board could be explained by the environmental context of the hospital. There are two functions of boards as mentioned previously—linkage with the environment and administration. The importance of these functions would be expected to vary with the context of the hospital. Some hospitals are dependent on their local community for funding and support, while others are less dependent. We would argue that those hospitals more dependent on local community support would have a greater likelihood of using the board for linkage with the environment rather than administration. On the other hand, hospitals less dependent on the local community would be less likely to use the board to obtain environmental support and would emphasize the administrative function of the board.

The chief administrator of each hospital was asked to rank from 1 to 4 in order of importance four possible functions of the board of directors and from 1 to 5, criteria by which board members should be selected. These two sets of questions can be used to assess the importance of the two functions of the board in the hospital. Administrators were also asked about the context of the hospital, including its ownership, source of funding, and size. There were three types of hospitals represented in the sample: private, nonprofit hospitals; private, nonprofit hospitals affiliated with religious denominations; and government hospitals. We expected that governmental and religious hospitals would be less dependent on their local communities. Governmental hospitals are linked to the governmental organizations that control their budgets, and while the community may be an important source of political support, it is not likely to be an important source of funds. Religious hospitals are somewhat less dependent on the local community also, as they are affiliated with national organizations that may provide support and control.

If boards are used to cope with those portions of the organization's environment most critical for survival, then we should find that fund raising will be more important for organizations which are private, nonprofit hospitals and which receive relatively more money from private contributions. For organizations which receive larger shares of their money from the government or are affiliated with the government or a religious denomination, we would expect that administration would be the more important board function. Also, size should affect the organization's dependence on the local community. Larger size would render the organization more visible, requiring more social support. Also, larger size probably means the organization would have larger financial requirements which might also increase dependence on the local environment.

In Table 7.3, simple correlations are presented between contextual variables and the two measures of the importance of environmental linkage as a function of the board. As can be seen in that table, the basic argument is supported. The importance of fund raising as a function of the board is more important to the extent the hospital obtains its capital budget from private donations and to the extent it is

TABLE 7.3   Correlations of the Importance of Fund Raising and the Recruiting of Board Members for Their Ability to Raise Money and Other Variables

Variable	Importance of Fund Raising as a Board Function	Importance of Selecting Board Members for Their Ability to Raise Money
Size of budget	.21°	.21°
Proportion of capital budget from private donations	.37°°	.33°°
Proportion of capital budget from the federal government	−.12	−.06
Religious classification	−.29°°	−.33°°
Private, nonprofit classification	.26°°	.31°°

° $p < .10$
°° $p < .05$

private and nonprofit. In Table 7.4, correlations between contextual variables and the function of the board in administration are presented. Administration is more important to the extent capital budget funds are obtained from the federal government, and less important to the extent funds are raised from private donations.

The size of the board is also predicted by the context of the hospital and the function the board is expected to serve. As we argued for the boards of corporations, board size is determined by the organization's need for integration with the environment. The greater the need for effective external linkage, the larger the board should be. For this sample of hospitals, the size of the board was positively associated with the size of the hospital ($r = .59, p < .001$) and was also associated with the importance of the function of the board for fund raising ($r = .46, p < .001$) and with the hospital being classified as private, nonprofit ($r = .39, p < .005$). Hospital boards were smaller to the extent that administration was perceived as a more important function of the board.

The composition of the board was related to the board's function and to the organizational context. Hospitals located in rural areas tended to have more persons from agriculture on their boards, while hospitals located in areas with large proportions of persons employed in manufacturing had more persons from manufacturing on the board. The proportion of persons employed in financial institutions was, as might be expected, correlated with the proportion of the capital budget obtained from private donations ($r = .43, p < .01$) and with the size of the budget ($r = .29, p < .05$). These results indicate that board members are chosen according to the functions they are ex-

TABLE 7.4   Correlations of the Importance of Administration and Recruiting of Board Members for Their Knowledge of Hospital Administration and Other Variables

Variable	Importance of Adminis-tration as a Function of the Board	Importance of Selecting Board Members for Their Knowledge of Hospital Administration
Size of the budget	−.12	−.23*
Proportion of capital budget from private donations	−.35**	−.17
Proportion of capital budget from the federal government	−.42***	.30**
Influence of the federal government on decisions	.28**	−.06
Religious classification	.21*	.12
Private, nonprofit classification	−.27**	−.19*

* $p < .10$
** $p < .05$
*** $p < .01$

pected to serve and in order to provide linkage between the organization and its social context.

Environmental Linkage and Organizational Effectiveness

We have argued that social linkages with external organizations are important for the organization as a means of stabilizing the environment and for ensuring favorable resource exchanges. We found in the case of interlocks among corporations that appropriate levels of linkage with the environment tended to be associated with higher levels of profitability. We can extend this question to our study of the 57 hospitals, and ask whether hospitals were differentially effective depending on how well integrated they were with their relevant social environments. One measure of effectiveness is whether the organization is able to sustain sufficient support from its environment to be able to acquire resources. This measure is similar to Yuchtman and Seashore's (1967) suggestion that the outcome of a generalized competition for resources provides a yardstick for measuring how well an organization is faring.

To examine the effectiveness of the hospitals, measures were collected concerning the growth in the number of beds and the budget during the preceding five years, as well as the addition of new facilities and services. All three measures constitute alternative indicators of the organization's effectiveness in acquiring resources. While growth is not the only, or a perfect, indicator of effectiveness, it does indicate the extent to which the organization can generate support and resources from the environment. In this instance, we hypothesized that the hospital's effectiveness would be greater when the board was selected for fund raising, community influence, and political connections, and would be less effective to the extent the board's primary function is administration and the composition of the board fails to match the hospital's social context. A board which does not represent the political and social interests of the community or does not coopt significant financial and political elites is not likely to be effective.

More detailed presentations of the effects of the board on the three measures of effectiveness and the other indicators of community support can be found in Pfeffer (1973). In summary, the analyses consistently substantiate the theoretical argument. Hospitals were found to have grown to the extent that they had political connections, financial institutional representation, and a board composition that was appropriate to the agricultural or manufacturing character of the area. With the exception that government hospitals tended to grow more, all of the factors associated with budget growth were dimensions of board composition and function and were consistently in the predicted directions.

To briefly summarize this study, the boards of directors from this particular sample of hospitals were selected quite explicity for their potential to link the organization to important sources of support, when the organization depended on the external environment more for support. Private hospitals, most dependent on the local community, selected directors who performed the task of integrating the institution with the environment. Government hospitals, less dependent on the local community, placed a greater emphasis on the administrative function of the board. Organizations that did not structure their board consistent with their requirements for integration with the social context were less effective than those that did. From this study and evidence on corporate boards, it would appear that cooptation as a strategy for managing the organization's environment is an important determinant of organizational support; and cooptation is itself explained by the organization's context and requirements for linkage with the environment.

ORGANIZED COORDINATION OF INTERDEPENDENCE: ASSOCIATIONS, COALITIONS, AND CARTELS

We have noted repeatedly that the development of tacit coordination among interdependent organizations is likely only when there are few organizations that must monitor each other. Even various interfirm linkages such as joint ventures and interlocking directorates can effectively coordinate interdependence only when there are a relatively few large participants in the market. When there are many firms, the organizing effectiveness of a few interfirm linkages is reduced, and coordination is more difficult to achieve except through some sort of centralized or hierarchical structure. We argue that it is under such conditions, when there are a large number of market participants to be organized, that the emergence of more formalized interorganizational mechanisms, with centralized structures of authority or information, such as trade associations or cartels, is likely.

A similar argument has been implicitly made by Phillips (1960). Noting the failure of traditional oligopoly theories, Phillips developed a theory of interfirm organization which took into account the environment in which the firms operated. Phillips argued that the parallel action of oligopolists comes when firms recognize their mutual interdependence and, therefore, consider themselves to be members of a group. He advanced four hypotheses about the structure of oligopolistic industries and the extent of formal interorganizational coordination. His first proposition was that the interfirm organization must become more formal, better planned, and better coordinated when there are a larger number of firms in the group (1960:607). Second, the more asymmetrical the distribution of power, given the number of firms, the less formal the interfirm organizations need to be to achieve efficient coordination (1960:608). Third, as the value systems of individual firms become more unlike, it is necessary to formalize the organization if the effectiveness of the oligopoly is to be maintained. One function of an interfirm organization may be to establish homogeneity through standardization of value systems, costing, and information (1960:609). Finally, Phillips argued that the better organized the groups from which purchases are made and to which sales are made, the more formal and more centralized must be the interfirm organization (1960:610).

Phillips' analysis hypothesizes some conditions under which oligopolies, if they are to effectively concentrate their power and co-ordinate actions, must use more formal and centralized structures for doing so. Williamson (1965) was also interested in the determinants of interfirm behavior. He developed a differential equation model which sought to account for alternative price wars and price stability in oligopolistic industries. He considered three variables: (1) a performance variable, (2) an adherence to group goals variable, and (3) an interfirm communication variable (1965:582). Williamson argued that the group socialization interpretation of oligopoly requires explicit attention to the communication process through which interfirm agreements are achieved and maintained. He found that environmental munificence appeared mainly responsible for firms shifting between cooperation and conflict (1965:580). When demand was expanding and the environment was relatively good to the business of each firm, the oligopoly was more likely to stay together. When business diminished and the profits in the group started to fall, it was more likely that the firms would begin to shade price and that price wars would occur.

It is interesting to contrast Williamson's approach with that taken by Litwak and Hylton (1962). Like Williamson, Litwak and Hylton saw the strategic problem in interorganizational analysis as that of analyzing coordination in a setting in which there were both elements of cooperation and elements of conflict. Their analysis focused on coordinating agencies like the United Fund as the device through which mutual conflicting interests were coordinated. They hypothesized that "co-ordinating agencies will develop and continue in existence if formal organizations are partly interdependent; agencies are aware of this interdependence, and it can be defined in standardized units of action" (1962:400). The principal point of contention derives from the following statement: "If the pool of resources in the community is suddenly decreased while the number of agencies remains the same or increases, then the agencies' competition for funds should increase and their interdependency increase accordingly" (1962:403). Litwak and Hylton's argument that community chest organizations should thrive during stringent times is exactly the opposite of Williamson's point about oligopolies. Litwak and Hylton's evidence for their hypothesis does not, however, really test it at all. They show a graph indicating that in times of major catastrophe, such as during the depression and during World War II, the amount of funds raised by the community chest was relatively greater. Their data really pertain to the amount of funds raised by the community chest, whereas their hypothesis refers to the proportion of local social agencies choosing to join or remain in the fund and the proportion of total charitable contributions developed through the coordinating agency.

A crucial question not discussed by Litwak and Hylton concerns how viable the coordinating mechanism is under different environmental conditions. One disadvantage of joining an interorganizational network is that the organization loses some autonomy. Part of the difference between Williamson's analysis and the analysis of Litwak and Hylton may be explainable by recognizing how the different environments of social service organizations and business organizations allow them to pursue individual goals when it is to their advantage to do so. When economic or other community conditions change to make charitable contributions scarce, the participating agencies may willingly exchange their autonomy for the promise of some funding rather than face drastically reduced resources. No other options are available to them. However, when economic conditions decline, industrial firms may be tempted to break away from the oligopoly and attempt to steal business from their competitors to increase profits. A comparable alternative is frequently not available to social service agencies. When such options for independent action are available, social service agencies may, in fact, act more like business firms. Litwak and Hylton, for instance, noted that agencies with national affiliation, such as the agencies concerned with diseases, may resist participating in coordinating agencies since such organizations have potential insulation from local fluctuations in the buffering provided by the national parent organization.

Trade Associations

The trade association is one collective structure that has developed to provide the centralized information and coordination that may be required in unconcentrated industries. Most industries, as well as professions, have associations whose major purpose is to exchange information and exert political influence for the benefit of their members. The formation of such associations has frequently coincided with major changes in the industry caused either by unexpected growth or decline or by threats from new external competition or the government. The American Hardboard Association, for example, was organized in 1952, some time after hardboard had become a viable, mass-produced building material and the postwar housing boom had made hardboard firms major materials suppliers. American psychologists formed the Association for the Advancement of Psychology in 1974 in response to various external pressures and threats. There had been cutbacks in federal funding for research, various federal legislation affecting the research and clinical practices of psychologists, and an attempt by the American Medical Association and the American Psychiatric Association to have the treatment of mental illness defined as a clinical practice limited to medical personnel. This latter move would have affected the payment of bills by Medicare and private insurers such as Blue Cross and would have harmed the business of many clinical psychologists, one of the largest groups within the American Psychological Association.

Gable (1953) has traced the rise and fall of membership in the

National Association of Manufacturers (NAM), a large and heterogeneous association of business firms, to the ebb and flow of political
activity relevant to business interests. When major legislation of interest to business is being contested, membership increases. For instance, when NAM was engaging in efforts to have the Taft-Hartley
collective bargaining legislation passed, membership increased. After
the legislation was passed and signed into law, membership declined
again, as business interest in political activity waned.

The growth of trade associations follows somewhat the same historical pattern as that of mergers. Many associations were founded
after the Civil War at a time of tremendous industrial development
and expansion. After the passage of the Sherman Act in 1890, trade
association formation diminished. The First World War caused another increase in association activity. In 1917, the War Industrial
Board actively encouraged the development of trade associations because it wished to deal with industry in organized groups to facilitate
war procurement. The number of associations grew from 800 to 2000
between 1914 and 1919. The prosperity and quiet of the 1920s caused
the number of associations to decline. The depression provided new
impetus for association activity. The National Industrial Recovery Act
of 1933 practically adopted trade associations as the mechanisms for
governmental control of industry.

While trade association activity rises and falls as conditions
change, it is also the case that trade associations at a point in time vary
across industries depending on the industry's need for government
action and for a mechanism to legally coordinate competition. Trade
associations do, indeed, have implications for competition. Associations serve as clearinghouses for information about industry sales,
prices, and costs. By explicitly sharing cost data and market information, organizations have at least some of the necessary information for
planning coordinated actions. Some associations actually have gone so
far as establishing pricing systems and attempting to enforce them. In
one such case reported by Latham (1952), the Cement Manufacturer's
Association established pricing to allocate markets. The Federal Trade
Commission successfully prosecuted this blatant attempt to fix price
but other, less obvious effects of information sharing may persist. Frequently, the mere publishing of price is sufficient to obtain compliance.
The American Bar Association, a professional association, regularly
published fee schedules and, furthermore, implied that charging less
than the minimum prescribed fees might be grounds for discipline for
professional misconduct. Recently, the justice department has begun
to attack the use of fee schedules, which can be found in a variety of
occupations and professions.

Industry associations also tend to reduce interorganizational variations by sponsoring research and product definition activities. Research and development jointly sponsored through industry associations allows new developments to be disclosed to all firms, avoiding surprises in design or technology that would disrupt competitive equilibria. Trade associations also restrain competition by providing standard definitions of products as well as guidelines on product quality. The American Hardboard Association, for instance, defines hardboard as "panel manufactured primarily from interfelted lignocellulose fibers consolidated under heat and pressure in a hot press to a density of at least thirty-one pounds per cubic foot." Failure to conform to industry standards can result in denial of approval for use in a variety of settings. Any action taken to standardize products would serve to diminish competitive uncertainty because one dimension of competition, differentiated product characteristics, has been eliminated. Furthermore, by providing standard definitions and operating characteristics, the association facilitates coordination of competitive activity among firms.

In spite of the pervasiveness of trade and industry associations, there is remarkably little literature about them. Stigler (1974), however, has surveyed some associations and provides some evidence that is not inconsistent with our earlier position about the conditions under which such associations are more likely to be important. We argued that associations, and other more formalized and centralized mechanisms of interfirm organization, were more likely to occur when there were too many participants in the industry to be coordinated either through tacit coordination or through semiformal interfirm linkages. In a study of some 60 trade associations, Stigler (1974:364) found that both the association budget and the size of the association staff were negatively related to industry concentration, though the relationship was not statistically significant. The direction of the relationship was as predicted, since we have argued that in more concentrated industries, less formal and centralized means of interfirm coordination can be used (e.g., Phillips, 1960). An important variable to examine is the extent to which firms need coordination. Stigler's analysis combines firms which impinge upon one another with those whose activities have little affect on each other.

Cartels

Cartels, which are even more overt attempts to organize a set of interdependent organizations, represent coalitions of organizations, with typically at least normative sanctions applied to members who deviate from proscribed cartel policies. In recent years, the most widely known cartel is OPEC, the Organization of Petroleum Exporting

Countries, but there are cartels of other raw material producers. While cartel arrangements are illegal under current United States antitrust legislation, they are acceptable and accepted ways of organizing markets in many parts of the world. Even in the United States some cartels have received specific exemption from antitrust regulations. For instance, the National Football League (NFL) for a long while enjoyed special privileges. The NFL faces the problem of keeping competition interesting and not letting teams get either too strong or too weak. To maintain competitive teams (if not competition among the team owners), the NFL has used a player draft system and a strong commissioner who can regulate the industry. The draft allows the weaker teams one year to acquire better players the next.

The United Fund is also a form of cartel, attempting to organize and coordinate social service agencies in a given community to avoid competition for donations and excessive overlapping of services. Like a cartel, the United Fund has come to define one of its most important objectives as being in control of as much of the local market for fund raising as possible. Also, like a cartel, member agencies enter or leave the United Fund as it suits their interests. The consequence of this is that the United Fund must distribute payoffs to agencies sufficient to maintain their participation. Such incentives are in the form of distributions from the United Fund collections. In a study of the allocations of 66 United Funds, Pfeffer and Leong (1977) found that the amount of money the agency could raise outside the fund, a measure of its ability to withdraw, was related to the amount of money obtained inside the fund, even after accounting for various measures of assumed community needs. Further, the relationship between outside support and the allocation from the fund was stronger for those agencies that were less dependent on the fund and on whom the fund was more dependent for visibility and fund-raising credibility.

The United Fund was an appropriate context in which to investigate interorganizational behavior because it was a public and legally sanctioned organization. Part of the problem involved in analyzing coordination of industrial organizations is that the analyst must investigate the phenomenon from the outside, developing hypotheses that test observable outcroppings of interorganizational activity. One does not distribute a questionnaire which asks, "How frequently do you collude with competitors?" Except for cartels that operate within the antitrust laws or in an international arena, coordination itself is not visible, but only its possible outcomes. However, since such outcomes, such as profits or stability, may be produced by a variety of other factors as well, the inference is always difficult. The relative invisibility of behavior, the reliance on ambiguous effects for determining whether or not behavior has occurred, and the historical precedents of economic theory, which argued that cartel activity had the single goal of maximizing joint income, have all served to impede the progress of understanding cartel and coalition behavior.

One notable exception is Macavoy's (1965) examination of the operation of the railroad cartels in the late 1800s. He noted that "when conditions in the market make it possible for an individual firm to make more money by being loyal to a cartel agreement than by being disloyal, the agreement is not likely to break down" (1965:14). Cartels that are successful guarantee a greater total amount of profits for all the firms involved, tend to lead to higher prices, and are accompanied by stable market shares for the participating firms.

Macavoy's principal contribution is an extremely clever analysis of railroad cartels, concluding that the formation of the Interstate Commerce Commission (ICC) resulted in a higher and more stable price than the cartel itself could maintain. Cartel behavior was measured by regressing actual prices charged against posted prices. When the cartel was effectively operating, the correlations were close to one. When the cartel was near dissolution, the correlations were quite small. Macavoy's study indicates that cartel behavior is potentially analyzable, and his conclusion about the effect of the regulatory agency is insightful.

Cartels, to remain effective, must punish cheaters. When a member firm breaks away from the cartel and offers a lower price to attract business, the cartel must match, and probably undercut, this new lower price. If cheating were permitted, all the firms might be tempted to try it, and the cartel would dissolve. Since the firms in the cartel know that when their cheating is discovered their price will be undercut, there would seem to be little reason for cutting price below that level set by the cartel. However, the price cut may be accidental or inadvertent, based on some mistake in the information received. The cheating may be difficult to detect, and the firm that cuts price may be able to make enough extra profits to compensate it for the fact that after the price cutting is discovered, the whole price structure of the industry will be substantially lower. Another reason for cheating may be that it is the first step in an agreement among participants reforming the cartel with a different allocation of market shares (Macavoy, 1965:23). If the reformation of the cartel leads to a higher market share for the first price cutter, then possibly it can be assumed that the destruction of the cartel was for the sake of the destruction.

Stigler (1964) has also considered the difficulty or ease of enforcing an oligopoly's higher price. For cartel or oligopoly arrangements, the problem is to maintain structure when any member can violate the price agreement, get away with it, and gain larger profits than by conforming. This is an inducement to break up the interorganizational organization, but the inducement is limited by the probability that the price cheater will get caught and have his profits reduced below that achieved by maintaining the cartel price.

Stigler noted that fixing market shares is the most efficient method of combating secret price reductions. "With inspection of output and an appropriate formula for redistribution of gains and losses from departures from quotas, the incentive to secret price-cutting is eliminated" (1964:46). Assigning buyers to sellers also eliminates the possibility of price cutting, but neither of these approaches are particularly viable where price fixing is illegal. Price cutting, Stigler argued, can be detected primarily from shifts in buyers from one seller to another. Thus, collusion is easiest to maintain when the buyers report fully and correctly the prices they were offered (the government placing contracts under competitive bidding), and collusion is most difficult to maintain when the significant buyers are constantly changing (1964:48). Stigler's most important conclusion is that since collusion depends upon being able to detect shifts in buyers, then the level of price is not responsive to the number of rivals, but rather is a function of the number of buyers, the proportion of new buyers, and the relative sizes of firms (1964:56).

An analysis of cartel arrangements must recognize that two sets of factors contribute to the creation and maintenance of the cartel—characteristics of the environment that affect the possibility of developing interfirm coordination and the motivation for organizing a cartel or belonging to one. The mere presence of conditions which might favor the development of a cartel does not mean that individual firms would be interested in joining. We suspect that the need for formal coordinating organizations would be greatest when conditions of uncertainty are greatest, organizations are interdependent, and the number of organizations to be coordinated, their differences in operating characteristics, or their similarity in size all require a more formal and centralized coordinating structure. The kinds of industries in which cartels have been discovered tend to be those that deal with undifferentiated products (oil, steel, cement, gypsum board). Product or market differentiation or segmentation reduces interdependence and makes cartels less necessary.

SUMMARY

In this chapter, we considered several strategies used by firms to manage environmental interdependence and uncertainty that do not involve the total absorption of portions of the environment. These strategies include the use of interlocking directorates, joint ventures, normative constraints on activity, and coordination achieved through more centralized structures such as as-

ׁociations and cartels. Semiformal interfirm linkages, such as joint ventures and director interlocks, were found to be used most frequently when industry structure was characterized by intermediate concentration. We indicated that it was in such circumstances that uncertainty resulting from interdependence would be most problematic. One of the striking things about this theoretical perspective on interfirm activities is that the same basic considerations, indeed the same variables, account for statistically significant proportions of the variation in a variety of different interorganizational linkage activities.

The common element in our consideration of strategies for developing a negotiated environment is communication. Both the need for and feasibility of interfirm communication is the single best predictor of interfirm activity. Since this is the case, one must reconsider the view that collusion among organizations is the consequence of evil or irresponsible corporate executives. In this reconsideration, we echo the thoughts of Leland Hazard (1961), expressed when he commented on the electrical machinery conspiracy case of 1961. Under some conditions, interfirm coordination is perceived to be a necessity for effective action. We have seen that joint venture activity and director interlocking does not occur randomly but, rather, in situations in which a set of interdependent organizations would adversely affect each other's performance if their actions were not coordinated. We have seen that the norms which develop as a consequence of stable exchanges among organizations arise to coordinate relationships so that they are more dependable and predictable for the organizations involved. And, we have seen from the discussion of associations and cartels that this management of interorganizational interdependence breaks down when the interests of the organizations are not served.

Explicit coordination among organizations is costly. When the external world is brought into the organization, through director interlocks, through the pooling of resources in a joint venture, or by giving authority to some interfirm organization, external influence over the organization is increased and its own discretion is simultaneously constrained even as it increases the certainty of its environment. Interorganizational coordination is both a natural and common phenomenon, and there is evidence that when one form of managing the environment is proscribed, another form will be adopted (Pate, 1969). Organizations are willing to bear the costs of restricted discretion for the benefits of predictable and certain exchanges.

One might ask why collusion is seen as so disturbing. Why are reciprocal trade agreements, cartels, and other forms of interfirm coordination considered to be undesirable? After all, the firms are just solving the problems of interdependence through establishing a negotiated environment. The problem is that the negotiated environment established is not one that includes the interests of all parties. If two organizations collude to reduce competition, they have created greater interdependénce for those who purchase their products. The problem with collusion, or coordination to establish negotiated environments, is that everyone is not freely and openly participating in the process. Only a few members of a market may be participating, and it is frequently the least powerful and the least organized whose interests are not served in the resultant interorganizational structure. As early as 1894, William Dean Howells remarked, "The struggle for life has changed from a free fight to an encounter of disciplined forces, and the free fighters that are left get ground to pieces between organized labor and organized capital." The truth of the statement is still evident, and the competing, organized interests include much more differentiated groups than merely labor and capital.

Solutions to interdependence lead to actions that create additional interdependence. As this interdependence, this interconnectedness, has increased, other solutions to the problem have been sought. One set of actions involves defining and mandating by law and social legitimacy how organizations shall operate and interact. We shall discuss this element of the external control of organizations in the next chapter.

REFERENCES

Aiken, M., and J. Hage. 1968. "Organizational interdependence and intra-organizational structure." *American Sociological Review*, 33:912–930.

Allen, M. P. 1974. "The structure of interorganizational elite cooptation: interlocking corporate directorates." *American Sociological Review*, 39: 393–406.

Bernstein, L. 1965. "Joint ventures in the light of recent antitrust developments: anti-competitive ventures." *The Antitrust Bulletin*, 10:25–29.

Bowman, E. H. 1963. "Consistency and optimality in managerial decision-making." *Management Science*, 9:310–321.

Boyle, S. E. 1968. "An estimate of the number and size distribution of domestic joint subsidiaries." *Antitrust Law and Economics Review*, 1: 81–92.

Brown, C. C., and E. E. Smith. 1957. *The Director Looks at His Job*. New York: Columbia University Press.

Cohen, K. J., and R. M. Cyert. 1965. *Theory of the Firm: Resource Allocation in a Market Economy*. Englewood Cliffs, N.J.: Prentice-Hall.

Cyert, R. M., and J. G. March. 1963. *A Behavioral Theory of the Firm*. Englewood Cliffs, N.J.: Prentice-Hall.

Dooley, P. C. 1969. "The interlocking directorate." *American Economic Review*, 59:314–323.

Dun and Bradstreet. 1969. *Reference Book of Corporate Managements*, 1969. New York: Dun and Bradstreet.

Federal Trade Commission. 1970. *Large Mergers in Manufacturing and Mining, 1948–1969*. Statistical Report No. 5. Washington, D.C.: Bureau of Economics, Federal Trade Commission.

Festinger, L. 1950. "Informal social communication." *Psychological Review*, 57:271–282.

Festinger, L. 1954. "A theory of social comparison processes." *Human Relations*, 7:117–140.

Gamson, W. A. 1968. *Power and Discontent*. Homewood, Ill.: Dorsey Press.

Garceau, O., and C. Silverman. 1954. "A pressure group and the pressured: a case report." *American Political Science Review,* 48:672–691.

Gouldner, A. W. 1960. "The norm of reciprocity: a preliminary statement." *American Sociological Review,* 25:161–178.

Granovetter, M. S. 1974. *Getting a Job.* Cambridge, Mass.: Harvard University Press.

Hazard, L. 1961. "Are big businessmen crooks?" *Atlantic Monthly,* 208: 57–61.

Hickson, D. J., C. R. Hinings, C. A. Lee, R. E. Schneck, and J. M. Pennings. 1971. "A strategic contingencies' theory of intraorganizational power." *Administrative Science Quarterly,* 16:216–229.

House of Representatives. 1965. Staff Report to the Antitrust Subcommittee of the Committee on the Judiciary, *Interlocks in Corporate Management.* Washington, D.C.: Government Printing Office.

Jacobs, R. C., and D. T. Campbell. 1961. "The perpetuation of an arbitrary tradition through several generations of a laboratory microculture." *Journal of Abnormal and Social Psychology,* 62:649–658.

Juran, J. M., and J. K. Louden. 1966. *The Corporate Director.* New York: American Management Association.

Kessel, R. A. 1958. "Price discrimination in medicine." *Journal of Law and Economics,* 1:20–53.

Kiesler, C. A., and S. B. Kiesler. 1969. *Conformity.* Reading, Mass.: Addison-Wesley.

Kiesler, C. A., S. B. Kiesler, and M. S. Pallak. 1967. "The effect of commitment to future interaction on reactions to norm violations." *Journal of Personality,* 35:585–599.

Koontz, H. 1967. *The Board of Directors and Effective Management.* New York: McGraw-Hill.

Latham, E. 1952. *The Group Basis of Politics.* Ithaca, N.Y.: Cornell University Press.

Leeds, R. 1964. "The absorption of protest: a working paper." In W. W. Cooper, H. J. Leavitt, and M. W. Shelly (eds.), *New Perspectives in Organization Research,* 115–135. New York: Wiley.

Levine, J. H. 1972. "The sphere of influence," *American Sociological Review,* 37:14–27.

Litwak. E., and L. F. Hylton. 1962. "Interorganizational analysis: a hypothesis on co-ordinating agencies." *Administrative Science Quarterly,* 6:395–420.

Macaulay, S. 1963. "Non-contractual relations in business: a preliminary study." *American Sociological Review,* 28:55–67.

MacAvoy, P. W. 1965. *The Economic Effects of Regulation.* Massachusetts Institute of Technology Press.

McDougal, W. J. (ed.). 1969. *The Effective Director.* School of Business Administration, University of Western Ontario.

Mead, W. J. 1967. "The competitive significance of joint ventures." *The Antitrust Bulletin,* 12:819–849

Pate, J. L. 1969. "Joint venture activity, 1960–1968." *Economic Review, Federal Reserve Bank of Cleveland,* 16–23.

Perrow, C. 1970. *Organizational Analysis: A Sociological View*. Belmont, Calif.: Wadsworth.

Pfeffer, J. 1972. "Size and composition of corporate boards of directors: the organization and its environment." *Administrative Science Quarterly*, 17:218–228.

Pfeffer, J. 1973. "Size, composition and function of hospital boards of directors: a study of organization-environment linkage." *Administrative Science Quarterly*, 18:349–364.

Pfeffer, J., and A. Leong. 1977. "Resource allocation in United Funds: an examination of power and dependence." *Social Forces*, 55:775–790.

Pfeffer, J., and P. Nowak. 1976. "Joint ventures and interorganizational interdependence." *Administrative Science Quarterly*, 21:398–418.

Phillips, A. 1960. "A theory of interfirm organization." *Quarterly Journal of Economics*, 74:602–613.

Price, J. L. 1963. "The impact of governing boards on organizational effectiveness and morale." *Administrative Science Quarterly*, 8:361–378.

Rabinowitz, L., H. H. Kelley, and R. M. Rosenblatt. 1966. "Effects of different types of interdependence and response conditions in the minimal social situation." *Journal of Experimental Social Psychology*, 2:169–197.

Salancik, G. R., 1977. "Commitment and the control of organizational behavior and belief." In B. M. Staw and G. R. Salancik (eds.), *New directions in organizational behavior*. Chicago: St. Clair, Press, pp. 1–54.

Selznick, P. 1949. *TVA and the Grass Roots*. University of California Press.

Sherif, M. 1935. "A study of some social factors in perception." *Archives of Psychology*, 27, No. 187.

Slovic, P., and S. Lichtenstein. 1971. "Comparison of Bayesian and regression approaches to the study of information processing in judgment." *Organizational Behavior and Human Performance*, 6:649–744.

Stern, L. W., and W. M. Morgenroth. 1968. "Concentration, mutually recognized interdependence and the allocation of marketing resources." *Journal of Business*, 41:56–67.

Stigler, G. J. 1964. "A theory of oligopoly." *Journal of Political Economy*, 72:44–61.

Stigler, G. J. 1974. "Free riders and collective action: an appendix to theories of economic regulation." *Bell Journal of Economics and Management Science*, 5:359–365.

Weiss, L. W. 1963. "Average concentration ratios and industrial performance." *Journal of Industrial Economics*, 11:237–254.

Wicklund, R. A. 1974. *Freedom and Reactance*. Potomac, Md.: Lawrence Erlbaum Associates.

Williamson, O. E. 1965. "A dynamic theory of interfirm behavior." *Quarterly Journal of Economics*, 79:579–607.

Yuchtman, E., and S. E. Seashore. 1967. "A system resource approach to organizational effectiveness." *American Sociological Review*, 32:891–903.

Zald, M. N. 1967. "Urban differentiation, characteristics of boards of directors and organizational effectiveness." *American Journal of Sociology*, 73:261–272.

Zald, M. N. 1969. "The power and function of boards of directors: a theoretical synthesis." *American Journal of Sociology,* 75:97–111.

Zucker, L. G. 1975. "The role of institutionalization in cultural persistence." Paper presented at the West Coast Conference on Small Group Research, Victoria, Canada, April 1975.

CHAPTER EIGHT

THE CREATED ENVIRONMENT:
Controlling Interdependence Through Law and Social Sanction

In the preceding chapters, we have argued that organizations deal with uncertainty and external constraint either by absorbing the interdependence or by negotiating an arrangement that adequately coordinates behavior. While such mechanisms may often be sufficient, in richly connected social systems they may not be effective. The solutions to the problems of some organizations can frequently create problems for others. In dense organizational networks, interests become entwined and interconnected. The feasibility of coordinating interests under such circumstances diminishes, and the possibility of absorbing all the necessary interdependencies disappears completely.

In 1974, Pan American and Trans World Airlines (TWA) were both in serious financial difficulty. Competition between them for foreign routes, the competition of foreign airlines, which frequently received government subsidies, and the absence of any domestic routes for Pan American, all had combined to make their business position precarious. While the two might have negotiated informally to reduce

188

competition, diversified into other routes, or reduced service on unprofitable routes, all of these actions were impossible because the companies operated in a regulated industry. Route adjustments can be made in the airline industry only with the approval of the Civil Aeronautics Board. In the same year, rapidly rising postal costs posed a threat to the survival of small magazine publishers. This time, the source of the problem was the United States Postal Service, which was raising its rates for all classes of mail service quite rapidly and could do so quite successfully because of its virtual monopoly position as a mail carrier. Since small magazines serving specialized audiences raise a larger proportion of their revenues from subscription sales, as contrasted with mass circulation magazines that obtain relatively more from advertising, the rise in postal rates was a serious problem. It could lead to charging higher subscription prices, which, in turn, would drive away subscribers. While the larger magazines might consider doing their own delivery or contracting with an independent firm, these actions are more readily possible when there is a large circulation in a limited geographic area. In both the airline and the magazine instance, the same solution was attempted: each went to the government and asked for special treatment. TWA and Pan American requested direct cash subsidies; the small magazine publishers requested exemption from the increased postal charges.

When dependence is not capable of being managed by negotiating stable structures of interorganizational action, organizations use yet one other class of strategies. Faced with otherwise unmanageable interdependence, organizations seek to use the greater power of the larger social system and its government to eliminate the difficulties or provide for their needs. The organization, through political mechanisms, attempts to create for itself an environment that is better for its interests. It may seek direct cash subsidies, market protection, or may seek to reduce competitive uncertainty by charging competitors with antitrust violations. In 1960, there were 255 private antitrust suits filed against corporations, or about 60 percent of all antitrust action. By 1972, the number of suits filed had jumped to 1299, which constituted 94 percent of all antitrust suits filed during that year. The courts and the government are increasingly replacing the market in determining which organizations will survive and prosper.

Zald (1970) has been one of the few theorists to explicitly develop a political economy framework for organizational analysis. He identified internal and external elements of both polity and economy. "Organizations, in attempting to achieve ends, form external alliances, curry favor, and conform to the requirements of agents having greater power" (1970:231). Zald noted that political relations may develop among significant suppliers or customers or among major competitors of the organization, much as they develop between the organization and the state (1970:233). What Zald leaves rather implicit is the fact that the external and internal political and economic components are inextricably bound up with each other. Organizations may use political means to alter the condition of the external economic environment. In turn, economic power may build political power in the external environment, to be used at some future time for the organization's interests in survival and resource acquisition. Thus, companies and trade unions contribute to political parties, serve in government, and are involved in the party organizations on many levels. If the political system is viewed as a collection of competing interest groups (Latham, 1952), then business firms and other formal organizations constitute an important segment of the constituency.

Organizational attempts to alter or adapt the external political or economic environment are almost limitless. As economic activity has become increasingly subject to government regulation or intervention, the attempts of formal organizations to adapt the environment, rather than adapting to changing environments, have become more frequent. In some respect, the activities of trade associations and the operation of informal interfirm organizations in industries are additional examples of organizational activity in the external political environment.

In this chapter, we argue not only that organizations are constrained by the economic, social, political, and legal environments but that in fact, law, social norms, values, and political outcomes reflect, in part, actions taken by organizations in their interests of survival, growth, and enhancement. "Environment" is not only a given, to be absorbed, avoided, or accepted. It is itself the dynamic outcome of the actions of many formal organizations seeking their own interests. The political environment is one important means by which the organization links itself into the social system from which it continually draws support and legitimacy. The political context is a place for formally institutionalizing the survival of the organization, guaranteeing it access to the resources it needs.

We shall illustrate these points by examining (1) organizational legitimacy and social values, (2) the history and effects of government regulation, and finally (3) the organization as a political actor, involved in lobbying to alter the environment. The perspective of the environment as outcome, as well as constraint, is not original with us. Hurst's (1964) review of the legal history of the lumber industry of Wisconsin noted how the government's desire for rapid economic development and the interests articulated by the timber firms brought about legal policies for incredibly rapid disposal of public lands. The laws of property and contract were written to encourage certain patterns of private usage. Conceptions of what was the public good changed, partially by actions of, and reactions to, the timber companies, altering regulations of property usage and the use of state funds for conservation. Neither laws nor social values are immutable. Any examination of how and why change occurs should consider the influences of formal organizations attempting to alter their environments for their advantage.

RATIONALIZATION OF POLITICAL CHOICE

There are, of course, some important differences between politically constructed environments and those which emerge from other methods of managing interdependence. In political decision contexts, a third party is involved in the situation, with discretion to act in ways which affect the interdependent organization but with no direct stake in the outcome. The decision maker, establishing a negotiated environment, directly experiences the consequences of the actions taken; political decision makers most often do not directly experience the consequences of their actions. Considering the decision maker in the political arena, the relevant interdependence is not the one which is affected by the decision, but rather the interdependence between those affected by the decision and those making the decisions. Access to the political decision makers and the possession of convincing arguments become more important determinants of outcomes.

A second major feature of third-party intervention is that decisions are most frequently applied across the board to entire classes of individuals and organizations, going well beyond the time and place of the original problem. When a cartel fixes a price, its impact is restricted to those organizations who consider it in their interests to be in the cartel, and the cartel can reset the price as changing economic conditions demand. When government regulation fixes a price, no one is free to charge any other price, and changes in the price must await the interminable delays of the administrative process. Thus, political decision making is much less adaptive, with considerably less flexibility and with a greater chance of spreading the effects of disasters (or benefits) among a greater number of individuals and organizations.

The fact that political solutions to organizational problems involve working through individuals and organizations who are themselves not party to the situation has important implications for organizational strategies. When two competitors have problems because of their interdependence, it is enough for them to know that each would be served by lessening competition. However, the benefit of a few actors is generally not sufficient grounds on which to base political action. The political decision maker may need to know that the reduced competition would benefit the general social welfare before he or she will take action. Thus, for the organizational strategist attempting to achieve organizational interests through a political mechanism, it may be more important to know about the pressures and interests of the decision maker and how they align with his or her own ends.

By operating in the political arena, the organization is forced to consider a much broader social reality than just its own interests. The political system expands the number of persons who must view as acceptable the organization's activities. The ability of the organization to link its interests or activities to the current social norms may be the most important aspect of ensuring its interests are served. Some limits are placed on the appeals which organizations may make upon political figures. Some implicit assessment of social worth of the desired action is made, and the concept of national need or national priority must be mustered to justify the action.

In one sense, the political process can be described as the search for rationalizations upon which to base actions and decisions. Recent United States aid to the shipbuilding industry and the unions of crew members presents an illustration of this point. The ship industry is served by a variety of special legislation. There are subsidies provided to construct ships in American shipyards. These subsidies make it possible for American shipbuilders to compete on the world market against foreign shipbuilders who can build a less expensive product. Legislation restricts the use of foreign registry vessels (with foreign, less expensive crews). For instance, foreign ships are restricted from carrying goods between two American cities, a provision which hurts Hawaii and Puerto Rico but few other localities. And, in the recent grain sales to Russia, one of the provisions specifies a certain amount of the purchased grain must be carried on American vessels. These laws are not justified in terms of the benefits they provide to the shipbuilding industry, which has received billions of dollars of direct cash subsidies, or to the unions who benefit. Rather, justification is always couched in terms of maintaining national security through having a strong merchant marine and a viable ship construction industry. Most, if not all, special interest legislation is justified in terms of some national policy benefiting the common good. Organizational strategists seeking to use political solutions to problems of dependence must develop arguments in such terms, or risk failure. Occasionally, as in the case of the removal of market protection for sugar, the situation is so absurd that the effort ultimately fails. It is easier to justify the need to have a strong merchant marine or to protect the domestic oil industry by import quotas than it is to claim that national security rests on protecting the domestic sugar industry.

ORGANIZATIONAL LEGITIMACY

Because organizations are only components of a larger social system and depend upon that system's support for their continued existence, organizational goals and activities must be legitimate or of worth to that larger social system. "Legitimation is the process whereby an organization justifies to a peer or superordinate system its right to exist, that is, to continue to import, transform, and export energy, material, or information" (Maurer, 1971:361). This legitimation is accomplished partially through the organization's espousing legitimate goals and partially through its own value system.

> In the most general sense the values of the organization legitimize its existence as a system. But more specifically they legitimize the main functional patterns of operation which are necessary to implement the values, in this case the system goal, under typical conditions of the concrete situation. Hence, besides legitimation of the goal-type and its primacy over other interests, there will be legitimation of various categories of relatively specific subgoals and the operative procedures necessary for their attainment. There will further be normative rules governing the adaptive process of the organization, the general principles on which facilities can be procured and handled, and there will be rules or principles governing the integration of the organization, particularly in defining the obligations of loyalty of participants to the organization as compared with the loyalties they bear in other roles (Parsons, 1956:68).

Legitimacy is bound up with social norms and values; and while it is not correlated perfectly with either law or economic viability, it bears some relationship to both. Actions or organizations may be legitimate, even though they are not specifically provided for in the law. Many customs of interpersonal and interorganizational behavior, such as reciprocity and fair but limited competition, are functional for the integration of the social system and hence are accepted but rarely codified into formal laws. Similarly, many economically viable activities are neither legitimate nor legal, such as selling narcotics. There are also instances when activities are both legitimate and economically viable, though not legal, such as the production and selling of liquor during prohibition. If an activity is legitimate to a large enough segment of the population, it will probably be economically viable as well.

Many norms and values governing formal organizations are only imperfectly formalized in the legal system. Perhaps the best example of this are the laws governing incorporation. The charters of incorporation granted and the powers and reasons for granting them are quite general and broad in scope. Whether or not the corporation, once established, can in fact survive depends upon whether it develops goals and operations perceived as legitimate by the larger society.

On occasion, the social acceptability that comes with legitimacy may be more important than economic viability. The Penn Central Railroad bankruptcy demonstrates the case of an organization which is not particularly economically viable, but which will not be allowed to die because the transportation provided is necessary to the nation. The airlines were subsidized by the government for quite some time to keep them in operation, and the protection of infant industries or industries vital to national defense also illustrates governmental or social actions to assist in the survival of enterprises which might otherwise collapse if left unprotected from the vagaries of the economic environment.

Legitimacy is a conferred status and, therefore, always controlled by those outside the organization. As with the existence of social norms generally, legitimacy is known more readily when it is absent than when it is present. When activities of an organization are illegitimate, comments and attacks will occur. While legitimation is a social process, it is not clear how large a part of the social system must confer its approval for an organization or its practices to be considered legitimate. We suspect that legitimacy need not be conferred by a large segment of society for the organization to prosper. If objections are raised by some groups regarding the acceptability of an organization, the problem of legitimacy will be a function of how widely the objections are dispersed and whether sufficient interest is generated to support the opposition.

It is also not clear by what process social collectivities come to judge an activity or an organization as being legitimate or illegitimate. Legitimation is, probably, a retrospective process, in which verbal justifications are mustered to provide approval for the organization in question. Organizations may themselves seek to establish their status in society by generating statements of their goals which in the current environment would be found to be acceptable by the relevant publics. When values change, organizations alter and restate their goals to give the appearance of supporting the new ideas. Thus, when the energy crisis was of great concern, one could observe many institutional advertisements for oil companies, automobile firms, and others which pointed out how the various organizations were contributing to the solution of the problem. A few years earlier, when the environment and its protection was the rage, the same organizations and the same advertising activity was directed toward showing how this problem was being handled.

The retrospective character of legitimacy or of social justification generally implies that an organization reviews its past actions and outputs in the context of current societal values and interests. For the most part, there is ambiguity in the nature of action so that it is feasible to provide new justifications as values change. There is also a great deal of diversity in the values held by a society and its various subgroups at any one point in time, so that the probability of an organization finding some subgroup espousing values consistent with its activities would be quite high. The retrospective nature of legitimacy also implies that the same activity can be seen as simultaneously legitimate and illegitimate, in that the multiplicity of values and the ambiguity of reality permit conflicting interpretations of organizational actions. When CBS paid H. R. Halderman, the aide to President Richard Nixon who was convicted for his role in illegal government and political activities, for an interview broadcast on "60 Minutes," the other networks attacked the practice of paying for news as illegitimate. On the other hand, the payment might be considered legitimate if you are concerned with the privacy of the individual and his right to refuse to discuss his life with others. One could see the act as a bribe to obtain exclusive coverage and competitive advantage or as a just payment for providing a public service. Legitimacy is determined as a function of other factors relating to the organizational action, such as self-interest or the desire to maintain the actions for reasons which may or may not be legitimate.

For the organizational strategist, the ambiguous, retrospective, and socially constructed nature of legitimacy are important features. The manipulation of social legitimacy to maintain social support can be achieved only if one is able to argue convincingly that what the organization is doing is just and worthy. The attempt by CBS to justify its payment to Halderman as payment for a personal memoir, while plausible, implicitly argued that the person was to be rewarded for being a participant in a national scandal. CBS might have had more success by adopting the position that Halderman should not be allowed to escape public questioning simply because he refused interviews without payment. Instead of being perceived as a competitor willing to violate industry norms for market advantage, it is possible that CBS could have presented itself as a public servant willing to bear the cost of blackmail to serve the public interest and bring details of the political scandals to light. Organizational legitimacy is not a given. It is the consequence of the interpretation of actions, and there is some latitude for describing actions in terms of legitimate social values.

An important part of the management of the organization's environment is the management of social legitimacy. While legitimacy is ultimately conferred from outside the organization, the organization itself may take a number of steps to associate itself with valued social norms. For one thing, the organization may alter or design its actions so that they fit a concept of established legitimacy. That is, the organization may conform to social values. Alternatively, the organization may attempt to change the social definition of legitimacy with respect to its own operations and objectives. Since the alteration of broad social norms and values is quite expensive and problematic, what typically occurs is that the organization attempts to have its operations redefined as legitimate by associating them with other generally accepted legitimate objectives, institutions, or individuals. We can illustrate both strategies.

Clark (1956), examining the operation of adult education in California, has noted that in the course of adapting to the demands of their environment, the organizations involved may have inadvertantly changed their norms and values. Organizations, he suggested, may transform their initial values in the process of adjusting to emergent problems. Social values are more likely to be altered when they are precarious because they are not strongly held or widely shared. Social values tend to be precarious when they are undefined, when the position of functionaries is not fully legitimized, and when they are unacceptable to the host population (1956:328–329). Clark makes the interesting observation that the precarious values are likely to evoke movements or crusades. Firm values require no efforts, but problematic norms or values require action to ensure their continuance. Similarly, legitimate organizations are less likely to have to take actions to legitimize themselves than are organizations which are on the fringes of legitimacy.

Adult education in California was viewed as a marginal activity. Nominal public funds were made available; administrators and instructors were accorded low status by their peers; and there were many who questioned whether it was even a legitimate school activity. This marginal status in part derived from the historical origins of adult education as remedial training for immigrants to learn English and other knowledge required for citizenship. As immigration gradually declined, this remedial function ceased to be important. But the organization did not simply go out of existence. State funding was allocated on the basis of attendance, and adult education confronted, on the one hand, an uncommitted clientele, and on the other, the fact that the students were the rationale for existence (Clark, 1956:333). Not surprisingly, there developed what Clark referred to as an "enrollment economy" (1956:333). Schools adapted their functioning to attract students, since students were the sine qua non of existence. Because of the diverse population served, the course offerings became increasingly heterogeneous, and the school adapted freely to changes in public taste. In other words, the adult educational system became primarily a service enterprise. This transformation, moreover, was completely at odds with common notions that educational direction was the educator's responsibility not the student's. Thus, in meeting short-term demands for enrollment, the adult educational system operated outside the norms of legitimate educational practice and thereby lost some of its claims for educational respectability (1956:335).

While the adult education system was quite able to justify its budget on the basis of enrollment, it began to find its role in the educational system challenged, and with it, its claim to resources. This forced the adult education system to develop rationales for its service function. One rationale was that adult education was a valuable public relations tool for the school system, as it involved more people with the schools. Another rationale was that adult education was geared to the demands of the public and thus could meet the complaints that schools were not relevant to public needs. As a consequence of the organizational adaptations to the environment, which required enrollment for funding, educational values were largely replaced by these new ideologies in adult educational programs. There is currently even some evidence that acceptance of these values is beginning to permeate the more traditional programs in education.

The Case of the American Institute for Foreign Study

The adult education system in California is a case of an organization adapting to environmental demands and then justifying its adaptations with an ideology more suitable than its former precarious educational values. In contrast, the American Institute for Foreign Study (AIFS) provides an example of an organization responding to a threatened illegitimacy by identifying itself, its methods of operation, and its output with other already legitimate social institutions. By associating with these institutions, the organization hoped to attain a similar legitimacy.

AIFS was, in 1965, affiliated with International Study Services, Inc., (ISS) a profit-making organization which was, in essence, a tourist agency catering to an educational clientele. ISS did not operate its tours under its own name, but worked closely with the nonprofit AIFS. The day-to-day affairs of ISS and AIFS were operated jointly, and the same men comprised the management of both organizations. ISS held an exclusive, noncancellable long-term contract with AIFS with "responsibility to plan the itineraries, reserve the necessary accommodations, engage the local guides, hire the buses, and reserve the airline and rail tickets" (AIFS, 1969:12). In short, AIFS provided the contact with the public and much of the legitimation. ISS, the travel agent, merely reaped the financial benefits.

The AIFS-ISS arrangement was designed to meet the problem of legitimacy faced by organizations in the business of arranging foreign study tours for high school students. Several attacks had been made on the operation of such tours and the entire concept. These attacks made legitimacy problematic and important for the arranging organizations. One attack came from Wallace Roberts in a February 15, 1969, *Saturday Review* article entitled, "Thirty Thousand Innocents Abroad." He criticized commercial summer foreign study programs, questioned both their value to the student and the legitimacy of running educational programs for profit. Roberts wrote, "Many people felt that education and commercialism are mutually exclusive" (1969:61). Four years earlier, Dr. Stephen Freeman pointed out that the ability of the teacher to sell the program might not be a good guide to whether he can adequately supervise students in Europe, and further, since reimbursement (and profits) increase with enrollment, there are pressures to admit any student regardless of qualifications or even lacking psychological maturity. Freeman concluded that the selection of the leader-chaperone should be totally separate from recruitment or financial considerations.

Further difficulties faced foreign study programs. In *A Guide to Study Abroad* (Garraty and Adams, 1962), a reference work on foreign study, the Freeman critique was repeated and the emphasis was on study abroad during the college, rather than the high school, years. Even the State Department entered the picture, publishing pamphlets urging careful consideration of summer study programs, especially with respect to the financial capabilities of the contracting organizations.

Confronted with such problems of legitimacy, AIFS-ISS took a number of steps to: (1) legitimate the organization, (2) legitimate the output, and (3) legitimate the methods of operation. AIFS approached the issue of incompatible goals in education and profit making most directly. They ran the foreign study program under a nonprofit organizational banner, and the business interests were under a separate organization. AIFS claimed to be a "nationwide non-profit association of students and teachers" (AIFS, 1969:3). ISS was created as a shareholder-owned, for profit Connecticut corporation. Once the nonprofit nature of AIFS was established, the organization employed a consistent and distinctive tone in its contacts with the environment. Students became "members," salespeople became "area secretaries," and pretrip orientation material became "an extensive information service on foreign countries." Through its nonprofit status, AIFS was able to use the social legitimacy lodged in the political system. It obtained endorsements from prominent politicians under the blanket of being a nonprofit educational organization. The specific mechanism used was a scholarship program. AIFS funded scholarships and asked prominent political figures to hand them out. The politicians, of course, obtained favorable publicity in return. According to an AIFS brochure:

> In 1968, on the suggestion of the late Senator Robert Francis Kennedy, a tax-exempt Scholarship Foundation was organized for the Institute. During 1969, the Foundation awarded scholarships to deserving students worth approximately $30,000. . . . For example, last year awards were administered by Senator Edward Kennedy, Senator Jacob Javits, Mayor John V. Lindsay, and Congressman Lowell Weicker. School systems involved in the scholarship program in 1969 included those in New York City, San Francisco, Chicago, Pittsburgh, Boston, and Detroit (AIFS, 1969:32).

The first payoff for coopting political support came in late 1967. President Johnson proposed a travel tax to improve the United States balance of payments. Johnson's proposal for a tax on overseas expenditures would have added approximately $7.50 a day to the costs of AIFS-ISS students and teachers, or about $300 to the cost of a program already priced at about $850. AIFS-ISS and the Foreign Study League made presentations seeking an educational exemption from the regulation to a congressional subcommittee holding hearings on the proposed legislation. Senator Javits, involved in administering the AIFS scholarship program, spoke out publicly indicating his strong support for a student-teacher exemption. There was also opposition from politicians not associated with AIFS; and eventually the entire idea was dropped.

The nonprofit umbrella and the scholarship program were also important in obtaining support from prominent educators and the organized educational system itself. Given the general unease about mixing education with private business, the active support of the educational establishment would be an important selling point with parents, while opposition from the establishment would have made the success of the program more difficult. AIFS-ISS used two strategies to obtain educator support. One was to give teachers and administrators the opportunity to travel through Europe free in return for recruiting students. Administrators and officials of higher rank could be retained as program evaluators or administrators. Such persons would be flown to Europe to evaluate or assist in the administration of the program. AIFS also used a traditional form of cooptation with its board of advisors in Europe and America. The American board was divided into a high school division and a college division. In 1969, the 22 members of the High School Advisory Board consisted of 10 principals, 8 superintendents or deputy superintendents, the executive secretary of the National Council of Teachers of English, the Deputy Commissioner of Education from Connecticut, the chairman of an English department, and the Director of Editorial Services for the National Association of Secondary School Principals. The advisors were well dispersed throughout the states and selected from large cities.

The issue of whether this cooptation was worth anything in enhancing the legitimacy of the organization can be raised. While a conclusive answer cannot be provided, there is some evidence AIFS was able to obtain considerable support from educators for planning and marketing programs. In addition to the regular AIFS summer study program, AIFS offered what were known as cooperative programs.

> The American Institute for Foreign Study offers school systems, teacher's associations and other educational organizations an opportunity to sponsor their own foreign study program without financial risk or logistical worries (AIFS, 1969:36).

In practice, the school system personnel themselves took most responsibility for designing the study program, planning the itinerary, and choosing the foreign campus. The travel planning was left to AIFS, which also assisted in recruiting participants. Cooperative programs tended to be large and, of course, legitimate, since the educational group itself did the planning. Of the six cooperative programs run in 1969, five of the districts or organizations running the program were represented on the United States Board of Advisors. In the case of the sole exception, the study tour was organized by the Distributive Education Clubs of America, a subsidiary of National Student Marketing which later purchased ISS.

To further ensure its legitimate image, AIFS selected fine European universities as study sites for regular programs, even though theoretically, any site in Europe could be used for study. European campuses offered some unique advantages. They could be listed in the AIFS brochure and thus increase the legitimacy of the educational operations. Participating institutions included the Hebrew University in Jerusalem, the University of Salzburg, and the Royal Academy of Music in London. Actual course operations were left in the hands of faculty from these universities. The schools themselves received some money during a time when their facilities would go either unutilized or underutilized.

AIFS also concerned itself with the legitimacy of its output—the students who had studied abroad. It was important to provide the feeling that the program was an educationally worthwhile experience. From a survey of participants of past programs, it was determined whether a chaperone (high school teacher) or a student who was in college received credit or advanced standing. If so, the school from which standing was received was listed in the AIFS brochure under the heading of Academic Credit (AIFS, 1969:9). It was pointed out in the third paragraph under that heading that advanced standing was the result of proficiency examinations and hence could not be directly attributed to AIFS. However, AIFS did provide certificates for the work completed and implied that these were instrumental in obtaining credit. It is not possible to determine what percentage of students enrolled in the program received credit or advanced standing, but the list of 144 universities is impressive, including Chicago, Stanford, Vassar, Brown, Vanderbilt, Northwestern, and Purdue.

In addition to the obvious implication that the program facilitated advanced standing in these various colleges and universities, the listing tells the reader that former AIFS participants attended these fine and select colleges.

From a management perspective, the problem of legitimation is to link the organization or its actions to beliefs about how the action will lead to values that are socially accepted. It is a problem similar to that faced by advertisers: convincing the buyer that the product will provide the experiences or features desired. While the advertiser has only the consumer to attend to, the legitimacy of an organization is assessed by many relevant publics. In the case of AIFS, without the implied support of the educational establishment, it is not likely that it could have attracted students, teachers, and parents. And while it may have been sufficient to attract students with the opportunity for travel in Europe, this would not have sufficed for parents and educators. AIFS was able to operate with low costs because of the support of the educational establishment—most of the marketing function was handled free by educators.

Organizational legitimacy appears to be especially problematic when organizations of different distinguishable types compete for the same resources or the same activities—in the words of Levine and White (1961), for the same domain. Thus, legitimacy may be an issue in competition between public and private organizations. Public organizations, like municipally owned utilities and the United States Postal Service, may find it easier to claim social worth than their private counterparts. Legitimacy affects the competition for resources. An organization which can convince relevant publics that its competitors are not legitimate can eliminate some competition. The issue of education versus commercialism is not merely of theoretical interest. There are bread-and-butter resource implications for organizations competing over appropriate organizational domain activities.

Legitimacy may also be a problem when an established organization begins new or different activities. With custom and time, social norms develop to legitimate the activity, but new ventures may confront problems of legitimating their operations and output, especially if the new activity is really something quite different and not an imitation of something already being done. Legitimacy is also problematic when the organization's methods of operation or output run counter to social norms.

In any case where organizational legitimacy is a problem, the organization may either adapt to conform to societal expectations or achieve legitimacy through identification with socially legitimate goals or institutions. In any case, the definition of legitimacy is likely to evolve and change as organizations and classes of organizations either adapt to social norms or to resource pressures, or attempt to identify with previously legitimated norms and institutions. Social legitimacy for an organization is, therefore, always somewhat problematic, because the definition of what is legitimate is continually changing and evolving, partially in response to the actions taken by organizations.

REGULATION: STATE MANAGEMENT OF THE ECONOMIC ENVIRONMENT

While organizational survival is enhanced by legitimacy, it is also enhanced by economic viability, especially in the case of private organizations. Classical economics suggests that economic viability is bound up with conditions such as low-cost production and meeting market demand better than the competition. This is not invariably the case. In large segments of United States industry, the market mechanisms that form the basis for economic theory are simply not permitted to work, as regulatory procedures and agencies are substituted.

Historically, regulation and government intervention in the marketplace have been the dominant forms of economic systems. Both the state and those who benefited from its decrees favored the administered and predictable controlled economy which regulation permits over the unpredictable, uncertain outcome of unrestrained competition. Adam Smith's *The Wealth of Nations* made the argument in 1776 that welfare would be better served through competition. That book has so much significance because its position was so unusual for that time. Some have suggested that the free market economy is an unusual form, and that the regulated, governmentally controlled economic system is not only the customary form of economic system but also the one that is likely to emerge in all countries as interdependence increases and resource scarcity becomes a greater problem. Certainly, there is evidence that in times of national crisis such as wars or rampant inflation, government intervention in the market increases.

The regulation evident in the United States often began from the intention to overcome the evils of unrestrained competition. Competition is a form of natural selection in which only firms suited to the environment survive. However, the disappearance of competitors is troublesome, particularly for those competitors that are disappearing or failing, and consequently, a variety of market interventions were designed to overcome the harsh effects of competition. Such things as loans to small businesses, the Fair Trade laws that forbade price cutting, and governmental attempts to give procurement contracts to smaller firms all helped soften the blow of competition.

When organizations are regulated by the state, the economic environment diminishes in importance as the importance of the political and administrative environment increases. Both attention and behavior shift accordingly. The decisions of consumers become less important than the decisions of lawmakers and government agents.

Two views have developed to explain why governments regulate or intervene in markets. "The first is that regulation is instituted primarily for the protection and benefit of the public at large or some large subclass of the public" (Stigler, 1971:3). While the regulatory process may be occasionally perverted, this line of reasoning holds that, over all, the goal of serving the public interest is met by government regulation. The second view concerning regulation is that, "as a rule, regulation is acquired by the industry and is designed and operated primarily for its benefit" (Stigler, 1971:3). Posner (1974) has extended this second view, noting that regulation may be equivalent to any other product or service, supplied at some price and facing some demand distribution. Like any other commodity, more regulation is purchased when its price is lower and the demand is higher.

The two views of regulation are not necessarily contradictory, as regulation may differ in its effects over time. It is possible that the initial impetus for regulation comes from outside the industry, motivated by general public welfare concerns, but that in time the industry captures the regulatory agency and then comes to demand the continuation of the regulation. A regulated industry is, of course, equivalent in many respects to a cartel, except that control is exercised by some governmental administrative apparatus rather than by a council of the producers. We would suspect that organizational support for regulation rises and falls with the effects of regulation on problematic interdependence. Regulation is likely to be viewed most favorably where it provides more benefits to the industry and when competitive uncertainty is greatest and cannot be managed by tacit interfirm arrangements.

Benefits of Regulation

Stigler has noted that the government can potentially provide four types of benefits to an industry. First, the government can furnish a direct cash subsidy. "The domestic airlines received 'air mail' subsidies (even if they did not carry mail) of $1.5 billion through 1968. The merchant marine has received construction and operation subsidies reaching almost $3 billions since World War II" (1971:4). But if the government is handing out money to firms in an industry, there is a temptation for other firms to enter the industry and share in the largesse. This dilutes the benefits to original industry members. Beneficiaries must then limit entry into the industry to avoid a situation where the government subsidy is divided among growing numbers of industry participants. Without restriction of entry, an industry is not likely to consider cash subsidies a preferred benefit from the government.

The second outcome the government can provide is restriction of entry by rivals. The theory of economics states that when firms are earning unusually large profits, these profits should act as a signal to attract new entry into the industry. New competition then eliminates any excess profits. Organizations, not wishing to experience these consequences, spend a great deal of time attempting to prevent such new entry. Advertising is one type of barrier; others are vertical integration arrangements and the practice of setting price below attractive levels. These actions themselves reduce profits, and an even better control is the requirement for governmental certification. The centralized decision structure of regulation makes entry restriction easier to implement. The Civil Aeronautics Board, for example, has not allowed a single new trunk line to be launched since it was created in 1938 (Stigler, 1971). The Interstate Commerce Commission has been equally vigilant. Volotta (1967) found that the number of truck carriers has persistently declined, despite more than 5000 applications per year for new certificates. The total number of carriers declined from 18,036 in 1957 to 15,426 in 1966. Such a decline at a time when the volume of motor freight was rising leads to fewer but larger carriers and an increasingly concentrated industry. Volotta (1967:123) noted that of the general commodities carriers, in 1957, 2.32 percent had over $5 million in revenues and accounted for 49.94 percent of total revenues of this class. Just seven years later, 3.47 percent of the large

carriers accounted for 66.42 percent of the revenues of general commodities carriers. A similar result holds for special commodities
carriers.

In reviewing the history of transportation regulation, Volotta uncovered some rather substantial gaps in governmental logic. "Justification, then, for governmental control over competition was established
for modes of transport with diametrically opposite economic and
operating characteristics: i.e., railroads tended toward monopoly, so
public interest was best served by fostering competition; and motor
carriers had highly competitive characteristics, therefore competition
should be restrained" (1967:3).

The third set of benefits government can provide are actions that
will affect substitutes and complements. The truckers have waged intense advertising campaigns pointing out the utility and social value of
the highway trust fund. Airlines are interested in improving airports.
And America's railroads would like to obtain the public funding of
rights of way—through government support for AMTRAK—that both
airlines and trucks enjoy through governmental maintenance of roads
and airport facilities. Another example of government action, this time
taken to diminish the attractiveness of substitute products, is the early
restriction on artificially coloring oleomargarine. When margarine was
first introduced, the dairy industry perceived it as direct competition
for butter. Regulations were implemented that resulted in margarine
being sold with a packet of food coloring that the individual purchasers could mix in. Buying a tub of some white substance and then
mixing in yellow food coloring, of course, is not nearly as attractive to
consumers as purchasing a product which is, in appearance at least,
indistinguishable from butter. Many states had restrictions on coloring
oleomargarine until the late 1950s, and Wisconsin, a dairy state,
dropped the regulation only relatively recently.

The final benefit the government can provide is the ability to fix
price legally to coordinate and manage competition. When one considers the enormous antitrust damage suits that have been won, it is
clear that the ability to fix price legally is quite an important benefit.
Regulation to fix price is likely to be most important when industries
face the maximum competitive uncertainty and interdependence, at
some level of moderate or intermediate concentration at which tacit or
semiformal interorganizational coordination mechanisms are less likely
to be effective. Without the ability to fix prices, competition might
depress the profits of firms in the industry. The classic study of price
regulation and its relationship to cartels is that done by Macavoy
(1965). Analyzing the price behavior of railroads in the late 1800s,
Macavoy concluded that there was a railroad cartel operating out of

Chicago to the east coast, but that it had some difficulty in maintaining the cartel price. With the advent of the Interstate Commerce Commission, however, railroad rates were legally enforced at a rate slightly higher than the previously highest cartel price, and since enforcement was in the hands of the government, the price was maintained without any variation or price wars.

That organizations attempt to control their economic environments politically through regulation has been documented by Stigler (1971). Regulated truck weight allowances suggest that economic interests, in part, determine regulatory policy. By the early 1930s, nearly all states regulated the weight and dimensions of trucks, regulations which are subject to controversy and lobbying to the present day. Weight and dimension limitations constrain the amount of freight hauled per trip. Trucking and railroad interests both attempted to adjust weight requirements to their own benefit. Railroads wanted low weight limits to restrict trucks to smaller hauls and limit competition for rail traffic; truckers wanted the more profitable larger dimensions and weight allowances. The public interest was presumably related to the problem of road maintenance and weight limitations were justified on the basis of road conditions. However, railroads were frequently the more powerful interest and were able to obtain policies they favored. "Sometimes the participation of railroads in the regulatory process was incontrovertible: Texas and Louisiana placed a 7000-pound payload limit on trucks serving (and hence competing with) two or more railroad stations, and a 14,000-pound limit on trucks serving only one station (hence, not competing with it)" (Stigler, 1971:8).

Stigler (1971) analyzed weight allowances as a function of the potency of three interest groups. On the truckers' side were farmers, who favored the allowance of heavy trucks. Trucks clashed with railroads, particularly on short hauls, since economies of operation made railroads favored on long hauls. The longer the average railroad haul, the less the railroads would need protection from truck competition. And finally, the surface of the road, which was ostensibly the reason for limiting weight at all, might be of interest to the public, which would not want its roads damaged by heavy trucks. Stigler combined these three variables in a regression equation and examined how they affected the weight limits set for four-wheel and six-wheel trucks. His results are reproduced in Table 8.1 and show how the three interests affected the weight allowances for trucks that were set in the 1930s.

Other evidence similarly concluded that regulation is an effective means of altering the economic environment of an industry to its benefit. Peltzman (1965) examined the entry restriction imposed on

TABLE 8.1   Regression Analysis of State Weight Limits on Trucks (t-Values Under Regression Coefficients)

Dependent Variable	N	Constant	X_3	X_4	X_5	r^2
X_1	48	12.28	0.0336	0.0287	0.2641	0.502
		(4.87)	(3.99)	(2.77)	(3.04)	
X_2	46	10.34	0.0437	0.0788	0.2528	0.243
		(1.57)	(2.01)	(2.97)	(1.15)	

SOURCE: Stigler (1971: 9) reprinted by permission.
X_1 = weight limit on 4-wheel trucks (thousands of pounds), 1932–1933
X_2 = weight limit on 6-wheel trucks (thousands of pounds), 1932–1933
X_3 = trucks on farms per 1000 agricultural labor force, 1930
X_4 = average length of railroad haul of freight (miles), 1930
X_5 = percent of state highways with high-type surface, December 31, 1930

commercial banking in 1935 after the bank failures of the Great Depression. He estimated that the entry rate into commercial banking was cut by 25 to 50 percent. There are about half as many banks as there might be had entry not been restricted. Demsetz (1968) contrasted early competition in the utility industry with the protection companies gained from regulation and legally protected market areas.

Stigler and Friedland (1962) attempted to assess whether regulation made a difference in the performance of utilities. They dated the start of regulation in a state from the creation of a special state commission empowered to regulate rates for electricity. Two-thirds of the states had commissions by 1915, and three-quarters by 1922. For the most part, the utilities themselves "provided most of the force behind the regulatory movement" (Demsetz, 1968:65). Stigler and Friedland attempted to assess the effect of regulation on rates. A simple comparison between rates in regulated and unregulated states may be misleading, as other economic factors may be involved, such as the size and density of the market, the price of fuel, and the incomes of consumers. Stigler and Friedland (1962), after adjusting for these variables, found *no* effect of regulation on rates. These authors also examined rate structure, particularly whether household users paid relatively lower rates compared to industrial users. Comparisons of the average ratio of charges per kilowatt hour to domestic users over charges to industrial users showed no effect for regulation. Finally, Stigler and Friedland examined the effect of regulation on investors in electric utility equities. There was a slight, insignificant effect of regulation tending to decrease share price, but again the essential conclusion was that there was no effect of regulation. The results suggest that there were no observable benefits to customers, investors, or the public coming from regulated rather than unregulated utilities.

Occupational Licensing

Yet another example of regulation to the benefit of the regulated is that achieved through occupational licensing of professions like medicine, law, and dentistry. Holen found that:

> (1) There is less movement between states among dentists and lawyers than among physicians; (2) there is a significant relationship between licensing-examination failure rates and average state professional incomes for dentistry and law (but not for medicine), indicating that mobility is impeded by exclusionary practices even apart from the structure of licensing arrangements; (3) dispersions of state average professional incomes for dentistry and law are consistent with the hypothesis that mobility restriction results in professional misallocation on a geographic basis; (4) barriers to interstate mobility prevent the benefits of geographical specialization in education from being fully realized in the field of law (1965:492).

The dilemma in occupational licensing has been recognized for some time (e.g., Council of State Governments, 1952). On the one hand, it is necessary to protect the public from harm and from frauds. On the other hand, licensing arranged by practitioners leads to state-sanctioned monopolies and a consequent increase in professional incomes. There are no easy solutions to the problem, and Holen's study does show that some monopoly profits accrue to professionals because of their licensed or regulated status.

Pfeffer (1974b) reviewed the literature on occupational licensing and attempted to examine four hypotheses derived from that literature concerning the relationship between licensing practices and occupational incomes. First, he investigated the effect of regulation on occupational incomes. To perform such an analysis, it is, of course, necessary to find occupations that are regulated in some states but unregulated in others and for which data on income by occupation by state are available. The stronger professions such as medicine and law are regulated in every state and have been for some time. The only three occupations that could be examined were plumber, real estate broker and salesman, and insurance broker and salesman. For these three occupations, controlling for state median income, there was no evidence that regulation had a statistically significant effect on occupational incomes.

Pfeffer next examined the effects of regulatory board composition, investigating the proportion of the board comprised of public representatives and the proportion comprised of occupational practitioners. While there was some support for the idea that public members on licensing boards tended to reduce occupational incomes, the support was quite weak. Of 17 correlations computed, only 6 reached a magnitude of .20 or higher in the expected direction, while 11 of the 17 were in the predicted direction. Again, however, there was no variance in many of the more powerful professions such as law and medicine— licensing boards were comprised solely of occupational practitioners in every state.

Pfeffer (1974b:108) also replicated Holen's analysis examining the correlation between the failure rate for applicants applying for licenses and occupational income. However, Pfeffer did control for state median income and examined some additional occupations not considered by Holen. This analysis was consistent with the argument that licensing restricting entry related to increased incomes. Five of the six correlations were in the expected direction, indicating the higher the proportion of applicants who actually received licenses, the lower the average income for the occupation in that state. Finally, Pfeffer (1974b:110) was able to show that the more professionalized the occupation, the less occupational income was affected by state median income, or in other words, general state economic conditions. While Pfeffer's study is, at times, consistent with the argument that regulation increases incomes, it does show that such a proposition is far too simplistic. The mere presence of regulation in the case of lower power occupations does not necessarily provide any benefits.

An analysis of the history of licensing of various occupations will reveal that over time, the requirements for licensure become more and more stringent and the effect is to reduce the total number of persons who can practice the occupation. This effect seems to appear regardless of whether the demand for licensing comes from the public or the occupation. The case of marriage counselors is an interesting illustration of the attempt to use state licensing to enhance occupational status and incomes. Marriage counselors have recently moved to achieve licensing in many major states. California was one of the first to license marriage counselors, taking that action in 1963. The achievement of licensing requirements for this occupation was difficult. First, marriage counseling is practiced by many different groups, including the clergy, doctors, lawyers, social workers, teachers, as well as marriage counselors. With so many diverse interests in the occupation, it is difficult to put together a coalition. Second, the states frequently hire social workers with only bachelor's degrees, and thus to have a law passed, it is necessary to explicitly exclude the state from the regulation. Licensing is introduced by first writing a bill that excludes practically no currently powerful group practicing the occupation. Over time, requirements are tightened to restrict the entry of new practitioners. Such is the history of the California law. While there is no evidence on whether the quality of service has increased with the requirements, it is clear that marriage counselors' incomes have increased while the divorce rate has increased as well.

Relationship Between the Regulated and the Regulator

Surprisingly enough, there have been very few studies which have attempted to examine the relationship between the regulator and the regulated industry, or to ask the question: Why does regulation typically favor, or at least not harm, the industry being regulated? Stigler and Friedland concluded that there was no effect of regulation on electric utilities because: (1) the individual utility system did not possess any large amount of long-run monopoly power because of competition from other power sources; and (2) the regulatory body, because it does not control operating decisions, cannot force the utility to operate at a specified combination of output, price, and cost (1962:11). Jordan (1972) has suggested that under conditions of producer monopoly, regulation will have no effect as the producer is already obtaining monopoly returns, while when there is oligopoly or competition, regulation will increase producer returns by effectively transforming the industry into a cartel.

There may be a third reason why regulation does not operate to benefit consumers or the general public. The regulatory commissions become captives of the regulated companies. The commissions must face the task of doing day-to-day business with the companies they are regulating. Accommodation would be the rule, rather than the exception, particularly when commissions are so poorly funded they must rely on the regulated companies for the data to make their decisions. Leiserson (1942) noted that in the regulatory process, the client groups typically give social and technical support to the agency by providing information and participating in some administrative functions. Such client involvement comes from resource constraints on the regulatory agency. The Federal Power Commission must generally obtain its information on the amount of gas reserves from the gas companies themselves. Few of these agencies, with staffs numbering in the several hundreds at most, are able to develop data about an industry of many multibillion dollar organizations. The regulated organizations find themselves in the position of supplying the data the regulators use to regulate them. In the midst of the energy crisis, it emerged that government estimates of proven gas reserves and industry estimates were vastly different, with the industry estimates being much lower, implying higher prices for the gas.

Insufficient regulatory resources, of course, are not the entire cause. The nature of the enduring relationship between the regulatory agency and the companies tends to promote cooperation. The participants come to know each other and they share common interests, as they depend on one another. Without the support of the industry, the regulatory commission may find it harder to obtain budget, and furthermore, the cooperation of the industry is necessary for the agency to do its job. Thus, a symbiotic relationship develops—less than 50 license renewals have been turned down by the Federal Communications Commission since that agency was founded in 1934.

Bernstein (1955) has noted how commissions, as they mature and public interest wanes, are left to face the regulated industry alone. The continued association between the two is almost inevitably going to lead to some accommodation being reached. "The single most important characteristic of regulation by commission is the failure to grasp the need for political support and leadership for the success of regulation in the public interest" (Bernstein, 1955:101). In the absence of external political support, the commission can either come to some accommodation with the regulated industry or attempt to fight it out with the organizations in that industry. But commissions, like any other organization, are interested in certainty and survival. In the absence of any support, they are not likely to operate long in conflict with the only group interested in their operations—the regulated industry.

The missing social and political support of an active public is supplied by the industry. Various mechanisms of environmental linkage are used by regulated organizations to obtain favorable outcomes. Organizations which are regulated frequently supply their own personnel to the regulatory agencies as either advisors or as actual regulators. Overt conflict of interest is denied. Robert C. Bowen, an employee of Phillips Petroleum who worked for the Federal Energy Administration while on leave from Phillips, told a congressional subcommittee that his duties were carefully defined to avoid policy making and his superiors at the agency denied any conflict of interest. Obtaining expertise by drawing on the regulated industry's own employees is frequently observed.

Another mechanism, already discussed, is cooptation. Although it is not legally permissible for regulators to sit on boards of organizations being regulated, it is quite possible to use the company's board to develop a coalition of significant political support which may itself influence regulation. This would be particularly important for organizations confronted by regulatory agencies that set rates and allowable rates of return. Since rates are determined after public hearings, commissions are likely to be responsive to important political interests in the area. A possible strategy for organizations operating in the regulated industry would be to coopt important political interests. Our earlier analyses of cooptation have already indicated that there tend to be more outside directors on the boards of firms which are regulated. It is also possible to examine cooptation in a regulated industry more directly.

Pfeffer (1974a) analyzed 96 privately owned electric utilities in 1967 and 1968, obtaining operating data on the utilities from the Federal Power Commission (1969) and on the composition of utility boards from Dun and Bradstreet (1969). Average revenues of the 96 utilities were $128.29 million in 1968, with 39.4 percent coming from residential customers, 27.6 percent from commercial customers, 23.1 percent from industrial users, and 4.6 percent from sales to other utilities. The average board had 11 members, with two-thirds of the directors coming from outside the organization's management.

If electric utilities were following a strategy of coopting important political interests, we would expect them to select directors covering segments of the population in proportion to their dependence on these segments for political support. Thus, for a utility operating within a state dominated by agriculture, the proportion of agricultural directors on the board should be higher than for a utility operating in a manufacturing area. Some evidence consistent with this argument emerged from the analysis of the composition of the boards of the 96 utilities in the sample. There was a positive correlation between the proportion of board members with agricultural backgrounds and the proportion of the population engaged in agriculture, and a relationship between the proportion of persons on the board from manufacturing organizations and the proportion of the population employed in manufacturing. Moreover, members were sampled from different cities in the state as a function of the extent to which the population was dispersed or concentrated.

Of course, it might be that representatives were being selected for the board because they are important customer groups. While plausible, this is not likely to be the entire explanation. The proportion of manufacturing representatives on the board was more highly correlated with the proportion of the population in manufacturing ($r = .54$) than with the proportion of the utility's revenues from industrial customers ($r = .31$), a statistically significant difference between the two correlations. This indicates that the utilities were coopting political interests necessary for dealing with the regulatory agency, not only with customers.

Regulation is only one specific outcome of a political process that involves the government in the management of economic conditions. Our examination of regulation, then, is only a part of the total examination of political actions taken by organizations to manage their environments for their benefit.

THE ORGANIZATION AS A POLITICAL ACTOR

Implicit in the observation that organizations attempt to obtain advantages from government regulators is the notion that formal organizations have interests and make demands on government just as individual citizens do. There is little doubt that organizations have been heavily involved in American government and American politics for a long time and will continue to be involved. The importance and pervasiveness of corporate political involvement has generated very little systematic empirical research on the causes or consequences of such involvement. Most of the material published has been case studies, and most of these have dealt with corporate involvement in electoral politics. However, it is likely that organizational attempts to affect the decisions made by government bureaucracies are equally important to, if not more so than, direct interventions in elections.

The fact that political activities of organizations are not considered in textbooks on management and organizational behavior tells us something about the beliefs of writers of these books. Apparently, political activity of organizations is not considered because it is not taken to be a normal and legitimate administrative function. Of course, the institutional function of management generally has been neglected in texts which have typically focused on problems of supervising and motivating workers. And, it is certainly not in the interests of organizations to call these omissions to anyone's attention. Given current attitudes and values, corporate attempts to manage their environments are, from their point of view, better left unexplored. Yet, it is undoubtedly true that organizations are involved in political activity, with different degrees of effectiveness.

Some organizations may have a large staff in Washington to gather information on governmental activity and lobby the administrative and legislative branches. Other organizations may have only a dim awareness of what actions are being taken and may limit their efforts to influence governmental policies. At times, one can document how private economic interests are reflected in governmental activity, such as Stigler's (1971) analysis of truck weight limits to prevent competition with railroads. Other times, corporate involvement in the political process has virtually no discernible impact. Thus, the issues of why organizations are involved in political activity and what consequences such involvement has for governmental decisions are important problems posed when the focus is on organizations as political actors.

Why do some organizations attend to the political environment and others do not? The answer is probably that the political environment is a greater source of interdependence for some organizations. Some may depend on the government for sales or for market protection. The political system becomes relevant for the organization when the system begins to affect organizational outcomes. There are two types of effects of government actions on organizations. One is direct action supplying money to the organizations, either through the purchase of goods and services, as from defense contractors, or through the provision of various cash subsidies. The second effect is action that protects markets from foreign or domestic competition or from competition from complementary or substitute goods and services, such as the building of roads for truckers or the use of tariffs to restrict imports in various industries.

One might predict that political involvement would be directly related to the extent that these two forms of governmental action are important for the successful operation of the organization. Measuring the effects of governmental action on industry, or individual firm, results is likely to be difficult, but consideration of the major contributors to political campaigns provides at least some support for this position. Because of the campaign finance reform law of 1971 and the Watergate scandals from the Nixon White House in 1972, more information about corporate activity in the 1972 campaign was developed than ever before. Epstein (1976) reviewed the status of the campaign reform laws, and provided information about political contributions. An examination of these patterns of contribution provide some interesting insights.

Secret contributions to the Nixon campaign of over $2 million were recorded by President Nixon's personal secretary Rose Mary Woods. Of the 28 companies on this list, 6 were defense contractors, and these 6 accounted for 23.4 percent of the total money contributed by all the firms listed. Two other firms were in electronics, two were in the oil industry, two were in the automobile industry, and two were in the chemical industry. All 28 firms faced significant interdependence with the government. The electronics and chemical firms may also have been major suppliers of the defense department, while oil was facing price regulation and environmental constraints, and the automobile industry was contending with safety and pollution regulations as well as with competition from abroad.

The Senate Watergate Committee's hearings and related investigations revealed that industry-wide solicitations by Herbert Kalmbach and others working for the Committee to Reelect the President produced more than $5 million just from the top nine industries. These industries and their amount of contributions were (Epstein, 1976:68):

Pharmaceuticals	$885,000
Petroleum products	809,600
Investment banking	690,812
Trucking	674,504
Textiles	600,000
Carpets	375,000
Auto manufacturers	353,900
Home builders	334,059
Insurance	319,000

Each of these industries receives some form of benefit from the government. Trucking, of course, is regulated by the ICC. Home builders and the carpet industry both rely on home construction, which in turn is affected by government policies including various programs to directly stimulate construction, urban renewal projects, and programs that affect the availability of mortgage money and its cost. Textile firms and automobile manufacturers face severe foreign competition; the latter also face various pollution control and safety regulations that affect sales and profit margins. Petroleum companies operate overseas, requiring governmental protection, and faced at the time of their contributions domestic price regulations, as well as concern over the depletion allowance and the regulation of natural gas, which is largely produced by the major oil companies. With the government getting into medical insurance, the pharmaceutical business was profoundly affected by governmental activity, including FDA licensing, payment provisions in various social insurance programs, and protection provided by the patent and licensing laws (see Hirsch, 1975). Investment banking is partly regulated and, moreover, handles major government agency financings, while insurance was seeking to remain unregulated by the federal government, so it could deal with the more easily negotiated state regulatory bodies. Furthermore, as Epstein (1976:19) pointed out, this list did not include contributions of over $5 million from oil company executives, contributions of over $2.5 million from officers and directors of the largest 25 defense contractors, or the contributions made by milk producers.

As government impact on industry has become more pervasive, so have the political activities of firms and industries.

One might suspect that organizational involvement in political activities is not a preferred mechanism for dealing with the environment because it has several disadvantages. First, political activity is relatively visible, due to stringent campaign finance laws. Visibility both increases the probability of influence attempts being directed at the organization and also facilitates influencing the organization since actions that are public are more easily constrained. Another major disadvantage of political action is that solutions to problems found in this arena may take longer and are not subject to the organization's demands for scheduling. Court cases wind their way through the system slowly, and regulatory actions take time and move at their own pace. Getting special legislation through committees and Congress is time consuming and a process that may be interrupted by other pressing events, vacations, or elections, which frequently require that the process begin anew.

Perhaps the most significant disadvantage of political intervention is that the system invites opposition from groups or organizations who themselves have interests affected by the government. Thus, when an organization requests some special action, for example, to protect it from foreign competition, this action becomes public, and opposition can be mustered. The public forum of political debate makes opposition more likely, and the shifting positions of political figures, interested primarily in reelection, makes obtaining favorable political outcomes uncertain.

Epstein (1969) has noted that involvement by business corporations in American political activity has come about partially as an unintended consequence of the increasingly pervasive government intervention in economic affairs. Large government virtually assures large intervention on the part of organizations in political activity. The two are inevitably related. Such corporate or organizational involvement in political activity, moreover, is not frivolous use of organizational slack, like plush carpets or executive limosines. For many industries, governmental actions so profoundly affect their economic environment that these policies may make the difference between profit or loss or between survival and disappearance.

Prior to the action taken by OPEC to raise oil prices, Senator Kennedy, among others, maintained that the oil import quotas excluding inexpensive foreign oil added $5 billion a year to the cost of fuel for consumers. Import quotas on textile products, particularly from the Far East, enhances the profitability of domestic textile producers and also assures the jobs of their employees. Import quotas on steel, meat (until July 1972), sugar (until June 1974), and manufactured items as well as other raw material play an important part in the maintenance of domestic corporation profits. The use of quotas, rather than tariffs, does not even have the redeeming virtue of producing any revenue for the treasury.

Import quotas can be so important to an industry that it is not reluctant to spend some money to keep the political system informed about the need for the protection. Martin Lobel, a former energy office aide, told of a meeting he once had with oil industry representatives. When Lobel first started working for Senator Proxmire he had some questions about the oil import quota system and called up an Exxon lobbyist. The lobbyist called headquarters and flew five experts to Washington to brief Lobel. They met at a very plush club and presented an elaborate slide show, as well as liquor and good food (Gruenstein and West, 1975).

Protection from foreign competition is only one area of organizational political activity. Another is taxation. Organizations and products are frequently subjected to differential rates of taxation. It is in the interests of organizations to press for some benefits. Liquor, gasoline, and cigarettes are all taxed heavily, and therefore, assuming negatively sloped demand curves, sales of these products are reduced. There are a variety of depletion allowances for virtually all mineral products which serve to reduce the taxes paid by corporations. Within the various states, there may be differing rates of taxation on incomes, sales, or products, and again corporations may find it desirable to work to shift the burden elsewhere.

Business corporations are not the only organizations to engage in political activity. Cities and states continually lobby the federal government for funds. Agencies of the executive branch itself lobby in Congress and conduct massive public relations campaigns to let their constituency know how well they are being served and to create more demand for their services. Public relations is not only the province of the Pentagon—public service advertisements (promotions) are run by Social Security, Housing and Urban Development, and the Equal Employment Opportunity Commission, among others. Universities and school systems are major sources of influence concerning bills affecting the funding of education, while hospitals have developed, through their associations, mechanisms for exerting influence on legislation affecting funding for health care.

Political intervention has typically been classified into two categories: (1) election activity, or (2) governmental activity.

> Governmental activities . . . include both political involvement intended to influence the formulation and execution of policy by governmental decision makers and efforts designed to create a public opinion favorable to the corporation's political goals. Electoral activities center around the selection and support of candidates or of issues that come before the public (Epstein, 1969:67).

Most investigations have concluded that organizational attempts to influence policy do not arise principally through participation in election activities. While much public concern has been voiced about corporate and union contributions to political campaigns, such activity may have relatively unimportant effects on political decisions.

With respect to what Epstein called governmental activities, there are again two categories. Organizations may lobby or petition the legislators, or organizations may lobby or petition the various administrative or executive agencies of the government. Again, it is not clear that the area which has received the most attention—lobbying of legislators —is really the most important. As Bauer et al. (1963:267) have commented, "business bureaucrats would rather deal with government bureaucrats, without being bothered by the temperamentally differing politician as an intermediary."

The models of organizational interest groups influencing the government are many and varied. There is, however, little theory or empirical research to aid in the understanding of when one might be used rather than another. Along one dimension, organizations may engage in their political activities alone through their own resources or collectively pooling their resources with other organizations which have similar interests. As with any collective effort, the danger exists that the interorganizational organization may not represent the interests of all the members, and for those coordinating mechanisms that develop formal staffs and structures, control of the lobbying organization itself becomes, at times, an organizational objective. We suspect that collective organizations are used when the individual organizations represented are small, for there are undoubtedly economies of scale in lobbying which would make collective efforts more efficient for all. Furthermore, collective efforts are more likely when firms in the industry are relatively homogeneous, so that the interests of all are likely to coincide. Group representation is also more feasible when group members share common interests. A third variable might be the extent of governmental importance to the firm and the industry. Here, we might expect a curvilinear relationship. If the organization were highly dependent on governmental actions, then it might find it worthwhile to conduct its own political activities. When the organization is affected but not quite as much, it may find it desirable to share its efforts with others. And, when the organization is not affected at all, it would not support efforts to represent its interests. Thus, the importance of group representation of corporate interests is more likely, other things being equal, when corporations are moderately affected by governmental activities.

The National Association of Manufacturers (NAM) and the United States Chamber of Commerce are two well-known, broadly based business associations that work to influence the economic environment through political action. Many trade associations also lobby and conduct public relations campaigns to build a favorable climate for the particular industry. Gable (1953) attempted to analyze the influence of NAM in passage of the Taft-Hartley Act, a bill long favored by manufacturers. Gable stated that "a political interest group tends to exercise a guiding influence in the determination of public policy when it succeeds in identifying its conception of the needs of the moment with the prevailing attitudes of the public, and has access to the major centers of policy decision so that its proposals can reach government . . . a political interest group may either manipulate public opinions so that they approximate group opinions or else adjust group opinions to conform to public opinions or both" (1953:255). Gable viewed political influence as a process of legitimation, one of establishing a congruence between the interests of the organizations and the interests of the general public. Gable also defined some variables that may affect how much influence on policy an organized group can have: "The effectiveness of these efforts is related to such internal factors as: the size of the group; the alliances it can make with other groups; its structure, organization, and policy-making procedures; the quality of its leadership; its financing, and its cohesion" (1953:256).

The strength of associations like NAM may diminish both with their success and with their perceived inability to meet external threats. If the organization cannot deal effectively with the environment, then the members are likely to withdraw support. On the other hand, when, or if, the organization removes a major environmental difficulty for the member organizations, they may no longer see any reason for participating and may withdraw. With respect to NAM, an organization which has been particularly active in opposing the extension of labor union power, Gable found that membership fluctuations have coincided rather remarkably with fluctuations in the membership of labor unions. Each new threat from labor has induced NAM to expand. When the union growth diminished, membership in NAM fell. For instance, after the passage of the Taft-Hartley Act, NAM membership declined by a thousand firms from 1947 to 1949 (Gable, 1953:260).

Gable's treatment of the Taft-Hartley issues illustrates how difficult it is to assess the influence of any one set of interests on legislative outcomes. The final bill looked remarkably like several legislative proposals which NAM actively supported. Not all NAM-favored provisions, however, remained in the final version. The difficulty of inferring organizational power from legislative similarity is: If the organization tends to support bills that are consistently passed, it may be because the organization really has the power to influence legislation, or it may be simply that the organization is able to identify prevailing opinion and line up behind it.

NAM represents one model of influence, an association of organizations directly representing their interests through lobbying and public relations. Another way in which such industry associations may operate is by directly negotiating with the various other interested parties outside the legislative process and then jointly presenting a compromise agreement to the legislature for its formal ratification into law. Since legislation typically does require compromise, it may be fruitful for the interested parties to deal with each other directly, rather than working through the legislator-intermediaries. An example of such interaction is provided in the study of the Associated Industries of Vermont (AIV) (Garceau and Silverman, 1954). This organization represented about 450 concerns in 1951, about half the total payroll of the state of Vermont. Vermont's legislative apportionment left the legislature dominated by the Farm Bureau, representing agricultural interests. Labor had almost no voice in the legislature; and only a few representatives were friendly to their interests. AIV's principal concern in 1951 was a bill proposed by labor to include certain occupational diseases under the Workman's Compensation Act. When the session opened, AIV had planned to introduce three bills aimed at tightening the qualifications for workers claiming benefits under the Unemployment Compensation Law. Labor, on the other hand, hoped for an increase in both the duration and the amount of unemployment benefits (1954:677–678). The leader of AIV negotiated directly with the CIO representative, and an agreement was reached under which AIV would get the occupational disease bill it wanted and it would drop the bills tightening up requirements for benefits under Workman's Compensation. In turn, labor agreed to drop its quest for higher unemployment benefits. "These negotiations were carried on completely outside the legislative hall with only two legislative participants." (1954:678). Since each group was interdependent with the other, with labor's access to the legislature almost entirely through AIV, they reconciled their differences outside of the legislative process.

While these studies focused on the use of organizations that represent the interests of others, Epstein (1969) noted that organizations frequently engage in direct political activities. This direct activity is, in part, a consequence of the increasing size of major organizations, which makes self-representation economically and politically feasible. It is also partially the consequence of the growing political sophistication on the part of organizational managers and of the fact that when organizations join together in some intermediary organization, none of their interests are perfectly served. Stigler (1971), for instance, has shown that many political benefits tend to be distributed more equally among the organizations on the principle of one organization, one share, rather than on the basis of relative size.

Another form of organizational influence in the political process is the hiring of former government officials by industry or the government's hiring of former industry officials. Cross movements between government and other organizations help build some common understanding. The actual cross movement of personnel, however, may be more of consequence than a cause of a mutual pattern of interaction and understanding that has developed. When personnel from two organizations are constantly in contact because of the interdependence between the organizations, it is likely that they and their organizations will develop stable structures of interaction and behavior to manage the interdependence and reduce uncertainty. These stable patterns of expectation, interaction, and structure of behavior facilitate movement between the organizations. And while such interorganizational flows of personnel may, in turn, further ratify the existing interorganizational relationships, the fact that such interchanges may be an effect, as well as a cause, of interorganizational collaboration should not be overlooked.

Two other points need to be made about the organization as a political actor. The first is that organizations, especially large, diversified organizations, seldom have a unified structure of interests. One division of an organization may favor one side of an issue and another division may favor the other side. Trade legislation is one setting where such controversies within the organization may occur. One division may be a major exporter, dependent upon reciprocal trade agreements for entry into foreign markets. Another division may be selling primarily domestically and would like to exclude the threat of competition from foreign manufacturers. Organizations are, after all, coalitions of various interests, and to the extent these interests exert different pressures for the organization, the organization itself may avoid a unified, determined position on any issue.

The second point is that organizations are limited in their exercise of political influence, often because they appear to be so powerful. Dexter (1960) has noted this about DuPont's political activities in Delaware (see Bauer, Pool, and Dexter, 1963). When an organization is quite large relative to its environment and possesses conspicuous economic or social power, the very fact of that power constrains its behavior. General Motors is constrained in its competitive behavior because of its near monopoly of the automobile industry. And DuPont is constrained in its attempts at influence because of its unique position in Delaware. Even though, for example, DuPont owns the Wilmington papers through a holding company, the editors took a stand on the foreign trade issue opposite to that of DuPont. DuPont is quite circumspect and proper in its attempts to communicate its positions to Delaware senators and representatives. This is not to say that DuPont exerts no influence on political activities, but merely that because of the visibility of the organization and its power, such influence is likely to be constrained by the attention it generates.

SUMMARY

We have argued that when the problems stemming from interdependence are otherwise unmanageable or when the resources ncessary to achieve co-ordinated action are widely dispersed, organizations will attempt to use the larger social power of the state to benefit its operating environment. Organizations are also likely to become involved in political activity when governmental intervention begins to affect their economic well-being and certainty.

The view that organizations are constrained by their political, legal and social environments is only partially correct. We have argued that organizations are not only constrained by their environments but that, in fact, law, legitimacy, and political outcomes somewhat reflect the actions taken by organizations to modify their environments for their interests of survival, growth, and certainty. Rather than taking the environment as a given to which the organization then adapts, it is considerably more realistic to consider the environment as an outcome of a process that involves both adaptation to the environment and attempts to change that environment.

Organizational efforts have been made to establish favorable environments through regulation as well as through other forms of political activity. Furthermore, organizations act to achieve social legitimacy and occasionally achieve this legitimacy through a process involving identification with other legitimate social actors. While the basic theoretical position we have developed in the earlier chapters has not been explicitly applied to test hypotheses relating to these dimensions of organizational activity, the case evidence and data presented do indicate the possibility that these organizational actions can also be explained by the situation of interdependence, uncertainty, and resource munificence confronting the organizations.

REFERENCES

American Institute for Foreign Study. 1969. *1969 Summer School Programs, High School Division*. Greenwich, Conn.: American Institute for Foreign Study.

Bauer, R. A., I. Pool, and L. A. Dexter. 1963. *American Business and Public Policy*. Massachusetts Institute of Technology Press.

Bernstein, M. H. 1955. *Regulating Business by Independent Commission*. Princeton University Press.

Clark, B. R. 1956. "Organizational adaptation and precarious values: a case study." *American Sociological Review*, 21:327–336.

Council of State Governments. 1952. *Occupational Licensing Legislation in the States*. Chicago: Council of State Governments.

Demsetz, H. 1968. "Why regulate utilities?" *Journal of Law and Economics*, 11:55–65.

Dexter, L. A. 1960. "Where the elephant fears to dance among the chickens: business in politics? the case of Du Pont." *Human Organization*, 19: 188–194.

Dun and Bradstreet. 1969. *Reference Book of Corporate Managements, 1969*. New York: Dun and Bradstreet.

Epstein, E. M. 1969. *The Corporation in American Politics*. Englewood Cliffs, N.J.: Prentice-Hall.

Epstein, E. M. 1976. "Corporations and labor unions in electoral politics." *Annals*, 425:33–58.

Federal Power Commission. 1969. *Statistics of Privately Owned Electric Utilities in the United States*. Washington, D.C.: Government Printing Office.

Gable, R. W. 1953. "NAM: influential lobby or kiss of death?" *Journal of Politics*, 15:254–273.

Garceau, O., and C. Silverman. 1954. "A pressure group and the pressured: a case report." *American Political Science Review*, 48:672–691.

Garraty, J. A., and W. Adams. 1962. *A Guide to Study Abroad*. New York: Channel.

Gruenstein, P., and D. West. 1975. "Anything you can eat, drink, or fornicate in one afternoon." *Washington Monthly*, 7:11–15.

Hirsch, P. M. 1975. "Organizational effectiveness and the institutional environment." *Administrative Science Quarterly*, 20:327–344.

Holen, A. S. 1965. "Effects of professional licensing arrangements on interstate labor mobility and resource allocation." *Journal of Political Economy*, 73:492–498.

Hurst, J. W. 1964. *Law and Economic Growth: The Legal History of the Lumber Industry in Wisconsin, 1836 to 1915*. Cambridge, Mass.: Harvard University Press (Belknap Press).

Jordan, W. A. 1972. "Producer protection, prior market structure and the effects of government regulation." *Journal of Law and Economics*, 15: 151–176.

Latham, E. 1952. *The Group Basis of Politics*. Ithaca, N.Y.: Cornell University Press.

Leiserson, A. 1942. *Administrative Regulation: A Study in Representation of Interests*. University of Chicago Press.

Levine, S., and P. E. White. 1961. "Exchange as a conceptual framework for the study of interorganizational relationships." *Administrative Science Quarterly*, 5:583–610.

MacAvoy, P. W. 1965. *The Economic Effects of Regulation*. Massachusetts Institute of Technology Press.

Maurer, J. G. 1971. *Readings in Organization Theory: Open-System Approaches*. New York: Random House.

Parsons, T. 1956. "Suggestions for a sociological approach to the theory of organizations." *Administrative Science Quarterly*, 1:63–85.

Peltzman, S. 1965. "Entry in commercial banking." *Journal of Law and Economics,* 8:11–50.

Pfeffer, J. 1974a. "Cooptation and the composition of electric utility boards of directors." *Pacific Sociological Review,* 17:333–363.

Pfeffer, J. 1974b. "Some evidence on occupational licensing and occupational incomes." *Social Forces,* 53:102–111.

Posner, R. A. 1974. "Theories of economic regulation." *Bell Journal of Economics and Management Science,* 5:335–358.

Roberts, Wallace. 1969. "Thirty thousand innocents abroad." *Saturday Review,* 52 (February 15):61–62 ff.

Stigler, G. J. 1971. "The theory of economic regulation." *Bell Journal of Economics and Management Science,* 2:3–21.

Stigler, G. J., and C. Friedland. 1962. "What can regulators regulate? the case of electricity." *Journal of Law and Economics,* 5:1–13.

Volotta, A. 1967. *The Impact of Federal Entry Controls on Motor Carrier Operations.* Pennsylvania State University, Center for Research of the College of Business Administration.

Zald, M. N. 1970. "Political economy: a framework for comparative analysis." In M. N. Zald (ed.), *Power in Organizations,* 221–261. Nashville, Tenn.: Vanderbilt University Press.

CHAPTER NINE

EXECUTIVE SUCCESSION:
A Mechanism for
Environmental Effects

We have argued that to understand organizations, it is necessary to understand the external constraints they face. These constraints, deriving from the organization's interdependence with other organizations, both influence organizational actions and create a need to manage the environment. To say that organizations are externally controlled or constrained, however, does not specify how. If we are to understand organizational actions, the processes by which environmental factors affect organizational actions must be specified. It is the purpose of this chapter to suggest one important mechanism of environmental influence on organizational change. The mechanism is that of executive succession, and we will present evidence suggesting that environmental contingencies affect the selection and removal of top organizational administrators to make the organization more aligned with its environment.

Much current literature about organization-environment relations does not hypothesize mechanisms of environmental effects. One can read studies about uncertainty and structure (e.g., Duncan, 1972), competitiveness and structure (e.g., Pfeffer and Leblebici, 1973), or change and structure (e.g., Lawrence and Lorsch, 1967) without ever learning how these environmental dimensions produce effects on organizations. It is as if a Mr. Environment came into the organization, giving orders to change organizational structures and activities.

In the absence of any specified mechanism by which environmental changes have impact on organizations, readers are left with a feeling of inevitable environmental determinism. Two broad classes of models of organizational-environmental linkages tend to imply a deterministic view. These two classes are the adaptation-change models and the ecological, or natural selection, models. Adaptation-change models suggest that organizations change or adapt in response to environmental requirements. Ecological models suggest that environmental contingencies allow some organizations to survive while others disappear, thus selecting organizations that fit the environment at the expense of others that fit less well. Models of both kinds imply an empirical consistency between the nature of the environment and the organization. When such empirical consistencies are found, there is no way to distinguish between the two types of model. Moreover, without specifying the selection or adaptation process in more detail, small relationships between context and organizational features are not accounted for.

Without additional qualifying assumptions, such as arguments about lags and rigidities, both adaptation and ecological models imply that the organization is tightly linked to its environment. Perturbations of the environment lead to alterations in organizations, either because of managed change or because of differential survival and growth rates. There should be two empirical consequences if the assumption of organizations being tightly linked to environments is correct. First, the relationship between the environment and organizational structures and decisions should be almost perfect. As Child (1972) has correctly noted, correlations observed in studies of organization-environment relationships are far from perfect. Either the studies have been poorly done with much measurement error, or else the link between organizations and their environments is much less tight than has been implied.

The other implication of the tightly linked concept also tends to be empirically undemonstrated. If the environment changes rapidly, then adaptation models positing tight coupling between environments and organizations imply that organizations will change rapidly in response. This prediction seems inconsistent with the relatively pervasive belief that organizations are remarkably stable and that resistance to change seems to characterize most social institutions. Selection models imply a slightly different consequence of environmental change. Rather than change exhibited by individual organizations, natural selection models imply the differential failure and survival of organizational forms. If environments change to make new forms more appropriate, then failure of the old forms should be prevalent. This expectation also is at least somewhat inconsistent with the existence of organizational forms over long periods of time and with the fact that failure seems to be confined to relatively small business organizations.

Either environments do not change as rapidly as some writers have thought (e.g., Terreberry, 1968; Emery and Trist, 1965), or assumptions about the tight linkage between organizations and environments are incorrect. We conclude, in agreement with Child (1972), that the relationship between organizations and their environments is important but, at the same time, indeterminate. In other words, organizations are only loosely coupled with their environments (Weick, 1976). While there is some coupling, so that environmental effects must be considered, the coupling is loose, which means that the relationships are far from perfectly determinate. Consequently, it is necessary to devote attention to the manner in which the process of organizational change takes place. Without considering the specific forms of linkage between environmental factors and the consequences, it is not possible to develop an adequate causal explanation for the relationship between context and organizational activities and structure.

A perspective which merely posits some relationship between the environment and the organization does not provide theoretical understanding. There is an important distinction between a theory and the empirical predictions derived from the theory. What such a perspective misses is how change occurs. A focus on the "how" of change leads one to consider who brings change about and who resists it. We assume change is a consequence of individual decisions and the actions taken by specifiable individuals. If change is a consequence of decisions, who is empowered to take actions which alter the organization becomes critical. One is inevitably led to consider who controls the organization and how such power and influence distributions arise.

It is important to emphasize that while the adaptation models have not specified how change comes about, the ecological or natural selection perspective is unconcerned with how variations or change in organizational structures arise (Aldrich and Pfeffer, 1976). The natural selection model is concerned with the differential survival rate of alternative forms. How the different forms arose in the first place, whether they were managerially planned or accidentally constructed, is not important. The selection models focus only on the outcomes, achieved presumably in some equilibrium state when organizational forms have adjusted to environmental requirements. The low correspondence between environmental dimensions and organizational variables suggests, however, that the process of change may be an important, neglected variable in both formulations.

A MODEL OF ENVIRONMENTAL EFFECTS

There are a variety of possible mechanisms by which the organization's context can come to influence its structure and actions. While the environment (or, more correctly, actions of others in the environment) may present the contingencies that create problems for the organization, those actions must be enacted and considered by organizational members. In Chapter Four we discussed the enactment process and noted that the link between context and organizational perceptions of that context was itself partly indeterminate.

In this chapter we will present a model of one mechanism by which the environment is linked to organizational change and action. The model suggests that the relationship between environments and organizations is not random but is indeterminate, and that the very indeterminancy of environmental effects on organizations is potentially explainable. The model concerns the effects of executive succession in organizations on organizational change. By succession we mean the removal of one executive and the selection of another. We argue that both the removal and selection of top administrators is affected by the organization's context. The argument can be briefly summarized: (1) the environmental context, with its contingencies, uncertainties, and interdependencies, influences the distribution of power and control within the organization; (2) the distribution of power and control within the organization affects the tenure and selection of major organizational administrators; (3) organizational policies and structures are results of decisions affected by the distribution of power and control; and (4) administrators who control organizational activities affect those activities and resultant structures. Executives are a source of control, and it matters who is in control because control determines organizational activities. The environment affects organizational activities because it affects the distribution of control within the organization.

The mechanism by which organizational environments may affect organizations can be represented by the following diagram:

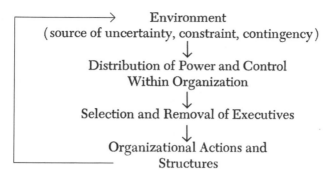

In specifying this model of organizational change, we naturally recognize that it is only one possible model. We use it to highlight three causal linkages that may lead from environmental factors to organizational characteristics. First, there is the link between the environment, a source of uncertainty and constraint, and the distribution of power and control within the organization. Second, there is the link between the distribution of power and control and the choice of executives and their tenure. Finally, there is the relationship between organizational administrators and the actions and structure of organizations. Given this causal sequence, one may not observe a perfect relationship between organizational actions and structures and the environment for several reasons. First, since each intermediate variable undoubtedly has other causes besides those specified, the relationship between environments and organizational actions and structures may be attenuated by these other factors. Second, because of the linked nature of the causal process, any indeterminacy or error in the process will be magnified because of the intermediate steps that link environments with organizations. For instance, even if each of the causal links were as strong as a .8 correlation, the overall correlation between environmental dimensions and organizational characteristics would be only .51. It is not surprising, therefore, that researchers often fail to find strong relationships between environmental characteristics and organizational outcomes.

The model indicates that organizational actions result from political processes within organizations, a view compatible with the political economy framework proposed by Zald (1970a; 1970b). As such, the model is inconsistent with theoretical positions that maintain that organizational actions and structures are inevitably constrained by environmental requirements. Such a position has been maintained by microeconomic theories of organizations operating in perfectly competitive environments and by the related ecological or natural selection models (e.g., Winter, 1971). In either model, the organization comes to match the environmental requirements, or else it fails. If, in fact, organizations were tightly linked to their environments, we could more easily neglect the intervening steps presented in the above model. Such intervening processes would be of interest only for their own sake; in equilibrium, it would be true that organizational results would be predicted by environmental factors. It is unlikely that organizations are so tightly constrained by their environments (Child, 1972). Organizations are only loosely coupled with their environments, and we believe that power is one important variable intervening between environments and organizations.

ORGANIZATIONAL CONTEXT AND INTRAORGANIZATIONAL POWER

The first link in the model of environmental effects on organizations is the effect of the environment on the distribution of power and control within the organization. Such an effect is posited in sociological analyses of organizations, most recently in the development of the strategic contingencies theory of intraorganizational power by Hickson and his colleagues (Hickson et al., 1971). Following Crozier (1964), Thompson (1967), and Perrow (1970), the strategic contingencies' theory argues that the most critical organizational function or the source of the most important organizational uncertainty determines power within the organization. Those subunits most able to cope with the organization's critical problems acquire power in the organization. Since many of the uncertainties and contingencies faced by organizations are a product of the environment, the environmental context partially determines the distribution of power within the organization. By power, we mean the ability of a subunit to influence organizational decisions in ways that produce outcomes favored by the subunit.

In its simplest form, the strategic contingencies' theory implies that for instance, when an organization faces a number of lawsuits and legal difficulties, the legal department will gain power and influence over organizational decisions. The theoretically interesting aspects of the development and conferral of power include the extent to which influence extends beyond the immediate functions of the subunit and the extent to which influence is used in the interest of the subunit independent of the goals and interests of the organization as a whole or of others in the organization. Thus, the power of a legal department derived from its handling of the organization's legal difficulties may extend beyond the legal function and involve the department in decisions about product design, advertising, and production. Such extensions of influence would, of course, be accompanied by justifications showing the importance of the legal department in such matters. It should be evident that any claims to influence and their accompanying justifications take place in a social context populated by other claimants. How the claims become resolved determines the distribution of control within the organization.

While the processes by which power develops have not been delineated, Hickson and his associates presented a multiplicative model for predicting subunit (departmental) power within organizations. The first element in their model is the ability of the subunit to cope with the organizational uncertainties or contingencies. The authors noted that it was not uncertainty that created power for a subunit, but the ability of the subunit to cope with that uncertainty, to actually solve the problems facing the organization. The second component of power is the substitutability of the subunit's capabilities. The subunit's ability to handle contingencies must be relatively unique. As Emerson (1962) and Blau (1964) have argued, if a needed resource or performance can be obtained from a large number of sources, the power of any single source is reduced. If the capability for coping with uncertainty were distributed widely throughout the organization, the power of any subunit would be small. The real meaning of Hickson's second condition is that power does not organize around abundant resources.

The third predictor of subunit power is the pervasiveness or importance of the contingency and uncertainty to the organization. Hickson et al. (1971) suggested that pervasiveness could be measured by noting how connected a given subunit is with other subunits, or in other words, how many other units are affected by its activities. The concept of pervasiveness is similar to the concept of criticality we introduced in Chapter Three. The argument is that a subunit will acquire more power by coping with uncertainties which affect larger areas of organizational activity. This means that power does not organize around unimportant or uncritical resources. It is sometimes difficult to operationalize the concepts of pervasiveness or criticality because what is critical depends, in part, on existing organizational dependencies and arrangements, themselves affected by conditions of scarcity and power. Thus, the definition of what is critical is itself open to a social contest and becomes an important focus in the contest for control.

Critical uncertainties and contingencies can arise from within or from outside the organization. Crozier (1964), for instance, studied a French cigarette factory and found that the maintenance engineers held considerable power in the organization because they controlled the one remaining uncertainty the organization faced—the repair of the machinery. Perrow (1970) provided evidence of power accruing from the handling of external contingencies. In a sample of 12 manufacturing firms, Perrow found that the marketing department was almost invariably the most powerful subunit, which he interpreted by noting the critical role of marketing in an American economy of affluence and consumerism.

One critical concern facing most organizations is that of obtaining sufficient resources. Considering this, it seems reasonable that those who contribute most to maintaining organizational resources would develop power in the organization. Resource exchanges are more directly measurable than some other components of uncertainty or contingency. In a study of the power of academic departments within the University of Illinois, Salancik and Pfeffer (1974) found that departmental power was best predicted by the proportion of outside grant and contract money the department brought into the university, closely followed by the department's national prestige and graduate program size. In a research-oriented university, the most critical resources are research funding and academic status. Both funding dollars and prestige are acquired from the organization's environment. Decisions taken at the national level providing physical sciences with more research support (Lodahl and Gordon, 1973) thus affect the ability of physical science departments to acquire grant and contract funds. The ability to acquire funding externally, in turn, leads to their power within universities and hence to their ability to obtain larger shares of internal budget allocations (Pfeffer and Salancik, 1974). The importance of the environment is that it sets the conditions that provide for the organizing of power within organizations.

Individual influence with an organizational subunit has been found to be determined in an analogous fashion. In a study of individual faculty influence within a single department, Salancik, Calder, Rowland, Leblebici, and Conway (1975) found that the national scholarly reputations of faculty members was the primary determinant. What is interesting about this case is that reputation, while mediated externally, is itself unmeasured but is assumed from more visible surrogate measures of activity, such as publication or attendance at meetings. In the same paper, an analysis of an insurance company showed that the influence of subunit managers was related not only to hierarchical position but also to the direct involvement of the subunit in maintaining the organization's revenues. Thus, underwriting managers were most influential, claims managers next most influential, and managers of functions unrelated to revenues, such as mailroom and payroll managers, were least influential.

The previously cited studies, while empirically and methodologically sophisticated, are all essentially case studies of single organizations or subunits. Pfeffer and Leong (1977) provide more direct

evidence for the power-dependence model by analyzing resource allocations to member agencies in 66 United Funds across the United States.
Pfeffer and Leong found that allocations to member agencies within
the fund were a function of the members' power, determined by their
dependence on the fund and the fund's dependence on them. For each
type of dependence, the meditating agent was the environmental context. Agencies were less dependent on the fund to the extent that they
could obtain outside support for their operations. The fund, on the
other hand, was more dependent on particular agencies to the extent
that those agencies brought legitimacy and visibility through their
participation. Again, the ability to obtain resources appears to be an
important determinant of subunit (agency) power within a social
structure.

In another study, Salancik, Pfeffer, and Kelley (in press) examined the distribution and correlates of influence in 17 organizations
deciding to purchase offset printing equipment. The decision to purchase equipment presented different kinds of problems to the organization as a function of the organizational context. From the basic idea
of strategic contingencies theory, it was expected that the influence of
individuals in making the decision would depend on the nature of
problematic uncertainty created by the decision context. An equipment
purchase can represent either of three decision contexts: a new purchase, a replacement purchase, or an additional purchase. In the case
of a new purchase, in which the firm buys the equipment for the first
time, information about the product was relatively more uncertain.
The prediction was that those with most contact with outside information sources or most involved in acquiring and communicating information would be most influential in the decision to purchase. For
replacing equipment, evaluation of competing machinery was thought
to be most critical uncertainty. The organization had expertise with
printing equipment, so information acquisition was not likely to be
important. But experience and knowledge of the equipment should be
important capabilities for making comparisons between the old and
the new and thus should be sources of influence in the decision. For
firms which were adding another piece of equipment, the determination of a need for more equipment was thought to be the most
problematic uncertainty faced by the organization, and it was expected
that individuals who did determine need would have the most influence in making the purchase. The analysis of variations in correlates of
influence in the organizations confirmed these expectations. The bases
of influence varied systematically across the 17 organizations as a function of the decision being concerned with a new, replacement, or additional purchase. Despite the small sample, the fact that the base of

influence varied with the nature of the critical uncertainty provides support for the strategic contingencies theory.

Indeterminacy in the Contingency-Power Relationship

The studies described above show consistent support for the first causal link in our model, the connection between environmental contingencies and internal power distributions. The link, however, may not be perfectly determined for several reasons. First, the environment does not come knocking on the organization's door announcing its critical contingencies. Rather, organizational participants must enact and interpret their environment and its effects on the organization. Since contingencies determine power and there are benefits to having control within the organization, one can be certain that enactments are not apolitical interpretations of events. As Thompson (1967) perceptively noted, it is not in the interest of those in power to call attention to changes in contingencies when such changes would diminish their own influence. Not only is it not in their interests, but the very structure of the organization's information system may prevent changes becoming known. Since information systems are themselves set up on the basis of past contingencies, as described in Chapter Four, change may be inaccurately perceived if perceived at all.

The fact that perception of environmental contingencies is an active process engaged in by organizational members does not mean that any subunit can enact the environment for its benefit and thereby lay claim to more power and resources. Such claims to importance take place in a social environment of other claimants, who are also likely to be affected by the current power structure of the organization. Pfeffer and Salancik (in press) examined the effect of advocating the use of criteria most favorable to the subunit on resource allocations, controlling for other bases of allocation such as power and objective criteria. These authors found that there was a positive correlation between advocating one's interests and resource allocations, but that this relationship was larger for more powerful subunits. The acceptance of arguments about what are the critical contingencies is itself determined by the distribution of power within the organization.

A second reason for expecting some indeterminacy in the relationship between environmental contingencies and internal power is that power can become institutionalized. By institutionalization we mean the establishment of relatively permanent structures and policies which favor one subunit's influence. One source of institutionalization of power is the definition of organizational contingencies and problems. Power distributions may be stable because problems from the environment tend to be perceived in ways that define them as similar to past problems. In part, this is a normal tendency for persons to categorize problems in ways that are familiar and tractable. Cyert and March (1963) argued that the search for solutions to problems would initially be localized in those parts of the organization identifying the problem. The cognitive bias leading to the identification of problems as being within one's specialty (Dearborn and Simon, 1958) and to searching for solutions requiring one's specialty would create stability in a power structure determined by the requirements for dealing with contingencies. As new problems arise, they would tend to be categorized in familiar ways and solutions created with current capabilities. The more ambiguous the situation and the more uncertain the information and the impact of any given proposal, the more likely power will be institutionalized as a result of the tendency to identify contingencies in familiar terms.

Power also may be institutionalized by the intentional actions of power holders. While in power, a dominant coalition has the ability to formulate constitutions, rules, procedures, and information systems that limit the potential power of others and ensure their own, continuing control. Political leaders frequently use their power first to change a country's constitution, claiming this is a necessary step, as a way of ensuring their continued tenure in office. Another source of institutionalization is the ability to coopt competing interest groups by offering small favors and rewards. The limited access and participation granted may be sufficient to ensure continued support even when new contingencies arise. Other sources of institutionalization include the ability to control and restrict the flow of information, both the flow from the environment and the distribution of information within the organization.

Whatever the source or form of institutionalization, the effect is to extend a subunit's power beyond its utility to the organization for its survival. Institutionalization is, of course, not absolute, and when confronted with persistent failure, no dominant coalition is permanently secure. The evidence of past failures and problems and the crises which mark turnover in control frequently only represent the surfacing of previously undisclosed problems of current power holders. Indeed, one might suggest that a measure of the extent to which power is institutionalized is the magnitude of the problem that must occur before the organization responds.

The institutionalization of power, a topic not empirically explored, would tend to weaken any direct link between environmental contingencies and intraorganizational power. Thus, there should be an imperfect relationship between the sources of organizational uncertainty and the distribution of influence.

EXECUTIVE SUCCESSION AND
ORGANIZATIONAL POWER

The second step in the model of organizational change specifies that one outcome of the distribution of power within the organization is the selection and tenure of individuals in major administrative positions. Since power conveys the ability to influence organizational decisions (e.g., Pfeffer and Salancik, 1974), it is likely that power will be used to influence the choice of top administrative personnel. Indeed, the designation of formal leaders is one of the most obvious ways of institutionalizing power in organizations.

We assume that the problems and difficulties facing the organization are likely to be attributed to the administrator, regardless of whether the administrator is the cause of such problems (e.g., Gamson and Scotch, 1964). Visible failure calls into question the competence of those in control, and the administrators become visible and, at times, arbitrary targets. One empirical implication of this assumption is that administrators will tend to be removed when organizational performance is below acceptable levels. However, performance and organizational problems are not the critical variables in administrator removal. The administrator's own perceived capacity or incapacity for dealing with the problems is important. Another critical factor is the importance of the problems facing the organization. The problems themselves must be important. And finally, another factor affecting the removal or tenure of administrators is the institutionalization of power; those who have institutionalized their positions of control should last longer given the same level of performance problems. In brief, the tenure and removal of administrators should be a function of the existence of critical difficulties, frequently deriving from the organization's context, and the ability of the administrator to cope with these problems or to maintain control independent of his coping capability.

The selection of new administrators should be similarly related to the environmental context of the organization. Those in power should tend to select individuals who are capable of coping with the critical problems facing the organization. Such selection may occur as a consequence of planning or it may occur unintentionally. Organizational members in power may intentionally select administrators who have characteristics that would be useful in coping with the organization's context and contingencies. However, a similar result would arise unintentionally from the decision situation. There is a tendency, under certain conditions, for decision makers to favor candidates who are similar to themselves (e.g., Byrne, 1969; Berscheid and Walster, 1969). If some organizational subunits have more influence than others, it is likely that the leader selected will tend to have characteristics similar to those with power in the organization. There will be a tendency for accountants to think that an accountant should head the organization, and for marketing personnel to favor a leader with a marketing background. The resolution of such differences in opinion would be that those with more power would have more influence in the decision, so the person selected would reflect characteristics of those in power. Since subunit power is derived from coping with critical contingencies, the selected administrators will tend to have characteristics appropriate for the organization's context. Therefore, for either intended or unintended reasons, the characteristics of administrators should be related to the context of the organization, and particularly in the case of recently selected administrators rather than those who have more institutionalized positions.

We view administrative succession as a political process of contested capability, where the contest is resolved by subunit power. Surprisingly, there is very little literature relevant to this position. Succession and tenure have most frequently been related to organizational size (Grusky, 1961; Gordon and Becker, 1964), with inconsistent results. Size itself may be confounded with political aspects of organizations. Large size may be correlated with a larger number of departments or subunits, which provide more bases of power and therefore more potential contests for control. Organizations differ in the extent to which they have clear-cut performance criteria, as well as in their actual performance. Size may be complexly related to both of these factors. The typical approach to examining administrator tenure does not provide information about the process or causes of change, but it is not necessarily inconsistent with the approach we are developing.

A notable exception to the size-turnover theme was the study by Zald (1965) of succession in a large social welfare organization. Zald argued that succession to the position of chief administrator was the outcome of political processes within the organization. Similarly, Perrow (1961) has noted that control in hospitals passed from the trustees to the doctors and then to the professional hospital administrators. There is some suggestion in Perrow's analysis that control has changed as environmental contingencies facing hospitals have changed. While hospitals first faced problems of obtaining funding and later problems of accreditation and quality, today hospitals face problems of cost controls that require professionally trained administrators.

Pfeffer and Salancik (1977) directly examined the relationship between an organization's context and the tenure and selection of administrators in 57 midwestern hospitals. This study related context directly to administrator succession, without examining the intervening causal linkage of the relationship of context to power and power to succession. Though not explicating this intervening step, the study represents the only empirical examination relating succession to organizational context.

Pfeffer and Salancik argued that the selection and tenure of chief executives in organizations are consequences of the organization's context and the ability of administrators to cope with the uncertainties and contingencies deriving from that context. Three hypotheses guided the study. First, the frequency of executive turnover should be a function of the stability and problems confronted by the organization (Gouldner, 1954). Second, the characteristics of the chief executive should be systematically related to the organization's requirements for dealing with critical contingencies (Thompson, 1967). And third, to the extent that power is institutionalized, the relationship between context and selection will be attenuated. To examine these hypotheses, questionnaires were given to the chief administrators of hospitals. Data were obtained on the hospital's sources of funding, ownership, size, and competitive conditions. Professional backgrounds of current administrators were obtained, and tenure was assessed by measuring the length of time the administator had served in that position.

Organizational Context and Administrator Tenure

There is some evidence that long tenure in office is negatively associated with organizational problems. Grusky (1963) studied turnover of baseball managers and found turnover to be negatively related to team performance, which Gamson and Scotch (1964) argued represented scapegoating. Pfeffer and Leblebici (1973) found that the average length of tenure of chief executives in business organizations decreased as the organization's debt to equity ratio increased. McEachern (1975) observed that turnover of chief executives is more likely when the firms managed suffered declines in profits four or more years in a row. In a university, Salancik, Staw, and Pondy (1975) observed that turnover was more likely in academic departments that needed resources and had difficulty in acquiring them. Departments characterized by high resource interdependence among members also had higher turnover in the leadership position.

The study by Salancik et al. (1975) attempted to show that turnover was not only associated with the presence of organizational difficulties, but that a critical variable was the ability of the administrator to cope with these difficulties. In addition to characterizing departments by their requirements for resources, departments were also characterized by their degree of paradigm development. It was assumed that departments in high paradigm disciplines should find it easier to resolve issues of resource allocation since such departments have well-developed frameworks within which to make such decisions (Lodahl and Gordon, 1972). Salancik and his colleagues found that over a twenty-year period, turnover was greater in departments characterized by poorly developed paradigms and high resource interdependence. Departments that had difficulties in obtaining requisite resources and that were also unable to resolve conflict because of the absence of shared judgments experienced twice the rate of administrator turnover of other departments. Administrators, removed when problems confronting the subunit could not be resolved, were scapegoated, since the lack of consensus is a function of the department's discipline and not the administrator.

In the study of hospital administrators, Pfeffer and Salancik (1976) attempted to relate tenure to hospital problems by examining three sources of external contingencies: competition for funding and staff; relationships with business and general community interests; and the condition of the hospital's operating budget, specifically whether surpluses or deficits were being run.

Correlations between administrator tenure and hospital context are displayed in Table 9.1. Tenure was longer in hospitals with less competition for funding and staff. Tenure was also longer for administrators in hospitals with better relationships with the business and local community. On the other hand, there was no simple relationship be-

TABLE 9.1   Correlations Between Tenure and Variables of
            the Organizational Context

Variable	Correlation
Amount of competition for funding	−.19#
Amount of competition for staff	−.35**
Amount of competition for patients	−.09
Hospital's relations with the local business community	.24*
Hospital's relations with the local community	.29*
Hospital's current operating budget in surplus	.10
Hospital's operating budget five years ago in surplus	.07
Affiliated with a religious denomination	−.29*
Private, nonprofit hospital	.19#
Government-owned hospital	.03

# $p < .10$
* $p < .05$
** $p < .01$

tween tenure in office and the state of the hospital's operating budget.

The lack of a relationship between tenure and the operating budget might at first appear to be inconsistent with the idea that executive tenure is reduced by organizational problems. A more sophisticated analysis, however, suggests that the operating budget is more or less critical for different hospitals. Some hospitals rely on operating surpluses for financing capital projects. Other hospitals, however, rely more on private contributions for capital expenditures. Clearly, private donations and operating funds represent alternative sources of financing, and the importance of operating funds for the hospital is contingent on the importance of private donations. Therefore, for hospitals which do not rely on private donations, tenure should be related to the status of the hospital's operating budget. For hospitals relying on private donations, tenure and the operating budget should be relatively uncorrelated. More important to hospitals relying on private donations should be the relationship with sources providing donations, such as the business community.

To examine the effect of funding sources on hospital administrator tenure, the 57 hospitals were divided into those with larger and those with smaller proportions of their capital budgets obtained from private donations. For hospitals relying more on donations, administrator tenure was highly correlated with the hospital's relations with the business community ($r = .43$) and was virtually independent of the status of the operating budget ($r = .01$). For hospitals relying less on donations and more on operating funds, administrator tenure was correlated with the operating budget condition ($r = .23$), and while also correlated with the hospital's relations with the business community, this correlation was smaller than for the other set of hospitals. The evidence suggests that it is not the presence of problems, but the criticality of the problems to the organization that affect administrator tenure.

Another factor we have suggested that might affect administrator tenure is the institutionalization of power in the organization. To the extent power becomes institutionalized, the administrator can continue even when confronted by unresolvable contingencies. This source of indeterminacy in the environmental-context–administrator-tenure relationship can be indirectly examined by considering the moderating effects of variables which might be associated with power institutionalization. One such variable is the ownership of the organization. In the study of hospitals, there was some relationship between ownership and tenure, with a positive association for administrators in private, non-profit hospitals and a negative association between tenure and administering a hospital affiliated with a religious denomination. There are a variety of ad hoc explanations that could be mustered for these relationships, including the fact that administrators of private, nonprofit hospitals are not embedded in a larger organization with a hierarchy of authority, as is the case for both religious and government hospitals.

Business organizations provide a better setting for observing the effects of ownership on tenure. In an insightful reexamination of the separation of ownership and control issue (e.g., Berle and Means, 1932), McEachern (1975) categorized firms as being: (1) owner-managed, in which the firm was both controlled and managed by the owners; (2) externally controlled, in which the firm was controlled by owners but managed by other managers; and (3) manager-controlled, in which the firm was both controlled and managed by nonowning managers. In the first case, dominant shareholders are involved in the management of the firm. For the owners to fire the managers would involve firing themselves. In the second case, there are dominant shareholders who control the firm but leave its management to others. In this case, the manager is readily fired since there is some concentration of power to accomplish the removal. It might be expected that tenure would be longer for executives in firms of the third type, in which the managers both controlled and ran the organization.

McEachern related the three types of ownership to executive turnover. Estimated equations for a sample of 96 firms and an industry sample of 48 firms are presented in Table 9.2. As expected, there are some dramatic differences between types of ownership and tenure. Tenure is about twice as long in the owner-managed firms than in either of the other two categories. While the coefficients in the two equations are in a direction indicating some effect of management control to lengthen tenure, neither coefficient is statistically significant.

Neither of the analyses reported by Pfeffer and Salancik (1977) or by McEachern (1975) test the more reasonable proposition that

TABLE 9.2   Executive Tenure and Organizational Control

$$T = 5.68 + 11.44\,OM + .65\,MC + .027\,D = .41\,P \qquad r^2 - \quad .19$$
$$(3.34)\quad\;\;(.24)\quad\;\;(.74)\quad\;(.15) \qquad\qquad n - 48$$
$$T = 4.59 + 10.97\,OM + .12\,MC \qquad\qquad\qquad\qquad r^2 - \quad .36$$
$$(6.46)\quad\;\;\;(.07) \qquad\qquad\qquad\qquad\qquad n - 96$$

Results taken from McEachern (1975).

T = manager-controlled dummy variable
OM = owner-managed dummy variable
MC = dummy variable for firms in drug industry
D = executive tenure
P = dummy variable for firms in petroleum industry

ownership has effects on tenure depending on the level of organizational performance. One possible reason why neither study found stronger results is that it would be expected that ownership would interact with organizational performance to determine tenure. If the administrator were handling the job brilliantly, he would remain in office regardless of ownership. It is only when the organization confronts difficulties that the institutionalization of power, represented by differences in ownership, would have a differential effect on tenure.

The length of an administrator's tenure in office is likely to be less when there is visible evidence of his inability to cope with critical contingencies and he is unable to institutionalize control. While there has been limited research directed to this issue, the available evidence is at least not inconsistent with this proposition.

Organizational Context and the Characteristics of Administrators

We have suggested that the organizational context tends to encourage the selection of administrators appropriate for coping with that context. Anecdotal evidence seems consistent with this position. At one time corporate executives tended to be drawn from the ranks of line production executives, who could cope with the problems of production. As production became increasingly routinized and mechanized, the problems changed to selling the products, and marketing executives became more prominent. Then, in the 1960s, financial concerns became more important because capital shortages, mergers and takeovers, and credit crunches made financing the critical organizational contingency. Financial executives came into power in organizations. Most recently, corporations have faced regulatory and legal problems, and lawyers have become increasingly powerful and prominent as chief executives. Pacific Gas and Electric, a public utility, formerly was dominated by engineers. Today, most of the engineers who populated the high administrative positions are gone, replaced by lawyers who can deal with the increasingly complex legal and regulatory environment.

If our argument is correct, and hospitals also select administrators who can cope with critical contingencies, then we should find systematic relationships between the hospital's context and the characteristics of its chief administrator. Pfeffer and Salancik (1977) examined the relationship between the hospital administrator's formal training in hospital administration and dimensions of the organizational context. The relevant correlations are displayed in Table 9.3. Training in hospital administration was related, as expected, to the context of the funding sources. Hospital administrators tended to have more training

TABLE 9.3   Correlations Between Amount of Training in Hospital Administration and Other Variables

Variable	Correlation	Level of Significance
Proportion of operating budget obtained from payments by private insurers	.47	.001
Proportion of operating budget obtained from private donations	−.23	.08
Proportion of operating budget obtained from government	−.44	.002
Proportion of capital budget obtained from donations	−.26	.10
Proportion of capital budget obtained from the federal government	−.24	.10
Classification as a government-owned hospital	−.30	.02
Hospital affiliated with a religious denomination	.29	.02
Private, nonprofit hospital	−.08	—
Surplus in operating budget	.41	.001

to the extent that the organizations received insurance funds and less training when private donations were more important.

The correlations in Table 9.3 are not very large, however. We have suggested that the extent to which administrators' capabilities will be aligned with environmental contingencies will vary with the institutionalization of control by the administrator. More recently appointed administrators should be more aligned with the environmental contingencies facing the hospital, for the longer-tenured administrators may, in part, reflect stable institutionalized structures of control.

The sample of 57 hospitals was divided according to the length of the administrator's tenure. The subsample of recently appointed administrators, constituting about one-half the sample, held office for four years or less. The correlations between context and training in hospital administration for the two subsamples of long-tenured and recently appointed administrators are displayed in Table 9.4. As expected, the relationships displayed in that table are stronger for more recently appointed administrators. This suggests that not only are administrator characteristics predicted by the organization's context, but that new appointments are even more strongly affected by the organizational environment. The study of hospital administrators is generally consistent with our argument that one manifestation of the environment's impact on organizations is through the selection of administrators.

TABLE 9.4   Correlations Between Training in Hospital Administration and Variables of Context for Two Subsamples

Variable	Hospitals with Low-tenured Administrators	Hospitals with High-tenured Administrators
Proportion of the operating budget obtained from payments by private insurers	.60**	.35#
Proportion of operating budget obtained from private donations	−.32#	−.23
Proportion of operating budget obtained from government	−.74***	−.13
Proportion of capital budget obtained from private donations	−.35#	−.25
Proportion of capital budget obtained from federal government	−.54*	.02
Classification as a government-owned hospital	−.36*	−.19
Hospital affiliated with a religious denomination	.20	.37*
Private, nonprofit hospital	.01	−.10

*** $p < .001$
** $p < .01$
* $p < .05$
# $p < .10$

EXECUTIVE DISCRETION AND ORGANIZATIONAL DECISION MAKING

The final link in the model of environment-organizational effects suggested that the administrator can affect decisions that direct the structure and activities of the organization. Presumably, such direction is to make the organization more consistent with the requirements of its environment. Thus, hospital administrators bring ideas for change, establishing elaborate inventory and cost accounting systems and investing in modern management systems and advanced equipment to reduce costs. They make decisions that redesign the organization in line with their views of what is needed. As in the case of the other linkages, the link between the administrator and organizational action is imperfect.

Child (1972) has noted that many researchers have posited various forms of technological or environmental determinism. Environmental or technological factors are presumed to place overwhelming constraints or requirements on the organization. The role of administrators can be safely ignored since the design and activities of organizations are dictated by these constraints. Although the few studies that have attempted to estimate the amount of variance in organizational performance attributable to administrators (Lieberson and O'Connor, 1972; Salancik and Pfeffer, 1977) have found that the administrator accounts for relatively little variation, there is some administrator effect. Complete determinism seems unlikely. Some change in organizational activities and performance is associated with administrators.

Although we are sympathetic with the view that the environment constrains the organization's design and activities—indeed, this is one of the points we have tried to emphasize throughout the book—we believe a more sophisticated and complex understanding of the process is required. There is some empirical evidence that organizational administrators can affect decisions, particularly for their own benefit. Stagner (1969), for instance, in a survey of business executives, reported that the executives claimed that powerful departments could get their way without regard to the welfare of the entire organization. Pfeffer and Salancik (1974) found that power of subunits was an important predictor of budget allocations in a university, and that even after accounting for subunit power, administrative strategies had statistically significant effects on resource allocations (Pfeffer and Salancik, in press). The various case studies of business firm decision making tend to indicate the importance of who is in control for predicting organizational actions. Cyert et al. (1956) found that forecasts were developed to justify the desired decisions, rather than having the decisions based on the forecasts. Baldridge's (1971) case study of an eastern university also suggests the applicability of a political model of organizational functioning, stressing the importance of who is in control.

A more realistic perspective on organizational action would recognize that organizational actors mold organizational activities, but do so within constraints which limit their discretion to take action. To explicate such a perspective it is necessary to develop a model that suggests how much constraint an administrator faces in formulating action. Both the omnipotent administrator and the impotent administrator are equally inaccurate representations of reality. It is necessary to develop a model specifying how much effect administrators can, or should, have and under what conditions.

Perhaps the most important thing to recognize about discretion is that it is rarely unilateral. Discretion, as well as power, is shared in organizations. The manager, though a leader, is also a follower who responds to the demands of those with whom he deals and upon whom he depends for support to accomplish his own activities. The subordinate, although sometimes thought of as dependent, can be seen as powerful, since the subordinate frequently controls resources or performances critical to the activities of the manager (e.g., Mechanic, 1962). Pfeffer and Salancik (1975) attempted to illustrate the external constraint on leader behavior in a study of first-line supervisors in a housing office in a large state university. The supervisors were asked to describe how they behaved with respect to a variety of activities and also how they thought their subordinates, bosses, and peers wanted them to act. Analyses indicated that supervisors were more likely to behave as their subordinates wanted when they were more similar to their subordinates (in sex and work activities) and more integrated with subordinates in the social network. The supervisors reported acting in conformity with the demands of their bosses to the extent that they were more similar to the boss and that they faced pressure for performance.

In another study conducted in an insurance company, Salancik et al. (1975) asked subordinates how they wanted their bosses to act and compared these demands with the managers' own reports of activities. The behaviors consisted of those commonly associated with work and supervision. Supervisors were classified according to how much their organizational position required them to coordinate their department's activities with other departments. The hypothesis stated that the more a given manager had to coordinate with other departments, the more constrained his behavior would be and the less likely he would be able to construct behaviors corresponding to the demands of subordinates. As predicted, an inverse relationship was observed between the extent of coordination with others and the supervisor's satisfaction of subordinate demands ($r = -.91$).

In another attempt to understand how administrators formulate actions in a political and social context, Pfeffer and Salancik (1976) examined the relative discretion of mayors on city budget items for a sample of 30 United States cities. They argued that the mayor should have more or less discretion depending upon the level of organized interests operating in the city. Measuring mayor effect as the amount of variation in budget categories attributable to the mayors from an analysis of variance procedure (e.g., Salancik and Pfeffer, 1977), Pfeffer and Salancik found that mayors confronting conditions associated with less organized interests had more effect on budget categories. Mayors with more discretion were in cities with a higher proportion of nonwhites, lower median income, and with a higher proportion of persons employed in government employment and construction. Mayors with less discretion were in cities with higher median income, more persons employed in manufacturing (a surrogate measure of unionization), and with a higher proportion of professional and managerial persons. These results indicate that administrator effects are reduced by organized, potent interests, and that factors associated with these interests therefore can be used to partially predict administrator effects.

Although there has been remarkably little attention to organizational decision making and managerial action, the information presented above suggests that a model of managerial behavior and its consequences can be developed. It will be necessary to take into account the social and political realities of organizations and to consider that actions are formulated under constraints mediated by others in the organization who have their own power and discretion. This model of decision making within organizations, it should be evident, is similar to the argument we have developed with regard to organizations operating in externally controlled environments. Power is shared and actions are consequences of power. Power, in turn, results from dependencies and interdependencies between actors attempting to achieve their own objectives.

Child (1972) has argued that a number of organizational structures and actions may be consistent with environmental requirements. His emphasis on strategic choice reintroduces the importance of control and power to the analysis of organizations. Of course, it is possible that the strategic variations resulting from choice are only short-term effects, and that over longer periods of time, environmental determinism such as that resulting from selection may predict the organization-environment relationship. Although this possibility warrants exploration, the available evidence indicates that organizational decisions differ depending on who controls the organization.

EXECUTIVE RECRUITMENT AND INTERFIRM COORDINATION

Thus far in this chapter we have described executive succession as a mechanism for organizational change, affected by the distribution of power within the organization and the organization's context and, in turn, affecting organizational designs and decisions. Another role served by executive succession is the integration of the organization with its environment and the development of coordinated structures of interorganizational behavior. We shall review some evidence consistent with this position and indicate how such results might be expected to emerge from the succession process.

In developing coordinated structures of interorganizational behavior, processes of communication and socialization are important. We argue that the movement of personnel, such as executives, between organizations is one important form of interorganizational communication that can facilitate the development of coordinated structures of behavior. Baty, Evan, and Rothermel (1971), who studied the movement of faculty between schools of business, wrote that "the recruitment of human resources, a universal and recurrent organizational process, gives rise to the flow of personnel, and concurrently, to a flow of information among organizations; for just as members of a society are carriers of the culture which they transmit consciously and unconsciously to the next generation, so members of an organization are carriers of its subculture, which they transmit to new members" (1971:430).

Executive succession, therefore, is itself one strategic response to environmental contingencies. Executive recruitment and succession patterns, much like other forms of interorganizational linkage activity, such as mergers or joint ventures, may derive from interorganizational interdependence. Characteristics of organizational contexts which hinder or assist in the development of collective structures of behavior should similarly affect executive movement between organizations. Just such an argument was explored in a study of executive recruitment by Pfeffer and Leblebici (1973).

Twenty randomly selected 4-digit Standard Industrial Classification Code (SIC) manufacturing industries were studied, with at least five companies sampled from each industry. Background data on executives from each company were obtained from the World Who's Who in Finance and Industry (1972) and from Who's Who in America (1972). Industry characteristics were also obtained. From the company data, the following variables were computed for each of the 20 industries: (1) the proportion of the top executives who had their previous job in the same company; (2) the proportion of top executives who had their previous job in the same industry; (3) the proportion whose previous job was in the government, including the military; (4) the proportion whose previous job was in finance or banking; (5) the average number of total job changes; (6) the average number of years spent in the same company; (7) the average number of years spent in the company before attaining the chief executive position; (8) the number of years spent in the corporate level chief executive position; (9) the number of years spent in the present position; and (10) the average number of years spent outside the company.

As argued previously in the case of mergers and joint ventures, two important conditions for developing interfirm organizations among competitors are the number of firms in the industry and their concentration. With numerous organizations, there is little possibility of developing a collective structure of interorganizational behavior without relying on formal mechanisms. A small number of firms, on the other hand, leads to the possibility of developing tacit coordination through personnel flows. Therefore, we hypothesize that a small number of firms will be associated with executive movements that could enhance communication among organizations. Executives would tend to move within the same industry, have a larger number of job changes, and tend to have been with the company a shorter period of time. Such personnel flows can socialize executives to industry practices and provide interfirm coordination.

Differences in concentration from a median value would tend to reduce both the possibility and the necessity of developing collective structures of behavior through executive movement. Therefore, one would expect executive movement which develops interfirm structures to be most prevalent in industries with intermediate concentration.

In Table 9.5, the correlations between measures of industry context and the characteristics of executive succession and recruitment are displayed. The examination of the results tends to support both the importance of context as an explanation for executive change and recruitment patterns and the relative importance of socialization and interfirm communication factors compared to variables such as firm size or financial structure.

In the first column of the table, the relationship between the number of firms in the industry and executive recruitment characteristics can be seen. As expected, there is a negative correlation with the proportion of executives with previous jobs in the same industry, indicating there is more recruitment within the industry the *smaller* the number of firms. This result is, of course, inconsistent with a relative supply argument. The supply of executives to be recruited from within the industry is larger the larger the number of firms in the industry. The average number of job changes is larger the smaller the number of firms, while the average time spent in the company before attaining the chief executive position and the average number of years spent in that position are both larger in industries with more firms.

A generally similar pattern of results emerges when one considers the second column in the table, the difference in concentration from a median value. Uncertainty is greatest when concentration is intermediate. There is a larger number of job changes in industries with intermediate levels of concentration; executives spend more time in the same company in very concentrated or very unconcentrated industries. More time is spent outside the company the closer industry concentration is to the median value. Both the number of firms results and concentration results support the idea that executive recruitment

TABLE 9.5   Correlations Between Variables of Organizational Size and Industry Context and Characteristics of Executive Recruitment

	Number of Organizations	Difference in Concentration from Median Value	Growth in Industry Sales	Growth in Industry Productivity	Debt/ Equity	Size
X1	−.04	.14	−.43*	−.15	.14	−.12
X2	−.32**	−.21	.49*	.49*	.32**	.32**
X3	−.11	−.12	.63***	.58***	.10	−.05
X4	−.32**	−.07	−.26	.25	.11	−.07
X5	−.36**	−.61***	.37**	.02	−.00	.24
X6	.31**	.58***	−.43*	−.13	−.12	−.11
X7	.53***	.62***	−.35**	−.37**	−.27	−.19
X8	.31**	.07	−.10	.39**	−.34**	.12
X9	−.14	−.29**	−.11	.03	−.30**	.01
X10	−.28	−.61***	−.39*	.03	−.09	.09

* $p < .05$
** $p < .10$
*** $p < .01$

X1 = proportion of executives with last job in the same company
X2 = proportion of executives with last job in the same industry
X3 = proportion of executives with last job in the government, including military
X4 = proportion of executives with last job in finance and banking
X5 = average number of job changes
X6 = average number of years spent in same company
X7 = average number of years spent in company before attaining chief executive position
X8 = average number of years spent in chief executive position
X9 = average number of years spent in the present position
X10 = average number of years spent outside the company

follows the environmental context, either as a strategic response of interfirm coordination or because of performance characteristics of firms operating in such industries.

Growth rate of industry sales and the rate of technological change, measured by growth in industry productivity (Gort, 1962), are both likely to upset industry equilibria, and therefore tend to be associated with more outside recruitment. Growth in industry sales is negatively associated with recruitment from within the same company and is positively associated with the number of job changes. Growth in industry sales tends to have both more statistically significant and more consistent effects than growth in industry productivity, the measure of technological change.

Finally, in spite of the importance of size in previous discussions of executive succession (e.g., Grusky, 1961), size has almost no statistically significant effect on any of the succession variables. There is no effect on tenure and no effect on inside versus outside succession for this sample of firms and industries.

The examination of executive recruitment indicates that there is more mobility associated with interfirm communication and socialization processes: (1) the smaller the number of firms; (2) the closer industry concentration is to the median value; (3) and the greater the growth rate of industry sales. These results are consistent with the idea that executives are recruited in response to the organizational context; executives seem to be more actively recruited from competitors when it is feasible to develop interfirm coordination through informal mechanisms (there are a small number of firms) and when it is necessary to do so (concentration is intermediate so competitive uncertainty is high; growth is relatively rapid so relative positions in the industry are changing unpredictably). The fact that the same contextual variables used to analyze mergers and joint ventures can again account for another dimension of interfirm behavior is quite important for its support of the basic theoretical argument.

Interfirm Coordination of the Model of Organizational Change

The discussion of the function of executive succession in managing organizational interdependence has been couched in terms that imply some intentional, strategic action taken by organizations to manage environmental uncertainty. Although such purposiveness may, in fact, be the case, it is not necessary to make any assumptions about intent to observe the results reported by Pfeffer and Leblebici (1973). Indeed, we can consider the tenure and selection of executives using the model developed to examine hospital administrators and can derive the results for the sample of industrial firms.

We have argued previously that turnover tends to be created by contingencies that present administrators cannot handle. In the case of hospitals, we saw the more problematic the organization's context (i.e., the greater the competition for funding and the poorer the relations with the local environment) the lower the average tenure for administrators. In the present case, concentration being intermediate is associated with greater uncertainty and unpredictability, as is rapid growth in industry sales. In highly concentrated industries, there tends to be more price stability, as well as stability in market shares. In very unconcentrated industries, there is little uncertainty arising from interdependence because there is little interdependence among competing organizations. Thus, as we have argued previously, competitive uncertainty deriving from interdependence is highest at intermediate levels of concentration. Similarly, the more rapidly sales change in the industry, the more instability in industry structure and operations introduced.

Uncertainty is related to both median concentration and rapid sales growth, and it is also the case that uncertainty is likely to lead to higher rates of turnover in executive positions. Other things being equal, the greater the level of uncertainty, the less likely it will be that any given executive can cope with that uncertainty successfully. Consequently, the greater uncertainty would tend to produce more problems and more executive turnover.

We have also argued that organizations will tend to select new administrators with characteristics likely to be associated with the capacity for dealing with current organizational problems. If organizations face uncertainty and instability deriving from competitive interdependence, then it is likely that these organizations will select new executives from within the industry, from competing firms, in an effort to reduce this competitive uncertainty. If there is little or no competitive uncertainty, because the industry is very concentrated or extremely unconcentrated, there would be less reason to recruit an executive from within the industry, since the management of competitive uncertainty would be less important.

Thus, we see that if median concentration and rapid growth are related to uncertainty, it is likely that there will be more turnover when these conditions obtain, and furthermore, executives selected will tend to be from within the industry to cope with the competitive uncertainty and interdependence. As a consequence of the operation of a series of processes not necessarily intentionally developed, it is likely that in this case, as in many others, organizations will take actions to align themselves with environmental requirements and take such actions in part through executive succession processes.

SUMMARY

We have considered one mechanism by which organizational context comes to affect organizations. We argued that there is a causal sequence that may occur in which environmental contingencies affect internal power distributions, internal power affects executive succession, and executive succession, through its effects on training, frame of reference, and information, comes to affect organizational behavior. While not the only mechanism of organizational change or the only process through which environments may affect organizations, we suggest that executive succession is a very important process by which organizations become aligned with their environments.

In a study of patterns of executive recruitment in manufacturing industries, it was found that executive recruitment may also be a strategic response to a need for interorganizational coordination among competitors. The movement of executives among organizations, viewed as information exchanges that enhance coordination, was most likely in industries of intermediate concentration, small number of firms, and high rates of sales growth. Such interorganizational coordination through the movement of personnel could be assumed to take place without assuming rational strategic action on the part of the organizations involved. High levels of competitive uncertainty may be expected to result in higher turnover, and executives would be more likely to be recruited from within the same industry to manage or cope with this competitive uncertainty.

It is clear that additional attention to the processes by which contexts come to affect organizations is warranted. The available empirical evidence is consistent with the model we have proposed and suggests the importance of executive succession. However, there is an astonishing lack of attention to developing models of administration and administrative effect on organizational structure and action. Sociological analyses tend to dismiss the administrator as unimportant and substitute a perspective of environmental determinism; industrial and organizational psychologists tend to concentrate on lower levels of management and on the supervisory component of administrative behavior. Reading the psychological literature, one might conclude that leadership was all important.

We have suggested that administrators have some discretion and operate within constraints. The important issues become what determines the amount of discretion and what are the administrative processes that both extend and limit the discretion available. Change comes through administrative succession because managers can, in fact, alter things. Such change is partially predictable, however, by the environmental context because administrators also operate within constraints, many of which come from the organization's context.

REFERENCES

Aldrich, H. E., and J. Pfeffer. 1976. "Environments of organizations." *Annual Review of Sociology*, 2:79–105.

Baldridge, J. V. 1971. *Power and Conflict in the University*. New York: Wiley.

Baty, G. B., W. M. Evan, and T. W. Rothermel. 1971. "Personnel flows as interorganizational relations." *Administrative Science Quarterly*, 16: 430–443.

Berle, A. A., and G. C. Means. 1932. *The Modern Corporation and Private Property*. New York: Macmillan.

Berscheid, E., and E. Walster. 1969. *Interpersonal Attraction*. Reading, Mass.: Addison-Wesley.

Blau, P. M. 1964. *Exchange and Power in Social Life*. New York: Wiley.

Byrne, D. 1969. "Attitude and attraction." In L. Berkowitz (ed.), *Advances in Experimental Social Psychology*, Vol. 4, 35–89. New York: Academic Press.

Child, J. 1972. "Organization structure, environment, and performance—the role of strategic choice." *Sociology*, 6:1–22.

Crozier, M. 1964. *The Bureaucratic Phenomenon*. University of Chicago Press.

Cyert, R. M., and J. G. March. 1963. *A Behavioral Theory of the Firm*. Englewood Cliffs, N.J.: Prentice-Hall.

Cyert, R. M., H. A. Simon, and D. B. Trow. 1956. "Observation of a business decision." *Journal of Business*, 29:237–248.

Dearborn, D. C., and H. A. Simon. 1958. "Selective perception: a note on the departmental identification of executives." *Sociometry*, 21:140–144.

Duncan, R. 1972. "Characteristics of organizational environments and perceived environmental uncertainty." *Administrative Science Quarterly*, 17:313–327.

Emerson, R. E. 1962. "Power-dependence relations." *American Sociological Review*, 27:31–41.

Emery, F. E., and E. L. Trist. 1965. "The causal texture of organizational environments." *Human Relations*, 18:21–32.

Gamson, W. A., and N. Scotch. 1964. "Scapegoating in baseball." *American Journal of Sociology*, 70:69–76.

Gordon, G., and S. Becker. 1964. "Organizational size and managerial succession: a reexamination." *American Journal of Sociology*, 70:215–223.

Gort, M. 1962. *Diversification and Integration in American Industry*. Princeton University Press.

Gouldner, A. W. *Patterns of Industrial Bureaucracy*. New York: Free Press.

Grusky, O. 1961. "Corporate size, bureaucratization, and managerial succession." *American Journal of Sociology*, 67:263–269.

Grusky, O. 1963. "Managerial succession and organizational effectiveness." *American Journal of Sociology*, 69:21–31.

Hickson, D. J., C. R. Hinings, C. A. Lee, R. E. Schneck, and J. M. Pennings. 1971. "A strategic contingencies' theory of intraorganizational power." *Administrative Science Quarterly*, 16:216–229.

Lawrence, P. R., and J. W. Lorsch. *Organization and Environment*. Boston: Harvard University Press.

Lieberson, S., and J. F. O'Connor. "Leadership and organizational performance: a study of large corporations." *American Sociological Review*, 37:117–130.

Lodahl, J., and G. Gordon. 1972. "The structure of scientific fields and the functioning of university graduate departments." *American Sociological Review*, 37:57–72.

Lodahl, J., and G. Gordon. 1973. "Funding the sciences in university departments." *Educational Record*, 54:74–82.

Marquis Who's Who. 1972a. *Who's Who in America*. Chicago: Marquis Who's Who.

Marquis Who's Who. 1972b. *World Who's Who in Finance and Industry*. Chicago: Marquis Who's Who.

McEachern, W. A. 1975. *Managerial Control and Performance*. Lexington, Mass.: Heath.

Mechanic, D. 1962. "Sources of power of lower participants in complex organizations." *Administrative Science Quarterly*, 7:349–364.

Perrow, C. 1961. "The analysis of goals in complex organizations." *American Sociological Review*, 26:854–866.

Perrow, C. 1970. "Departmental power and perspective in industrial firms." In M. N. Zald (ed.), *Power in Organizations*, 59–89. Nashville, Tenn.: Vanderbilt University Press.

Pfeffer, J., and H. Leblebici. 1973. "The effect of competition on some dimensions of organizational structure." *Social Forces*, 52:268–279.

Pfeffer, J., and A. Leong. "Resource allocations in United Funds: an examination of power and dependence." *Social Forces*, 55:775–790.

Pfeffer, J., and G. R. Salancik. 1974. "Organizational decision making as a political process: the case of a university budget." *Administrative Science Quarterly*, 19:135–151.

Pfeffer, J., and G. R. Salancik. 1975. "Determinants of supervisory behavior: a role set analysis." *Human Relations*, 28:139–154.

Pfeffer, J., and G. R. Salancik. 1977. "Organizational context and the characteristics and tenure of hospital administrators." *Academy of Management Journal*, 20:74–88.

Pfeffer, J., and G. R. Salancik. 1977. "Administrator effectiveness: the effects of advocacy and information on resource allocations." *Human Relations* (in press).

Salancik, G. R., B. J. Calder, K. Rowland, H. Leblebici, and M. Conway. 1975. "Leadership as an outcome of social structure and social process: a multidimensional approach." In J. G. Hunt and L. Larson (eds.), *Leadership Frontiers*, 81–102. Ohio: Kent State University Press.

Salancik, G. R., and J. Pfeffer. 1974. "The bases and use of power in organizational decision making: the case of a university." *Administrative Science Quarterly*, 19:453–473.

Salancik, G. R., and J. Pfeffer. 1977. "Constraints on administrator discretion: the limited influence of mayors on city budgets." *Urban Affairs Quarterly* (in press).

Salancik, G. R., J. Pfeffer, and J. P. Kelley. "A contingency model of influence in organizational decision making." *Pacific Sociological Review* (in press).

Salancik, G. R., B. M. Staw, and L. R. Pondy. 1975. "Administrative turnover as a response to unmanaged organizational interdependence: the department head as a scapegoat." Unpublished manuscript, University of Illinois.

Stagner, R. 1969. "Corporate decision making: an empirical study." *Journal of Applied Psychology*, 53:1–13.

Terreberry, S. 1968. "The evolution of organizational environments." *Administrative Science Quarterly*, 12:590–613.

Thompson, J. D. 1967. *Organizations in Action*. New York: McGraw-Hill.

Weick, K. E. 1976. "Educational organizations as loosely coupled systems." *Administrative Science Quarterly*, 21:1–19.

Winter, S. G. 1971. "Satisficing, selection, and the innovating remnant." *Quarterly Journal of Economics*, 85:237–261.

Zald, M. N. 1965. "Who shall rule? a political analysis of succession in a large welfare organization." *Pacific Sociological Review*, 8:52–60.

Zald, M. N. 1970a. *Organizational Change: The Political Economy of the YMCA.* University of Chicago Press.

Zald, M. N. 1970b. "Political economy: a framework for comparative analysis." In M. N. Zald (ed.), *Power in Organizations*, 221–261. Nashville, Tenn.: Vanderbilt University Press.

CHAPTER TEN

THE DESIGN AND MANAGEMENT OF EXTERNALLY CONTROLLED ORGANIZATIONS

The theme of this book has been: To understand organizational behavior, one must understand how the organization relates to other social actors in its environment. Organizations comply with the demands of others, or they act to manage the dependencies that create constraints on organizational actions. While not novel, the theoretical position advanced here differs from many other writings about organizations. The perspective developed denies the validity of the conceptualization of organizations as self-directed, autonomous actors pursuing their own ends and instead argues that organizations are other-directed, involved in a constant struggle for autonomy and discretion, confronted with constraint and external control.

Most current writers give only token consideration to the environmental context of organizations. The environment is there, somewhere outside the organization, and the idea is mentioned that environments constrain or affect organizations. It is sometimes mentioned that organizational environments are becoming more turbulent and this will presumably foster more decentralized management structures. Environment, and particularly environmental turbulence and uncertainty, is used as an arguing point by those wishing to promulgate their advocacy of participation. After this, the task of management is considered. Somehow, the things to be managed are usually within the organization, assumed to be under its control, and often have to do with the direction of low level hired personnel. When authors get down to the task of describing the running of the organization, the relevance of the environment fades. Yet, the idea that organizational actions are socially constrained means that part of the explanations for behavior can be found in the social context.

We take the view of externally controlled organizations much more seriously. This chapter will recapitulate the arguments derived from that perspective and then explore the role of management, the design of organizations, the design of organizational environments, and the likely future of organizational structures. In many instances, our theoretical orientation leads to expectations and recommendations discrepant with the dominant literature. While we have no particular style of management to promote and no appealing phrases like "human relations," "human resources," or "participation" to use to summarize our thoughts, we would suggest that the ideas developed are likely to be more empirically verifiable and more descriptive of the actual operation of interacting social actors.

A RESOURCE DEPENDENCE PERSPECTIVE

To survive, organizations require resources. Typically, acquiring resources means the organization must interact with others who control those resources. In that sense, organizations depend on their environments. Because the organization does not control the resources it needs, resource acquisition may be problematic and uncertain. Others who control resources may be undependable, particularly when resources are scarce. Organizations transact with others for necessary resources, and control over resources provides others with power over the organization. Survival of the organization is partially explained by the ability to cope with environmental contingencies; negotiating exchanges to ensure the continuation of needed resources is the focus of much organizational action.

Organizations themselves are the interlocking of the behaviors of the various participants that comprise the organization. Activities and behaviors, not social actors, are organized into structures. Because social actors can have some activities included in different structures, inclusion in an organization is typically partial. In this context, organizational boundaries can be defined by the organization's control over the actions of participants relative to the control of other social entities over these same activities. Control is the ability to initiate or terminate actions at one's discretion. An organization's control over activities is never absolute because there are always competing claims for the control of given activities. Attempts are made, however, to stabilize activities by institutionalizing exchanges into formal roles and using other control mechanisms. The set of interlocked activities controlled by the organization constitutes the organization. The organization's most important sources of control to achieve interlocked structures of behavior are the ability to empower individuals to act on its behalf and to regulate the use, access, and allocation of organizationally generated resources.

Organizations are coalitions of varying interests. Participants can, and frequently do, have incompatible preferences and goals. The question of whose interests are to prevail in organizational actions is crucial to determining those actions. Power is overlooked too frequently by attending to issues of effectiveness and efficiency. Effectiveness and organizational performance can be evaluated only by asking whose interests are being served.

Organizations, in addition to being coalitions of interests, are markets in which influence and control are transacted. When an organization is created, activities and outcome potential are created. Organizations, or the energy represented in organizations, are resources. It is in the interests of those who require resources to attempt to control and influence the organization. Participants attempt to exchange their own resources, their performances, for more control over the collective effort, and then, they use that control to initiate actions for their own interests. In organizations as in other social systems, power organizes around critical and scarce resources. To the extent participants furnish resources that are more critical and scarce, they obtain more control over the organization. Of course, the determination of what is critical and scarce is itself open to change and definition. Power is, therefore, determined by the definition of social reality created by participants as well as by their control over resources.

Participants differ in the extent to which the organization controls their activities. Some participants provide resources but are not tightly bound to the organization. These actors, which may be other organizations, groups, or individuals, constitute the social environment or context of the organization. To the extent that these actors control critical resources and certain other conditions are met, they are in a position to influence the actions of organizations. In this sense, we can speak of the social control of organizations. The conditions that facilitate this control of the organization include:

1) The possession of some resource by the social actor
2) The importance of the resource to the focal organization; its criticality for the organization's activities and survival
3) The inability of the focal organization to obtain the resource elsewhere
4) The visibility of the behavior or activity being controlled
5) The social actor's discretion in the allocation, access, and use of the critical resource
6) The focal organization's discretion and capability to take the desired action
7) The focal organization's lack of control over resource critical to the social actor
8) The ability of the social actor to make its preferences known to the focal organization

Each of these conditions can be altered by the parties to the relationship. The focal organization can attempt to avoid these conditions, and thereby enhance its discretion. The social actor seeking control over the organization can act to increase the conditions, and thereby increase its control over the organization. Organizations interacting with one another are involved in a dynamic sequence of actions and reactions leading to variations in control and discretion. Strategies of achieving control or discretion and sequences of interactions have rarely been examined.

The study of Israeli managers and their attitudes toward compliance with governmental demands, and the examination of the response of United States defense contractors to affirmative action pressures both support the idea that organizations are externally controlled. Organizational responses were predicted from the situation of resource interdependence confronting the various organizations.

Organizational environments, however, are not objective realities. Environments become known through a process of enactment in which perceptions, attention, and interpretation come to define the context for the organization. Enactments of dependencies, contingencies, and external demands are in part determined by organizational structures, information systems, and the distribution of power and control within organizations.

Assessments which are inconsistent with the actual potency and demands of various participants may be made by organizations. The cognitive and perceptual processes of individuals and the design of most information systems focus attention on familiar historical events, most frequently events that have occurred within the organization. Coupled with a tendency to attribute organizational outcomes to the actions of individuals within the organization, these characteristics of information processing tend to lead most organizations to look within their own domains for the definition and solution of problems. In addition, the contest for control within the organization intervenes to affect the enactment of organizational environments. Since coping with critical contingencies is an important determinant of influence, subunits will seek to enact environments to favor their position. Adjustments to environmental demands follow when visible problems erode the position of those in the dominant coalition. Such adjustments are slowed by the ability of those in power to institutionalize their control over the organization. When the organization's conceptions and responses to environmental constraints become too inappropriate, resource acquisition becomes increasingly difficult. We suggested in Chapter Four a systematic procedure for assessing organizational environments and for evaluating the potential consequences of various organizational activities.

The fact of competing demands, even if correctly perceived, makes the management of organizations difficult. It is clearly easier to satisfy a single criterion, or a mutually compatible set of criteria, than to attempt to meet the conflicting demands of a variety of participants. Compliance to demands is not a satisfactory answer, since compliance with some demands must mean noncompliance with others. Organizations require some discretion to adjust to contingencies as they develop. If behaviors are already completely controlled, future adjustments are more difficult. For this reason, organizations attempt to avoid influence and constraint by restricting the flow of information about them and their activities, denying the legitimacy of demands made upon them, diversifying their dependencies, and manipulating information to increase their own legitimacy.

At the same time organizations seek to avoid being controlled, they seek stability and certainty in their own resource exchanges. Indeed, it is usually in the interests of all participants to stabilize organizational resource exchanges and ensure the organization's survival. The organization, thus, confronts a dilemma. On the one hand, future adaptation requires the ability to change and the discretion to modify actions. On the other hand, the requirements for certainty and stability necessitate the development of interorganizational structures of coordinated behaviors—interorganizational organizations. The price for inclusion in any collective structure is the loss of discretion and control over one's activities. Ironically, to gain some control over the activities of another organization, the focal organization must surrender some of its own autonomy.

Organizations seek to avoid dependencies and external control and, at the same time, to shape their own contexts and retain their autonomy for independent action. The dilemma between the maintenance of discretion and the reduction of uncertainty leads to the performance of contradictory activities. The dilemma of autonomy versus certainty has been noted by Thompson and McEwen (1958) and is an important characteristic of organizational actions taken with respect to the environment. The demands for certainty and the quest for discretion and autonomy lead to the various actions we have described— merger, joint ventures, cooptation, growth, political involvement, the restriction on the distribution of information. All these activities can be understood from the same resource dependence framework.

To say that context affects organizational actions is to say little. The question is how context affects organizations, and the answer requires specifying some process for environmental effects. One model linking organizational environments with organizational actions suggests that environmental contingencies affect the distribution of power and control in the organization. In turn, power affects succession to leadership positions in the organization, and organizational leaders— the members of the dominant coalition—shape organizational actions and structures. This model suggests that executive succession both reflects environmental contingencies and helps the organization manage its interdependence with other social actors.

We have attempted to illustrate how a large number of phenomena can be understood within the resource dependence perspective. The empirical studies reviewed clearly only begins to investigate the various themes and ideas developed within this perspective. Many implications of our model of external control remain unexamined—the use of secrecy to avoid influence and reduce conflict, the limitation of discretion to avoid external control, the attempt to define for elements in the environment their demands and satisfaction, are only a few examples. It is clear that the environment, the context of the organization, is more important than many writers have implied by restricting their attention to the effects of uncertainty on decentralized decision making.

THREE MANAGERIAL ROLES

In the first chapter, we indicated what a model of administration might look like using the theoretical perspective developed in this book. We return to the three roles introduced then to see what we have learned about the importance and use of those roles. The three roles of management—symbolic, responsive, and discretionary—differ in the way organizational constraints and actions are related. In the symbolic role, actions are unrelated to constraints. The organization's outcomes are determined primarily by its context and the administrator's actions have little effect. In the responsive role, organizational actions are developed in response to the demands from the environment. Managers form actions according to the interdependencies they confront, and constraint and action are directly related. In the discretionary role, constraints and environments are managed to suit the interests of the organization. Management's function is to direct the organization toward more favorable environments and to manage and establish negotiated environments favorable to the organization. All three roles are typically involved in the management of organizations.

The Symbolic Role of Management

The manager is a symbol of the organization and its success or failure, a scapegoat, and a symbol of personal or individual control over social actions and outcomes. The symbolic role of management derives in part from a belief in personal causation as opposed to environmental determinism, a belief which is both pervasive and important to concepts of human action (e.g., Kelley, 1971; Lieberson and O'Connor, 1972). As a symbol of control and personal causation, managers and organizational leaders can be used as scapegoats, rewarded when things go well and fired when they go poorly. The knowledge that someone is in charge and that the fate of the organization depends on that person offers the promise of change in organizational activities and fortunes. When problems emerge, the solution is simple and easy—replace the manager. Such changes may not be accomplished readily, as the administrator's power and ability to control the interpretation of organizational outcomes can maintain tenure in office.

Organizations and social systems go to great lengths to invest managers with symbolic value. Leaders may be provided with special perquisites and designations of authority which serve not only to reward the leader but also to remind others of this person's importance by focusing their attention on him. When one leader leaves office, the search for the new leader may be elaborate, involving committees, elections, inaugurations, and the expenditure of time and resources. All of these activities tend to cause observers to attribute great consequences to the occupant of the particular administrative position. In this sense, the symbolic role of management is critical whether or not the manager actually accounts for variance in organizational results. The symbol of control and personal causation provides the prospect of stability for the social system. Belief in the importance of leaders would, logically, lead to the replacement of leaders when things went badly. But, while there is some disruption when turnover occurs, the disruption and alteration of organizational activities is clearly less than if the organization were redesigned and undertook new activities in new environments.

Beliefs in the potency of individual administrators, created through mythologies, symbols, and activities designed to create such beliefs, may be held by outsiders as well as by those individuals whose activities are structured within the organization. Not privy to information about the constraints on administrators, outsiders may have an even greater tendency to see organizational actions as under the control of one or a few persons. The various external interests will focus on the leader and attempt to influence the organization through him or her.

In creating the symbolic role of the manager, the organization also creates a mechanism for dealing with external demands. When external demands cannot be met because of constraints on the organization, the administrator can be removed. Replacing the leader, who has come to symbolize the organization to the various interest groups, may be sufficient to relieve pressures on the organization. As long as all believe that the administrator actually affects the organization, then replacement signals a change taken in response to external demands. The change communicates an intent to comply, and this intent may be as useful as actual compliance for satisfying external organizations.

Changing administrators offers a way of altering appearances, thereby removing external pressure, without losing much discretion. If the manager has little effect on organizational outcomes, his or her replacement will not change much, particularly if a person with similar views is chosen as the replacement. The manager is, therefore, a convenient target for external influences, and provides the organization with a relatively simple way of responding to external demands.

The argument that one of the manager's important roles is to serve as a symbol is a functionalist argument. Explication of the functions served (such as providing stability) must await additional research on the process of symbol creation and the actions taken to invest managers with the appearance of control over outcomes and activities. For the present, we can note that the capability of replacing managers who have been invested with symbolic importance affords the organization the possibility of coping with competing demands and constraints.

The belief in personal causation of events is also lodged in our legal system. Organizations are typically not criminally liable, only individual managers are. The electrical generating equipment price fixing case of the early 1960s illustrates well the manager as a symbol. Manufacturing generating equipment was a business with high fixed costs. When demand fell, price wars tended to occur. In an attempt to stabilize their environment, managers from the major manufacturers met and attempted to fix price and allocate markets. Such attempts were often unsuccessful and were at least in part a consequence of the structure of the industry. Managers were acting because of environmental contingencies and, it might be presumed, because of pressures from superiors for higher and more stable operating results. When the conspiracy was uncovered, the colluding managers were prosecuted, fined, occasionally imprisoned, and in almost every instance, fired by the employing organizations. While the firms themselves were liable for treble damage suits, the managers faced ruined careers. More recently, officials in Lockheed and Gulf Oil were removed following disclosures of bribery of foreign political officials. The corporations, by firing their agents, could claim that such illegal actions were not condoned and would not be permitted. More of the onus for the action was shifted to the individuals involved, who were fired and thereby separated from the company.

The symbolic role of management involves the process by which causality for events is attributed to various actors or external factors (e.g., Kelley, 1971). Studies of processes of attribution, including attention to the role of salient and relevant information, the differences in perceptions between actors and observers (Jones and Nisbett, 1971), and the tendency for persons to attribute control to personal actions (e.g., Langer, 1975) are all relevant for explaining the processes by which beliefs in the causal importance of administrators are created. The symbolic role of management is both important and empirically explainable.

The Responsive Role of Management

If managers were only symbols, it would not matter what they did. Such a position obviously underestimates the actual consequences of administrative action. Even though administrators or organizational leaders may not have tremendous effects on actions and outcomes (Salancik and Pfeffer, 1977), they do account for some variance. There are two roles of management that can be identified with this position of managerial impact, the responsive role and the discretionary role. By responsive role we mean that the manager is a processor and responder to the demands and constraints confronting the organization. In this role, the manager assesses the context, determines how to adapt the organization to meet the constraints of the context, and implements the adaptation.

The conceptualization of managers as responders must be carefully distinguished from the view of the all-knowing, all-seeing leader who directs organizational actions unconstrained by the context. To manage the organization's relationships with its environment, the manager in the responsive role must perceive the demands and dependencies confronting the organization, and then adjust the organization accordingly. To say that a leader is responsive to the demands of others is to say that the activities of the leader are structured and shaped by others. The responsive role of management posits the function of management as being an assimilator and processor of demands. Such a view is at variance with the image of great managerial leaders directing the organization, making decisions, and through the sheer force of will transforming organizations to achieve success.

The most appropriate activity of the responsive manager is not developing appropriate actions but deciding which demands to heed and which to reject. The actions to be taken are provided by the various participants and interests in the organization and its environment. There is no shortage of suggestions, if not demands, concerning what the organization should be doing. The manager's function is to decide which of these to follow. The choice is critical for organizational survival, for in responding to demands the organization necessarily gives up discretion. Our prediction is that administrators respond to demands as a function of the interdependence with various elements in the environment—the greater the interdependence with a given other social actor, the more likely the organization is to follow its demands. To maintain support from important suppliers of resources, organizations constrain their actions to comply with the requests of those with resource control. It is clear that such a course requires being aware of the situation of interdependence and the demands of those with whom the organization is interdependent.

Management is frequently described as decision making. This, of course, is correct. But the emphasis in such a view is often misplaced, focusing almost exclusively on choice. Choice, however, is only one step in the decision process. Prior to the exercise of choice, information about the environment and possible consequences of alternative actions must be acquired and processed. Once this is done, the choice is usually obvious. Instead of describing management as decision making, we could describe management as information gathering and be both consistent with the original position and possibly more descriptive of the actual emphasis of managers (e.g., Mintzberg, 1973). Decisions are made in a social context, and this context must inevitably constrain decisions if the decisions are to be effective in that context. The responsive role of management is not inconsistent with the more widely seen view of management as decision making. Rather, this role emphasizes the importance of processing and responding to the organization's context. The critical factor is that constraints are imposed on the actor.

The Discretionary Role of Management

As we have noted before, managers not only adapt their organizations to the context, but may take actions to modify the environment to which the organization then responds. In addition to a responsive role of management, therefore, we can speak of a discretionary role. Managerial action focuses on altering the system of constraints and dependencies confronting the organization. This discretionary role of management is involved when we think of organizations merging, lobbying, coopting, and doing all the various things that alter the interdependencies confronted by the organization.

In some respects, the discretionary role of management is not inconsistent with the responsive role. Both require accurate assessment of environmental constraints and contingencies. Whether one is going to respond to the environment or change it, effective action is more likely if the context is accurately perceived. Both the responsive and discretionary roles of management, then, emphasize the importance of the information processing tasks and the criticality of the accuracy of the manager's perception, his or her model of reality.

The discretionary role, however, places more emphasis on the possibility for managerial action actually to change the organization's context. The discretionary role is more fitting to some organizations than others. Only a few have enough resources and scale to attempt to alter their contexts in a significant fashion. For millions of small business organizations, voluntary associations, and nonprofit organizations, such change of the environment is virtually out of the question.

The three roles of management we have described are certainly not mutually exclusive. At some time all may be enacted. At one point, management may serve a symbolic value; while at others, it may respond to environmental demands; while at still others, it may engage in actions to modify the environment. Although each perspective may emphasize a slightly different set of skills and activities, all are potentially important. The critical issues involve under what circumstances one or the other role is likely to predominate and what factors appear to be associated with successfully performing each of the managerial roles.

Specifying these three roles does not mean that they can inevitably be handled to bring success to the organization. If there is one image we wish to provide the reader, it is that success is in the hands of many actors outside the control of the organization. Organizations exist in interdependent environments and require the interlocking of activities to survive. Control over this interlocking or structuring of activities is never in the hands of a single actor such as a manager. Books about how to manage or how to succeed are ill-advised because they give the impression that there is some set of rules or procedures that will guarantee success. The essence of the concept of interdependence means that this cannot be the case. In any interdependent situation, outcomes are at least partially in the control of other social actors, and the successful outcomes achieved through performing various managerial roles derives in part from actions taken by others outside the manager's control.

DESIGNING EXTERNALLY CONTROLLED ORGANIZATIONS

This is not a treatise on organizational design. However, some implications of the resource dependence perspective for design are worthy of consideration, if only because the adequacy and value of the perspective can be assessed. We will consider four implications: (1) the design of scanning systems; (2) designs for loosening dependencies; (3) designs for managing conflicting demands and constraints; and (4) designs of chief executive positions.

Scanning the Environment

Whether management plays a responsive role or attempts to alter the organization's environment, good information about the context will be required. Most organizations follow the easy course. Available data is collected and processed; information more difficult to gather is ignored. The information most frequently generated for other purposes—usually for accounting for the organization's internal operations—is all too frequently the only information available in the organization. Few organizations systematically seek out information about their context.

Academic literature on environmental scanning is notably sparse (e.g., Aguilar, 1967). Any recommendation, therefore, must be tentative; there is an insufficient empirical base on which to develop strong conclusions. Most writers will assert that since organizational environments are important, it is critical to scan them. Yet, the fact is that organizations typically do not do much environmental scanning. One must either question the advice or question the common practices of organizations. That there is so little literature in this area reinforces our conclusion that the allusion to the environment is frequently pro forma and seldom follows up the open systems perspective with anything remotely useful from a managerial or theoretical perspective. It may also be that scanning the environment is, in fact, not that necessary. One can imagine some advantage to ignoring environmental change. Knowing about the change puts the organization in the position of having to respond to it. It may be better to ignore changes rather than risk overresponding to every small, insignificant environmental fluctuation.

Scanning systems face two problems: (1) how to register needed information, and (2) how to act upon the information. Both problems affect the organization's ability to either adapt to or change the environment. Part of the problem of scanning environmental elements was implied in our earlier discussion about enactment. Subunits established to scan a particular part of the environment typically hire persons with expertise limited to one narrow segment. A market research department employs MBA or Ph.D. business graduates trained in marketing, survey research, and statistics. The firm will survey consumers, often a dominant focus in marketing training, and test-market various products. The firm will probably have excellent information about alternative communication channels, their costs and effectiveness, as well as all kinds of attitudinal data about potential consumers for the product. Communications data are prevalent in part because other organizations (advertising agencies, the media) collect them and make them available. What the firm is not likely to have are data on whether the product is stocked anywhere, whether the sales force is doing an adequate job promoting the product, or what kind of shelf space or display it is getting. After all, the performance of the sales force is a topic for industrial psychologists interested in motivation, while issues of distribution are the responsibility of those specializing in marketing channels.

A scanning unit frequently attends to only one portion of the environment. Yet, the environment has multiple facets. The obvious solution is to establish multiple scanning units or scanning units that have within them a variety of interests, backgrounds, and types of expertise. Although this solution is useful to overcome the problem of missing important aspects of the environment, the establishment of multiple scanning units does nothing to overcome, and may actually worsen, the second problem of acting on the information.

The greater problem in coping with organizational environments is that the needed information is not in the hands of those making the decisions or is not used by these persons. The causes of these difficulties are many and varied. One problem is that information is typically collected by staff departments (marketing research, long-range planning, etc.) and must be used by line personnel. Conflicts are common between line and staff. Information collected by specialized experts, with unique vocabularies and sophisticated methodological approaches, produces reports couched in terminology unfamiliar to the line managers who must use the information. Communication is difficult. Differences in perspective, vocabulary, and expertise all bar the use of information collected about organizational environments.

An additional problem is that those who provide information collect what they believe to be important. There is no assurance that similar judgments of importance hold for operating managers. Staff members may fail to ask managers what information is needed, and the information collected may be important only to those who collected it. This problem is not easily solved. A decision maker may be unable to predict what information he needs or would use. A likely response to the question of what information is needed is the information he has used in the past, obviously constrained by availability. Moreover, it is not clear that the manager is the best judge of what is needed, since he operates on the basis of what he has done before. Persons develop styles of operating and decision making; changing these styles may be difficult. Persons accustomed to making decisions using certain information are not likely to suddenly use new information, especially information they did not request.

A third problem facing operating managers and staff is that both implicitly may perceive information collection and acquisition as affecting their relative power and status. It is the case that if one controls the information used in decision making, one can control decision outcomes. To the extent that managers rely on staff, they lose discretion and admit the importance of the staff and the need for them. One way for managers to retain power is to ignore the staff information. For their part, the staff attempt to have their reports heeded to illustrate their importance and power within the organization. The contest for control over decision making is what is involved, and this contest is frequently exacerbated by the differences in backgrounds and ages of the parties involved.

The environmental perspective argues for the need for information about environments. Specialized scanning units, however, may be ineffective in meeting that need. Specialized units collect specialized information, so that to develop a comprehensive view of the environment, a variety of units may be required. At the same time, operating managers may use the collected information only under duress, and the problems of obtaining the attention of the managers are increased as the number of scanning units writing reports increases. Many reports are filed and forgotten, and few become incorporated in organizational decision making. Scanning highlights and narrows the organization's attention, so that the assignment of specific individuals to scan specific environmental segments may leave the organization more isolated and less informed than before. The scanners focus on routinized, quantitative data collection, prepare reports filled with jargon and complexity, and then struggle with operating personnel to have their efforts considered.

In writing of environmental enactment, we noted the difficulty of planning. Planning scanning systems is no less difficult, since such an activity presumes the organization already knows what it needs to know. We argue that the problem is not one of not having the necessary information. The expertise required to manage the organization's interdependence is often present in the organization. It is already possessed by the various operating managers themselves. Constantly confronted with problems from their own interactions with the environment, it is unlikely they are unaware of that environment. More probably, they are unable to consider the situation and its implications taking an overall, longer range view. Unfortunately, operating managers are most often involved in immediate, short-run problem solving (Mintzberg, 1973), and therefore, they seldom have the time or the inclination to engage in any kind of planning.

While the organization as a whole may possess the requisite information, the information may be widely dispersed throughout the organization in a variety of different functional areas and positions. One effective strategy for keeping up on major changes would be to bring together the various sources of expertise within the organization in a focused format to use this expertise in planning and decision making. Such techniques as the Delphi (Linstone and Turoff, 1975) and Nominal Group Technique (Delbecq, Van de Ven, and Gustafson, 1975), in which participants, chosen for their expertise, are systematically queried about judgments, potential actions, and forecasts, provide some advantages over the use of specialized staff departments. Commitment to the decisions and forecasts may be increased because operating personnel are themselves involved. The planning and decision making, moreover, can be done in language, and using data, familiar to the persons involved.

Loosening Dependencies

The external control of organizational behavior comes about, in part, from the organization's dependence on specific others. Discretion permits the organization to adapt to contingencies and to alter activities as conditions change. It is likely that the maintenance of discretion should be a crucial organizational activity. Some latitude in the organization's behavior will be useful and organizations will seek to minimize external control.

The loosening of external control can be accomplished, we have suggested, through the loosening of dependencies. Organizations are controlled by an external source to the extent they depend on that source for a large proportion of input or output. Dependence diminishes through diversification. Organizations with many small suppliers are potentially less controlled than ones with a few major suppliers. From the above considerations, it might appear that organizational designs that reduce organizational dependencies would be highly differentiated structures, organizations performing a variety of activities in a variety of contexts. If diversification loosens dependence and provides the focal organization with more discretion, and if discretion is both sought and useful for survival and adaptation, then it should be the case that over time more diversified structures should emerge, particularly for those organizations dealing with concentrated input or output markets. This result might occur either because less diversified organizations were more likely to fail or because organizations systematically adapted and became more diversified.

It does appear that there have been trends toward increasing diversification. Consider Berman's (1973) history of merger waves. The first wave was described as an attempt to consolidate and control markets. In this first wave, many of the giant enterprises which today control sectors of the economy were created. Various steel producers combined to form U.S. Steel, and tobacco manufacturers combined to form the major tobacco firms. In the second wave of merger, vertical integration was accomplished with the organizations extending to take over sources of supply and distributors. The third major wave involved conglomerate mergers, or mergers made for purposes of diversification, involving firms such as Tenneco, Gulf and Western Industries, and LTV. Such a pattern of merger activity would suggest that organizations first secure their competitive position, then attempt to manage interdependence with supply and distribution channels, and finally, turn their attention to diversification to diminish the external control of others over their activities. The situation is more complex, however. These different merger movements took place under different legal conditions. Vertical integration followed the passage and more vigorous enforcement of the Sherman Act, and the conglomerate mergers followed the passage of more stringent antimerger regulations. The regulations themselves were in response to the perceived threat of economic concentration posed by earlier mergers. While legal constraints may provide some explanation for the pattern of activities undertaken by industrial firms, other types of organizations not subject to antitrust laws have also diversified. Downs (1967), for instance, has noted that public agencies expand their domains and take on additional activities to ensure their survival. Such expansion provides the agencies with more independence.

Coping with Conflicting Demands

The pursuit of diversification or organizational growth, both designed to lessen dependence on elements of the organization's environment, will probably lead to an increase in the number of groups and organizations interested in the focal organization. This can increase the diversity and number of demands on the organization. Size, however, is not the critical variable affecting the complexity of demands. Even small, less diversified organizations are confronted by a variety of interests with different preferences for organizational action. Rather, the critical variable is the extent to which the organization represents a resource or potential tool to be used by others. The more useful the resources of an organization are to others, the more demands the organization will face. According to the theoretical perspective we have developed, organizational designs which disperse dependence through the environment also link the organization to more elements which might seek to use it in their service, creating more competing and conflicting interests.

Fortunately, the very differentiation that reduces the organization's dependence on external groups also helps the organization manage the conflicting demands thus created. First, diversification, while not reducing demands, does reduce the organization's need to respond to any given demand. By dispersing dependency among numerous others, the impact of the organization's not responding to given demands is reduced. A second advantage, obtained through the creation of a differentiated, loosely coupled organizational structure is that various groups may be satisfied simultaneously. The critical factor is that the diverse interests be loosely coupled and not interdependent within the organization. When interests are not tightly interconnected and there is no need for actions to be consistent with all interests simultaneously, then it is possible to satisfy conflicting demands by establishing subunits to cope with each interest. Consumers may demand better quality products and more control over product policies. In response, the organization may establish a consumer affairs department. Demands are registered and consumers or their organizations are provided with access and a feeling of participation. At the same time, workers wanting more control can appeal to the personnel or industrial relations department, while minorities can articulate their interests through affirmative action offices. This differentiation process can go on indefinitely, subject only to the constraint imposed by limited resources. Thompson (1967) has argued that organizations do exactly what we have described—establish subunits to deal with homogeneous subsegments of the environment.

Structural differentiation, from this perspective, derives not directly as a consequence of organizational size but as a function of the number and importance of different interests that must be coopted. This number may, in turn, be related to organizational size. And size, in turn, may be a function of growing differentiation and diversification. Differentiating an organization to simultaneously satisfy multiple constituencies is a practice evident in many organizations. Universities, for example, establish research institutes to obtain money from various sources, academic departments to serve disciplinary interests, and various student and community service units to meet the demands of those groups.

It is important to note that differentiation provides a satisfactory solution to the problem of competing demands only when the differentiated subunits are themselves relatively independent. Each subunit must be in a position to take actions unconstrained by the actions taken by other subunits. Loose-coupling assists organizations in coping with their environments by permitting new subunits to absorb protest without a requirement to rationalize the relationship among all the various subunits. Of course, it is also true that if subunits are loosely coupled then most organizational practices will be buffered from changes created by any single subunit in response to interest group demands. The organization can thus make small accommodations to interest groups without redirecting the activities of the entire organization. A consumer affairs department can deal with complaints about the product with a letter and a free sample, but the production and development departments remain unaffected.

A second benefit achieved by establishing a special department to handle particular subsegments of the environment is that each subsegment becomes partially coopted. The interest group or organization develops an interest in the subunit with which it deals. Since the established subunit is the primary access to the organization, its survival becomes defined as critical for the interest group's purposes. As a consequence, the external interest may make less extreme demands on the subunit and become interested in preserving its limited access and representation within the organization. The differentiation of organizational structures to cope with homogeneous environmental elements can both buffer the organization and lessen the force of the external influences.

Another strategy for coping with interdependence with external groups making conflicting demands is through the use of slack resources (Galbraith, 1973). Organizations can more readily cope with conflicting demands when they have sufficient resources, so that many demands can be at least partially satisfied simultaneously. Organizational slack, frequently apparent in the form of extra profits or resources, is useful not only to make the owners and managers happy but to facilitate managing the environment of competing demands. Conflict is reduced when interdependence is reduced, and interdependence is reduced when resources are plentiful. As we already noted, the elaboration of structure to include differentiated, loosely coupled subunits to cope with the various environmental elements also requires resources to support the various subunits thereby created. Again, then, the importance of slack resources for managing conflicting demands is evident.

The structural solution to conflicting demands is a differentiated organization of loosely coupled subunits, each of which deals with special environmental interests, and each of which is only slightly interdependent with other subunits within the organization. This solution depends on the availability of slack resources, for without slack, subunits could not be loosely connected and could not respond to their immediate environments without affecting the entire system.

Neither the differentiation of the organization into subunits nor the diversification of activities reduces the organization's dependence on the environment. What such actions accomplish is to alter the nature of the interdependence and structure organizational dependence so that it is more readily managed. By having numerous interests make demands on the organization, the organization reduces its need to respond to any specific interest because each represents only a small part of the total organization and its activities. While there are still resource acquisition consequences of not complying, the effects are diminished.

Moreover, diversification shifts interdependence from the organization's relationship with the environment to greater interdependence among elements in the environment. By making previously unrelated activities or markets now related under a single management or control structure, diversification makes previously unrelated environmental subsegments more interdependent. Linked through the organization, environmental subsegments now compete with each other as well as facing competition within the subsegment. If there are insufficient slack resources across the entire economy, such interlocking of organizations can actually cause problems. Organizations dealing with a large set of diverse environmental elements without sufficient slack resources face difficulties in managing and resolving the competing groups therefore confronted.

The Chief Executive Position

In Chapter Nine we argued that environments affect organizational change through alteration of the distribution of influence and consequent changes in administrators. As a symbol of the organization and its policies, administrators can be removed when participants demand it as a condition for continuing to support the organization. If it is indeed true that adaptation to environmental interest comes about in part through changes in administration, then the institutionalization of power and control can be seen as detrimental to the organization's ability to cope with the environment. Structures which inhibit the institutionalization of power should survive change more readily. Structures which permit power to be maintained beyond the point of being useful to the organization are less likely to be adaptable.

While the trend in organizational forms has been to more diversified structures and activities, the trend in organizational power structures appears to be in the direction of increasing centralization. In industry, stock companies are increasingly owned by diffuse ownership interests or by trust departments and pension funds that are unwilling and unable to exercise strong influence on management. As a result, managers have acquired more control over the organization. The diffusion of control over a number of small investors enhances the manager's ability to institutionalize his power. Earlier, we noted that there was some tendency for turnover in administrators to be reduced when the corporation was management-controlled compared to the situation where managers faced a few, nonmanaging dominant ownership interests. It is likely to be true in general that the diffusion of the organization's activities will permit more centralized administrator control. This is because any single other group or organization now has less interest in the total organization and its activities and, therefore, should be less willing to spend the resources and effort necessary to control the organization. Such reasoning may be another explanation for the emergence of differentiated, diffused organizational structures.

If differentiation in organizational structures is useful for dealing with competing demands, it would be logically possible to extend that argument and suggest the usefulness of differentiation even in the chief executive position. Instead of having a single chief executive or chief administrator, the organization might have several, each with his or her own expertise and the ability to cope with some segment of the environment. Multiple chief executives have seldom been tried, and when tried, have often not succeeded. In part, this is because the idea of multiple chief executive officers, while useful for dealing with the various environments confronted by the organization, is inconsistent with the concept of the administrator as the symbol of organizational action. After all, when we want to fire the administrator for some problem in the organization, we would prefer to fire one, clearly visible, target rather than several persons who share responsibility and through this sharing avoid responsibility.

One way of achieving both accountability and adaptability may be to have a single figurehead but have the actual organizational control lodged in a multiparty executive position. This would require giving each executive an independent and sufficient power base to survive the struggle for dominance which would undoubtedly ensue. Of course, such an organizational design is completely at variance with the traditional prescriptions for unity of command. Indeed, the type of political decision making likely to be produced by the structure we have described may be viewed as irrational or inefficient. Of course, the trade-off must be made between some loss of order and efficiency to achieve the capability of organizational adaptability.

In the absence of the ability or desire to establish multiple centers of control and authority, the next best solution requires ensuring that executives can be replaced easily when environmental conditions require new skills or a new symbol. Such replacement is obviously facilitated when power is decentralized in the organization, or when the chief executive cannot control the appointment of all subordinates so as to people the organization with dedicated loyalists. Overlapping political districts common to some United States cities represents an example of this form of shared power. The mayor controls the hiring of some personnel, but other boards and commissions control other hiring.

Power is also more likely to be institutionalized when the executive controls the definition of reality through a control over the information system in the organization. It is interesting that authors have not more frequently noted the connection between decentralization of authority and the decentralization of information systems. The connection is direct. If the chief executive is allowed to control the social distribution of information through secrecy and selective presentation of information, then he can control the definition of the situation. By defining organizational contingencies, his power can be institutionalized beyond both the formal authority structure and the contingencies of the environment.

The institutionalization of control is a process that has not been empirically examined and is only imperfectly understood. Yet, it is clear that organizational responsiveness will increase when power and control are not institutionalized and new skills, competencies, and interests can emerge with changing environmental contingencies.

At the same time, stability and predictability in the organization is desirable. After all, continual change would be as destructive as no change at all. Thus, some institutionalization of power and control is necessary to achieve stability. It prevents the organization from changing to meet minor environmental contingencies of short duration. However, it is likely that most organizations err on the side of stability. Those in control, certainly, would favor such a position.

Organizational and Political Structures

Many of the structural attributes described as desirable for organizational adaptability and for coping with an environment of conflicting demands and interests are represented in political organizations in the

United States. Institutionalization of control is inhibited by the requirement for confronting elections, and multiple control structures are designed into the system by providing at the federal level the three branches of government and the host of commissions and boards, and at other governmental levels through overlapping, autonomous political districts and organizations. Structural elaboration into various departments and committees permits various interests to be heeded, while the existence of organizational slack and a loosely coupled system facilitates the absorption of protest and the incorporation of change without profoundly disturbing the entire system.

We are not the first to note structural parallels between political organizations and other types of organization or the similarities in their governance and adaptation. To carry the analogy to its logical conclusion, however, suggests that one should design organizations with features of representative political structures, particularly when adaptation rather than stability or efficiency is of primary concern. Even current writing about decentralization and delegation typically speaks of such passing of power as a gift, conferred upon lower level participants. Despite awareness of surface similarities, there remain fundamental differences in the control structure of representative democracies and those of formal organizations. The belief in the requirement for absolute authority and unity of command prevents the development of designs which incorporate representative forms of control. We suspect it is mainly when the problems confronted by formal organizations become increasingly the management of conflicting demands and adaptation to changing social contexts that structural similarities to political organizations emerge.

DESIGNING ORGANIZATIONAL
ENVIRONMENTS

If organizational actions are responses to their environments, then the external perspective on organizational functioning argues strongly that organizational behavior is determined through the design of organizational environments. The focus for attempts to change organizations, it would appear, should be the context of the organizations. By changing the context, the behavior of the organizations can be changed. The profoundly important topic of designing organizational environments is almost completely neglected. The idea of changing organizations by changing their environments is scarcely found in the literature on organizational change.

Among the few social scientists who have not neglected environmental design as a way of affecting organizational behavior are economists. Their basic model presumes that persons seek their self-interest, and therfore, environments must be so structured that in seeking their own interests, individual actors also behave so as to increase social welfare. Such a realization of the importance of the design of context for determining behavior is in refreshing contrast to the frequently encountered prescriptions for training, T-groups, or other individually oriented internal change approaches advocated most frequently by organizational behavior authors.

The analogy we would like to make is between our perspective and social psychology. In the study of human behavior, originally time was spent attempting to predict and analyze such behavior using concepts that presumably were related to the internal state of the individual, such as personality, motivation, and attitudes. Growing evidence, however, indicated that persons, regardless of individual differences, would respond similarly to similar environmental conditions. This outcome suggested that behavior could be controlled by its context, through the use of appropriate reinforcers as in operant conditioning or through other physical and social designs. Similarly, the analysis of organizational behavior has focused on internal states of organizations, their climate, leadership, even structures. Yet, if organizations are affected by their social contexts, one might expect that one efficacious way to accomplish organizational change would be through the redesign of that context. This is the position we are advocating.

The appropriate design for organizational environments depends, of course, upon what activities and interests are to be served. Consider the problem of collusion among business firms. Price fixing cases have involved pharmaceutical companies, chemical firms, food processors, and many other industries and firms. Collusion, while a violation of the antitrust laws, is a dominant form of behavior. Even when there is not overt collusion, organizations may attempt to achieve the benefits of collusion—the creation of collective structures of behavior—through joint ventures, trade associations, mergers, director interlocks, and other devices. These interfirm structures may serve the interests of the various participants quite well. Indeed, if the interests were not served, the structures would probably not persist. However, economists have argued that the welfare of all participants and the efficient allocation of resources in an economic system is best served when competition prevails. If we accept the economists' position, then what can be done to assure competition?

It is clear what can not be done. Legislating against collusion, attempting to legally restrict mergers or joint ventures, is probably not an effective solution. First, such laws must be obeyed to have any impact. Reid (1968) has noted that few mergers are ever prosecuted given the limited resources of the antitrust agencies. Price fixing conspiracies are only occasionally uncovered, and when found out, the companies are frequently permitted to plead no contest, which leaves the burden of proving ultimate guilt on those who would sue for treble damages. Second, laws typically attack one type of presumably anticompetitive practice at a time. This leaves the organization with the option of developing substitutes for the practice now proscribed. Pate (1969) noted that when the antimerger laws were strengthened, more joint ventures were formed. And, Pfeffer (1976) has argued that tightening up restrictions against joint ventures would probably just cause the organizations affected to develop alternative methods for accomplishing interfirm coordination. In many ways, passing a law is a symbolic act like firing a manager. It provides the feeling that something has been done but does not affect the source of the activity.

If behavior is affected by its context, then a more adequate strategy to change behavior would involve redesigning the context. In the present case, we have seen that the tendency for firms to attempt to develop interfirm organizations is most pronounced when concentration is intermediate, a result which helped explain mergers and joint ventures among competitors, director interlocks among competing firms, and the movement of executives. If the policy outcome desired is to diminish this activity, the most effective strategy would involve making the industry less concentrated by creating new competitors either by breaking up existing firms into smaller companies or by encouraging the founding of new enterprises in the same industry.

Or, consider another example. Employment agencies, both private and state services, have frequently assisted employing firms in pursuing discriminatory hiring policies by sending applicants of only one sex or race as requested. There have been some efforts to enforce nondiscrimination regulations by threatening to take away the agency's license to operate and by actually investigating and fining the offending agencies. If the situation is examined carefully, however, the futility of such efforts can be seen. Employment agencies are numerous and the cost of entry into the business is relatively low. Because there are so many agencies and so many persons typically looking for work, what is scarce are job orders, the positions to be filled given to the agency by an employer. If the agency does not go along with the employer's request, the employer can simply move the hiring to another of the many agencies available. In the case of the state employment services, legislatures evaluate them according to placements, so again the organizations compete for job orders. In this instance, the behavior is predicted by the context. The employers have power with respect to the agencies and can obtain the behaviors they desire. Applying enforcement against the agencies only puts them in an untenable position but does not resolve their problem. Enforcement directed against the employer organizations is much more likely to change the situation of discriminatory referrals.

We could provide numerous other examples, but the point should be clear. Behavior is a consequence of the context confronting the organization. The design and change of organizational behavior, therefore, can profitably be approached from the perspective of analyzing and designing the context to produce the desired activities. Of course, such a strategy of organizational change is more difficult than attempting to enforce the law against single organizations or preaching values and norms. On the other hand, it is more likely to be effective. If behavior is externally controlled, then the design of the external system of constraints and controls is the place to begin to determine organizational actions and structures.

ORGANIZATIONAL FUTURES

The literature is littered with predictions about what future organizations will look like and how they will operate and be managed. The fact that most of these predictions have not been realized is, we believe, a consequence of the inadequate theoretical base underlying them. We would like to conclude our exposition of the resource dependence perspective by considering one of the more frequently seen predictions concerning organizational futures and then consider what the evidence we have developed suggests about this forecast.

Recently, humanists such as Warren Bennis, Abraham Maslow, and Douglas McGregor have predicted the demise of bureaucracy as an organizational form. In a climate of social values that stress participation and democracy, bureaucracies, with their centralized structures of authority and control, are anachronistic. With a more skilled and more educated work force, with increasingly sophisticated technologies, the prediction has been that professional, rather than bureaucratic, organizational forms would emerge. Power would be based on skills and knowledge, and consistent with the professional model, self-control or collegial control would be emphasized over control by the organizational hierarchy. Unfettered by inappropriate strategies of motivation and rigid, dehumanizing structures, the new workers, educated and creative, would adjust their activities to the needs of the organization and realize their creative potential in the process.

Originally, this prediction was based more on beliefs and values than on anything else. But then, these authors discovered the environment and found, they thought, a whole new, empirically based foundation for their beliefs and the associated application of those beliefs, organizational development. Miles has summarized this argument quite well:

> The environment, as they (OD theorists) see it, is becoming increasingly turbulent and this, they argue, makes it especially important that organizations adopt the kinds of structure and processes mentioned above. . . . OD writers tend to believe that the linkage among the elements in most organizational environments are becoming more numerous and more complex, that the rate of change in environmental conditions is increasing, and that traditional bureaucratic structures are becoming less and less adequate. It is argued that new and more adaptive structures and processes are required and that these in turn demand new levels of interpersonal skill and awareness which OD (organizational development) can best provide (1974:170–171).

Unfortunately, the issue of what effects uncertainty has on the structure of organizations, and even if uncertainty is increasing, is more complicated than suggested by numbered systems (Likert, 1967) and two-category archetypes (McGregor, 1960). We attempt below to provide some thought about these complexities, not because we envision better views of the future but because different futures appear more probable.

A recurrent theme reported in this book has been that organizations attempt to manage or avoid uncertainty. Rather than accepting uncertainty as an unavoidable fate, organizations seek to create around themselves more stable and predictable environments. Thus, to forecast increasingly turbulent and unpredictable environments is to simultaneously predict attempts to create negotiated, predictable environments. Greater turbulence produces greater efforts to manage the environment. The implied contradiction in that statement can be understood by considering the nature of interdependence in social systems and how interdependence changes form without changing in magnitude.

We have described how organizations cope with the uncertainty created by interdependence by managing interdependence through interorganizational coordination. By law, collusion, merger, cooptation, and other strategies, organizations seek to avoid uncertainty arising from their need to acquire and maintain resources. Managing interdependence, however, does not avoid interdependence. Indeed, it is the case that the solution to one problem frequently creates different difficulties. The typical solution to problems of interdependence is to structure and coordinate the organization's behavior more closely with other organizations. This strategy, however, creates its own problems.

For example, steel manufacturers depend upon coal as a resource. Seeking to remove uncertainty of supply, the manufacturers may integrate backward and purchase coal mines or coal companies. Although the purchase of a coal mine reduces the organization's dependence on uncertain suppliers, the dependence on coal itself has not been eliminated. In fact, if major technological changes in steel manufacturing eliminate the need for coal, the vertically integrated firm with its own source of coal may be less able to change. And, as a consequence of being more heavily invested in resources used in the manufacture of steel, the organization is now more dependent on the steel market. Also, since the merged organization is presumably larger, capital requirements may be greater, as is the organization's visibility to regulators and others who will make demands of it.

Solving the uncertainty deriving from interdependence with suppliers leads the organization to create an environment which makes it even more important to stabilize than the other elements in the environment. To assure markets, the organization may press to have laws passed restricting competition. The organization may invite major clients or financial institutions to sit on its board of directors, or it may invest in joint ventures in partnership with major competitors. The immediate effects of these efforts may be to stabilize the flow of resources to the steel manufacturer and reduce the uncertainty confronted by the organization in the short run.

A closer examination of the situation, however, reveals that the interdependence and uncertainty has merely been shifted not eliminated. By merging with coal companies, the organization's problematic dependence is shifted from one resource to others and from suppliers to markets. By restricting competition through legislation, the organization now depends on legislators. The organization becomes more connected to elements of its environment, and the environment itself becomes more interconnected over time as various organizations engage in these strategies. The more tightly connected the system becomes, the more the fate of each is linked to the fate of all other organizations. Linked to a particular financial institution for capital, the steel manufacturer now needs the survival and health of that particular financial institution. Linked to a particular legislator, the company requires the political survival and health of that person.

If one considers the consequences of the actions for other organizations, it is even more evident how interdependence is shifted rather than eliminated. The steel manufacturer who acquired the coal company gains control over the supply and leaves other steel firms less able to acquire their own coal. The others become more interdependent with other suppliers and may find it necessary to increasingly coordinate their behaviors. Essentially, the merging organization has shifted the costs of interdependence to other parts of the system. The same thing occurs when market coordination occurs; the interdependence of sellers is shifted to make buyers more interdependent and more dependent on the sellers as a collectivity.

The only changes which alter the amount of interdependence are those which (1) increase the amount of available resources and (2) decrease the number of contenders for those resources. If there is a scarcity of some resource, the fact that one organization stabilizes its acquisition of the resource through some form of social coordination does not alter the fact of the scarcity. It solves one organization's problem by transferring the problem to others. One can see this illustrated in the recent "energy crisis" (more properly, a shortage of inexpensive oil). Most of the changes made in response to that crisis were attempts to redistribute the problem of not having enough cheap oil. Some organizations stored reserves in larger amounts, while others sought new forms of energy. However, the changes that reduce conditions of scarcity are those that lead to new sources of energy or less use of energy; other changes merely reallocate the cost of scarcity.

Social systems can be evaluated according to how the burdens and costs of interdependence are allocated. Those who suffer the costs are those with the least power in the social system, and indeed, social power becomes defined and determined in the process of managing interdependence. Power is the ability to organize activities to minimize uncertainties and costs, and as mentioned previously, power is inevitably organized around the most critical and scarce resources in the social system. Solutions to problems of interdependence require the concentration of power. Strategies to manage interdependence require interlocking activities with others, and such interlocking produces concentrated power. Those organizations not involved in the resultant structure are less powerful and less able to cope with their problems of interdependence.

Because the problems facing one organization are generally due to the activities of another organization, it is inevitable that the solution to problems involve interlocking activities among the organizations and an attempt to influence the other organization's activities to the focal organization's benefit. This interlocking of activities develops a concentration of power. Those who are least powerful in a social system are those who are least able to organize and structure the activities of other social actors for their own interests. The resulting environment is one which is increasingly structured and interlocked, coordinated, comprised of larger and larger organizations and greater concentrations of social power. The burdens of interdependence are shifted to the less organized and less powerful actors. In the modern economic environment. the least organized group of social actors are consumers, and contrary to the view of consumers portrayed in some economic and marketing theories, the consumer is increasingly likely to bear the cost of interdependence in the economic system. One might think that a solution to the consumers' problems is to concentrate power, and many actions of consumer interest groups are attempts to accomplish just that. However, while coordination makes the consumer more powerful, it also makes influence more possible. It is easier to target influence to affect a few organizations than millions of independent actors. Thus, ironically, the very structuring of activities that produces social power makes the social actors so interconnected that they are more likely targets for influence.

If all organizations attempted to solve their own problems of critical uncertainties and dependencies by interlocking behaviors with others, the resulting environment is one of more tightly coordinated organizational action. Decision structures developed for initiating and coordinating actions must, of necessity, become more centralized with greater concentrations of power. The system is too complex, too interconnected, and too potent to rely on haphazard adjustments made by its components.

Therefore, the net result of various organizational actions would appear to be the creation of larger organizations operating in environments that are increasingly regulated and politically controlled. A single organization's larger size and increased commitment to given areas of activity make it less able to adapt and means that any failure is more consequential. Thus, there is increased need for coordination with other critical actors. This increased need for coordination leads to an increasingly interconnected environment in which power is increasingly concentrated. One might project from this that the environment that will evolve will be a stable and cooperative set of actors. Such will be the case as long as none of the parties have interests which conflict, and this circumstance is more likely to the extent that resources are plentiful. If there is a scarcity of critical resources, the consequence of greater interconnectedness is greater uncertainty. The response to that uncertainty will be even more interlocking of behavior and an even greater concentration of power.

This scenario does not suggest an increase in decentralized, participative management structures as a result of turbulent organizational environments. Rather, we would suggest that uncertainty will result in greater efforts at coordination, which require the concentration of power and decision discretion. We would argue that in the first place, uncertainty is managed so that the prediction of increasing environmental uncertainty is questionable. In the second place, increasing interconnectedness is likely to be met with increasingly concentrated decision structures, not decentralized structures as many have predicted. There is some evidence that external pressure is accompanied by decision centralization (Hamblin, 1958; Korten, 1962;

Pfeffer and Leblebici, 1973). If turbulence and uncertainty is perceived as stress or pressure, then centralization is a more correct prediction than decentralization.

Before we can have confidence in the preceding description, there are a number of other variables that must be considered. Ultimately, the need for coordination is a function of environmental munificence. Scarcity is not itself a given, but depends in part on the definition of the organization's requirements and the number of organizations contending for those resources. Definitions of required resources can change and do so as organizations adapt to their environments. A second unknown is the extent to which power can be increasingly concentrated. At some point, concentration must cease as the cost of coordination becomes too high, threatening the survival of individual social actors and posing too great a loss of autonomy consistent with survival. Moreover, the ability to coordinate must have limits also, perhaps determined by the ability to see the relationship between sets of actors and activities.

Unfortunately, speculations about the evolution of social systems require facts and knowledge that are not presently available. Because it has not been studied, there is little information about how organizational responses and environments evolve over time. The cycle of contextual effect, organizational response, and new contexts must be examined more fully in the future to describe adequately the external control of organizations.

REFERENCES

Aguilar, F. J. 1967. *Scanning the Business Environment.* New York: Macmillan.

Berman, L. 1973. "What we learned from the great frenzy." *Fortune,* 87: 70–73 ff.

Delbecq, A. L., A. H. Van de Ven, and D. H. Gustafson. 1975. *Group Techniques for Program Planning.* Glenview, Ill.: Scott, Foresman.

Downs, A. 1967. *Inside Bureaucracy.* Boston: Little, Brown.

Galbraith, J. 1973. *Designing Complex Organizations.* Reading, Mass.: Addison-Wesley.

Hamblin, R. L. 1958. "Leadership and crises." *Sociometry,* 21:322–335.

Jones, E. E., and R. E. Nisbett. 1971. *The Actor and the Observer: Divergent Perceptions of the Causes of Behavior.* Morristown, N.J.: General Learning Press.

Kelley, H. H. 1971. *Attribution in Social Interaction.* Morristown, N.J.: General Learning Press.

Korten, D. C. 1962. "Situational determinants of leadership structure." *Journal of Conflict Resolution,* 6:222–235.

Langer, E. 1975. "The illusion of control." *Journal of Personality and Social Psychology,* 32:311–328.

Lieberson, S., and J. F. O'Connor. 1972. "Leadership and organizational performance: a study of large corporations." *American Sociological Review,* 37:117–130.

Likert, R. 1967. *The Human Organization: Its Management and Value.* New York: McGraw-Hill.

Linstone, H. A., and M. Turoff. 1975. *The Delphi Method: Techniques and Applications.* Reading, Mass.: Addison-Wesley.

McGregor, D. 1960. *The Human Side of Enterprise.* New York: McGraw-Hill.

Miles, R. E. 1974. "Organization development." In G. Strauss, R. E. Miles, C. C. Snow, and A. S. Tannenbaum (eds.), *Organizational Behavior: Research and Issues,* 165–191. New York: Industrial Relations Research Association.

Mintzberg, H. 1973. *The Nature of Managerial Work.* New York: Harper & Row.

Pate, J. L. 1969. "Joint venture activity, 1960–1968." *Economic Review, Federal Reserve Bank of Cleveland,* 16–23.

Pfeffer, J. 1976. "Patterns of joint venture activity: implications for antitrust policy." Testimony presented before the Subcommittee on Monopolies and Commercial Law of the House Committee on the Judiciary, February 11, 1976.

Pfeffer, J., and H. Leblebici. 1973. "The effect of competition on some dimensions of organizational structure." *Social Forces,* 52:268–279.

Reid, S. R. 1968. *Mergers, Managers, and the Economy.* New York: McGraw-Hill.

Salancik, G. R., and J. Pfeffer. 1977. "Contraints on administrator discretion: the limited influence of mayors on city budgets." *Urban Affairs Quarterly* (in press).

Thompson, J. D. 1967. *Organizations in Action.* New York: McGraw-Hill.

Thompson, J. D., and W. J. McEwen. 1958. "Organizational goals and environment." *American Sociological Review,* 23:23–31.

SUBJECT INDEX

NAME INDEX